Classic and Contempo

Classic and Contemporary Readings in Sociology

Edited by
Ian Marsh **with Rosie Campbell & Mike Keating**

Addison Wesley Longman Limited
Edinburgh Gate
Harlow
Essex CM20 2JE
United Kingdom
and Associated Companies throughout the world

Published in the United States of America
by Addison Wesley Longman, New York

First published 1998

ISBN 0 582 32023 2

British Library Cataloguing-in-Publication Data

A catalogue record for this book is available from the British Library

Library of Congress Cataloging-in-Publication Data

Marsh, Ian, 1952–
Classic and contemporary readings in sociology / Ian Marsh, Rosemary Campbell, and Mike Keating.
p. cm.
Includes bibliographical references and index.
ISBN 0-582-32023-2 (alk. paper)
1. Sociology. 2. Sociology—Research. I. Campbell, Rosemary, 1967– . II. Keating, Mike, 1950– . III. Title.
HM15.M344 1998
301—dc21 98-13328
CIP

Set by 35 in 10/12pt New Baskerville
Printed in Malaysia, PP

Contents

Preface

Aims

The intention behind this book is to provide students with the opportunity to examine sociological theories, ideas and arguments in more depth than is possible through the summaries provided in introductory textbooks. It will enable students to read more substantial extracts from first hand sources – both classic sociological theorising and more recent sociological work.

The editors of any compilation of readings are faced by the dilemma of what to include and, more awkwardly, what to omit. And there is a particular danger that an introductory reader in sociology might try to cover too much, be too eclectic and not 'work'. In attempting to avoid this, we have aimed for a coherent thread to run through the reader – a clear focus on sociological theory and research, both classic and contemporary. The book is divided into four main sections. Part One, Origins and Concepts, looks at the history of the discipline of sociology and at some of the key themes that have influenced sociological theorising and investigation: in particular, social control, culture and socialisation. Parts Two and Four, Sociological Theories and Sociological Research, include a number of readings from founding theorists and investigators, including Auguste Comte, Emile Durkheim, Karl Marx, Max Weber and Charles Booth, and readings that illustrate more recent theoretical writing and research approaches. The focus on theory and research is extended by a selection of readings centred around the theme of Differences and Inequalities (Part Three); these readings provide students with substantive examples of work from an area where sociological theorising and research has been widely and fruitfully applied.

Sociological theory and research is a major part of all undergraduate sociology courses; as well as being the basis of the core/compulsory courses that feature on many Sociology degree programmes. However, it is often difficult to get students to read from original sources in this area and we feel that this collection illustrates the clarity and accessibility of some of the best examples of past and present sociological work and will help to overcome any such reluctance. While the majority of sources from which the readings have been taken are well-known sociological sources, we have included a number that would perhaps not be thought of as obviously sociological. We make no apologies for this: we feel it is important for students to be aware that valuable sociological insights can be gained from a range of sources. Indeed, it is often the more unusual, non-mainstream sources that particularly grab our attention; and, of course, many classic theorists and writers who are now seen as key figures in Sociology did not necessarily see themselves as sociologists, or at least as solely sociologists. There are also a number of readings from feminist writers who may not see themselves as sociologists. Again, we see this as a strength of this collection, given the extensive critique of conventional sociological theory provided by feminist writers and the importance of feminist explanations for the divisions between men and women in society. As well as a balance between classic sociological work and contemporary pieces, the selection has an international flavour with readings from British, American and European sources.

The basic aim, then, is to encourage students in a deeper reading and understanding of original sociological work and it is hoped that these extracts will encourage students to locate and delve into the books from which they are taken.

Readership

The reader can be used as a text for a variety of courses on sociological theory, research methods and inequality. It is especially suited for courses on sociological theory and research provided for second- and third-year undergraduates – core and/or compulsory courses on sociological analysis, for instance. Equally, it could be used in conjunction with a more general introductory textbook by students following first-year undergraduate courses in Sociology.

Features

We have tried to provide some consistency of structure across the four parts with certain features included in each.

Each part starts with an **introduction** providing an overview of the area being looked at and setting the context for each of the individual readings – including how it relates to the other extracts and to the development of sociology in that particular area. These introductions explore the general areas being examined, explain why particular readings have been chosen and set those readings in context.

Each of the readings is preceded by a short **summary** highlighting some of the points and issues that students might consider when reading it. These summaries also remind readers of why the sources have been used and why the particular extracts have been chosen from them.

The **readings** themselves vary in length although we have tried to ensure that each is substantial enough to enable students to get a real flavour of the arguments being advanced without being so long as to necessitate cutting down on the range of sociological writing included. Obviously each source has had to be edited considerably and such editing is inevitably likely to have an effect on the character of that particular text. While we have tried to avoid distorting the meaning and sense of the work we have included, it is inevitable that some of the depth and subtlety of the work of the writers included in this collection will be lost in the editing. Having made that disclaimer, the basic aim of the reader is to introduce students to original sociological sources.

In trying to remain faithful to the spirit of the readings we have had to face the question of sexist language. The majority of the writers whose work we have included have routinely used male terms – man, he, him, his – when referring to the person or people in general. However, as the intention is for students to read original sources we did not feel it appropriate to alter the text to 'correct' such language. In order to gain a fuller understanding of the extracts it is important that students are aware of the social and historical context from which they were written – a context that included explicit sexism, reflected in gender-blindness in language.

(Note: Where readings have been edited we have used the convention of [. . .] to indicate an omission from the source. Any words or phrases that have been added have been put in square brackets.)

We feel that the writers included in the book will provide students with a flavour of 'real' sociology and thereby stimulate reflection on the nature of sociology. To encourage this, after each reading there are **questions** that encourage students to reflect on the extract and the issues raised by it. These are not intended to be essay questions, rather questions which can be used for group discussion and/or individual consideration.

At the end of each section there is a more general student **activity** that can be used for students to address some of the issues raised by the readings and look for patterns and connections between them. They could (and hopefully will) be adapted according to the structure of the particular course the student is following: they might be undertaken individually or as a group activity and could form the basis of fuller classroom or seminar discussion.

As well as reading more from the sources of the extracts themselves, other suggestions for **further reading** are provided at the end of each section.

References and notes. We have edited these down to a minimum to avoid too many interruptions to the readings. However, we have had to keep many references – when, for instance, a work is either directly referred to or quoted from in a particular reading. To ensure consistency, all the sources referred to in the readings are listed, reading by reading, at the end of the book (pages 360–70).

Ian Marsh
Liverpool Hope University College
April 1998

Acknowledgements

We are grateful to the following for permission to reproduce copyright material:

Addison Wesley Longman Limited for an extract from *Disability and Society: Emerging Issues and Insights* edited by L. Barton (Longman, 1996), an extract from *Social Europe* (2nd edition) edited by J. Bailey (Longman, 1998) and an extract from *Conflicts about Class: Debating Inequality in Late Industrialism* by D.J. Lee and B.S. Turner (Longman, 1996); Blackwell Publishers for an extract from *Inside the British Police: A Force at Work* by Simon Holdaway (1983); Georges Borchardt, Inc for an extract from *Sexual Politics* by Kate Millet (Virago, 1977); Doubleday for an extract from *An Invitation to Sociology* by Peter Berger (Penguin, 1966), copyright Peter L. Berger 1963; the Controller of Her Majesty's Stationery Office for an extract from *Inequalities in Health* by P. Townsend and N. Davidson (Penguin, 1982) and extracts from *Gender and the Criminal Justice System*; Institute of Economic Affairs Health and Welfare Unit for an extact from *Unequal but Fair?: A Study of Class Barriers in Britain* by P. Saunders (IEA, 1996); Karl Popper Charitable Trust for an extract from *The Poverty of Historicism* by K. Popper (Routledge, 1961); Lawrence and Wishart for an extract from *Collected Works* by K. Marx and F. Engels (1976); Low Pay Unit for an extract from *Poverty and Labour in London* by P. Townsend, P. Corrigan and U. Kowarzik (1987); Open University Press for an extract from *Sex Work on the Streets: Prostitutes and their Clients* by N. McKeganey and M. Barnard (1996); Oxford University Press for an extract from *The Sociological Imagination* by C. Wright Mills (1959), an extract from *Witchcraft, Oracles and Magic Among the Azande* by E.E. Evans-Pritchard (Clarendon Press, 1976), an extract from the article 'Sex, sentencing and reconviction' from *British Journal of Criminology*, 23, 3.7.83 (Oxford University Press Journals) and an extract from the article 'Women, crime and dependency, from *British Journal of Criminology* (1982) (Oxford University Press Journals); Penguin Books Limited for an extract from *How the Other Half Dies: The Real Reason for World Hunger* by S. George (Pelican,

1991) and an extract from *Double Deviant, Double Damned: Society's Treatment of Violent Women* by A. Lloyd (Penguin, 1995); Peters Fraser and Dunlop Group Ltd for an extract from *The Rules of Sociological Method* by E. Durkheim (Free Press, 1964); Pluto Press for an extract from *Staying Power: The History of Black People in Britain* by P. Fryer (Pluto Press, 1984); Policy Studies Institute for an extract from *Ethnic Minorities* in Britain by T. Modood, R. Berthoud *et al.* (Policy Studies Institute, 1997); Progress Publishers for an extract from *The Manifesto of the Communist Party* by K. Marx and F. Engels (1952); Random House for an extract from *Civilization and its Discontents* by S. Freud (The Hogarth Press, 1975); Routledge for an extract from *Classes in Modern Society* by T. Bottomore (Allen and Unwin, 1965), an extract from *Breaking Out Again: Feminist Ontology and Epsitemology* by L. Stanley and S. Wise (Routledge, 1993), an extract from *Suicide: A Study in Sociology* by E. Durkheim (Routledge and Kegan Paul, 1952), an extract from *Young, Female and Black* by H.S. Mirza (Routledge, 1992) and an extract from *Black Feminist Thought: Knowledge Consciousness and the Politics of Empowerment* by P. Hill Collins (Unwin Hyman, 1990); Sage Publications for an extract from *Researching Social Life* edited by N. Gilbert (1993); Sheil and Associates Ltd for an extract from *Blood and Belongings: Journeys into the New Nationalism* by Michael Ignatieff (Vintage, 1994); Simon and Schuster for an extract from *Violence Against Wives: A Case Against Patriarchy* by R. Emerson and R. Dobash (The Free Press, 1979); South End Press for an extract from *Feminist Theory: From Margin to Centre* by bell hooks (1984); Stanford University Press for an extract from *Class and Class Conflict in Industrial Society* by R. Dahrendorf (Routledge and Kegan Paul, 1959); The University of Chicago Press for an extract from *Mind, Self and Society* by G.H. Mead (1934) and The Women's Press for an extract from *There's a Good Girl: Gender Stereotyping in the First Three Years of Life: A Diary* by M. Grabrucker (1988).

Part I

Origins and Concepts

1

Introduction

Sociology as a separate area of study is a relatively new discipline and there has been a tendency to see it as a less essential subject than more traditional disciplines. This view is perhaps due to the fact that relatively few people will have encountered sociology at school. However, the areas and issues that it investigates – including, for example, the relationship of the family unit to wider society, the causes of deviant behaviour, the role of religion – have long been a source of intellectual examination and debate and to that extent we would argue that sociology has a rich and diverse history. The readings in this section illustrate how contemporary sociology has been influenced and shaped from a number of directions.

The Social Sciences in general, and sociology as a distinct academic discipline, developed in response to the massive technical, economic and social changes of the eighteenth and nineteenth centuries: changes that transformed the social order of the Western world. Scientific and technological developments encouraged the hope that scientific methods would be able to explain the social as well as natural worlds. The Industrial Revolution that began in Britain in the late eighteenth century led to the growth of mechanised industry and a population migration to urban areas to work in the new factories. All of the major 'classic' sociological writers reflected on and offered analyses of these drastic changes and of the transformation from 'simple' societies to complex, industrial ones.

In his analysis of the origins of sociology, Robert Nisbet (1970) suggests that it was in the years 1830 to 1900 that the conceptual framework of modern sociology was created. He argues that 'the fundamental ideas of European sociology are best understood as responses to the problem of order created at the beginning of the nineteenth century by the collapse of the old regime under the blows of industrialism and revolutionary democracy'. The Industrial Revolution and the democratic revolutions in France and America were the key events in the history of sociological thought. Indeed, it would be hard to find any area of thought and writing in the nineteenth century that was not affected by one or both of these events. As Nisbet puts it: 'The cataclysmic nature of each is plain enough if we look at the responses of those who lived through the revolutions and their immediate consequences.' Today we tend to see particular historical events, including revolutions, as part of the long-term process of change; we tend to emphasise evolution rather than revolution. Nisbet points out that to intellectuals of that age, radical and conservative alike, the changes were of almost millennial abruptness. 'Contrast between present and past seemed stark – terrifying and intoxicating, depending upon one's relation to the old order and to the forces at work on it.' Reading 2 is taken from Nisbet's analysis of 'The Two Revolutions' and their influence on the development of sociology.

Nisbet's argument that sociology developed in response to the 'problem of order' of the newly industrialised Western world suggests that social control is at the heart of society and sociology. This is the focus of the second reading, taken from Peter Berger's introduction to sociology, *Invitation to Sociology: A Humanistic Perspective,* in which Berger provides a personal argument for studying sociology. Although only brief, and freely written, this introductory book had a tremendous impact on the expansion of sociology in the 1960s and 1970s. Along with C. Wright Mill's *The Sociological Imagination,* Berger's book captured the excitement and challenge of studying society and inspired a generation of students and teachers. As he says at the end of the first chapter, 'Sociology is more like a passion. The sociological perspective is more like a demon that possesses one, that drives one compellingly, again and again, to the questions that are its own. An introduction to sociology is, therefore, an invitation to a very special kind of passion.' This excitement is well illustrated in the extract here (Reading 3) in which Berger introduces the key sociological concept of social control. He describes various systems of social control, including physical violence, economic pressure, ridicule, gossip, morality, custom and manners, and examines how they can influence our day-to-day lives.

In their attempts to understand how societies 'worked' – how they developed and held together – many of the early, 'classic' sociologists studied pre-modern societies; perhaps in the hope that finding out how 'simpler' societies were structured and organised would help an understanding of modern, industrial societies. Durkheim's study of Australian aborigines (from written reports, not his own fieldwork) helped him develop his views on social solidarity and the collective conscience. Marx, Weber, Tonnies and Spencer, among others, all referred to earlier forms of society in their analyses of social development.

This tradition was continued in the pioneering work of social anthropologists such as Margaret Mead and Bronislaw Malinowski (both of whom carried out fieldwork in the Pacific in the first half of this century), Alfred Radcliffe-Brown (whose work included studies of the Andaman Islanders, 1922, Australian tribes, 1931, and African kinship systems, 1950) and Edward Evans-Pritchard (who carried out extensive fieldwork in Africa in the 1930s and 1940s). As well as providing a model from which comparison with modern societies can be made, such studies also reveal the extent of cultural diversity. They illustrate very graphically that terms such as 'acceptable' or 'normal' are difficult to apply across time or space. Evans-Pritchard's believed that systems of magic and religion had their own internal logic and Reading 4, taken from his famous work *Witchcraft, Oracles and Magic among the Azande,* shows how practices that we may regard as cruel or ridiculous were used by the Azande to explain everyday misfortunes. Margaret Mead's work on child-rearing in the Pacific made an enduring contribution to the nature/nurture; although Mead did not deny the importance of biology and the natural environment, her research demonstrated the central role of culture in shaping human behaviour and attitudes. Reading 5 is taken from her study *Growing up in New Guinea* and, in particular, her examination of the way in which gender-specific behaviour is learned by the 'untouched people' on the island of Manus, north of New Guinea.

Introductory texts in sociology rarely spend much time looking at the contribution of Sigmund Freud to the discipline. This is perhaps not surprising given that Freud is most famous for his psychoanalytic approach to personal problems and that much of his work focused on the instinctual dispositions of individuals. However, from about 1914, after his earlier work on hysteria and dreams and after his break with Jung, Freud began thinking and writing more about the social implications of his theories (evidenced in his studies *The Ego and the Id,* 1923, and *Civilization and Its Discontents,* 1929). Freud's description of the characteristics of contemporary civilisation in *Civilization and its Discontents* is the subject of Reading 6; and it is a description that is very close to the way in which sociologists use the term culture. Essentially, he sees civilisation as the sum of achievements and regulations that distinguish the lives of humans from those of animals. Freud was convinced of the inherent conflict between civilisation and instinctual pleasure, suggesting that civilisation was built on a renunciation of instinctual pleasure and thus demands instinctual sacrifice. It is worth noting here that Freud's ideas on the family, socialisation and gender are also of particular relevance to sociology, perhaps especially through their impact on feminism, either through those who have criticised him (over his notions of patriarchy and 'mothering', for instance) or those who have been influenced by him (in psychoanalytic work, for example).

In general usage, the term 'culture' is associated with the traditional arts such as ballet, literature, classical music and painting. However, in sociology a much broader usage is adopted, with 'culture' referring to the values, customs and modes of behaviour of a society or of a particular social grouping. Sociologists emphasise the importance of culture, rather than biological instinct, as the key to understanding human behaviour and lay great stress on the processes by which individuals learn and internalise the culture of the society and social groupings to which they belong. Socialisation is the term given to this learning process and is, therefore, one of the key sociological concepts; it helps explain social cohesion and cultural endurance. There are various agencies of socialisation, including the family, the education system and the mass media. Reading 7 is taken from Marianne Grabrucker's diary of her first three years of motherhood in which she recounts her experience of trying to bring up her daughter free from gender stereotyping. It includes her comments on her reasons for keeping the diary and on how her best intentions were 'subverted', and extracts from the diary itself. Although a personal reflection, Grabrucker's account illustrates some of the many influences outside her control that communicated messages about gender differences. In Reading 8, American sociologist Jack Levin reflects on the role of the media, and in particular television soap operas, in the socialisation process. From an initially hostile view of 'soaps', as a sort of modern day 'opiate of the masses' socialising young people to accept the *status quo*, Levin explains how and why he has reconsidered his opinion.

Reading 2

The two revolutions

ROBERT NISBET

The two revolutions (the title of the second chapter of Nisbet's study), that Nisbet is referring to are the Industrial Revolution and French Revolution, both of which begun in the late eighteenth century. Although there were other democratic revolutions around this period, most notably the American Revolution, the French Revolution, according to Nisbet, was the 'first thoroughly ideological revolution' (the aim of the American Revolution was limited almost completely to independence from England). These revolutions, Nisbet argues, stimulated the birth of sociology.
In the first section of this extract he highlights a number of key elements that emerged as a social response to the conditions created by rapid industrialisation; the second part focuses on the French Revolution as an example of 'Democracy as Revolution' and examines some of the changes in the relationship of individuals to the state; the final part summarises three of the processes that Nisbet feels particularly characterised the 'two revolutions'.

The Themes of Industrialism

[. . .]

What were the aspects of the Industrial Revolution that were to prove most evocative of sociological response, most directive in the formation of sociological problems and concepts? Five, we may judge, were crucial: the *condition of labour*, the *transformation of property*, the *industrial city*, *technology*, and the *factory system* [. . .]

Beyond question, the most striking and widely treated of these aspects was the condition of the working class. For the first time in the history of European thought, the working class (I distinguish 'working class' from the poor, the downtrodden, the humble, which, of course, form timeless themes) becomes, in the nineteenth century, the subject of both moral and analytical concern. Some recent scholarship has suggested that the condition of the working class under even the first stages of industrialism was better than that which had prevailed for a couple of centuries before. This may be true. But it was rarely the view of independent observers in the early nineteenth century. For radical and conservative alike, it was the undoubted degradation of labour, the wrenching of work from the protective guild, village, and family, that was the most fundamental, and shocking, characteristic of the new order [. . .]

The likeness between the conservative Southey and the radical Cobbett here is reflective of a certain affinity between conservatism and radicalism that was to last throughout the century. (I am referring, of course, to the evaluation of industrialism and its byproducts. There was little if any affinity when it came to political matters.) What conservatives such as Tocqueville, Taine, and the American Hawthorne were to write in horrified reaction to the scene presented in Manchester and other cities of the Midlands in England did not differ in descriptive character or emotional intensity from what Engels was to write [. . .]

(Indeed) the indictment of capitalism that comes from the conservatives in the nineteenth century is often more severe than that of the socialists. Whereas the latter accepted capitalism at least to the point of regarding it as a necessary step from past to future, the traditionalists tended to reject it outright, seeing any development of its mass industrial nature – either within capitalism or a future socialism – as but a continued falling away from the superior values of Christian-feudal society [. . .]

The second of the themes to emerge from the Industrial Revolution has to do with property and its influence on the social order . . . For conservatives, property was the indispensable basis of family, church, state, and all other major groups in society. For radicals, increasingly, the abolition of property, save as a vague collective sentiment, became the prime goal of their aspirations [. . .]

But the affinity between conservative and radical went further. It extended to hatred of a certain type of property: large-scale industrial property, but more especially the abstract and impersonal type of property that was represented by shares bought and sold on the market [. . .]

In the nineteenth century conservative and radical alike distrusted industrial and financial capital. But whereas radicals tended more and more, after Marx, to see this mode of property as an essential step in the evolution toward socialism and its capitalistic evils subject to the cure of revolutionary liquidation of the privateness of its ownership, conservatives thought that it was the very nature of such capital to create instability and alienation in a population, and that this was quite unaffected by the mere matter of public or private ownership [. . .]

A third theme to emerge from the Industrial Revolution was urbanism . . . Prior to the early nineteenth century the city, insofar as it was dealt with at all in humanistic writing, was seen as the repository of civilised graces and virtues . . . But actual revulsion for the city, fear of it as a force in culture, and forebodings with respect to the psychological conditions attending it – these are states of mind hardly known before the nineteenth century . . . It is, as we shall repeatedly see, the city that forms the context of most sociological propositions relating to disorganisation, alienation, and mental isolation – all stigmata of loss of community and membership [. . .]

In the beginning, radicals and conservatives were largely united in their distaste for urbanism . . . But as the century progresses, one cannot but be struck by the increasingly 'urban' character of radicalism [. . .]

Marx regarded the onset of urbanism as one of the blessings of capitalism, something to be spread even further in the future socialist order . . . If modern radicalism is urban in its mentality, conservatism is largely rural.

Two themes, equally alive, equally freighted with ideological passion in nineteenth century thought, must be mentioned: technology and the factory system. Under the impact of the former and within the confines of the latter, conservatives and radicals alike could see changes occurring that affected the historic relations between man and woman, that threatened (or promised) to make the traditional family obsolete, that would abolish the cultural separation between town and countryside, and that would make possible, for the first time in history, a liberation of man's productive energies from the restraints that both nature and traditional society had imposed [. . .]

Democracy as Revolution

The French Revolution was no less shattering in its impact upon cherished dogma and traditionalist feeling. And the political revolution in France had what the economic revolution largely lacked: dedicated emissaries and disciples who made it the first great ideological revolution in Western history . . . By its very nature the French Revolution was possessed of a suddenness and dramatic intensity that nothing in the Industrial Revolution could match [. . .]

It was the ideological character of the Revolution that made it the obsession of intellectuals for decades afterward. Mere events, even those involving dethronement, expropriation, and beheading, do not captivate the hopes of romantics, idealists, and visionaries for generations, nor torment the apprehensions of traditionalists. Dogmas and heresies are required, and these the Revolution had in abundance. It was the Revolution that contributed to Western Europe states of mind about political good and evil that had previously been reserved to religion and demonology [. . .]

The family also underwent profound change in law during the Revolution. Like the *philosophes*, the Revolutionary legislators found patriarchal customs and the indissolubility of the marriage tie 'against nature and contrary to reason'. In a law of 1792 marriage was designated a civil contract and several grounds for divorce were made available. The arguments for such measures invariably rested on natural law with frequent citation of philosophy. That the relaxation was not unwelcome in some quarters may be inferred from the fact that in the sixth year of the Republic the number of divorces in Paris exceeded the number of marriages. But there was more to follow in reform of the family. Strict limitations were placed upon paternal power, and in all cases the authority of the father ceased when the child reached legal age [. . .]

As one more expression of its dedication to the liberation of individuals from the ancient authorities, the government of 1793, took from the family the control of education . . . The successive governments of the Revolution, believing with Danton that 'after bread, education is the chief need of the people,' passed numerous measures designed to centralize and broaden education simultaneously, making it not merely the right but the political duty of all citizens [. . .]

Religion also was deeply affected . . . At the outbreak of the Revolution there was no manifest wish to abolish Christianity, but there was plainly desire to regulate it completely. If there was to be a church, it must reflect the character of the new political order . . . Bishops and clerics were to be elected like ordinary officials. It was ruled that clerics must accept their living from the state, and in such capacity must take an oath of fidelity to the state [. . .]

Individualization, Abstraction, Generalization

If one looks at the two revolutions from the point of view of the most fundamental and widespread processes they embodied in common, three are especially striking. I shall call them *individualization, abstraction,* and *generalization.* Together these terms convey a great deal of what revolutionary change meant to philosophers and social scientists of the nineteenth century. And the relevance of each has lasted well into the twentieth century.

INDIVIDUALIZATION Everywhere in the modern world, the clear direction of history seemed to be toward the separation of individuals from communal or corporate structures: from guild, village community, historic church, caste of estate, and from patriarchal ties in general. Some, perhaps most, people saw this separation in the progressive terms of liberation, of emancipation from tradition grown oppressive . . . Not the group but the *individual* was the heir of historical development; not the guild but the *entrepreneur*; not class or estate but the *citizen*; not corporate or liturgical tradition but *individual reason* [. . .]

ABSTRACTION This is related to individualization, but refers primarily to moral values. What struck a great many minds in the century was not merely the tendency of historic values to become ever more secular, ever more utilitarian, but increasingly separated from the concrete and particular roots which for many centuries had given them both symbolic distinctness and means of realization. Honor – as Tocqueville was to show in a masterly chapter of *Democracy in America* – and loyalty and friendship and decorum had all begun, as values, in the highly particular contexts of locality and rank . . . Many of these values had depended for their effect on man's direct experiencing of nature: of its rhythms and cycles of growth and decay, of cold and warmth, of light and dark. Now a technological system of thought and behaviour was coming between man and the directness of natural habitat [. . .]

GENERALIZATION The nation and even the international sphere come to be seen more and more as essential areas of man's thought and allegiance. From family and local community to nation, to democracy, to visions of international order: this is the course of thought in the age. Loyalties become broadened, along with interests and functions. So do perceptions. Men saw their fellows less as particular individuals and more as members of a general aggregate or class . . . What the Industrial Revolution accomplished in the economic sphere, revolutionary democracy did in the political. In each instance the particularism of the old order – the tendency to think in terms of concrete, *identifiable* rich or powerful, poor or helpless – disappeared along with its localism. The same tendency to think now increasingly in terms of 'the working class', 'the poor', 'the capitalists' expressed itself with equal force in the tendency to think in terms of 'voters', 'bureaucracy', the 'citizenry', and so on.

From R.A. Nisbet (1970) *The Sociological Tradition*, London: Heinemann, pp. 23–44.

Questions

1. Nisbet suggests that there was a certain affinity between conservatives and radicals as regards their views of the 'main themes of industrialism' (which he lists in the first paragraph of the extract).
   (a) What were the areas of agreement between conservatives and radicals? How could you account for them?
   (b) How did conservatives and radicals differ in their views and interpretations of these themes?

2. What similarities are there between the social changes and developments encouraged by the French Revolution and those that have occurred in modern Western society 200 years on?
3. To what extent have the processes of individualisation, abstraction and generalisation continued in contemporary society? What factors have worked against them?

Reading 3

Social control

PETER BERGER

In this reading, Peter Berger explores one of the key sociological concepts: social control. In particular he considers the relative importance of the internal, more intimate mechanisms of social control, such as family or friends, and the external, more formal mechanisms, such as occupation or the legal system. While reading this extract you might reflect on the extent to which each of the elements of social control that Berger discusses impinges on your own behaviour and attitudes.

Social control is one of the most generally used concepts in sociology. It refers to the various means used by a society to bring its recalcitrant members back into line. No society can exist without social control. Even a small group of people meeting but occasionally will have to develop their mechanisms of control if the group is not to dissolve in a very short time. It goes without saying that the instrumentalities of social control vary greatly from one social situation to another. Opposition to the line in a business organization may mean what personnel directors call a terminal interview, and in a criminal syndicate a terminal automobile ride. Methods of control vary with the purpose and character of the group in question. In either case, control mechanisms function to eliminate undesirable personnel and (as it was put classically by King Christophe of Haiti when he had every tenth man in his forced-labour battalion executed) 'to encourage the others'.

The ultimate and, no doubt, the oldest means of social control is physical violence. In the savage society of children it is still the major one. But even in the politely operated societies of modern democracies the ultimate argument is violence. No state can exist without a police force or its equivalent in armed might. This ultimate violence may not be used frequently. There may be innumerable steps before its application, in the way of warnings and reprimands. But if all the warnings are disregarded, even in so slight a matter as paying a traffic ticket, the last thing that will happen is that a couple of cops show up at the door with handcuffs and a Black Maria. Even the moderately courteous cop who hands out the initial traffic ticket is likely to wear a gun just in case. And even in England, where he does not in the normal course of events, he will be issued one if the need arises.

In Western democracies, with their ideological emphasis on voluntary compliance with popularly legislated rules, this constant presence of official violence is under-emphasized. It is all the more important to be aware of it. Violence is the ultimate foundation of any political order. The commonsense view of society senses this, and this may have something to do with the widespread popular reluctance to eliminate capital punishment from the criminal law (though this reluctance is probably based in equal measure on stupidity, superstition and the congenital bestiality that jurists share with the bulk of their fellow citizens). However, the statement that political order rests ultimately on violence is just as true in states that have abolished capital punishment [. . .]

Since the constant use of violence would be impractical and also ineffective, the official organs of social control rely mostly on the restraining influence of the generally known availability of the means of violence [. . .]

In any functioning society violence is used economically and as a last resort, with the mere threat of this ultimate violence sufficing for the day-to-day exercise of social control. For our purposes in this argument, the most important matter to underline is that nearly all men live in social situations in which, if all other means of coercion fail, violence may be officially and legally used against them.

If the role of violence in social control is thus understood, it becomes clear that the, so to speak, penultimate means of coercion are more important for more people most of the time. While there is a certain uninspired sameness about the methods of intimidation thought up by jurists and policemen, the less-than-violent instrumentalities of social control show great variety and sometimes imagination. Next in line after the political and legal controls one should probably place economic pressure. Few means of coercion are as effective as those that threaten one's livelihood or profit. Both management and labour effectively use this threat as an instrumentality of control in our society. But economic means of control are just as effective outside the institutions properly called the economy. Universities or churches use economic sanctions just as effectively in restraining their personnel from engaging in deviant behaviour deemed by the respective authorities to go beyond the limits of the acceptable. It may not be actually illegal for a minister to seduce his organist, but the threat of being barred forever from the exercise of his profession will be a much more effective control over this temptation than the possible threat of going to jail. It is undoubtedly not illegal for a minister to speak his mind on issues that the ecclesiastical bureaucracy would rather have buried in silence, but the chance of spending the rest of his life in minimally paid rural parishes is a very powerful argument indeed.

Naturally such arguments are employed more openly in economic institutions proper, but the administration of economic sanctions in churches or universities is not very different in its end results from that used in the business world.

Where human beings live or work in compact groups, in which they are personally known and to which they are tied by feelings of personal loyalty (the kind that sociologists call primary groups), very potent and simultaneously very subtle mechanisms of control are constantly brought to bear upon the actual or potential deviant. These are the mechanisms of persuasion, ridicule, gossip and opprobrium. It has been discovered that in group discussions going on over a period of time individuals modify their originally held opinions to conform to the group norm, which corresponds to a kind of arithmetic mean of all the opinions represented in the group. Where this norm lies obviously depends on the constituency of the group. For example, if you have a group of twenty cannibals arguing over cannibalism with one noncannibal, the chances are that in the end he will come to see their point and, with just a few face-saving reservations (concerning, say, the consumption of close relatives), will go over completely to the majority's point of view. But if you have a group discussion between ten cannibals who regard human flesh aged over sixty years as too tough for a cultivated palate and ten other cannibals who fastidiously draw the line at fifty, the chances are that the group will eventually agree on fifty-five as the age that divides the *déjeuner* from the *débris* when it comes to sorting out prisoners. Such are the wonders of group dynamics. What lies at the bottom of this apparently inevitable pressure towards consensus is probably a profound human desire to be accepted, presumably by whatever group is around to do the accepting. This desire can be manipulated most effectively, as is well known by group therapists, demagogues and other specialists in the field of consensus engineering.

Ridicule and gossip are potent instruments of social control in primary groups of all sorts. Many societies use ridicule as one of the main controls over children – the child conforms not for fear of punishment but in order not to be laughed at. Within our own larger culture, 'kidding' in this way has been an important disciplinary measure among Southern Negroes. But most men have experienced the freezing fear of making oneself ridiculous in some social situation. Gossip, as hardly needs elaboration, is especially effective in small communities, where most people live their lives in a high degree of social visibility and inspectability by their neighbours. In such communities gossip is one of the principal channels of communication, essential for the maintenance of the social fabric. Both ridicule and gossip can be manipulated deliberately by any intelligent person with access to their lines of transmission.

Finally, one of the most devastating means of punishment at the disposal of a human community is to subject one of its members to systematic opprobrium and ostracism. It is somewhat ironic to reflect that this is a favourite control mechanism with groups opposed on principle to the use of violence.

An example of this would be 'shunning' among the Amish Mennonites. An individual who breaks one of the principal taboos of the group (for example, by getting sexually involved with an outsider) is 'shunned'. This means that, while permitted to continue to work and live in the community, not a single person will speak to him ever. It is hard to imagine a more cruel punishment. But such are the wonders of pacifism.

One aspect of social control that ought to be stressed is the fact that it is frequently based on fraudulent claims. Later, we shall take up further the general importance of fraud in a sociological understanding of human life; here we will simply stress that a conception of social control is incomplete and thus misleading unless this element is taken into account. A little boy can exercise considerable control over his peer group by having a big brother who, if need be, can be called upon to beat up any opponents. In the absence of such a brother, however, it is possible to invent one. It will then be a question of the public-relations talents of the little boy as to whether he will succeed in translating his invention into actual control. In any case, this is definitely possible. The same possibilities of fraudulence are present in all the forms of social control discussed. This is why intelligence has some survival value in the competition with brutality, malice and material resources. We shall return to this point later.

It is possible, then, to perceive oneself as standing at the centre (that is, at the point of maximum pressure) of a set of concentric circles, each representing a system of social control. The outer ring might well represent the legal and political system under which one is obligated to live. This is the system that, quite against one's will, will tax one, draft one into the military, make one obey its innumerable rules and regulations, if need be put one in prison, and in the last resort will kill one. One does not have to be a right-wing Republican to be perturbed by the ever-increasing expansion of this system's power into every conceivable aspect of one's life. A salutary exercise would be to note down for the span of a single week all the occasions, including fiscal ones, in which one came up against the demands of the politico-legal system. The exercise can be concluded by adding up the sum total of fines and/or terms of imprisonment that disobedience to the system might lead to. The consolation, incidentally, with which one might recover from this exercise would consist of the recollection that law-enforcement agencies are normally corrupt and of only limited efficiency.

Another system of social control that exerts its pressures towards the solitary figure in the centre is that of morality, custom and manners. Only the most urgent-seeming (to the authorities, that is) aspects of this system are endowed with legal sanctions. This does not mean, however, that one can safely be immoral, eccentric or unmannered. At this point all the other instrumentalities of social control go into action. Immorality is punished by loss of one's job, eccentricity by the loss of one's chances of finding a new one, bad manners by remaining uninvited and uninvitable in the groups, that respect what they consider good manners. Unemployment and loneliness may be minor penalties compared to being dragged away by the cops, but they may not actually appear so to the individuals thus punished. Extreme defiance against the *mores* of our particular society, which is quite sophisticated in its control apparatus, may lead to yet another consequence – that of being defined, by common consent, as 'sick' [. . .]

The social control of one's occupational system is so important because the job decides what one may do in most of the rest of one's life – which voluntary associations one will be allowed to join, who will be one's friends, where one will be able to live. However, quite apart from the pressures of one's occupation, one's other social involvements also entail control systems, many of them less unbending than the occupational one, but some even more so. The codes governing admission to and continued membership in many clubs and fraternal organizations are just as stringent as those that decide who can become an executive at IBM (sometimes, luckily for the harassed candidate, the requirements may actually be the same). In less exclusive associations, the rules may be more lax and one may only rarely get thrown out, but life can be so thoroughly unpleasant for the persistent nonconformist to the local folk-ways that continued participation becomes humanly impossible. The items covered by such unwritten codes will, naturally, vary greatly. They may include ways of dressing, language, aesthetic taste, political or religious convictions, or simply table manners. In all these cases, however, they constitute control circles that effectively circumscribe the range of the individual's possible actions in the particular situation.

Finally, the human group in which one's so-called private life occurs, that is the circle of one's family and personal friends, also constitutes a control system. It would be a grave error to assume that this is necessarily the weakest of them all just because it does not possess the formal means of coercion of some of the other control systems. It is in this circle that an individual normally has his most important social ties. Disapproval, loss of prestige, ridicule or contempt in this intimate group has far more serious psychological weight than the same reactions encountered elsewhere. It may be economically disastrous if one's boss finally concludes that one is a worthless nobody, but the psychological effect of such a judgement is incomparably more devastating if one discovers that one's wife has arrived at the same conclusion. What is more, the pressures of this most intimate control system can be applied at those times when one is least prepared for them. At one's job one is usually in a better position to brace oneself, to be on one's guard and to pretend than one is at home. Contemporary American 'familism', a set of values that strongly emphasizes the home as a place of refuge from the tensions of the world and of personal fulfillment, contributes effectively to this control system. The man who is at least relatively prepared psychologically to give battle in his office is willing to do almost anything to preserve the precarious harmony of his family life. Last but not least, the social control of what German sociologists have called the 'sphere of the intimate' is particularly powerful because of the very factors that have gone into its construction in the individual's biography. A man chooses a wife and a good friend in acts of essential self-definition. His most intimate relationships are those that he must count upon to sustain the most important elements of his self-image. To risk, therefore, the disintegration of these relationships means to risk losing himself in a total way. It is no wonder then that many an office despot promptly obeys his wife and cringes before the raised eyebrows of his friends.

If we return once more to the picture of an individual located at the centre of a set of concentric circles, each one representing a system of social control, we can understand a little better that location in society means to locate one-self with regard to many forces that constrain and coerce one. The individual who, thinking consecutively of all the people he is in a position to have to please, from the Collector of Internal Revenue to his mother-in-law, gets the idea that all of society sits right on top of him, had better not dismiss that idea as a momentary neurotic derangement. The sociologist, at any rate, is likely to strengthen him in this conception, no matter what other counsellors may tell him to snap out of it.

From P.L. Berger (1967) *Invitation to Sociology: A Humanistic Perspective*, Harmondsworth: Penguin, pp. 83–94.

Questions

1. Berger suggests a 'model' for understanding the various mechanisms of social control is to see them as a series of concentric circles. Each circle would represent a different system of social control, with the individual at the centre – the outer ring would be represented by the legal and political system which, in the last resort, could exercise physical violence to ensure conformity.

   Putting yourself at the centre draw in the layers of social control that affect your life, starting from the more personal and moving out.

   Which of these systems of control have the most influence on you? Why?

2. How can violence be officially and legally used in Britain today?

3. Berger describes the social control exercised by one's occupation. How can the following occupations influence other areas of the worker's life: (a) teacher; (b) sales representative; (c) police officer?

Reading 4

Cultural diversity (1): Religion and witchcraft

EDWARD EVANS-PRITCHARD

Evans-Pritchard's research in South Sudan during the late 1920s has become one of the most important references for works on witchcraft and sorcery. This reading suggests and describes how a belief in witchcraft provided explanations for various natural occurrences that faced the Azande people and for the relationships that characterised their society. It also illustrates how witchcraft can offer an explanation for a range of unfortunate events and accidents and how magic and witchcraft can be used on a regular basis to guide everyday behaviour and decision-making.

Witches, as the Azande conceive them, clearly cannot exist. None the less, the concept of witchcraft provides them with a natural philosophy by which the relations between men and unfortunate events are explained and a ready and stereotyped means of reacting to such events. Witchcraft beliefs also embrace a system of values which regulate human conduct.

Witchcraft is ubiquitous. It plays its part in every activity of Zande life; in agricultural, fishing, and hunting pursuits; in domestic life of homesteads as well as in communal life of district and court; it is an important theme of mental life in which it forms the background of a vast panorama of oracles and magic; its influence is plainly stamped on law and morals, etiquette and religion; it is prominent in technology and language; there is no niche or corner of Zande culture into which it does not twist itself. If blight seizes the ground-nut crop it is witchcraft; if the bush is vainly scoured for game it is witchcraft; if women laboriously bale water out of a pool and are rewarded by but a few small fish it is witchcraft; if termites do not rise when their swarming is due and a cold useless night is spent in waiting for their flight it is witchcraft; if a wife is sulky and unresponsive to her husband it is witchcraft; if a prince is cold and distant with his subject it is witchcraft; if a magical rite fails to achieve its purpose it is witchcraft; if, in fact, any failure or misfortune falls upon anyone at any time and in relation to any of the manifold activities of his life it may be due to witchcraft. The Zande attributes all these misfortunes to witchcraft unless there is strong evidence, and subsequent oracular confirmation, that sorcery or some other evil agent has been at work, or unless they are clearly to be attributed to incompetence, breach of a taboo, or failure to observe a moral rule.

To say that witchcraft has blighted the ground-nut crop, that witchcraft has scared away game, and that witchcraft has made so-and-so ill is equivalent to saying, in terms of our own culture, that the ground-nut crop has failed owing to blight, that game is scarce this season, and that so-and-so has caught influenza. Witchcraft participates in all misfortunes and is the idiom in which Azande speak about them and in which they explain them. To us witchcraft is something which haunted and disgusted our credulous forefathers. But the Zande expects to come across witchcraft at any time of the day or night. He would be just as surprised if he were not brought into daily contact with it as we would be if confronted by its appearance. To him there is nothing miraculous about it. It is expected that a man's hunting will be injured by witches, and he has at his disposal means of dealing with them. When misfortunes occur he does not become awe-struck at the play of supernatural forces. He is not terrified at the presence of an occult enemy. He is, on the other hand, extremely annoyed. Someone, out of spite, has ruined his ground-nuts or spoilt his hunting or given his wife a chill, and surely this is cause for anger! He has done no one harm, so what right has anyone to interfere in his affairs? It is an impertinence, an insult, a dirty, offensive trick! It is the aggressiveness and not the eerieness of these actions which Azande emphasize when speaking of them, and it is anger and not awe which we observe in their response to them.

Witchcraft is not less anticipated than adultery. It is so intertwined with everyday happenings that it is part of a Zande's ordinary world. There is nothing remarkable about a witch – you may be one yourself, and certainly many of your closest neighbours are witches. Nor is there anything awe-inspiring about witchcraft. We do not become psychologically transformed when we hear that someone is ill – we expect people to be ill – and it is the same with Zande. They expect people to be ill, i.e. to be bewitched, and it is not a matter for surprise or wonderment.

I found it strange at first to live among Azande and listen to naïve explanations of misfortunes which, to our minds, have apparent causes, but after a while I learnt the idiom of their thought and applied notions of witchcraft as spontaneously as themselves in situations where the concept was relevant. A boy knocked his foot against a small stump of wood in the centre of a bush path, a frequent happening in Africa, and suffered pain and inconvenience in consequence. Owing to its position on his toe it was impossible to keep the cut free from dirt and it began to fester. He declared that witchcraft had made him knock his foot against the stump. I always argued with Azande and criticized their statements, and I did so on this occasion. I told the boy that he had knocked his foot against the stump of wood because he had been careless, and that witchcraft had not placed it in the path, for it had grown there naturally. He agreed that witchcraft had nothing to do with the stump of wood being in his path but added that he had kept his eyes open for stumps, as indeed every Zande does most carefully, and that if he had not been bewitched he would have seen the stump. As a conclusive argument for his view he remarked that all cuts do not take days to heal but, on the contrary, close quickly, for that is the nature of cuts. Why, then, had his sore festered and remained open if there were no witchcraft behind it? This, as I discovered before long, was to be regarded as the Zande explanation of sickness.

Shortly after my arrival in Zanderland we were passing through a government settlement and noticed that a hut had been burnt to the ground on the previous night. Its owner was overcome with grief as it had contained the beer he was preparing for a mortuary feast. He told us that he had gone the previous night to examine his beer. He had lit a handful of straw and raised it above his head so that light would be cast on the pots, and in so doing he had ignited the thatch. He, and my companions also, were convinced that the disaster was caused by witchcraft [. . .]

Men whose habits are dirty, such as those who defecate in the gardens of others and urinate in public, or who eat without washing their hands, and eat bad food like tortoise, toad, and house-rat, are the kind of people who might well bewitch others. The same is thought of unmannerly persons who enter into a man's hut without first asking his permission; who cannot disguise their greed in the presence of food or beer; who make offensive remarks to their wives and neighbours and fling insults and curses after them; and so on.

Not everyone who displays these unpleasant traits is necessarily regarded as a witch, but it is these sentiments and modes of behaviour which make people suspicious of witchcraft, so that Azande know that those who display them have the desire to bewitch, even if they do not possess the power to do so. Since it is these traits which antagonize neighbours against those who show them it is their names which are most frequently placed before the oracles when the neighbours fall sick, and they are therefore likely to be accused frequently of witchcraft and to acquire a reputation as witches. Witches tend to be those whose behaviour is least in accordance with social demands. For though Azande do not consistently think of neighbours who have once or twice bewitched them as witches, some people are so frequently exposed by oracles that they gain a sustained reputation for witchcraft and are regarded as witches outside specific situations of misfortune. Those whom we would call good citizens – and, of course, the richer and more powerful members of society are such – are seldom accused of witchcraft, while those who make themselves a nuisance to their neighbours and those who are weak are most likely to be accused of witchcraft [. . .]

Where Zande moral notions differ profoundly from our own is in the range of events they consider to have a moral significance. For to a Zande almost every happening which is harmful to him is due to the evil disposition of someone else. What is bad for him is morally bad, that is to say, it derives from an evil man. Any misfortune evokes the notion of injury and desire for retaliation. For all loss is deemed by Azande to be due to witches. To them death, whatever its occasion, is murder and cries out for vengeance, for the event or situation of death is to them the important thing and not the instrument by which it was occasioned, be it disease, or a wild beast, or the spear of an enemy.

In our society only certain misfortunes are believed to be due to the wickedness of other people, and it is only in these limited situations of misfortune that we can retaliate through prescribed channels upon the authors of them. Disease or failure in economic pursuits are not thought by us to be injuries inflicted on us by other people. If a man is sick or his enterprises fail he cannot retaliate upon anyone, as he can if his watch has been stolen or he has been assaulted. But in Zanderland all misfortunes are due to witchcraft, and all allow the person who has suffered loss to retaliate along prescribed channels in every situation because the loss is attributed to a person. In situations such as theft or adultery or murder by violence there is already in play a person who invites retaliation. If he is known he is sued in the courts, if unknown he is pursued by punitive magic. When this person is absent notions of witchcraft provide an alternative objective. Every misfortune supposes witchcraft, and every enmity suggests its author [. . .]

Keeping our eyes fixed on the dynamic meaning of witchcraft, and recognizing therefore its universality, we shall better understand how it comes about that witches are not ostracized and persecuted; for what is a function of passing states and is common to most men cannot be treated with severity. The position of a witch is in no way analogous to that of a criminal in our own society, and he is certainly not an outcast living in the shadow of disgrace and shunned by his neighbours. On the contrary, confirmed witches, known for miles around as such, live like ordinary citizens. Often they are respected fathers and husbands, welcome visitors to homesteads and guests at feasts, and sometimes influential members of the inner-council at a prince's court. Some of my acquaintances were notorious witches.

A witch may enjoy a certain amount of prestige on account of his powers, for everyone is careful not to offend him, since no one deliberately courts disaster [. . .]

Belief in witchcraft is a valuable corrective to uncharitable impulses, because a show of spleen or meanness or hostility may bring serious consequences in its train. Since Azande do not know who are and who are not witches, they assume that all their neighbours may be witches, and are therefore careful not to offend any of them without good cause.

The poison oracle, *benge*, is by far the most important of the Zande oracles. Zande rely completely on its decisions, which have the force of law when obtained on the orders of a prince. A visitor to Zanderland hears as much of the poison oracle as he hears of witchcraft, for whenever a question arises about the facts of a case or about a man's well being they at once seek to know the opinion of the poison oracle on the matter. In many situations where we seek to base a verdict upon evidence or try to regulate our conduct by weighing of probabilities the Zande consults, without hesitation, the poison oracle and follows its directions with implicit trust.

No important venture is undertaken without authorization of the poison oracle. In important collective undertakings, in all crises of life, in all serious legal disputes, in all matters strongly affecting individual welfare, in short, on all occasions regarded by Azande as dangerous or socially important, the activity is preceded by consultation of the poison oracle.

When I say that the poison oracle, or some other oracle, must be consulted on the occasions listed below, I mean that if a Zande were not to consult it he would be acting contrary to custom and might suffer in social prestige. He might even incur legal penalties. The following situations are typical occasions of consultation:

To discover why a wife has not conceived.
During pregnancy of wife, about place of delivery, about her safety in childbirth, and about the safety of her child.
Before circumcision of son.
Before marriage of daughter.
Before sending son to act as page at court.
In sickness of any member of family. Will he die? Who is the witch responsible? etc.
To discover the agent responsible for any misfortune.
At death of kinsman in the old days. Who killed him? Who will execute the witch? etc.
Before exacting vengeance by magic. Who will keep the taboos? Who will make the magic? etc.
In cases of sorcery.
In cases of adultery.

[. . .]

It is not only about what we would consider the more important social activities that Azande consult their oracles, but also about their smaller everyday affairs. If time and opportunity permitted many Azande would wish to consult one or other of the oracles about every step in their lives.

I found that when a Zande acted towards me in a manner that we would call rude and untrustworthy his actions were often to be accounted for by obedience to his oracles. Usually I have found Azande courteous and reliable according to English standards, but sometimes their behaviour is unintelligible till their mystical notions are taken into account. Often Azande are tortuous in their dealings with one another, but they do not consider a man blameworthy for being secretive or acting contrary to his declared intentions.

On the contrary, they praise his prudence for taking account of witchcraft at each step and for regulating his conduct after the direction of his oracles. Hence it is not necessary for one Zande to explain to another his waywardness, for everybody understands the motives of his conduct [. . .]

I never found great difficulty in observing oracle consultations. I found that in such matters the best way of gaining confidence was to enact the same procedure as Azande and to take oracular verdicts as seriously as they take them. I always kept a supply of poison for the use of my household and neighbours and we regulated our affairs in accordance with the oracles' decisions. I may remark that I found this as satisfactory a way of running my home and affairs as any other I know of. Among Azande it is the only satisfactory way of life because it is the only way of life they understand.

From E. Evans-Pritchard (1976) (1937) *Witchcraft, Oracles and Magic among the Azande,* Oxford: Clarendon Press, pp. 18–20, 52–5, 121–6.

Questions

1. What explanations for human misfortune (such as the failure of a harvest or the festering of a cut) are provided by (a) the Zande and (b) ourselves/Western society?
2. To what extent do both forms of explanation provide an answer to the question 'Why has this happened to me/us at this particular time?'
3. What social functions does witchcraft play for the Zande?
4. What support can you find in the extract for Evans-Pritchard's comment that he found the oracle consultations of the Zande 'as satisfactory a way of running my home and affairs as any other I know of'?

Reading 5

Cultural diversity (2): Learning sex roles

MARGARET MEAD

Margaret Mead's book Growing Up In New Guinea *examines the isolated community of the Manus of the Admiralty Islands, north of New Guinea. This extract includes her reflections on family life among the Manus and in particular the role of the mother and father in bringing up children. It highlights the very different relationships that girls and boys have with their mothers and fathers.*

If a long line of devoted biologists had been breeding guinea-pigs or fruit-flies for a hundred years and recording the results, and some careless vandal burnt the painstaking record and killed the survivors, we would cry out in anger at the loss to science. Yet, when history, without any such set purpose, has presented us with the results of not a hundred years' experiment on guinea-pigs, but a thousand years' experiment on human beings, we permit the records to be extinguished without a protest.

Although most of these fragile cultures which owed their perpetuation not to written records but to the memories of a few hundred human beings are lost to us, a few remain. Isolated on small Pacific islands, in dense African jungles or Asiatic wastes, it is still possible to find untouched societies which have chosen solutions of life's problems different from our own, which can give us precious evidence on the malleability of human nature.

Such an untouched people are the brown sea-dwelling Manus of the Admiralty Islands, north of New Guinea. In the vaulted thatched houses set on stilts in the olive-green waters of the wide lagoon, their lives are lived very much as they have been lived for unknown centuries. No missionary has come to teach them an unknown faith, no trader has torn their lands from them and reduced them to penury. Those white men's diseases which have reached them have been few enough in number to be fitted into their own theory of disease as a punishment for evil done. They buy iron and cloth and beads from the distant traders; they have learned to smoke the white man's tobacco, to use his money, to take an occasional dispute into the District Officer's Court. Since 1912 war has been practically abolished, an enforced reformation welcome to a trading, voyaging people. Their young men go away to work for two or three years in the plantations of the white man, but come back little changed to their own villages. It is essentially a primitive society without written records, without economic dependence upon white culture, preserving its own canons, its own way of life.

The manner in which human babies born into these water-dwelling communities gradually absorb the traditions, the prohibitions, the values of their elders and become in turn the active perpetuators of Manus culture is a record rich in its implications for education. Our own society is so complex, so elaborate, that the most serious student can, at best, only hope to examine a part of the education process. While he concentrates upon the method in which a child solves one set of problems, he must of necessity neglect the others. But in a simple society, without division of labour, without written records, without a large population, the whole tradition is narrowed down to the memory capacities of a few individuals. With the aid of writing and an analytic point of view, it is possible for the investigator to master in a few months most of the tradition which it takes the native years to learn.

From this vantage point of a thorough knowledge of the cultural background, it is then possible to study the educational process, to suggest solutions to educational problems which we would never be willing to study by experimentation upon our children. But Manus has made the experiment for us; we have only to read the answer.

I made this study of Manus education to prove no thesis, to support no preconceived theories. Many of the results came as a surprise to me. This description of the way a simple people, dwelling in the shallow lagoons of a distant South Sea island, prepare their children for life, is presented to the reader as a picture of human education in miniature. Its relevance to modern educational interest is first just that it is such a simplified record in which all the elements can be readily grasped and understood, where a complex process which we are accustomed to think of as written upon too large a canvas to be taken in at a glance can be seen as through a painter's diminishing glass. Furthermore in Manus certain tendencies in discipline or accorded licence, certain parental attitudes, can be seen carried to more drastic lengths than has yet occurred within our own society. And finally these Manus people are interesting to us because the aims and methods of Manus society, although primitive, are not unlike the aims and methods which may be found in our own immediate history.

The family picture in Manus is also strange and revealing, with the father taking the principal role, the father the tender solicitous indulgent guardian, while the mother takes second place in the child's affection. Accustomed as we are to the family in which the father is the stern and distant dictator, the mother the child's advocate and protector, it is provocative to find a society in which father and mother have exchanged parts. The psychiatrists have laboured the difficulties under which a male child grows up if this father plays patriarch and his mother madonna. Manus illustrates the creative part which a loving tender father may play in shaping positively his son's personality. It suggests that the solution of the family complex may lie not in the parents assuming no roles, as some enthusiasts suggest, but in their playing different ones.

This account is the result of six months' concentrated and uninterrupted field work. From a thatched house on piles, built in the centre of the Manus village of Peri, I learned the native language, the children's games, the intricacies of social organization, economic custom, and religious belief and practice which formed the social framework within which the child grows up. In my large living-room, on the wide verandas, on the tiny islet adjoining the houses, in the surrounding lagoon, the children played all day and I watched them, now from the midst of a play group, now from behind the concealment of the thatched walls. I rode in their canoes, attended their feasts, watched in the house of mourning and sat severely still while the mediums conversed with the spirits of the dead. I observed the children when no grown-up people were present, and I watched their behaviour towards their parents. Within a social setting which I learned to know intimately enough not to offend against the hundreds of name taboos, I watched the Manus baby, the Manus child, the Manus adolescent, in an attempt to understand the way in which each of these was becoming a Manus adult.

Manus Attitudes towards Sex

The father treats his young children with very slight regard for differences in sex. Girls or boys, they sleep in their father's arms, ride on his back, beg for his pipe, and purloin betel from his shoulder bag. When they are three or four he makes them small canoes, again regardless of sex. Neither boys nor girls wear any clothing except tiny bracelets, anklets, necklaces of dogs' teeth, and beaded belts. These are usually worn only on state occasions, as continued wear chafes the skin and produces an ugly eruption. The adults emphasize sex differences from birth in their speech – a boy is a *nat*, a girl is a *ndrakein*, at an hour of age. Before birth only is the term *nat* used to denote child. These terms are used so frequently by women – who are likely to wax voluble about 'boy of mine', or 'girl of mine' – that a child of three will gravely correct the misapplication of a term to the baby of the house.

But before three, no other distinctions are made between the sexes. At about three maternal pride makes a new bid for the small girl. A tiny curly grass skirt is fashioned with eager hands and much comment, and the solemn-eyed baby arrayed in it for a feast day. The assumption of this costume unites the daughter with the mother in a way that has never happened before. Her mother is addressed as *pen*, woman, but she is a *ndrakein*, similarly her father is called a *kamal*, and her brother is a *nat*. The differences between her body and her brother's are obvious, as both sexes go naked. But as adults are clothed and most prudish about uncovering, and her undeveloped breasts are more like her father's than her mother's, mere anatomy does not give her nearly as good a clue to sex as does clothing.

The children were asked to draw pictures of men and women, or of girls and boys; where differences were shown – far more often they were ignored – the male anatomy was drawn correctly and the female was indicated by drawing a grass skirt.

From the moment when the baby girl and her slightly older sisters are dressed identically with their mother, although it is only for an hour, the girls begin to turn to their mothers more, to cling to their older sisters.

Little girls are not forced to wear grass skirts until they are seven or eight; they put them on, go swimming, get them wet, put on green leaves instead, lose the leaves, run about naked for a while, go home and put on dry skirts. Or they will take their grass skirts off and wade through the water at low tide, grass skirts high and dry on top of their curly heads. Not until twelve or thirteen is the sense of shame at being uncovered properly developed.

At about the age of three little boys begin to punt their fathers to the lee of the island which all the men of the village use as a latrine. Girls and women never go there, and the boy child learns thus early to slip apart from the women to micturate.

But little boys' great realization of maleness comes when they learn the phallic athleticism practised by their elders in the dance. A child grown suddenly proficient wriggles and prances for days and the adults applaud him salaciously. This is learned at about the age of three or four. Soon after this age, the boys are given bows and arrows and small fish spears; very tiny girls and boys wander about the lagoon at low tide playing with sticks and stones, imitating the more purposeful play of the older children without regard to sex. But little girls are never given real fishing toys. They are given small canoes and are as proficient in paddling and punting as the boys, but they never sail toy canoes of their own. From the time of this differentiation in play and dress the sex groups draw apart a little. There is no parental ban upon playing together nor is there any very deep antagonism between the groups. The line is drawn more in terms of activities. Round games and water games are played by both groups; fist fights as frequently cross sex lines as not: on moonlight nights boys and girls race shrieking over the mudflats of the lagoon laid bare by tide.

But as the adolescent girls are drawn more and more into the feminine activities of their households, the twelve-year-olds, eight-year-olds, five-year-olds, tend to follow in a long straggling line. When a girl reaches puberty all the younger girls down to the age of eight or nine go to sleep in her house for a month. This draws the girls closer together. There was one little island in the village reserved for the women. Here they went occasionally to perform various industrial tasks, and here on a grass plot at the peaked summit of the small steep cone, the little girls used to dance at sunset, taking off their grass skirts and waving them like plumes over their heads, shouting and circling, in a noisy revelry, high above the village.

The boys would be off stalking fish in the reedy shallows and sternly schooling the crowd of small boys who followed in their wake. Between the boys' group and the girls' there would be occasional flare-ups, battles with sea animal squirt guns or swift flight and pursuit. Very occasionally, as we have seen, they united in a semi-amorous play, choosing mates, building houses, making mock payments for their brides, even lying down cheek to cheek, in imitation of their parents. I believe that fear of the spirit wrath over sex prevented this play from ever developing into real sex play. Each group of children, believe that the young people who are now grown engaged in much more intriguing play when they were young. But as this golden age theme is investigated, each group pushes it back a generation further to the days just before their time when the spirits were not so easily angered. This play is always in groups. There is no opportunity for two children to slip away together; the group is too clamorous of all its members.

With the child's increased consciousness of belonging to a sex group and greater identification with adults of the same sex comes a rearrangement of the family picture. Up to the time a little girl is five or six, she accompanies her father as freely as would her brother. She sleeps with her father, sometimes until she is seven or eight. By this time she is entering the region of taboo. If she is not engaged herself, younger sisters and cousins may be engaged, and she will be on terms of avoidance with the boys to whom they are betrothed. If she is engaged herself, there will likely be several men in the village from whom she must hide her face. She is no longer the careless child who rode upon her father's back into the very sanctuary of male life, the ship island. More and more her father tends to leave her at home for her younger brothers and sisters, or to go more staidly, babyless, about his business. But she is used to adult attention, dependent upon the sense of pleasant power which it gives her. Gradually deserted by her father, she comes to identify herself either with her mother or with some older woman of her kindred. It is curious how much more frequent this latter adjustment is, except where the mother is a widow. It is as if the girl had so thoroughly passed over her mother in preference to her father that she could not go back and pick up the dropped thread. These attachments to older women have nothing of the nature of a 'crush' in them: they are very definitely in terms of the family picture. Often a grandmother is chosen. The older women are freer to teach the girls beadwork, to start them at work for their trousseaux. The younger women are more preoccupied with baby tending, which does not interest the little girls and in which their help is not enlisted. Little girls have no dolls and no pattern of playing with babies. We bought some little wooden statues from a neighbouring tribe and it was the boys who treated them as dolls and crooned lullabies to them.

From M. Mead (1963) (1930) *Growing Up In New Guinea: A Study of Adolescence and Sex in Primitive Societies*, Harmondsworth: Penguin, pp. 10–16, 117–20.

Questions

1. How would you describe Margaret Mead's attitude to the Manus? What 'evidence' is there for your description?
2. List the main similarities and differences between the Manus' and Western approaches to child-rearing. (Refer in particular to child-rearing and sex roles.)
3. What evidence does Mead provide to indicate that gender-specific behaviour is learned rather than innate?

Reading 6

Culture and civilization

SIGMUND FREUD

In this extract from Civilization and Its Discontents *Freud outlines some of the key features of contemporary civilisation (remember that he wrote this in the 1920s). He focuses on the role of science and technology in providing man with power and control through developments in communication and motor power and, crucially, in advancing human civilisation (in reading this you might also note the extent to which Freud, as with most other early theorists in the Social Sciences and elsewhere, routinely uses sexist language throughout his writing). Civilisation can be 'measured', Freud suggests, by comparing the advanced form of modern towns and cities with those of Shakespeare's or Dickens' times. He then raises the issue of whether, in terms of interpersonal relationships, the modern world is 'more civilized'. When reading this extract, consider how you would define civilisation and what you feel constitutes a civilised society.*

It is time for us to turn our attention to the nature of this civilization on whose value as a means to happiness doubts have been thrown. We shall not look for a formula in which to express that nature in a few words, until we have learned something by examining it. We shall therefore content ourselves with saying once more that the word 'civilization' describes the whole sum of the achievements and the regulations which distinguish our lives from those of our animal ancestors and which serve two purposes – namely to protect men against nature and to adjust their mutual relations [. . .]

We recognize as cultural all activities and resources which are useful to men for making the earth serviceable to them, for protecting them against the violence of the forces of nature, and so on. As regards this side of civilization, there can be scarcely any doubt. If we go back far enough, we find that the first acts of civilization were the use of tools, the gaining of control over fire and the construction of dwellings. Among these, the control over fire stands out as a quite extraordinary and unexampled achievement, while the others opened up paths which man has followed ever since, and the stimulus to which is easily guessed. With every tool man is perfecting his own organs, whether motor or sensory, or is removing the limits to their functioning. Motor power places gigantic forces at his disposal, which, like his muscles, he can employ in any direction; thanks to ships and aircraft neither water nor air can hinder his movements; by means of spectacles he corrects defects in the lens of his own eye; by means of the telescope he sees into the far distance; and by means of the microscope he overcomes the limits of visibility set by the structure of his retina. In the photographic camera he has created an instrument which retains the fleeting visual impressions, just as a gramophone disc retains the equally fleeting auditory ones; both are at bottom materializations of the power he possesses of recollection, his memory. With the help of the telephone he can hear at distances which would be respected as unattainable even in a fairy tale. Writing was in its origin the voice of an absent person; and the dwelling-house was a substitute for the mother's womb, the first lodging, for which in all likelihood man stir longs, and in which he was safe and felt at ease.

These things that, by his science and technology, man has brought about on this earth, on which he first appeared as a feeble animal organism and on which each individual of his species must once more make its entry . . . as a helpless suckling – these things do not only sound like a fairy tale, they are an actual fulfilment of every – or of almost every – fairy-tale wish. All these assets he may lay claim to as his cultural acquisition. Long ago he formed an ideal conception of omnipotence and omniscience which he embodied in his gods. To these gods he attributed everything that seemed unattainable to his wishes, or that was forbidden to him. One may say, therefore, that these gods were cultural ideals. To-day he has come very close to the attainment of this ideal, he has almost become a god himself [. . .]

Future ages will bring with them new and probably unimaginably great advances in this field of civilization and will increase man's likeness to God still more. But in the interests of our investigations, we will not forget that present-day man does not feel happy in his Godlike character.

We recognize, then, that countries have attained a high level of civilization if we find that in them everything which can assist in the exploitation of the earth by man and in his protection against the forces of nature – everything, in short, which is of use to him – is attended to and effectively carried out. In such countries rivers which threaten to flood the land are regulated in their flow, and their water is directed through canals to places where there is a shortage of it. The soil is carefully cultivated and planted with the vegetation which it is suited to support; and the mineral wealth below ground is assiduously brought to the surface and fashioned into the required implements and utensils. The means of communication are ample, rapid and reliable. Wild and dangerous animals have been exterminated, and the breeding of domesticated animals flourishes. But we demand other things from civilization besides these, and it is a noticeable fact that we hope to find them realized in these same countries. As though we were seeking to repudiate the first demand we made, we welcome it as a sign of civilization as well if we see people directing their care too to what has no practical value whatever, to what is useless – if, for instance, the green spaces necessary in a town as playgrounds and as reservoirs of fresh air are also laid out with flower-beds, or if the windows of the houses are decorated with pots of flowers. We soon observe that this useless thing which we expect civilization to value is beauty. We require civilized man to reverence beauty wherever he sees it in nature and to create it in the objects of his handiwork so far as he is able. But this is far from exhausting our demands on civilization. We expect besides to see the signs of cleanliness and order. We do not think highly of the cultural level of an English country town in Shakespeare's time when we read that there was a big dungheap in front of his father's house in Stratford; we are indignant and call it 'barbarous' (which is the opposite of civilized) when we find the paths in the Wiener Wald[1] littered with paper. Dirtiness of any kind seems to us incompatible with civilization. We extend our demand for cleanliness to the human body too. We are astonished to learn of the objectionable smell which emanated from the *Roi Soleil*[2] and we shake our heads on the Isola Bella[3] when we are shown the tiny wash-basin in which Napoleon made his morning toilet. Indeed, we are not surprised by the idea of setting up the use of soap as an actual yardstick of civilization. The same is true of order. It, like cleanliness, applies solely to the works of man. But whereas cleanliness is not to be expected in nature, order, on the contrary, has been imitated from her. Man's observation of the great astronomical regularities not only furnished him with a model for introducing order into his life, but gave him the first points of departure for doing so. Order is a kind of compulsion to repeat which, when a regulation has been laid down once and for all, decides when, where and how a thing shall be done, so that in every similar circumstance one is spared hesitation and indecision. The benefits of order are incontestable. It enables men to use space and time to the best advantage, while conserving their psychical forces. We should have a right to expect that order would have taken its place in human activities from the start and without difficulty; and we may well wonder that this has not happened – that, on the contrary, human beings exhibit an inborn tendency to carelessness, irregularity and unreliability in their work, and that a laborious training is needed before they learn to follow the example of their celestial models.

Beauty, cleanliness and order obviously occupy a special position among the requirements of civilization. No one will maintain that they are as important for life as control over the forces of nature or as some other factors with which we shall become acquainted. And yet no one would care to put them in the background as trivialities. That civilization is not exclusively taken up with what is useful is already shown by the example of beauty, which we decline to omit from among the interests of civilization. The usefulness of order is quite evident. With regard to cleanliness, we must bear in mind that it is demanded of us by hygiene as well, and we may suspect that even before the days of scientific prophylaxis the connection between the two was not altogether strange to man. Yet utility does not entirely explain these efforts; something else must be at work besides.

No feature, however, seems better to characterize civilization than its esteem and encouragement of man's higher mental activities – his intellectual, scientific and artistic achievements and the leading role that it assigns to ideas in human life. Foremost among those ideas are the religious systems, on whose complicated structure I have endeavoured to throw light elsewhere. Next come the speculations of philosophy; and finally what might be called man's 'ideals' – his ideas of a possible perfection of individuals, or of peoples or of the whole of humanity, and the demands he sets up on the basis of such ideas.

The last, but certainly not the least important, of the characteristic features of civilization remains to be assessed: the manner in which the relationships of men to one another, their social relationships, are regulated – relationships which affect a person as a neighbour, as a source of help, as another person's sexual object, as a member of a family and of a State. Here it is especially difficult to keep clear of particular ideal demands and to see what is civilized in general. Perhaps we may begin by explaining that the element of civilization enters on the scene with the first attempt to regulate these social relationships. If the attempt were not made, the relationships would be subject to the arbitrary will of the individual: that is to say, the physically stronger man would decide them in the sense of his own interests and instinctual impulses. Nothing would be changed in this if this stronger man should in his turn meet someone even stronger than he. Human life in common is only made possible when a majority comes together which is stronger than any separate individual and which remains united against all separate individuals. The power of this community is then set up as 'right' in opposition to the power of the individual, which is condemned as 'brute force'. This replacement of the power of the individual by the power of a community constitutes the decisive step of civilization. The essence of it lies in the fact that the members of the community restrict themselves in their possibilities of satisfaction, whereas the individual knew no such restrictions. The first requisite of civilization, therefore, is that of justice – that is, the assurance that a law once made will not be broken in favour of an individual. This implies nothing as to the ethical value of such a law. The further course of cultural development seems to tend towards making the law no longer an expression of the will of a small community – a caste or a stratum of the population or a racial group – which, in its turn, behaves like a violent individual towards other, and perhaps more numerous, collections of people.

The final outcome should be a rule of law to which all – except those who are not capable of entering a community – have contributed by a sacrifice of their instincts, and which leaves no one – again with the same exception – at the mercy of brute force.

The liberty of the individual is no gift of civilization. It was greatest before there was any civilization, though then, it is true, it had for the most part no value, since the individual was scarcely in a position to defend it [. . .]

The urge for freedom, therefore, is directed against particular forms and demands of civilization or against civilization altogether. It does not seem as though any influence could induce a man to change his nature into a termite's. No doubt he will always defend his claim to individual liberty against the will of the group. A good part of the struggles of mankind centre round the single task of finding an expedient accommodation – one, that is, that will bring happiness – between this claim of the individual and the cultural claims of the group; and one of the problems that touches the fate of humanity is whether such an accommodation can be reached by means of some particular form of civilization or whether this conflict is irreconcilable [. . .]

Finally, and this seems the most important of all, it is impossible to overlook the extent to which civilization is built up upon a renunciation of instinct, how much it presupposes precisely the non-satisfaction (by suppression, repression or some other means?) of powerful instincts. This 'cultural frustration' dominates the large field of social relationships between human beings.

From S. Freud (1975) (1929) *Civilization and its Discontents*, London: The Hogarth Press, pp. 26–34.

Notes

1. The wooded hills on the outskirts of Vienna.
2. Louis XIV of France.
3. The island in Lake Maggiore, visited by Napolean a few days before the battle of Marengo.

Questions

1. Summarise Freud's arguments about the role of each of the following as key characteristics and requirements of civilisation: beauty; cleanliness; order; ideas; and community.
2. Freud suggested that a 'high level of civilization' is achieved if man (*sic*) is able to 'exploit the earth' and protect himself against the forces

of nature. To what extent have events in the years since Freud's work supported or undermined this argument?

3. In what ways might civilisation involve a renunciation of instincts? (Consider how Freud's notion of civilisation undermines and restricts individual freedom.)

Reading 7

Socialisation and gender roles

MARIANNE GRABRUCKER

Can children be brought up in a gender-neutral manner? However well-intended parents may be, is it unrealistic to bring up a baby girl free from gender stereotyping? Those are the sort of issues that Marianne Grabrucker addresses in the diary she kept during the first three years of bringing up her daughter, Anneli. The reading below highlights some of the compromises Grabrucker had to make in bringing up Anneli. Given that Grabrucker made a conscious effort to be 'gender neutral', when reading these extracts you might consider how much more subject to gender socialisation the majority of children will be.

Introduction

A child is born, a new woman has arrived. And her future is going to be different.

These were more or less the thoughts that I and women friends and acquaintances had when my daughter was born. It was like starting school, the New Year, a new job or a new love affair; it was all going to be different this time – better. I was going to avoid all the old mistakes, or at least those we thought we understood. I would be cautious and diplomatic, would employ tact and the right sense of balance, so that a 'new woman' could unfold naturally.

I was, of course, simply following relevant theories of social conditioning, proceeding on the assumption that it is education which forms man and woman. For my daughter things were going to be different. She was not going to become like us, that is, women who were born in the post-war period. I did not want her to accept from her male contemporaries what we had accepted as regards education, work and personal relationships. I did not want her to be compliant, to keep her opinions to herself and to smile sweetly instead of contradicting. I did not want her to be always checking and rethinking her ideas before daring to open her mouth, unlike her male counterparts who would say everything three times and then repeat it once again. And I did not want her to be completely devoted to some man who would be continually finding fault with and criticising her until she lost faith in herself. I wanted her to avoid having plans for the future which were modest and which fitted in neatly with the reality of women's lives. My daughter was going to reach for the stars!

The theory was that our generation and the thousands of generations of women before us had been prevented from achieving all these things by a process of gender conditioning determined by centuries of patriarchy. This process had to be broken. My daughter's socialisation was going to be different – this was to be a new start and traditional influences were going to be eliminated as far as possible. I myself was determined to make no mistakes in this respect and I really believed that I was capable of this. I thought that my involvement and growth in the second wave of the women's movement in the late sixties, my own experience of personal relationships and of discrimination in my studies and in my profession as a lawyer had made me proof against any risk of my bringing up a child to be a typical girl. I had thought and talked about it too much to believe myself susceptible to that. If everything were caused by education then everything could equally well be avoided through education – such was the conclusion I came to [. . .]

I kept a diary about the development of my daughter. In the course of time I grew less sure and began to doubt my premises. I was often on the point of abandoning my theories and accepting a belief in innate gender-specific behaviour, for so many 'feminine' aspects of my daughter's behaviour could not possibly have been learned from me. And I was confirmed in this by many critical and emancipated mothers who were absolutely convinced that they were bringing up their children in a manner free of gender prejudice. For they too seemed to find, especially if they had both a daughter and a son, that there really were innate boy and girl traits. Nothing could be done about this, it simply had to be accepted. We shared many a sigh. But the mothers of boys seemed less concerned than the mothers of girls [. . .]

At the end of each day I began to make a precise account of everything that had happened, what I had said and done and what had been passed on to Anneli and her male and female friends – always from the point of view of what part these trivial, often insignificant, events might play in role creating. My sensitivity grew in direct ratio to my understanding. Days teemed with role-enforcing events, concealed and obvious, for which I was only rarely responsible.

An accumulation of such experiences provides the child with a pattern, in accordance with which it is bound to adjust its own behaviour within its environment. Only when I had gained this general view from three years of observing quite chance events, and grasped all the details as part of a whole picture, did I realise that I and the world around were building brick by brick a woman governed by patriarchy, and not a human being with female or male components. And so much of this happened unconsciously, unintentionally, without reflection or real understanding of the situation. For these reasons the mothers I spoke to about it denied that their approach to their children's upbringing was gender differentiated, as I would also no doubt have done without the diary. For the first time I recognised many things in everyday life as being gender stereotyped and realised that everything happened like a computer program set to 'girl upbringing'.

I am therefore now convinced that mothers who proceed from a belief in the innate differences in behaviour of the sexes are falling victim to a mechanism which keeps on reproducing itself. Behaviour patterns are handed on unconsciously. The result is then labelled 'innate' and it is here that the mistake is made. I therefore think it both mistaken and dangerous when progressive and thoughtful mothers begin to believe that there are innate differences just because, despite the best of intentions, they themselves are having no apparent success in rearing their children differently from traditional patterns [. . .]

The events described here happened principally in Berlin and Munich. Our home is in Munich and there Anneli lived in the father-mother-child nuclear family, where her father earned the money and was away from home from Monday to Friday and was available only in the evenings and at weekends. Since I was not earning and had more freedom I took the opportunity to visit friends and family in Berlin quite often, and there Anneli lived in the society of emancipated feminist women, with me but without her father. We also spent some time each year in the nearby Alps, in villages in the Tyrol or Switzerland. Anneli was thus exposed to a wide spectrum of behaviour and attitudes, between the progressive north and the ultra conservative south [. . .]

19 August 1981 (birth)

When I see her for the first time, when I look into her face and she into my eyes – she's lying on my stomach and the umbilical cord has just been cut – I think: 'She's beautiful, she has well proportioned features, she's pretty.' And I'm overwhelmed with relief and think 'Well, that'll make things a bit easier for her.' Because I've learned from personal experience that a woman has to look good to justify her existence in this world. Only then has she any right to open her mouth, to make demands without being laughed at (more than otherwise), is permitted to have wishes and to be choosy, not just making do with what happens to come her way. She can expect things of men, because she's got something to offer. Above all in the choice of partner. I'm full of vague fears for my daughter and worry that she will, after all, end up dependent on some man, on the benevolence and understanding of one partner, and I'm afraid things will only turn out okay if she can make her choice and not make do with second best.

These are all my own fears and problems I thought I'd got over long ago but which are now resurfacing. Apparently such anxieties, in the best patriarchal tradition, were latent; deep down I'm ready to pass them on to the next generation [. . .]

Winter 1981–82 (3 to 7 months)

I regularly meet one of my women colleagues, a lawyer, who had a son three weeks after I had Anneli.

Every time we meet, Karin admires Anneli, saying how pretty she is, how dainty and graceful her legs are, and what a good ballet dancer she'd make. She admires Anneli's long eyelashes and blue eyes and says that later on her flirtatious glance, her smile and delicate figure will turn men's heads and they'll run after her. 'Anneli will be able to twist men round her little finger', she says.

But neither his mother nor I say anything like this about her son. Neither of us paints a picture of a future geared to his appearance or of his market value with women. In his case we are amused when he pees in a wide arc as his nappy is being changed, or we just talk about his eating and sleeping habits.

Later I discuss this with Uschi, the mother of one-year-old Annalena, and she has a similar tale to tell. During a visit to a friend who has a son they talk first about how adorable Annalena looks – this is their main topic of conversation – and then about the boy's abilities, his progress and development.

Then I suddenly remember Margaret Mead, who said that a girl was important to the tribe, or society, by her very existence, because of her reproductive function; she doesn't need to achieve anything to justify herself, as men and boys do. Is this what's at the bottom of our behaviour? A girl is admired simply because she exists, because of her beauty, but a boy has to do something more than simply be there to attract attention; he has to define himself by playing with objects and by acquiring skills [. . .]

14 February 1983 (18 months)

We're walking in the centre of Munich. On an advertising hoarding there's a large advertisement for a film showing a picture of a half naked woman. Once again Anneli announces 'Woman nothing on.' The fact that she says this so often is beginning to get on my nerves. But she has obviously recognised naked women as a fact of life and feels a need to communicate to me her moments of recognition. I myself have become so blunted to the sight of naked women that I hardly register them any more.

In the evening there is a meeting of a club I'm a member of. I can't find a babysitter and Anneli wants to come with me. Since I'm chairperson I have to go and I take her with me. Inevitably we're fifteen minutes late and a man is just speaking when we arrive. He continues for another five minutes before handing over to me. During this time Anneli whispers to me 'Man talk.' After that I speak for a while and then everyone joins in. On the way home I ask Anneli whether she liked the meeting and all she says is 'Man talk.' I'm simply furious that the man's five minutes of talking have remained the determining factor of the evening for her.

I am depressed by the fact that her perception of how women and men live together can be reduced to one simple formula: 'Woman nothing on – man talk.' She's never said 'Man nothing on', and 'Woman talk' only once [. . .]

3 May 1983 (21 months)

Grandma is visiting us and is playing with Anneli. Some soft toys have been wrapped up and are being rocked to sleep. Grandma shows Anneli how to do it and she copies eagerly. Grandma would never have done this with a boy.

She's brought Anneli a present of a little shopping basket. When we set off to do the shopping in the afternoon I'm on the point of giving it to her and saying 'There, now you've got a shopping basket just like Mummy's', when it occurs to me that by doing so I'm identifying her with me and again defining her in terms of myself and my own activities. Of course, this isn't the first time. How often have I passed on the idea of being 'just like Mummy' in my daily activities as a housewife?

This sense of being just like Mummy, handed on in the daily intimacy between mother and daughter, stays with us all our lives [. . .]

28 December 1983 (2 years 4 months)

Anneli is playing with the Duplo pieces she got for Christmas and realises that one of the building units is a dredger. Now she needs a 'dredger man', to go with it. Klaus suggests that she use the figure of the girl as it would do just as well and hands her it. She rejects it with exasperation. 'That's a girl.'

Klaus: 'Can't girls drive dredgers?'

Anneli: 'No, because women would get their hands dirty then.' I'm shocked but recognise my own dislike of the grease, oil and dirt involved in car repairs . . . .

I'm sure I never actually said as much and am inclined to think she got this from Grandma. Or was my behaviour itself enough to lead her to this conclusion? I can hardly believe so [. . .]

Epilogue

One thing that made a strong impression on me was, on the one hand, girls' mothers' willingness to experiment and, on the other, the conservatism of boys' mothers. Gender limits are being extended for girls and their horizons broadened in comparison with former generations. And there are enough directions being made clear, since girls have a lot to gain in the experiment. Girls' mothers want change for their daughters, a new future, a different identity from the feminine one prescribed in the past. So they set off together with their little daughters on a search following first one and then another route, without really knowing whether they will achieve their goals. There is plenty of experimentation in the upbringing of girls. This means that girls are confronted with the two 'worlds' prescribed for the sexes, and are expected to feel at home in both. On the one hand many of the messages they receive require them to be and behave like girls. On the other hand they are also expected to feel at home in the boys' world. And all this at an age when they are struggling to find their own sexual identity and trying to find their way to one of the two poles.

The fact that little girls wear both trousers and dresses whilst anything other than traditionally masculine clothing is out of the question for boys makes clear how girls are forced to adapt to masculine lifestyles, and the demands this makes on them. This is the symbol of being a woman and at the same time being allowed, able, expected and obliged to do everything the masculine world decides for us. If the image of the independent self-confident professional woman requires it, we put on our tailored suit; if the sporting image and increased interest in technology so requires it, then we put on our dungarees or tracksuit. We change roles, in fact we change our very identity, because we learned early on how to do everything.

It's different for a boy. The mother and the people about him, who are all so concerned about his sexual identity, create no tension with his environment and its message by giving him varied clothes and toys. Identity development is for a small boy more or less straightforward and clear, following prescribed models. Whereas a girl might be praised for behaviour that exceeds traditional role expectations, the same is at best ignored in a boy. At worst he is put right at the first opportunity, but a boy will never – however progressive his parents may be – encounter positive reactions in those around him if he behaves like a girl [. . .]

Therefore, although there is no doubt that the liberation of girls from the chains of conventional upbringing can only be seen as positive, as long as no major effort is made to change boys' education as well, the pressure on girls to adapt will continue. As long as boys are not challenged, exposed to risk and to insecurity, placed outside the seclusion of patriarchal culture, we will be stuck with girls' skill at adapting. This means all sexual liberation is required of the incredible strength of small girls, of their carrying the burden of change on their shoulders. Unless boys are challenged they will again come up against the brick wall of masculine ignorance and lack of sensitivity and experience men's complete inability to question and change themselves. Men have never learned what it is like to feel one's way into different roles, to be laughed at, to take second place. They have always been in the winning team, they are insiders.

As long as mothers recoil in horror at the thought of their sons wearing their older sisters' nightdresses, beautiful though they may be, *nothing* will change in men. As long as Anneli is proud of wearing the cast-off clothing of Martin, nothing will change in her two-fold struggle to be both a woman and like a man.

I think it is time, now that a start has been made to change the upbringing of girls, to start a new gender approach with boys. Many examples have shown us that emancipatory education directed only at girls is doomed to failure and will never lead to any significant change in the relationship between the sexes. Only when both sexes from childhood on are engaged in a continual process of change, moving forward together step by step, is there any hope for a future of real equality.

From M. Grabrucker (1988) *There's a Good Girl: Gender Stereotyping in the First Three Years of Life: A Diary*, London: Women's Press, pp. 7–12, 17–19, 24–5, 35, 82, 159–61.

Questions

1. In her first diary entry (19 August 1981), Grabrucker comments on the looks of her daughter, Anneli, and comments 'I've learned from personal experience that a woman has to look good to justify her existence in the world.'
   (a) What evidence is there to support or refute this comment?
   (b) To what extent do you think 'looking good' is more important for girls/women than boys/men?
2. Grabrucker suggests that mothers are more conservative in bringing up boys than girls: for example they are less likely to discourage girls wearing trousers than they are to discourage boys from wearing dresses.
   (a) What other examples of the conservatism (with regard to gender) of parents in bringing up boys can you think of?
   (b) Why do you think parents might be more conservative in bringing up boys?

Reading 8

Culture and socialisation: The role of the soap opera

JACK LEVIN

Jack Levin's introductory book Sociological Snapshots *contains a series of short essays that examine the social structures and processes that underpin our everyday lives and experiences. In this essay Levin looks at the relationship between the 'fantasy' of TV soap operas and the reality of everyday life. While reading it, consider the extent to which it is justifiable to lump all serialised programmes together as soap operas; and consider what distinguishes soap operas from other drama (and perhaps ask yourselves why some forms of drama are seen as more 'acceptable' or 'cultural' than others).*

Confessions of a Soap Opera Addict

The daytime serials are more than I bargained for

I've been watching *Days of Our Lives* each day of my life for the last 22 years. It all started in 1968, when I took a year off to finish my doctoral dissertation. Each afternoon my wife and I sat together in the living room of our small apartment: She watched soap operas; I wrote my thesis. Working at home was tough enough, and eavesdropping on midday melodrama didn't help. In fact, it only reinforced my long-held impression that soaps were at about the same intellectual level as Saturday-morning cartoons – but those, at least, had action. Did anyone really care whether Julie and David got together again, when Marie would discover that her fiancé was actually her long-lost brother, or whether Missy was pregnant with 'another man's' child?

I didn't think so. Soap operas were television's 'opiate of the masses', I had decided: that medium through which too many Americans vicariously escaped their dreary existence into the make-believe world of the rich and beautiful. While the pressing economic and social problems of our society went ignored, millions of *General Hospital* groupies became Luke and Laura, if only for a few minutes a day. They needed that soap opera 'fix' to make their lives seem exciting and worthwhile. America's daytime serial fanatics were being distracted from improving their own lives by a particularly insidious form of fantasy and escapism.

I was especially annoyed by the depiction of women. They seemed always to be getting pregnant, not for the purpose of having children, but to manipulate and control the men in their lives. They used pregnancy to trap boyfriends into unwanted marriages, or husbands into maintaining unwanted marriages. In addition, any woman who dared have a career in a field traditionally dominated by men – medicine, law, business – was either mentally ill or evil. The sex role socialization message was unmistakable: Women were to stay out of the boardrooms and executive offices and stay in the kitchens and bedrooms 'where they belonged'.

It occurred to me that, in some perverse way, soap operas were a mass form of socializing young people to accept the *status quo*. Even while college students of the 1980s were scheduling or skipping courses to accommodate *General Hospital*, the majority of daytime serial watchers were high school graduates who had never attended college, mostly middle-aged women. Many used the characters on soaps as role models for how to handle their spouses. But what they learned frightened me: first, that infidelity and promiscuity were acceptable, even desirable, modes of sexual behavior; second, that divorce was the answer to any difference, no matte how trivial. If your marriage wasn't smooth as glass, get a divorce. Or a lover. Better yet, get a lover, then a divorce.

By the third or fourth week of watching out of the corner of my eye, I noticed something peculiar was happening to me. If I had to be away during a weekday afternoon, I'd call home for a rundown of that day's episodes. I scheduled meetings with colleagues so I wouldn't miss a particular serial. It got to the point where my wife would have to tear me away from my show to take a phone call or answer the door. It was painful to admit, but I was hooked. I was brainwashed – 1 had become a socialized 'soapie'.

Perhaps as a sort of therapy, I spent a good part of the next few years immersed in the study of soap operas. It was legitimate: I was teaching a course in mass communication and the students were discussing the impact of television on society. I read what the experts – psychologists, sociologists, and assorted communications specialists – had to say. I even assigned student projects that involved analysing the characters on daytime serials.

Surprising, to me at least, was their conclusion that soap operas were much better than prime-time dramatic series in representing women, minorities, and older people in central roles. While young and middle-aged males were vastly overrepresented on prime-time television, in soap operas one-half of the characters were women. Even more to their credit, soap operas featured actors and actresses who remained on the shows for decades. Many of them aged gracefully and remained thoroughly attractive while they continued to play roles central to the plot. Indeed, older people were treated much better on soap operas than on most other television fare. And the daytime serials frequently focused on a range of social problems: intergroup conflict, juvenile delinquency, alcoholism, organized crime – issues that were all but ignored by soaps' prime-time counterparts.

It was soon clear to me why soaps are so appealing to so many. For one, they provide us with the things we find lacking in modern life. Monday through Friday, without fail (barring an occasional hijaking or a presidential news conference) we follow our 'good friends' into their offices, living rooms, and bedrooms. We attend their weddings and funerals, visit them in the hospital after surgery or childbirth. We watch them argue with their spouses, make love with their mistresses, and punish their children. We often get to know more about the personal lives of our favorite soap opera characters than we know abut our real neighbors. In an era of anonymity, soap operas give us intimacy. Sadly, for those who are socially isolated, this may be the one and only source of intimacy in their lives, but perhaps this is better than nothing.

Soap operas make us feel good about ourselves. Misery loves miserable company, and our own problems are somehow less painful when we're able to compare them with the troubles of those we admire. The world of the daytime serial is the world of the wealthy, beautiful, and powerful – our cultural heroes, the people we aspire to become. Yet these characters have problems with their families and friends, much worse than ours. So we feel better – at their expense, of course.

Soap opera intimacy often takes the form of snooping, but only in the most positive sense. By eavesdropping, we're given the opportunity to rehearse our own emotional reactions to problems that may confront us in everyday life. Observing untimely deaths, kidnappings, divorces, and mental illness on television, we learn something about how we might handle similar problems in our own lives.

At least part of the influence of daytime serials can be attributed to the credibility of television as a form of mass communication. Study after study shows that Americans trust the authenticity of the images they see on the tube. In the process, however, heavy viewers often develop distorted views of social reality. They tend to exaggerate, for example, the amount of violence they are likely to encounter in everyday life, the proportion of criminal cases that end in jury trials, and the likelihood that physicians will perform miracle cures. For these viewers, the fantasy world on television becomes the reality. During the five years that Robert Young played Dr Marcus Welby, the actor received more than 250,000 letters asking him for medical advice. Admiring fans were apparently unable to distinguish actor Young from character Welby.

This incredible power of soap operas as an agent of socialization was brought home to me last year when I met two longtime stars of *Days of Our Lives,* Susan and Bill Hayes (Doug and Julie). As an interested observer, I couldn't resist asking them the questions that might confirm what I always suspected: Do soap opera addicts confuse the fantasy world of the daytime serials with the real world in which they live? Yes, and often. Whenever a *Days of Our Lives* star gives birth (it's only a pillow), gets married (a rhinestone wedding ring), or dies (usually a failure to renegotiate the actor's contract), cards and gifts appear at the studio, they said.

For me soaps have a special appeal. As a sociologist, I investigate problems that have no easy solutions. I spend years studying serial killers, for example, and am troubled that we can't predict from childhood experience who will eventually commit hideous crimes. I research the causes of prejudice and discrimination, and still see the number of racist acts of vandalism and desecration increasing. And, like others, I see criminals too often get suspended sentences while their victims suffer, the rich get richer as homelessness grows, and the questionable ethics of politicians go unpunished.

And that's where soaps are different. Warm, friendly, predictable, they make sure people get what they deserve.

From J. Levin (1993) *Sociological Snapshots,* Newbury Park CA: Pine Forge Press, pp. 34–7.

Questions

1. In the first paragraph, Jack Levin suggests that soap operas are 'low culture': 'the same intellectual level as Saturday-morning cartoons' as he puts it. Why do you think that he initially held this view?
2. List arguments for and against the view that 'soap operas (are) a mass form of socialising young people to accept the *status quo*'. (Give examples from specific soaps if you can.)
3. Consider one (or more) soap opera that you are familiar with:
   (a) How would you describe the portrayal of women; ethnic minorities; old people? Do you agree with Levin's suggestion that soap operas give a better representation of these groups than other television programming?
   (b) What personal and social problems have been dealt with in recent episodes? How balanced and helpful would you say that this coverage was?

Part I Origins and Concepts

Further Reading

There are a number of studies that could be used to complement and reflect on Robert Nisbet's analysis of the origins of sociology, including:

Hawthorn, G. (1976) *Enlightenment and Despair: A History of Sociology*, Cambridge: Cambridge University Press.

Hobsbawm, E.J. (1962) *The Age of Revolution: Europe 1789–1948*, London: Weidenfeld & Nicolson.

Kent, R. (1981) *A History of British Empirical Sociology*, Aldershot: Gower.

Swingewood, A. (1991) *A Short History of Sociological Thought*, 2nd edn, London: Macmillan.

Hobsbawm's classic historical text traces the transformation that the dual revolutions – the French Revolution of 1789 and the Industrial Revolution – brought to almost every sphere of European life. It would be particularly useful for those whose history is a bit weak or rusty! The other two studies focus more directly on the history of sociology. Hawthorn begins with what he terms the 'prehistory' of the subject, particularly the work of Rousseau, Kant and Hegel, and considers how this influenced the founding theorists, including Marx, Durkheim and Weber.

Swingewood's text details the rise of sociological thought from its origins in eighteenth-century philosophy to the classical sociology of Marx, Durkheim and Weber and the development of their work in the modern perspectives of functionalism, interactionism, structuralism and critical Marxism. Kent's work has a narrower remit, focusing on the origins of British empirical sociology. While theoretical sociology is generally associated with European writers, Kent argues that although Britain may not have produced her Durkheim or Weber it was here that empirical sociology (sociology based on research that reveals facts and data that can be tested) first developed. The best examples of empirical sociology can be found, he argues, in the detailed studies undertaken in the new industrial cities of Britain by researchers such as Charles Booth (see Reading 47, Part Four).

It is difficult to recommend particular further reading on concepts such as social control, socialisation and culture in that the terms themselves and the ideas they encompass are very diffuse. One starting point would be to look at some of the sociology dictionaries and encyclopedias that are available. A particularly full discussion of all three of these concepts is given in the following:

Mann, M. (ed.) (1983) *The Macmillan Student Encyclopedia of Sociology*, London: Macmillan.

A greater understanding would also, of course, be gained by reading more from the sources of the readings chosen for this section.

One general text that provides an up-to-date and international introduction to sociological traditions and concepts and that we would particularly recommend is:

Ballard, C., Gubbay, J. and Middleton, C. (eds) (1997) *The Student's Companion to Sociology*, London: Blackwell.

It is a collection written by an international team (and with an American editor, Ballard, and British editors, Gubbay and Middleton) that conveys the excitement of studying sociology and provides practical advice for students new to the subject and for those hoping to use their sociological education to enhance their employment prospects.

Activity

This activity involves you looking at the way in which introductory sociology texts deal with some of the key concepts. Start with at least two sociology textbooks you have used.

1. Look up social control and socialisation (the terms should be referenced in the index; however this is not always the case and you may have to skim through sections of the book). How similar are the definitions? In what topics or areas of sociology are the terms most usually referred to and discussed?
2. With regard to cultural diversity, find out how much space is devoted to discussing the following:
   - non-Western societies
   - pre-industrial societies
   - Western but non-British or American societies.

Note: You could take specific chapters (e.g. on the Family, Education, etc.) in a number of textbooks and compare their coverage of the above.

Part II

Sociological Theories

9

Introduction

Introductory texts in sociology naturally provide students with an overview of a variety of sociological theories, perhaps following a general distinction between classic/old and more contemporary theorising. The work of key theorists is summarised in what is hoped to be an accessible, user-friendly way. Thus students are presented with secondary reviews (albeit often very clearly and concisely written) perhaps interspersed with a few quotes to give a flavour of the 'real thing'. While this is inevitable given the dictates of space and time on introductory courses, it is a pity that students can complete courses in sociology without reading any original theoretical work in the subject. However, to gain a fuller understanding and appreciation of theoretical positions and arguments we have to look at original sources, many of which are far more accessible and interesting than might initially be thought. The readings included in this section provide examples of the 'real thing'; they provide a more substantial 'taste' of the work of some of the key social theorists, both classic and modern.

Just as there are a wide range of sociological theories, so there are a number of different ways of classifying them and, so, of organising introductory chapters on theory. A general practice in introducing sociological theory is to start with a 'macro–micro' categorisation. This division is seen as a basic dualism in social theory and essentially highlights a society–individual distinction – a division between theories that focus on society and those that focus on the individual. Macro theories emphasise the large-scale, more general features of society including social institutions and organisations; and hence are sometimes categorised under headings such as 'social systems' or 'structural' theories. Micro theories centre on the personal, immediate aspects of everyday life and are sometimes known as 'social action' theories. While this is an important distinction, in this section we introduce different theoretical writings in a roughly chronological manner and then relate them to the macro–micro dualism. This is because the early, 'classic' theories in sociology were essentially 'grand theories' adopting a macro approach to their analyses and, given the importance of these classic theories, there would be clear imbalance toward the macro side of the dualism. While we agree that the society–individual distinction is a useful analytic tool, there are some difficulties with it. It is clearly impossible to see individuals as completely separate from society and social influences. As Layder (1994) puts it 'there is no such thing as society without the individuals who make it up just as there are no individuals existing outside the influence of society' (p. 3). However, he warns against simply abandoning this distinction: 'to neglect this distinction would be to merge the individual with social forces to such an extent that the idea of unique self-identities would disappear along with the notion of "subjective experience" as a valid category of analysis.'

We start this section with a reading from Auguste Comte, who has perhaps as great a claim as anyone to be called the founder of sociology in that he 'invented' the terms 'sociology', which he included in his 'Cours de Philosophie Positive', published in 1838, and 'positivism', which he used as the equivalent of scientific. Comte was born in 1798 and grew up in an age when science was making massive strides in 'explaining' nature. He read widely around the history of science and believed that the methods established in the natural sciences could be applied to the study of society's origins and development. Although Comte did not develop a theoretical perspective in the way of Durkheim, Marx or Weber (and receives little coverage on introductory courses in sociology) he made an important contribution to theories of social development. Comte provided an evolutionary account of how society developed and changed: he believed that the development of the human mind, and thereby of knowledge and belief, was closely related to the way in which society was organised. He argued that different types of society and different forms of human thought emerged in sequences that reflected different types of knowledge. Comte's view was, essentially, an optimistic one of inevitable human progress, with humankind gradually freeing itself from the remnants of theology and metaphysics and evolving to a positive (scientific) state, with scientific rationality becoming the dominant mode of thought. As society became more complex and differentiated, Comte felt that sociology (and particularly positive sociology) should and would develop as the natural discipline to analyse social development, social institutions and then interaction between them. As the first 'grand theorist' in sociology Comte's work influenced later, more widely acknowledged, social theorists who have attempted to explain the nature of modern industrial society by examining how different forms of society evolve. This influence can be seen in Durkheim's account of the move from mechanical to organic forms of social solidarity and in Marx's historical materialist analysis of social change.

Although many theorists and writers have been influential in the establishment and development of sociology, Durkheim, Marx and Weber are generally seen as the key classic theorists. Readings 11 to 16 provide examples of the work of these theorists; work that continues to play an important part in contemporary sociology. In attempting to understand and explain industrial society, Durkheim focused on the moral basis of social order and stability – the basis of what he termed social solidarity. He believed that social order was based on a core of shared values. This concern with social solidarity runs through all of Durkheim's major works, as does his other main 'theme' – the establishment of sociology as an autonomous subject centred on the study of social facts (rather than individuals). His famous study *Suicide* (written in 1897) brings these two themes together. He suggests that different forms of social solidarity can be used to provide a sociological explanation for apparently individual decisions to commit suicide. To explain what is generally taken to be a very private act sociologically would, Durkheim believed, help to establish the value of sociology. Reading 11 contains a series of extracts from *Suicide* that describe and illustrate the three major forms of suicide he categorised and then examines the notion of a social suicide rate that exists separately to and cannot be explained by individual peculiarities.

Marx's analysis of society and history was, essentially, an attempt to discover and explain the principles of change in society. Although he emphasised the conflicts that existed in all societies he did not aim just to explain the divisions in society, but also to discover which groups had strong interests in maintaining the existing structures in their societies and which in trying to change them. These groups Marx saw as social classes and, not surprisingly, social class plays a key role in Marx's analysis. In various of his writings, Marx grapples with defining and describing what constitutes a social class – at both the general, theoretical level and in relation to specific societies at specific periods of history. In the *Communist Manifesto* (Reading 12) Marx suggested a very simplified class model based on a polarity between two, opposed hostile classes – in capitalist society these two classes were the numerically small bourgeoisie and the immense proletariat majority. As capitalism developed intermediate groups would disappear into one or other of these two classes. Elsewhere in his writings Marx provided a much more detailed and complex class analysis. Reading 13 is taken from *The Eighteenth Brumaire of Louis Bonaparte* in which Marx provides an account of historical change in terms of class relationships and class struggle. The study focuses on the French Revolution of 1848 and its aftermath. This period encompassed the fall of Louis Philippe, the establishing of a provisional government composed of various sectors of society united against the domination of the aristocracy and the formation of the 'party of order' with Bonaparte as its figurehead. However a *coup d'état* and his dictatorship had always been Bonaparte's obsession and this happened on 2 December 1851 after a period of struggle between the parliamentary bourgeoisie and the Bonaparte party.

Marx's analysis of these political developments aimed to explain why different classes in French society represented themselves in particular ways in the political arena. In France at this time capitalism was still very undeveloped with the great majority of the population still involved in either peasant or artisan production. There was no clear division into the industrial proletariat and the bourgeoisie and thus there was a much richer variety of classes and fractions of classes. Marx's account and analysis of the peasantry as a passive class of Bonapartism is the focus of our Reading 13. Marx saw the 'Bonapartes' as the dynasty of the peasants: 'Bonaparte represents a class, indeed he represents the most numerous class of French society, the small peasant proprietors.'

All of the early, founding writers reflected on the role of religion in the developing capitalist societies of their time. Durkheim, Marx and Weber were concerned about the consequences of what they felt to be the diminishing hold of religion on social life and the spread of rationalism in place of religious thought and practice. Although there are clear differences in their analyses, both Durkheim and Marx examined the role of religion in maintaining and reinforcing the *status quo* in society. Durkheim emphasises the role of religion in binding communities together, focusing on the integrative function of religion. His argument that religion fulfils a social need through promoting social solidarity and cohesion was elaborated in his classic study *The Elementary Forms of the Religious Life.* Reading 14 is taken from the introduction to this work, in which Durkheim argues that studying the most elementary form of religion (in this case the totemic religion of the Australian aborigines) would provide an understanding of the essential religious nature of humankind in general and contemporary society in particular. Marx did not write widely on religion but referred to it here and there in his work; he saw religion as a tool for manipulating and controlling the mass of the population, benefiting the powerful at the expense of the less powerful and thereby strengthening divisions rather than promoting integration. Reading 15 is taken from the introduction to his *Contribution to the Critique of Hegel's Philosophy of Law* and, in the space of a few paragraphs, includes Marx's most famous comments on the role of religion.

With Durkheim and Marx, Max Weber is the third of the 'holy trinity' of classic sociologists who have had the greatest influence on modern sociology. Weber felt that the basis of sociological analysis should be meaning: the social world had to be understood in terms of the meaning individuals gave to their social behaviour. Sociology should aim to understand human action and this would involve interpreting the meaning of action for those involved. Weber used the term *verstehen* to describe this procedure of interpretive understanding which he argued sociology should adopt. Because of this emphasis on interpretation, Weber is generally regarded as the major influence on the interpretive approach in sociology. Weber's analytical approach is illustrated in his famous study *The Protestant Ethic and the Spirit of Capitalism* in which he applies the concept of *verstehen* to a specific socio-historical process. In this study Weber tried to demonstrate the influence that ideas and beliefs could have on major historical events and change. Reading 16 includes extracts from two sections of *The Protestant Ethic and the Spirit of Capitalism*: the

Introduction, in which Weber discusses the nature of Western (or Occidental as Weber puts it) capitalism, and his discussion of the Protestant conception of 'the calling', the nature of asceticism and their links with capitalism.

Grand theory did not end with the writing of the founding theorists. Durkheim's work, for instance, was developed as the cornerstone of the functionalist theoretical perspective – the dominant sociological perspective from the 1930s up to the 1960s. It was the work of the American sociologist, Talcott Parsons, that established functionalism as the pre-eminent theoretical position in sociology. Parsons, along with Robert Merton, was the leader of the 'golden age' of American sociology of the 1940s and 1950s; his ideas and theoretical approach dominated the sociological scene of this period. Of particular significance for the development of the 'grand' theoretical perspective of functionalism was Parsons' work on the social system and its power to influence the behaviour of individuals. Although Parsons saw the individual as an important unit of analysis, individual action was constrained by the social system and the complex interrelations of the structured parts of the system. Indeed, his work provides an interpretation of the connection between the macro and micro aspects of social life. While not denying Parsons' huge influence on sociology, his written work can perhaps most politely be described as difficult. Reading 17 is taken from C. Wright Mills' summary of Parsons' text *The Social System* (1951) – which Mills perhaps somewhat cheekily suggests could be distilled into a few pages. Our extract gives a flavour of Parsons' writing while Mills' commentary provides an interpretation of the gist of Parsons' argument.

Symbolic Interactionism is the most established of the sociological theories that fit under the broad heading of interpretive sociology: theories that focus on the micro level of social life as a basis for explaining human behaviour. Symbolic Interactionism developed from the writings of sociologists working at the University of Chicago in the 1920s and 1930s; in particular the work of George Herbert Mead on the relationship between the individual and society. Mead did not write any key texts or classic studies (indeed, when he died in 1931 he had not published any books) and it is his lectures that were used by sociologists and graduate students at the University of Chicago to introduce his writings into the mainstream of sociological theory and to establish him as the founder of Symbolic Interactionism. The concept of the self was developed by Mead in an attempt to understand how individuals relate to one another. He saw the self as being made up of two essential elements which he called the 'I' and the 'Me'. The nature of the 'I' and the 'Me' and their relationships to the important sociological concepts such as social control and socialisation are explored in Reading 18.

While Mead and fellow social scientists at the University of Chicago played a key role in the development of an interpretive approach in sociology, Erving Goffman's work from the 1950s until his death in 1982 established the place of interpretive sociology, and particularly Symbolic Interactionism, in the mainstream of sociological theorising. The influence of Mead is evident in Goffman's concern with the sociology of everyday life and his analyses of interpersonal relationships. Through his analysis Goffman developed what has become known as the dramaturgical approach, based on the notion that in everyday life individuals have to be 'actors' – playing roles, negotiating situations and dealing with audiences. Goffman emphasised the social order underlying relationships and encounters and how it is based on strongly held norms; he also looked at the consequences when this order is disrupted. We all like to think of ourselves as 'normal' and Goffman's collection of essays *Stigma* (1970), from which Reading 19 is taken, examined the strategies used by people with what he termed 'spoiled identities' (such as the mentally ill or the physically disabled) to cope with being stigmatised.

As well as the development of Symbolic Interactionism and interpretive sociology in post-First World War USA, another important school of social theorising developed during this period based on the work of social researchers at Frankfurt University. The 'Frankfurt School' represented an attempt by Marxist theorists to explain the failure of working-class revolution in capitalist societies. It developed a critical approach to both capitalism and Soviet communism, advocating a critical analysis of all forms of domination in modern society: an approach that earned this school of thought the name 'critical theory'. The critical theorists were strongly affected by their experiences in Hitler's Germany. They argued that modern society had to be examined critically in order to understand modern life and that one of the realities of modern life was that knowledge was not necessarily a social good, but that it could be and was implicated in evil. Critical theory aimed to revitalise rather than undermine traditional, 'official' Marxism and to some extent critical theory became synonymous with neo-Marxism. The leading members of the Frankfurt School of critical theorists included Max Horkheimer, Theodore Adorno and Herbert Marcuse, all of whom were forced into exile in the USA as a result of Hitler's successes in the 1930s. Reading 20 is taken from Herbert Marcuse's *One-Dimensional Man* (1964), one of the most accessible texts from the Frankfurt School writers, in which Marcuse argues that modern societies gave the working classes a false consciousness through generating artificial needs.

So far in this section we have included ten readings from social theorists and they have all been males. Yet sociology is not generally seen as a 'male subject': indeed, more females than males take introductory sociology courses. Perhaps part of the reason for this imbalance is that only relatively recently has feminism begun to impact on and reshape sociology. One of the key texts that has helped the establishment of feminist social theory has been Simone de Beauvoir's *The Second Sex* (first published in 1949). Reading 21 is taken from Book Two of *The Second Sex,* which looks at 'Woman's Life Today', and from the chapter on 'The Married Woman'. In this extract de Beauvoir expresses the view shared by many contemporary feminists that marriage is 'better' for men than for women and that the subordination of women is the product of social conditioning rather than a fact of nature. In response to such texts and to the fictional writings of authors such as Virginia Woolf, feminist sociologists have produced an extensive critique of conventional sociological theory. Kate Millett's *Sexual Politics* was one of the classic texts of the 'second wave' of feminism. It influenced many feminists in the late 1960s and early 1970s who were trying to make sense of why women remained relatively powerless. *Sexual Politics* was a significant book because it presented all relationships between men and women, even those considered the most personal and intimate, as power relations based on the systematic oppression of women by men. Millett felt that no aspect of society was free from patriarchal influence and Reading 22 highlights the role of the family, and violence within it, in perpetuating male supremacy and female subjugation. Millett's emphasis on the enduring nature of patriarchy and on gender inequality as the fundamental inequality has meant that she has been identified with radical feminism.

As feminist theory developed in the 1970s and 1980s the universalising approach of Millett and other feminists, who positioned all women as sharing an oppressed social position and all men as equally powerful, received criticism from feminists striving to acknowledge and theorise differences between women and the relationship between gender and other dynamics of inequality. bell hooks is an American Black feminist whose work has highlighted the racism and ethnocentrism of the predominantly White feminist movements and theories. She and other Black feminists have pointed out that many White feminists have developed theories based on a White experience and have inaccurately generalised this to all women. Lumping women together as an oppressed group with a shared experience has meant that much feminist theory has neglected differences between women and specifically the impact of race and racism on women's lives. Reading 23 is taken from *Feminist Theory: from Margin to Center* in which hooks challenges the ethnocentrism of much White feminist theory. hooks is also critical of what she refers to as opportunist feminism, which does not fundamentally challenge inequality but simply enables a small group of privileged women to gain status and power. In this extract hooks stresses that an examination of the position and experience of Black women within social relations provides real insights into social structures, insights which can enrich feminist theory. Such experiences, including the exposure to sexist, racist and class oppression, demonstrate the difficulty of identifying one form of inequality as more fundamental or oppressive than another and the inadequacy of a feminism which focuses simply on gender.

This section started with extracts from the sociological 'classics'. Post-modernism rejects this notion of classic or grand theory and advocates a relativist position that treats all such theories (or metanarratives) as 'texts' rather than gospels. All theoretical points of view are valid; they merely represent different ways of looking at things. Marxism, functionalism, interactionism or indeed sociology itself have no special claim to truth.

One of the consequences for sociology of this relativist position is that postmodernism cannot be seen as a unified theory but rather as a collection of different ideas and perspectives. In his study *Consumer Culture and Postmodernism* Mike Featherstone (Reading 24) argues that the emphasis on consumption, led by the mass media and advertising, is a key determinant of everyday life. He looks for the roots of this postmodern consumer culture through an examination of the theories of consumption and postmodernism of writers such as Bourdieu, Baudrillard, Lyotard and Jameson. This reading is taken from his discussion of how changes in culture have encouraged the development of 'postmodern lifestyles' in contemporary cities.

Like many of the most influential writers and theorists, it is not easy to categorise Michel Foucault under a neat theoretical heading. Indeed, Foucault did not see himself as a practitioner of the social sciences; rather they were the object of his study and his work has provided a major critique of the conventional methodology and assumptions of sociology and other of the human sciences. However, to the extent that Foucault was not interested in finding a general theory of history, nor in unveiling the 'truth', in his detailed studies of, for instance, the asylum, the prison and sexuality, his work can be seen as taking a 'postmodernist' position. Foucault's work can be seen as a rejection of the macro–micro dualism in that it involves a rejection of both structural theories and of theories that centre on the analysis of the individual subject. Reading 25 is taken from Foucault's *Discipline and Punish* in which he analyses how 'disciplinary technology' is imposed and used as a means for regulation and subjection. Although Foucault relates the spread of disciplinary control – through institutions such as prisons, hospitals and schools – to the development of capitalism, the emphasis of his work is on the individual subject and power.

Reading 10

The law of human progress

AUGUSTE COMTE

This reading looks at Comte's preoccupation with evolutionary progress. It is taken from the introduction to The Positive Philosophy *in which Comte sets out the aims of his work and his evolutionary view of society and thought, that later became known as the 'law of three stages'. The aim of establishing and understanding the law of human development and the positive philosophy which characterises modern society led Comte himself to describe his area of study as 'vast and hitherto indeterminate'. Such a grand aim, together with the fact that Comte was writing some 150 years ago, does not make Comte's study an easy read. However, given Comte's influence on later 'grand theorists', and in particular Emile Durkheim, it is worth reading his own summary of the different stages of human development and how one leads inevitably to the next, and considering how it relates to the major sociological theories you have already encountered. In this extract, Comte defines and discusses the three stages of human society and thought: first, theological society, dominated by primitive religious thought, with intuition and feeling being all important; second, metaphysical society, characterised by the beginnings of critical thought and the search for some sort of ultimate reality; and third, positive society, based on the rejection of religious belief and the pre-eminence of scientific thought.*

Introduction – Account of the Aim of the Work – View of the Nature and Importance of the Positive Philosophy

A general statement of any system of philosophy may be either a sketch of a doctrine to be established, or a summary of a doctrine already established. If greater value belongs to the last, the first is still important, as characterizing from its origin the subject to be treated. In a case like the present, where the proposed study is vast and hitherto indeterminate, it is especially important that the field of research should be marked out with all possible accuracy. For this purpose, I will glance at the considerations which have originated this work, and which will be fully elaborated in the course of it.

In order to understand the true value and character of the Positive Philosophy, we must take a brief general view of the progressive course of the human mind, regarded as a whole; for no conception can be understood otherwise than through its history.

Law of human progress

From the study of the development of human intelligence, in all directions, and through all times, the discovery arises of a great fundamental law, to which it is necessarily subject, and which has a solid foundation of proof, both in the facts of our organization and in our historical experience. The law is this: that each of our leading conceptions – each branch of our knowledge – passes successively through three different theoretical conditions: the Theological, or fictitious; the Metaphysical, or abstract; and the Scientific, or positive. In other words, the human mind, by its nature, employs in its progress three methods of philosophizing, the character of which is essentially different, and even radically opposed: viz., the theological method, the metaphysical, and the positive. Hence arise three philosophies, or general systems of conceptions on the aggregate of phenomena, each of which excludes the others. The first is the necessary point of departure of the human understanding; and the third is its fixed and definitive state. The second is merely a state of transition.

First stage In the theological state, the human mind, seeking the essential nature of beings, the first and final causes (the origin and purpose) of all effects – in short, Absolute knowledge – supposes all phenomena to be produced by the immediate action of supernatural beings.

Second stage In the metaphysical state, which is only a modification of the first, the mind supposes, instead of supernatural beings, abstract forces, veritable entities (that is, personified abstractions) inherent in all beings, and capable of producing all phenomena. What is called the explanation of phenomena is, in this stage, a mere reference of each to its proper entity.

Third stage In the final, the positive state, the mind has given over the vain search after Absolute notions, the origin and destination of the universe, and the causes of phenomena, and applies itself to the study of their laws – that is, their invariable relations of succession and resemblance. Reasoning and observation, duly combined, are the means of this knowledge. What is now understood when we speak of an explanation of facts is simply the establishment of a connection between single phenomena and some general facts, the number of which continually diminishes with the progress of science.

Ultimate point of each

The Theological system arrived at the highest perfection of which it is capable when it substituted the providential action of a single Being for the varied operations of the numerous divinities which had been before imagined. In the same way, in the last stage of the Metaphysical system, men substitute one great entity (Nature) as the cause of all phenomena, instead of the multitude of entities at first supposed. In the same way, again, the ultimate perfection of the Positive system would be (if such perfection could be hoped for) to represent all phenomena as particular aspects of a single general fact; such as Gravitation, for instance.

The importance of the working of this general law will be established hereafter. At present, it must suffice to point out some of the grounds of it.

Evidences of the law

There is no science which, having attained the positive stage, does not bear marks of having passed through the others. Some time since it was (whatever it might be) composed, as we can now perceive, of metaphysical abstractions; and, further back in the course of time, it took its form from theological conceptions. We shall have only too much occasion to see, as we proceed, that our most advanced sciences still bear very evident marks of the two earlier periods through which they have passed.

The progress of the individual mind is not only an illustration, but an indirect evidence of that of the general mind. The point of departure of the individual and of the race being the same, the phases of the mind of a man correspond to the epochs of the mind of the race. Now, each of us is aware, if he looks back upon his own history, that he was a theologian in his childhood, a metaphysician in his youth, and a natural philosopher in his manhood. All men who are up to their age can verify this for themselves.

Besides the observation of facts, we have theoretical reasons in support of this law.

The most important of these reasons arises from the necessity that always exists for some theory to which to refer our facts, combined with the clear impossibility that, at the outset of human knowledge, men could have formed theories out of the observation of facts. All good intellects have repeated, since Bacon's time, that there can be no real knowledge but that which is based on observed facts. This is incontestable, in our present advanced stage; but, if we look back to the primitive stage of human knowledge, we shall see that it must have been otherwise then. If it is true that every theory must be based upon observed facts, it is equally true that facts cannot be observed without the guidance of some theory. Without such guidance, our facts would be desultory and fruitless; we could not retain them; for the most part we could not even perceive them.

Thus, between the necessity of observing facts in order to form a theory, and having a theory in order to observe facts, the human mind would have been entangled in a vicious circle, but for the natural opening afforded by Theological conceptions. This is the fundamental reason for the theological character of the primitive philosophy. This necessity is confirmed by the perfect suitability of the theological philosophy to the earliest researches of the human mind. It is remarkable that the most inaccessible questions – those of the nature of beings, and the origin and purpose of phenomena – should be the first to occur in a primitive state, while those which are really without our reach are regarded as almost unworthy of serious study. The reason is evident enough: that experience alone can teach us the measure of our powers; and if men had not begun by an exaggerated estimate of what they can do, they would never have done all that they are capable of. Our organization requires this. At such a period there could have been no reception of a positive philosophy, whose function is to discover the laws of phenomena, and whose leading characteristic it is to regard as interdicted to human reason those sublime mysteries which theology explains, even to their minutest details, with the most attractive facility. It is just so under a practical view of the nature of the researches with which men first occupied themselves. Such inquiries offered the powerful charm of unlimited empire over the external world – a world destined wholly for our use, and involved in every way with our existence. The theological philosophy, presenting this view, administered exactly the stimulus necessary to incite the human mind to the irksome labour without which it could make no progress. We can now scarcely conceive of such a state of things, our reason having become sufficiently mature to enter upon laborious scientific researches, without needing any such stimulus as wrought upon the imaginations of astrologers and alchemists. We have motive enough in the hope of discovering the laws of phenomena, with a view to the confirmation or rejection of a theory. But it could not be so in the earliest days; and it is to the chimeras of astrology and alchemy that we owe the long series of observations and experiments on which our positive science is based. Kepler felt this on behalf of astronomy, and Berthollet on behalf of chemistry. Thus was a spontaneous philosophy, the theological, the only possible beginning, method, and provisional system, out of which the Positive philosophy could grow. It is easy, after this, to perceive how Metaphysical methods and doctrines must have afforded the means of transition from the one to the other.

The human understanding, slow in its advance, could not step at once from the theological into the positive philosophy. The two are so radically opposed, that an intermediate system of conceptions has been necessary to render the transition possible. It is only in doing this, that Metaphysical conceptions have any utility whatever. In contemplating phenomena, men substitute for supernatural direction a corresponding entity. This entity may have been supposed to be derived from the supernatural action: but it is more easily lost sight of, leaving attention free for the facts themselves, till, at length, metaphysical agents have ceased to be anything more than the abstract names of phenomena. It is not easy to say by what other process than this our minds could have passed from supernatural considerations to natural; from the theological system to the positive.

From A. Comte (1853) *The Positive Philosophy of Auguste Comte*, freely translated and condensed by H. Martineau, Vol. 1, London: John Chapman, pp. 1–5.

Questions

1. Comte suggests that the modern state of mind has abandoned 'the vain search after Absolute notions', such as the origin and destination of the universe. Do you think he is correct to suggest this? Can you think of any examples which indicate that modern humankind is still interested in such questions?
2. What 'evidence' can you suggest that would support Comte's assertion that 'each of us is aware, if he (*sic*) looks back upon his own history, that he was a theologian in his childhood, a metaphysician in his youth, and a natural philosopher in his manhood'?

Reading 11

The social suicide rate

EMILE DURKHEIM

In his famous study Suicide, *Durkheim argues that different types of social context, in particular different forms of social solidarity, can explain the variation in rates of suicide in different societies. Suicide is a social fact and has to be explained (or more correctly its distribution has to explained) by other social facts. How else could we explain the differing suicide rates between, say, England and Italy, women and men or Catholics and Protestants? This reading starts with extracts from Durkheim's categorisation and description of three different main types of suicide: egoistic, reflecting a lack of integration to society and social groups; altruistic, where individuals are so integrated that they are happy to sacrifice their lives out of a sense of duty to the society; and anomic, where society does not adequately integrate and regulate individuals. In the last section of the reading, Durkheim argues that in spite of there being a multiplicity of individual 'reasons' for suicide, the suicide rate remains stable in specific societies from year to year, demonstrating the suicide rate to be a social fact. When reading these extracts consider how Durkheim's explanation includes very stereotypical (to put it kindly!) views of women; for instance, their ability to endure isolation better than men because their 'sensibility is rudimentary rather than highly developed'.*

Egoistic Suicide

This type of suicide well deserves the name we have given it. Egoism is not merely a contributing factor in it; it is its generating cause. In this case the bond attaching man to life relaxes because that attaching him to society is itself slack. The incidents of private life which seem the direct inspiration of suicide and are considered its determining causes are in reality only incidental causes. The individual yields to the lightest shock of circumstance because the state of society has made him a ready prey to suicide.

Several facts confirm this explanation. Suicide is known to be rare among children and to diminish among the aged at the last confines of life [. . .]

We shall likewise see in the next chapter that, though lower societies practise a form of suicide of their own, the one we have just discussed is almost unknown to them. Since their social life is very simple, the social inclinations of individuals are simple also and thus they need little for satisfaction. They readily find external objectives to which they become attached. If he can carry with him his gods and his family, primitive man, everywhere that he goes, has all that his social nature demands.

This is also why woman can endure life in isolation more easily than man. When a widow is seen to endure her condition much better than a widower and desires marriage less passionately, one is led to consider this ease in dispensing with the family a mark of superiority; it is said that woman's affective faculties, being very intense, are easily employed outside the domestic circle, while her devotion is indispensable to man to help him endure life. Actually, if this is her privilege it is because her sensibility is rudimentary rather than highly developed. As she lives outside of community existence more than man, she is less penetrated by it; society is less necessary to her because she is less impregnated with sociability. She has few needs in this direction and satisfies them easily. With a few devotional practices and some animals to care for, the old unmarried woman's life is full. If she remains faithfully attached to religious traditions and thus finds ready protection against suicide, it is because these very simple social forms satisfy all her needs. Man, on the contrary, is hard beset in this respect. As his thought and activity develop, they increasingly overflow these antiquated forms. But then he needs others. Because he is a more complex social being, he can maintain his equilibrium only by finding more points of support outside himself, and it is because his moral balance depends on a larger number of conditions that it is more easily disturbed.

Altruistic Suicide

It has sometimes been said that suicide was unknown among lower societies. Thus expressed, the assertion is inexact. To be sure, egoistic suicide, constituted as has just been shown, seems not to be frequent there. But another form exists among them in an endemic state.

Bartholin, in his book, *De Causis contemptae mortis a Danis*, reports that Danish warriors considered it a disgrace to die in bed of old age or sickness, and killed themselves to escape this ignominy. The Goths likewise believed that those who die a natural death are destined to languish forever in caverns full of venomous creatures. On the frontier of the Visigoths' territory was a high pinnacle called *The Rock of the Forefathers*, from the top of which old men would throw themselves when weary of life [. . .]

Suicide, accordingly, is surely very common among primitive peoples. But it displays peculiar characteristics. All the facts above reported fall into one of the following three categories:

1. Suicides of men on the threshold of old age or stricken with sickness.
2. Suicides of women on their husbands' death.
3. Suicides of followers or servants on the death of their chiefs.

Now, when a person kills himself, in all these cases, it is not because he assumes the right to do so but, on the contrary, *because it is his duty.* If he fails in this obligation, he is dishonoured and also punished, usually, by religious sanctions. Of course, when we hear of aged men killing themselves we are tempted at first to believe that the cause is weariness or the sufferings common to age. But if these suicides really had no other source, if the individual made away with himself merely to be rid of an unendurable existence, he would not be required to do so; one is never obliged to take advantage of a privilege. Now, we have seen that if such a person insists on living he loses public respect; in one case the usual funeral honours are denied, in another a life of horror is supposed to await him beyond the grave. The weight of society is thus brought to bear on him to lead him to destroy himself. To be sure, society intervenes in egoistic suicide, as well; but its intervention differs in the two cases. In one case, it speaks the sentence of death; in the other it forbids the choice of death. In the case of egoistic suicide it suggests or counsels at most; in the other case it compels and is the author of conditions and circumstances making this obligation coercive.

This sacrifice then is imposed by society for social ends [. . .]

For society to be able thus to compel some of its members to kill themselves, the individual personality can have little value. For as soon as the latter begins to form, the right to existence is the first conceded it; or is at least suspended only in such unusual circumstances as war. But there can be only one cause for this feeble individuation itself. For the individual to occupy so little place in collective life he must be almost completely absorbed in the group and the latter, accordingly, very highly integrated. For the parts to have too little life of their own, the whole must indeed be a compact, continuous mass [. . .]

We thus confront a type of suicide differing by incisive qualities from the preceding one. Whereas the latter is due to excessive individuation, the former is caused by too rudimentary individuation. One occurs because society allows the individual to escape it, being insufficiently aggregated in some parts or even in the whole; the other, because society holds him in too strict tutelage. Having given the name of *egoism* to the state of the ego living its own life and obeying itself alone, that of *altruism* adequately expresses the opposite state, where the ego is not its own property, where it is blended with something not itself, where the goal of conduct is exterior to itself, that is, in one of the groups in which it participates. So we call the suicide caused by intense altruism *altruistic suicide.* But since it is also characteristically performed as a duty, the terminology adopted should express this fact. So we will call such a type *obligatory altruistic suicide* [. . .]

Anomic Suicide

It is well-known fact that economic crises have an aggravating effect on the suicidal tendency.

In Vienna, in 1873 a financial crisis occurred which reached its height in 1874; the number of suicides immediately rose. From 141 in 1872, they rose to 153 in 1873 and 216 in 1874. The increase in 1874 is 53 per cent above 1872 and 41 per cent above 1873. What proves this catastrophe to have been the sole cause of the increase is the special prominence of the increase when the crisis was acute, or during the first four months of 1874.

This relation is found not only in some exceptional cases, but is the rule. The number of bankruptcies is a barometer of adequate sensitivity, reflecting the variations of economic life. When they increase abruptly from year to year, some serious disturbance has certainly occurred. From 1845 to 1869 there were sudden rises, symptomatic of crises, on three occasions. While the annual increase in the number of bankruptcies during this period is 3.2 per cent, it is 26 per cent in 1847, 37 per cent in 1854 and 20 per cent in 1861. At these three moments, there is also to be observed an unusually rapid rise in the number of suicides. While the average annual increase during these 24 years was only 2 per cent, it was 17 per cent in 1847, 8 per cent in 1854 and 9 per cent in 1861.

But to what do these crises owe their influence? Is it because they increase poverty by causing public wealth to fluctuate? Is life more readily renounced as it becomes more difficult? The explanation is seductively simple; and it agrees with the popular idea of suicide. But it is contradicted by facts.

Actually, if voluntary deaths increased because life was becoming more difficult, they should diminish perceptibly as comfort increases. Now, although when the price of the most necessary foods rises excessively, suicides generally do the same, they are not found to fall below the average in the opposite case. In Prussia, in 1850 wheat was quoted at the lowest point it reached during the entire period of 1848–81; it was at 6.1 marks per 50 kilograms; yet at this very time suicides rose from 1,527 where they were in 1849 to 1,736, or an increase of 13 per cent, and continued to increase during the years 1851, 1852 and 1853 although the cheap market held [. . .]

So far is the increase in poverty from causing the increase in suicide that even fortunate crises, the effect of which is abruptly to enhance a country's prosperity, affect suicide like economic disasters [. . .]

The state of conjugal anomy, produced by the institution of divorce, thus explains the parallel development of divorces and suicides. Accordingly, the suicides of husbands which increase the number of voluntary deaths in countries where there are many divorces, form a division of anomic suicide. They are not the result of the existence of more bad husbands or bad wives in these societies, that is, of more unhappy households. They result from a moral structure *sui generis,* itself caused by a weakening of matrimonial regulation [. . .]

The Social Element of Suicide

There is first the external situation of the agent. Sometimes men who kill themselves have had family sorrow or disappointments to their pride, sometimes they have had to suffer poverty or sickness, at others they have had some moral fault with which to reproach themselves, etc. But we have seen that these individual peculiarities could not explain the social suicide-rate; for the latter varies in considerable proportions, whereas the different combinations of circumstances which constitute the immediate antecedents of individual cases of suicide retain approximately the same relative frequency. They are therefore not the determining causes of the act which they precede. Their occasionally important role in the premeditation of suicide is no proof of being a causal one. Human deliberations, in fact, so far as reflective consciousness affects them are often only purely formal, with no object by confirmation of a resolve previously formed for reasons unknown to consciousness.

Besides, the circumstances are almost infinite in number which are supposed to cause suicide because they rather frequently accompany it. One man kills himself in the midst of affluence, another in the lap of poverty; one was unhappy in his home, and another had just ended by divorce a marriage which was making him unhappy. In one case a soldier ends his life after having been punished for an offence he did not commit; in another, a criminal whose crime has remained unpunished kills himself. The most varied and even the most contradictory events of life may equally serve as pretexts for suicide. This suggests that none of them is the specific cause. Could we perhaps at least ascribe causality to those qualities known to be common to all? But are there any such? At best one might say that they usually consist of disappointments, of sorrows, without any possibility of deciding how intense the grief must be to have such tragic significance. Of no disappointment in life, no matter how insignificant, can we say in advance that it could not possibly make existence intolerable; and, on the other hand, there is none which must necessarily have this effect. We see some men resist horrible misfortune, while others kill themselves after slight trouble. Moreover, we have shown that those who suffer most are not those who kill themselves most. Rather it is too great comfort which turns a man against himself. Life is most readily renounced at the time and among the classes where it is least harsh. At least, if it really sometimes occurs that the victim's personal situation is the effective cause of his resolve, such cases are very rare indeed and accordingly cannot explain the social suicide-rate.

Accordingly, even those who have ascribed most influence to individual conditions have sought these conditions less in such external incidents than in the intrinsic nature of the person, that is, his biological constitution and the physical concomitants on which it depends. Thus, suicide has been represented as the product of a certain temperament, an episode of neurasthenia, subject to the effects of the same factors as neurasthenia. Yet we have found no immediate and regular relationship between neurasthenia and the social suicide-rate.

The two facts even vary at times in inverse proportion to one another, one being at its minimum just when and where the other is at its height. We have not found, either, any definite relation between the variations of suicide and the conditions of physical environment supposed to have most effect on the nervous system, such as race, climate, temperature. Obviously, though the neuropath may show some inclination to suicide under certain conditions, he is not necessarily destined to kill himself; and the influence of cosmic factors is not enough to determine in just this sense the very general tendencies of his nature.

Wholly different are the results we obtained when we forgot the individual and sought the causes of the suicidal aptitude of each society in the nature of the societies themselves. The relations of suicide to certain states of social environment are as direct and constant as its relations to facts of a biological and physical character were seen to be uncertain and ambiguous. Here at last we are face to face with real laws, allowing us to attempt a methodical classification of types of suicide. The sociological causes thus determined by us have even explained these various concurrences often attributed to the influence of material causes, and in which a proof of this influence has been sought. If women kill themselves much less often than men, it is because they are much less involved than men in collective existence; thus they feel its influence – good or evil – less strongly. So it is with old persons and children, though for other reasons. Finally, if suicide increases from January to June but then decreases, it is because social activity shows similar seasonal fluctuations. It is therefore natural that the different effects of social activity should be subject to an identical rhythm, and consequently be more pronounced during the former of these two periods. Suicide is one of them.

The conclusion from all these facts is that the social suicide-rate can be explained only sociologically. At any given moment the moral constitution of society establishes the contingent of voluntary deaths. There is, therefore, for each people a collective force of a definite amount of energy, impelling men to self-destruction. The victim's acts which at first seem to express only his personal temperament are really the supplement and prolongation of a social condition which they express externally.

From E. Durkheim (1952) (1897) *Suicide: A Study in Sociology*, London: Routledge & Kegan Paul, pp. 214–21, 241–3, 297–9.

Questions

1. How does each of the three types of suicide described by Durkheim relate to the degree of social integration and social control in society?
2. What criticisms could you make of Durkheim's description and explanation of egoistic, altruistic and anomic suicide?
3. What 'evidence' does Durkheim provide to demonstrate that suicide rates can be related to certain states of social environment?

Reading 12

Bourgeois and proletarians: Marx's analysis of class relationships (1)

KARL MARX AND FREDERICK ENGELS

One of the difficulties of reading and interpreting Marx is due to his prolific and wide-ranging writing. In essence, Marx's work can be seen as an attempt to explain the nature of modern society, and how one form of production (and hence society) leads inevitably to another. In the Communist Manifesto, *Marx asserts that capitalism is a necessary stage prior to the establishment of communism in all modern societies (just as feudalism was a necessary forerunner to capitalism). This evolution of one form of society to another comes as result of conflict around the system of production, and especially in the relations of production. The emphasis on conflict in Marx's theory of social revolution highlights the key role of social classes, and the struggle between classes with different and opposed interests. For Marx, a social class was a group of people who occupied a similar position in relation to the forces of production in society. The basis of social class, then, lay in the relations of production – the relations between employers and employees, for example. These relations of production will vary from one society to another and will, in turn, lead to different class relationships. In the* Communist Manifesto, *Marx presents a basic model of two classes – the Bourgeoisie and Proletarians – and describes the increasing polarisation between them. This reading is taken from the section of the* Communist Manifesto *in which Marx describes the growth of the Bourgeoisie and explains how this growth has created the conditions for the development of an urban proletariat.*

The history of all hitherto existing society is the history of class struggles.

Freeman and slave, patrician and plebian, lord and serf, guild-master and journeyman, in a word, oppressor and oppressed, stood in constant opposition to one another, carried on an uninterrupted, now hidden, now open fight. A fight that each time ended, either in a revolutionary re-constitution of society at large, or in the common ruin of the contending classes.

In the earlier epochs of history, we find almost everywhere a complicated arrangement of society into various orders, a manifold gradation of social rank. In ancient Rome we have patricians, knights, plebians, slaves; in the Middle Ages, feudal lords, vassals, guild-masters, journeymen, apprentices, serfs; in almost all of these classes, again, subordinate gradations.

The modern bourgeois society that has sprouted from the ruins of feudal society has not done away with class antagonisms. It has but established new classes, new conditions of oppression, new forms of struggle in place of the old.

Our epoch, the epoch of the bourgeoisie, possesses, however, this distinctive feature: it has simplified the class antagonisms. Society as a whole is more and more splitting up into two great hostile camps, into two great classes directly facing each other: Bourgeoisie and Proletariat.

From the serfs of the Middle Ages sprang the burghers of the earliest towns. From these burgesses the first elements of the bourgeoisie were developed.

The discovery of America, the rounding of the Cape, opened up fresh ground for the rising bourgeoisie. The East-Indian and Chinese markets, the colonisation of America, trade with the colonies, the increase in the means of exchange and in commodities generally, gave to commerce, to navigation, to industry, an impulse never before known, and thereby, to the revolutionary element in the tottering feudal society, a rapid development.

The feudal system of industry, under which industrial production was monopolised by closed guilds, now no longer sufficed for the growing wants of the new markets. The manufacturing system took its place. The guildmasters were pushed on one side by the manufacturing middle class; division of labour between the different corporate guilds vanished in the face of division of labour in each single workshop.

Meantime the markets kept ever growing, the demand ever rising. Even manufacture no longer sufficed. Thereupon, steam and machinery revolutionised industrial production. The place of manufacture was taken by the giant, Modern Industry, the place of the industrial middle class, by industrial millionaires, the leaders of whole industrial armies, the modern bourgeois [. . .]

We see, therefore, how the modern bourgeoisie is itself the product of a long course of development, of a series of revolutions in the modes of production and exchange [. . .]

The bourgeoisie, historically, has played a most revolutionary part.

The bourgeoisie, wherever it has got the upper hand, has put an end to all feudal, patriarchal, idyllic relations. It has pitilessly torn asunder the motley feudal ties that bound man to his 'natural superiors', and has left remaining no other nexus between man and man than naked self-interest, than callous 'cash payment'. It has drowned the most heavenly ecstasies of religious fervour, of chivalrous enthusiasm, of philistine sentimentalism, in the icy water of egotistical calculation. It has resolved personal worth into exchange value, and in place of the numberless indefeasible chartered freedoms, has set up that single, unconscionable freedom – Free Trade. In one word, for exploitation, veiled by religious and political illusions, it has substituted naked, shameless, direct, brutal exploitation.

The bourgeoisie has stripped of its halo every occupation hitherto honoured and looked up to with reverent awe. It has converted the physician, the lawyer, the priest, the poet, the man of science, into its paid wage-labourers.

The bourgeoisie has torn away from the family its sentimental veil, and has reduced the family relation to a mere money relation [. . .]

The bourgeoisie, during its rule of scarce one hundred years, has created more massive and more colossal productive forces than have all preceding generations together. Subjection of Nature's forces to man, machinery, application of chemistry to industry and agriculture, steam navigation, railways, electric telegraphs, clearing of whole continents for cultivation, canalisation of rivers, whole populations conjured out of the ground – what earlier century had even a presentiment that such productive forces slumbered in the lap of social labour?

We see then: the means of production and of exchange, on whose foundation the bourgeoisie built itself up, were generated in feudal society. At a certain stage in the development of these means of production and of exchange, the conditions under which feudal society produced and exchanged, the feudal organisation of agriculture and manufacturing industry, in one word, the feudal relations of property became no longer compatible with the already developed productive forces; they became so many fetters, they were burst asunder.

Into their place stepped free competition, accompanied by a social and political constitution adapted to it, and by the economical and political sway of the bourgeois class [. . .]

The weapons with which the bourgeoisie felled feudalism to the ground are now turned against the bourgeoisie itself.

But not only has the bourgeoisie forged the weapons that bring death to itself, it has also called into existence the men who are to wield those weapons – the modern working class – the proletarians.

In proportion as the bourgeoisie, i.e., capital, is developed, in the same proportion is the proletariat, the modern working class, developed – a class of labourers, who live only so long as they find work, and who find work only so long as their labour increases capital. These labourers, who must sell themselves piecemeal, are a commodity, like every other article of commerce, and are consequently exposed to all the vicissitudes of competition, to all the fluctuations of the market.

Owing to the extensive use of machinery and to division of labour, the work of the proletarians has lost all individual character, and, consequently, all charm for the workman. He becomes an appendage of the machine, and it is only the most simple, most monotonous, and most easily acquired knack, that is required of him. Hence, the cost of production of a workman is restricted, almost entirely, to the means of subsistence that he requires for his maintenance, and for the propagation of his race. But the price of a commodity, and therefore also of labour, is equal to its cost of production. In proportion, therefore as the repulsiveness of the work increases, the wage decreases. Nay more, in proportion as the use of machinery and division of labour increases, in the same proportion the burden of toil also increases, whether by prolongation of the working-hours, by increase of the work exacted in a given time or by increased speed of the machinery, etc.

No sooner is the exploitation of the labourer by the manufacturer, so far, at an end, that he receives his wages in cash, than he is set upon by the other portions of the bourgeoisie, the landlord, the shopkeeper, the pawnbroker, etc.

The lower strata of the middle class – the small tradespeople, shopkeepers, and retired tradesmen generally, the handicraftsmen and peasants – all these sink gradually into the proletariat, partly because their diminutive capital does not suffice for the scale on which Modern Industry is carried on, and is swamped in the competition with the large capitalists, partly because their specialised skill is rendered worthless by new methods of production. Thus the proletariat is recruited from all classes of the population.

The proletariat goes through various stages of development. With its birth begins its struggle with the bourgeoisie. At first the contest is carried on by individual labourers, then by the workpeople of a factory, then by the operatives of one trade, in one locality, against the individual bourgeois who directly exploits them. They direct their attacks not against the bourgeois conditions of production, but against the instruments of production themselves; they destroy imported wares that compete with their labour, they smash to pieces machinery, they set factories ablaze, they seek to restore by force the vanished status of the workman of the Middle Ages.

At this stage, the labourers still form an incoherent mass scattered over the whole country, and broken up by their mutual competition [. . .]

But with the development of industry the proletariat not only increases in number; it becomes more concentrated in greater masses, its strength grows, and it feels that strength more. The various interests and conditions of life within the ranks of the proletariat are more and more equalised, in proportion as machinery obliterates all distinctions of labour, and nearly everywhere reduces wages to the same low level. The growing competition among the bourgeois, and the resulting commercial crises, make the wages of the workers even more fluctuating. The unceasing improvement of machinery, ever more rapidly developing, makes their livelihood more and more precarious; the collisions between individual workmen and individual bourgeois take more and more the character of collisions between two classes. Thereupon the workers begin to form combinations (Trades' Unions) against the bourgeois; they club together in order to keep up the rate of wages; they found permanent associations in order to make provision beforehand for these occasional revolts. Here and there the contest breaks out into riots.

Now and then the workers are victorious, but only for a time. The real fruit of their battles lies, not in the immediate result, but in the ever expanding union of workers [. . .]

Of all the classes that stand face to face with the bourgeoisie today, the proletariat alone is a really revolutionary class. The other classes decay and finally disappear in the face of modern industry; the proletariat is its special and essential product.

The lower middle class, the small manufacturer, the shopkeeper, the artisan, the peasant, all these fight against the bourgeoisie, to save from extinction their existence as fractions of the middle class. They are therefore not revolutionary, but conservative. Nay more, they are reactionary, for they try to roll back the wheel of history. If by chance they are revolutionary, they are so only in view of their impending transfer into the proletariat, they thus defend not their present, but their future interests, they desert their own standpoint to place themselves at that of the proletariat [. . .]

All the preceding classes that got the upper hand, sought to fortify their already acquired status by subjecting society at large to their conditions of appropriation. The proletarians cannot become masters of the productive forces of society, except by abolishing their own previous mode of appropriation. They have nothing of their own to secure and to fortify; their mission is to destroy all previous securities for and, insurances of, individual property.

All previous historical movements were movements of minorities, or in the interest of minorities. The proletarian movement is the self-conscious, independent movement of the immense majority, in the interest of the immense majority. The proletariat, the lowest stratum of our present society, cannot stir, cannot raise itself up, without the whole superincumbent strata of official society being sprung into the air [. . .]

The essential condition for the existence, and for the sway of the bourgeois class, is the formation and augmentation of capital; the condition for capital is wage labour. Wage labour rests exclusively on competition between the labourers. The advance of industry, whose involuntary promoter is the bourgeoisie, replaces the isolation of the labourers, due to competition, by their revolutionary combination, due to association. The development of Modern Industry, therefore, cuts from under its feet the very foundation on which the bourgeoisie produces and appropriates products. What the bourgeoisie, therefore, produces, above all, is its own grave-digger. Its fall and the victory of the proletariat are equally inevitable.

From Marx, K. and Engels, F. (1952) (1848) *The Manifesto of the Communist Party*, Moscow: Progress, pp. 40–60.

Reading 13

The French peasantry of the mid-nineteenth century: Marx's Analysis of class relationships (2)

KARL MARX

Marx's basic model for all 'developed' societies was of a broad division into two classes, one of which exploits the other – the model set out in the Communist Manifesto. *This was, though, only a model and Marx was well aware that in 'real' societies the picture was more complicated with several social classes coexisting, including some left over from previous forms of society. This more complex class analysis is illustrated in 'The eighteenth brumaire of Louis Bonaparte' which describes and analyses the role of class relationships and class struggles both before and after the French Revolution of 1848. Capitalism was very undeveloped in France at this time and the rural peasantry still constituted the largest 'class grouping'. In this extract, note Marx's graphic description of the peasants and his argument that the lack of collective interests among them worked against the formation of a social class with a true class consciousness.*

Bonaparte represents a class, indeed he represents the most numerous class of French society, the *small peasant proprietors.*

Just as the Bourbons were the dynasty of big landed property and the Orleans the dynasty of money, so the Bonapartes are the dynasty of the peasants, i.e. of the mass of the French people [. . .]

The small peasant proprietors form an immense mass, the members of which live in the same situation but do not enter into manifold relationships with each other. Their mode of operation isolates them instead of bringing them into mutual intercourse. This isolation is strengthened by the wretched state of France's means of communication and by the poverty of the peasants. Their place of operation, the smallholding, permits no division of labour in its cultivation, no application of science and therefore no diversity of development, variety of talent, or wealth of social relationships. Each individual peasant family is almost self-sufficient; it directly produces the greater part of its own consumption and therefore obtains its means of life more through exchange with nature than through intercourse with society. The smallholding, the peasant, and the family; next door, another smallholding, another peasant, and another family. A bunch of these makes up a village, and a bunch of villages makes up a department. Thus the great mass of the French nation is formed by the simple addition of isomorphous magnitudes, much as potatoes in a sack form a sack of potatoes. In so far as millions of families live under economic conditions of existence that separate their mode of life, their interests and their cultural formation from those of the other classes and bring them into conflict with those classes, they form a class. In so far as these small peasant proprietors are merely connected on a local basis, and the identity of their interests fails to produce a feeling of community, national links, or a political organization, they do not form a class. They are therefore incapable of asserting their class interest in their own name, whether through a parliament or through a convention. They cannot represent themselves; they must be represented. Their representative must appear simultaneously as their master, as an authority over them, an unrestricted governmental power that protects them from the other classes and sends them rain and sunshine from above. The political influence of the small peasant proprietors is therefore ultimately expressed in the executive subordinating society to itself [. . .]

After the first revolution had transformed the peasants from a state of semi-serfdom into free landed proprietors, Napoleon confirmed and regulated the conditions under which they could exploit undisturbed the soil of France, which had now devolved on them for the first time, and satisfy their new-found passion for property. But the French peasant is now succumbing to his smallholding itself, to the division of the land, the form of property consolidated in France by Napoleon. It was the material conditions which made the feudal French peasant a small proprietor and Napoleon an emperor. Two generations have been sufficient to produce the inevitable consequence: a progressive deterioration of agriculture and a progressive increase in peasant indebtedness. The 'Napoleonic' form of property, which was the condition for the liberation and enrichment of the French rural population at the beginning of the nineteenth century, has developed in the course of that century into the legal foundation of their enslavement and their poverty. And precisely this law is the first of the 'Napoleonic ideas' which the second Bonaparte has to uphold. If he still shares with the peasants the illusion that the cause of their ruin is to be sought, not in the smallholding itself, but outside it, in the influence of secondary circumstances, his experiments will burst like soap bubbles at their first contact with the relations of production.

The economic development of the smallholding has profoundly distorted the relation of the peasants to the other classes of society. Under Napoleon the fragmentation of landed property in the countryside supplemented free competition and the beginning of large industry in the towns. The peasant class was the ubiquitous protest against the landed aristocracy which had just been overthrown. The roots which the smallholding struck in French soil deprived feudalism of all nutriment. Its fences formed the bourgeoisie's system of natural fortifications against surprise attacks on the part of its old overlords. But in the course of the nineteenth century the urban usurer replaced the feudal lord; the mortgage on the land replaced its feudal obligations; bourgeois capital replaced aristocratic landed property. The peasant's smallholding is now only the pretext that allows the capitalist to draw profits, interest and rent from the soil, while leaving the tiller himself to work out how to extract the wage for his labour. The mortgage debt burdening the soil of France imposes on the French peasantry an interest payment equal to the annual interest on the entire British national debt. Owing to this enslavement by capital, inevitably brought about by its own development, small peasant property has transformed the mass of the French nation into troglodytes. Sixteen million peasants (including women and children) live in hovels, many of which have only one opening, others only two, and the rest, the most fortunate cases, only three. Windows are to a house what the five senses are to a head. The bourgeois order, which at the beginning of the century made the state do sentry duty over the newly arisen smallholding, and manured it with laurels, has become a vampire that sucks out its blood and brains and throws them into the alchemist's cauldron of capital. The Code Napoléon is now merely the lawbook for distraints on chattels, forced sales, and compulsory auctions. To the four million (including children, etc.) officially admitted paupers, vagabonds, criminals and prostitutes in France must be added five million who totter on the precipice of non-existence and either wander around the countryside itself or, with their rags and their children, continually desert the country for the towns and the towns for the country. The interests of the peasants are therefore no longer consonant with the interests of the bourgeoisie, as they were under Napoleon, but in opposition to those interests, in opposition to capital. They therefore find their natural ally and leader in the *urban proletariat*, whose task is the overthrow of the bourgeois order.

From K. Marx (1973) (1869) 'The eighteenth brumaire of Louis Bonaparte', in D. Fernbach (ed.) *Karl Marx: Survey from Exile, Political Writings, Vol. 2*, Harmondsworth: Penguin, pp. 238–43.

Questions on Readings 12 and 13

1. Why does Marx suggest in the *Communist Manifesto* that the growth of the bourgeoisie inevitably led to the growth of the urban proletariat?
2. To what extent does the French peasantry described in 'The eighteenth brumaire' constitute a distinct social class?
3. Summarise the main similarities and differences between the peasants and the urban proletariat that Marx highlights in 'The eighteenth brumaire'. To what extent do these differences undermine Marx's prediction in the *Communist Manifesto* of a socialist revolution?

Reading 14

The role of religion (1)

EMILE DURKHEIM

In The Elementary Forms of the Religious Life, *from which this reading is taken, Durkheim develops his views on social solidarity and cohesion and sets out to demonstrate how religion fulfils the vital social function of promoting social solidarity and cohesion. He argues that primitive religion embodies the basic idea of society: religious ceremonies establish and strengthen collective values and sacred objects are symbols of the wider community. The empirical base for the book is a study (from written reports rather than Durkheim's own first hand research) of Australian totemism – for Durkheim an example of religion in its most 'elementary form'. Totemism, he argued, contains within it all the major features which are found in more 'developed' religions, such as Christianity. In order to 'understand' religion, the best method is to examine religious beliefs in 'lower societies'; as Durkheim puts it 'primitive civilizations offer privileged cases . . . because they are simple cases'. In this extract from the Introduction to* The Elementary Forms of the Religious Life, *Durkheim starts by highlighting the importance of taking an objective, scientific approach to the study of religion and spells out his view that all religions fulfil the same functions: all 'respond to the same needs, they play the same role, they depend upon the same causes'. The fact that all religions are equally valid reinforces Durkheim's argument that an understanding of contemporary religions can come from the examination of previous and different forms of religion, particularly religions in 'lower societies' that lack the confusion of complex contemporary religions.*

Introduction

Subject of our Study: Religious Sociology and the Theory of Knowledge

In this book we propose to study the most primitive and simple religion which is actually known, to make an analysis of it, and to attempt an explanation of it. A religious system may be said to be the most primitive which we can observe when it fulfils the two following conditions: in the first place, when it is found in a society whose organization is surpassed by no others in simplicity; and secondly, when it is possible to explain it without making use of any element borrowed from a previous religion.

We shall set ourselves to describe the organization of this system with all the exactness and fidelity that an ethnographer or an historian could give it. But our task will not be limited to that: sociology raises other problems than history or ethnography. It does not seek to know the past forms of civilization with the sole end of knowing them and reconstructing them. But rather, like every positive science, it has as its object the explanation of some actual reality which is near to us, and which consequently is capable of affecting our ideas and our acts: this reality is man; and more precisely, the man of to-day, for there is nothing which we are more interested in knowing. Then we are not going to study a very archaic religion simply for the pleasure of telling its peculiarities and its singularities. If we have taken it as the subject of our research, it is because it has seemed to us better adapted than any other to lead to an understanding of the religious nature of man, that is to say, to show us an essential and permanent aspect of humanity [. . .]

When only the letter of the formulae is considered, these religious beliefs and practices undoubtedly seem disconcerting at times, and one is tempted to attribute them to some sort of a deep-rooted error. But one must know how to go underneath the symbol to the reality which it represents and which gives it its meaning. The most barbarous and the most fantastic rites and the strangest myths translate some human need, some aspect of life, either individual or social. The reasons with which the faithful justify them may be, and generally are, erroneous; but the true reasons do not cease to exist, and it is the duty of science to discover them.

In reality, then, there are no religions which are false. All are true in their own fashion; all answer, though in different ways, to the given conditions of human existence. It is undeniably possible to arrange them in a hierarchy. Some can be called superior to others, in the sense that they call into play higher mental functions, that they are richer in ideas and sentiments, that they contain more concepts with fewer sensations and images, and that their arrangement is wiser. But howsoever real this greater complexity and this higher ideality may be, they are not sufficient to place the corresponding religions in different classes. All are religions equally, just as all living beings are equally alive, from the most humble plastids up to man. So when we turn to primitive religions it is not with the idea of depreciating religion in general, for these religions are no less respectable than the others. They respond to the same needs, they play the same role, they depend upon the same causes; they can also well serve to show the nature of the religious life, and consequently to resolve the problem which we wish to study.

But why give them a sort of prerogative? Who chose them in preference to all others as the subject of our study? It is merely for reasons of method.

In the first place, we cannot arrive at an understanding of the most recent religions except by following the manner in which they have been progressively composed in history. In fact, historical analysis is the only means of explanation which it is possible to apply to them. It alone enables us to resolve an institution into its constituent elements, for it shows them to us as they are born in time, one after another. On the other hand, by placing every one of them in the condition where it was born, it puts into our hands the only means we have of determining the causes which gave rise to it. Every time that we undertake to explain something human, taken at a given moment in history – be it a religious belief, a moral precept, a legal principle, an aesthetic style or an economic system – it is necessary to commence by going back to its most primitive and simple form, to try to account for the characteristics by which it was marked at that time, and then to show how it developed and became complicated little by little, and how it became that which it is at the moment in question [. . .]

Besides this, outside of these indirect reactions, the study of primitive religions has of itself an immediate interest which is of primary importance.

If it is useful to know what a certain particular religion consists in, it is still more important to know what religion in general is. This is the problem which has aroused the interest of philosophers in all times; and not without reason, for it is of interest to all humanity. Unfortunately, the method which they generally employ is purely dialectic: they confine themselves to analysing the idea which they make for themselves of religion, except as they illustrate the results of this mental analysis by examples borrowed from the religions which best realize their ideal. But even if this method ought to be abandoned, the problem remains intact, and the great service of philosophy is to have prevented its being suppressed by the disdain of scholars. Now it is possible to attack it in a different way. Since all religions can be compared to each other, and since all are species of the same class, there are necessarily many elements which are common to all. We do not mean to speak simply of the outward and visible characteristics which they all have equally, and which make it possible to give them a provisional definition from the very outset of our researches; the discovery of these apparent signs is relatively easy, for the observation which it demands does not go beneath the surface of things. But these external resemblances suppose others which are profound. At the foundation of all systems of beliefs and of all cults there ought necessarily to be a certain number of fundamental representations or conceptions and of ritual attitudes which, in spite of the diversity of forms which they have taken, have the same objective significance and fulfil the same functions everywhere. These are the permanent elements which constitute that which is permanent and human in religion; they form all the objective contents of the idea which is expressed when one speaks of *religion* in general. How is it possible to pick them out?

Surely it is not by observing the complex religions which appear in the course of history. Every one of these is made up of such a variety of elements that it is very difficult to distinguish what is secondary from what is principal, the essential from the accessory. Suppose that the religion considered is like that of Egypt, India or the classical antiquity. It is a confused mass of many cults, varying according to the locality, the temples, the generations, the dynasties, the invasions, etc. Popular superstitions are there confused with the purest dogmas. Neither the thought nor the activity of the religion is evenly distributed among the believers; according to the men, the environment and the circumstances, the beliefs as well as the rites are thought of in different ways. Here they are priests, there they are monks, elsewhere they are laymen; there are mystics and rationalists, theologians and prophets, etc. In these conditions it is difficult to see what is common to all. In one or another of these systems it is quite possible to find the means of making a profitable study of some particular fact which is specially developed there, such as sacrifice or prophecy, monasticism or the mysteries; but how is it possible to find the common foundation of the religious life underneath the luxuriant vegetation which covers it? How is it possible to find, underneath the disputes of theology, the variations of ritual, the multiplicity of groups and the diversity of individuals, the fundamental states characteristic of religious mentality in general?

Things are quite different in the lower societies. The slighter development of individuality, the small extension of the group, the homogeneity of external circumstances, all contribute to reducing the differences and variations to a minimum. The group has an intellectual and moral conformity of which we find but rare examples in the more advanced societies. Everything is common to all. Movements are stereotyped; everybody performs the same ones in the same circumstances, and this conformity of conduct only translates the conformity of thought. Every mind being drawn into the same eddy, the individual type nearly confounds itself with that of the race. And while all is uniform, all is simple as well. Nothing is deformed like these myths, all composed of one and the same theme which is endlessly repeated, or like these rites made up of a small number of gestures repeated again and again. Neither the popular imagination nor that of the priests has had either the time or the means of refining and transforming the original substance of the religious ideas and practices; these are shown in all their nudity, and offer themselves to an examination, it requiring only the slightest effort to lay them open. That which is accessory or secondary, the development of luxury, has not yet come to hide the principal elements. All is reduced to that which is indispensable, to that without which there could be no religion. But that which is indispensable is also that which is essential, that is to say, that which we must know before all else.

Primitive civilizations offer privileged cases, then, because they are simple cases. That is why, in all fields of human activity, the observations of ethnologists have frequently been veritable revelations, which have renewed the study of human institutions. For example, before the middle of the nineteenth century, everybody was convinced that the father was the essential element of the family; no one had dreamed that there could be a family organization of which the paternal authority was not the keystone. But the discovery of Bachofen came and upset this old conception [. . .]

To return to religions, the study of only the most familiar ones had led men to believe for a long time that the idea of god was characteristic of everything that is religious. Now the religion which we are going to study presently is, in a large part, foreign to all idea of divinity; the forces to which the rites are there addressed are very different from those which occupy the leading place in our modern religions, yet they aid us in understanding these latter forces [. . .]

But primitive religions do not merely aid us in disengaging the constituent elements of religion; they also have the great advantage that they facilitate the explanation of it. Since the facts there are simpler, the relations between them are more apparent. The reasons with which men account for their acts have not yet been elaborated and denatured by studied reflection; they are nearer and more closely related to the motives which have really determined these acts [. . .]

The remainder of this book will be an illustration and a verification of this remark on method. It will be seen how, in the primitive religions, the religious fact still visibly carries the mark of its origins: it would have been well-nigh impossible to infer them merely from the study of the more developed religions.

The study which we are undertaking is therefore a way of taking up again, *but under new conditions*, the old problem of the origin of religion. To be sure, if by origin we are to understand the very first beginning, the question has nothing scientific about it, and should be resolutely discarded. There was no given moment when religion began to exist, and there is consequently no need of finding a means of transporting ourselves thither in thought. Like every human institution, religion did not commence anywhere. Therefore, all speculations of this sort are justly discredited; they can only consist in subjective and arbitrary constructions which are subject to no sort of control. But the problem which we raise is quite another one. What we want to do is to find a means of discerning the ever-present causes upon which the most essential forms of religious thought and practice depend. Now for the reasons which were just set forth, these causes are proportionately more easily observable as the societies where they are observed are less complicated. That is why we try to get as near as possible to the origins. It is not that we ascribe particular virtues to the lower religions. On the contrary, they are rudimentary and gross; we cannot make of them a sort of model which later religions only have to reproduce. But even their grossness makes them instructive, for they thus become convenient for experiments, as in them, the facts and their relations are easily seen.

From Durkheim, E. (1915) (1912) *The Elementary Forms of the Religious Life: A Study in Religious Sociology*, translated by J.W. Swain, London: Allen & Unwin; New York: Macmillan, pp. 1–8.

Questions

1. Describe Durkheim's view of 'primitive religion'. What criticisms could you make of his view?
2. Durkheim suggests that all religions contain a certain number of fundamental concepts and ritual attitudes which fulfil the same functions everywhere. They are the 'permanent elements which constitute what is permanent and human in religion'. List as many permanent elements of religion as you can and consider their role and function in a number of different religions.
3. The study of 'primitive religion' can provide us with an understanding of the 'essential and permanent aspect of humanity'. What do you think are the strengths and weaknesses of this argument?

Reading 15

The role of religion (2)

KARL MARX

Like Durkheim, Marx considered the extent to which religion helped to reinforce social order. Although Marx did not write specifically or in great detail on religion, he criticised its conservative role in his general writing. In this short extract, Marx explains his view that religion is a human construction developed to support the interests of the powerful against those of the less powerful; and that it is used by the powerful to promote a false consciousness among the working population.

For Germany the criticism of religion is in the main complete, and criticism of religion is the premise of all criticism.

The profane existence of error is discredited after its heavenly *oratio pro aris et focis* (speech for the altars and hearths) has been disproved. Man, who looked for a superhuman being in the fantastic reality of heaven and found nothing there but the reflection of himself, will no longer be disposed to find but the semblance of himself, only an inhuman being, where he seeks and must seek his true reality.

The basis of irreligious criticism is: Man makes religion, religion does not make man. Religion is the self-consciousness and self-esteem of man who has either not yet found himself or has already lost himself again. But man is no abstract being encamped outside the world. Man is the world of man, the state, society. This state, this society, produce religion, an inverted world-consciousness, because they are an inverted world. Religion is the general theory of that world, its encyclopaedic compendium, its logic in a popular form, its spiritualistic *point d'honneur*, its enthusiasm, its moral sanction, its solemn complement, its universal source of consolation and justification. It is the fantastic realisation of the human essence because the human essence has no true reality. The struggle against religion is therefore indirectly a fight against the world of which religion is the spiritual aroma.

Religious distress is at the same time the expression of real distress and also the protest against real distress. Religion is the sigh of the oppressed creature, the heart of a heartless world, just as it is the spirit of spiritless condition. It is the opium of the people.

To abolish religion as the illusory happiness of the people is to demand their real happiness. The demand to give up illusions about the existing state of affairs is the demand to give up a state of affairs which needs illusions. The criticism of religion is therefore in embryo the criticism of the vale of tears, the halo of which is religion.

Criticism has torn up the imaginary flowers from the chain not so that man shall wear the unadorned, bleak chain but so that he will shake off the chain and pluck the living flower. The criticism of religion disillusions man to make him think and act and shape his reality like a man who has been disillusioned and has come to reason, so that he will revolve round himself and therefore round his true sun. Religion is only the illusory sun which revolves round man as long as he does not revolve round himself.

The task of history, therefore, once the world beyond the truth has disappeared, is to establish the truth of this world. The immediate task of philosophy, which is at the service of history, once the holy form of human-estrangement has been unmasked, is to unmask self-estrangement in its unholy forms. Thus the criticism of heaven turns into the criticism of the earth, the criticism of religion into the criticism of law and the criticism of theology into the criticism of politics.

From Marx, K. (1976) (1843–44) 'Contribution to the critique of Hegel's philosophy of law', in K. Marx and F. Engels *Collected Works*, vol. 3, London: Lawrence & Wishart, pp. 174–5.

Questions

1. What human, social needs does Marx suggest that religion meets?
2. Why do you think Marx believes that religion produces an 'illusory happiness' among people? How would 'real happiness' differ from this 'illusory happiness'?

Reading 16

Verstehen and the Protestant ethic

MAX WEBER

The Protestant Ethic thesis is perhaps the most famous of Max Weber's ideas. Weber argued that in trying to 'explain' the massive social and economic changes that led to the development of modern, industrial society, the influence of religious ideas and values should not be overlooked. In particular, he highlighted the importance of the ethics of Protestantism in encouraging the development of the Industrial Revolution and of Western capitalism. While capitalism had existed before, modern, Western (Occidental) capitalism was of a uniquely rational kind according to Weber. In the first part of this extract, Weber explores and attempts to define the spirit of capitalism and to explain how 'the Occident has developed capitalism . . . in types, forms and directions which have never existed elsewhere'. The second part looks at the ways in which the early Protestant reformers believed work to be both a virtue and an obligation – to be a 'calling'; with industriousness seen as a sign of respectability and worth. This belief encouraged an ascetic lifestyle – a lifestyle based on self-denial and abstinence – which, Weber argued, provided industry with sober, conscientious workers and thus helped the rational organisation of labour that characterised Western capitalism.

The impulse to acquisition, pursuit of gain, of money, of the greatest possible amount of money, has in itself nothing to do with capitalism. This impulse exists and has existed among waiters, physicians, coachmen, artists, prostitutes, dishonest officials, soldiers, nobles, crusaders, gamblers, and beggars. One may say that it has been common to all sorts and conditions of men at all times and in all countries of the earth, wherever the objective possibility of it is or has been given. It should be taught in the kindergarten of cultural history that this naïve idea of capitalism must be given up once and for all. Unlimited greed for gain is not in the least identical with capitalism, and is still less its spirit. Capitalism may even be identical with the restraint, or at least a rational tempering, of this irrational impulse. But capitalism is identical with the pursuit of profit, and forever *renewed* profit, by means of continuous, rational, capitalistic enterprise. For it must be so: in a wholly capitalistic order of society, an individual capitalistic enterprise which did not take advantage of its opportunities for profit-making would be doomed to extinction.

Let us now define our terms somewhat more carefully than is generally done. We will define a capitalistic economic action as one which rests on the expectation of profit by the utilization of opportunities for exchange, that is on (formally) peaceful chances of profit. Acquisition by force (formally and actually) follows its own particular laws, and it is not expedient, however little one can forbid this, to place it in the same category with action which is, in the last analysis, oriented to profits from exchange. Where capitalistic acquisition is rationally pursued, the corresponding action is adjusted to calculations in terms of capital. This means that the action is adapted to a systematic utilization of goods or personal services as means of acquisition in such a way that, at the close of a business period, the balance of the enterprise in money assets (or, in the case of a continuous enterprise, the periodically estimated money value of assets) exceeds the capital, i.e. the estimated value of the material means of production used for acquisition in exchange [. . .]

Now in this sense capitalism and capitalistic enterprises, even with a considerable rationalization of capitalistic calculation, have existed in all civilized countries of the earth, so far as economic documents permit us to judge. In China, India, Babylon, Egypt, Mediterranean antiquity, and the Middle Ages, as well as in modern times. These were not merely isolated ventures, but economic enterprises which were entirely dependent on the continual renewal of capitalistic undertakings, and even continuous operations. However, trade especially was for a long time not continuous like our own, but consisted essentially in a series of individual undertakings. Only gradually did the activities of even the large merchants acquire an inner cohesion (with branch organizations, etc.). In any case, the capitalistic enterprise and the capitalistic entrepreneur, not only as occasional but as regular entrepreneurs, are very old and were very widespread.

Now, however, the Occident has developed capitalism both to a quantitative extent, and (carrying this quantitative development) in types, forms, and directions which have never existed elsewhere. All over the world there have been merchants, wholesale and retail, local and engaged in foreign trade. Loans of all kinds have been made, and there have been banks with the most various functions, at least comparable to ours of, say, the sixteenth century. Sea loans, *commenda*, and transactions and associations similar to the *Kommanditgesellschaft*, have all been widespread, even as continuous businesses. Whenever money finances of public bodies have existed, moneylenders have appeared, as in Babylon, Hellas, India, China, Rome. They have financed wars and piracy, contracts and building operations of all sorts. In overseas policy they have functioned as colonial entrepreneurs, as planters with slaves, or directly or indirectly forced labour, and have farmed domains, offices, and, above all, taxes. They have financed party leaders in elections and *condottieri* in civil wars. And, finally, they have been speculators in chances for pecuniary gain of all kinds. This kind of entrepreneur, the capitalistic adventurer, has existed everywhere. With the exception of trade and credit and banking transactions, their activities were predominantly of an irrational and speculative character, or directed to acquisition by force, above all the acquisition of booty, whether directly in war or in the form of continuous fiscal booty by exploitation of subjects.

The capitalism of promoters, large-scale speculators, concession hunters, and much modern financial capitalism even in peace time, but, above all, the capitalism especially concerned with exploiting wars, bears this stamp even in modern Western countries, and some, but only some, parts of large-scale international trade are closely related to it, to-day as always.

But in modern times the Occident has developed, in addition to this, a very different form of capitalism which has appeared nowhere else: the rational capitalistic organization of (formally) free labour [. . .]

Rational industrial organization, attuned to a regular market, and neither to political nor irrationally speculative opportunities for profit, is not, however, the only peculiarity of Western capitalism. The modern rational organization of the capitalistic enterprise would not have been possible without two other important factors in its development: the separation of business from the household, which completely dominates modern economic life, and closely connected with it, rational book-keeping [. . .]

However, all these peculiarities of Western capitalism have derived their significance in the last analysis only from their association with the capitalistic organization of labour. Even what is generally called commercialization, the development of negotiable securities and the rationalization of speculation, the exchanges, etc., is connected with it. For without the rational capitalistic organization of labour, all this, so far as it was possible at all, would have nothing like the same significance, above all for the social structure and all the specific problems of the modern Occident connected with it. Exact calculation – the basis of everything else – is only possible on a basis of free labour.

And just as, or rather because, the world has known no rational organization of labour outside the modern Occident, it has known no rational socialism. Of course, there has been civic economy, a civic food-supply policy, mercantilism and welfare policies of princes, rationing, regulation of economic life, protectionism, and *laissez-faire* theories (as in China). The world has also known socialistic and communistic experiments of various sorts: family, religious, or military communism, State socialism (in Egypt), monopolistic cartels, and consumers' organizations. But although there have everywhere been civic market privileges, companies, guilds, and all sorts of legal differences between town and country, the concept of the citizen has not existed outside the Occident, and that of the bourgeoisie outside the modern Occident. Similarly, the proletariat as a class could not exist, because there was no rational organization of free labour under regular discipline. Class struggles between creditor and debtor classes; landowners and the landless, serfs, or tenants; trading interests and consumers or landlords, have existed everywhere in various combinations. But even the Western medieval struggles between putters-out and their workers exist elsewhere only in beginnings. The modern conflict of the large-scale industrial entrepreneur and free-wage labourers was entirely lacking. And thus there could be no such problems as those of socialism.

Hence in a universal history of culture the central problem for us is not, in the last analysis, even from a purely economic view-point, the development of capitalistic activity as such, differing in different cultures only in form: the adventurer type, or capitalism in trade, war, politics, or administration as sources of gain. It is rather the origin of this sober bourgeois capitalism with its rational organization of free labour. Or in terms of cultural history, the problem is that of the origin of the Western bourgeois class and of its peculiarities, a problem which is certainly closely connected with that of the origin of the capitalistic organization of labour, but is not quite the same thing. For the bourgeois as a class existed prior to the development of the peculiar modern form of capitalism, though, it is true, only in the Western hemisphere [. . .]

Now naturally the whole ascetic literature of almost all denominations is saturated with the idea that faithful labour, even at low wages, on the part of those whom life offers no other opportunities, is highly pleasing to God. In this respect Protestant Asceticism added in itself nothing new. But it not only deepened this idea most powerfully, it also created the force which was alone decisive for its effectiveness: the psychological sanction of it through the conception of this labour as a calling, as the best, often in the last analysis the only means of attaining certainty of grace. And on the other hand it legalized the exploitation of this specific willingness to work, in that it also interpreted the employer's business activity as a calling. It is obvious how powerfully the exclusive search for the Kingdom of God only through the fulfilment of duty in the calling, and the strict asceticism which Church discipline naturally imposed, especially on the propertyless classes, was bound to affect the productivity of labour in the capitalistic sense of the word. The treatment of labour as a calling became as characteristic of the modern worker as the corresponding attitude toward acquisition of the business man. It was a perception of this situation, new at his time, which caused so able an observer as Sir William Petty to attribute the economic power of Holland in the seventeenth century to the fact that the very numerous dissenters in that country (Calvinists and Baptists) 'are for the most part thinking, sober men, and such as believe that Labour and Industry is their duty towards God' [. . .]

One of the fundamental elements of the spirit of modern capitalism, and not only of that but of all modern culture: rational conduct on the basis of the idea of the calling, was born – that is what this discussion has sought to demonstrate – from the spirit of Christian asceticism [. . .]

The Puritan wanted to work in a calling; we are forced to do so. For when asceticism was carried out of monastic cells into everyday life, and began to dominate worldly morality, it did its part in building the tremendous cosmos of the modern economic order. This order is now bound to the technical and economic conditions of machine production which to-day determine the lives of all the individuals who are born into this mechanism, not only those directly concerned with economic acquisition, with irresistible force. Perhaps it will so determine them until the last ton of fossilized coal is burnt. In Baxter's view the care for external goods should only lie on the shoulders of the 'saint like a light cloak, which can be thrown aside at any moment'. But fate decreed that the cloak should become an iron cage.

Since asceticism undertook to remodel the world and to work out its ideals in the world, material goods have gained an increasing and finally an inexorable power over the lives of men as at no previous period in history. To-day the spirit of religious asceticism – whether finally, who knows? – has escaped from the cage. But victorious capitalism, since it rests on mechanical foundations, needs its support, no longer. The rosy blush of its laughing heir, the Enlightenment, seems also to be irretrievably fading, and the idea of duty in one's calling prowls about in our lives like the ghost of dead religious beliefs. Where the fulfilment of the calling cannot directly be related to the highest spiritual and cultural values, or when, on the other hand, it need not be felt simply as economic compulsion, the individual generally abandons the attempt to justify it at all. In the field of its highest development, in the United States, the pursuit of wealth, stripped of its religious and ethical meaning, tends to become associated with purely mundane passions, which often actually give it the character of sport.

No one knows who will live in this cage in the future, or whether at the end of this tremendous development entirely new prophets will arise, or there will be a great rebirth of old ideas and ideals, or, if neither, mechanized petrification, embellished with a sort of convulsive self-importance. For of the last stage of this cultural development, it might well be truly said: 'Specialists without spirit, sensualists without heart; this nullity imagines that it has attained a level of civilization never before achieved.'

But this brings us to the world of judgements of value and of faith, with which this purely historical discussion need not be burdened. The next task would be rather to show the significance of ascetic rationalism, which has only been touched in the foregoing sketch, for the content of practical social ethics, thus for the types of organization and the functions of social groups from the conventicle to the State. Then its relations to humanistic rationalism, its ideals of life and cultural influence; further to the development of philosophical and scientific empiricism, to technical development and to spiritual ideals would have to be analysed. Then its historical development from the medieval beginnings of worldly asceticism to its dissolution into pure utilitarianism would have to be traced out through all the areas of ascetic religion. Only then could the quantitative cultural significance of ascetic Protestantism in its relation to the other plastic elements of modern culture be estimated.

Here we have only attempted to trace the fact and the direction of its influence to their motives in one, though a very important point. But it would also further be necessary to investigate how Protestant Asceticism was in turn influenced in its development and its character by the totality of social conditions, especially economic. The modern man is in general, even with the best will, unable to give religious ideas a significance for culture and national character which they deserve. But it is, of course, not my aim to substitute for a one-sided materialistic an equally one-sided spiritualistic causal interpretation of culture and of history. Each is equally possible, but each, if it does not serve as the preparation, but as the conclusion of an investigation, accomplishes equally little in the interest of historical truth.

From M. Weber (1974) (1902) *The Protestant Ethic and the Spirit of Capitalism*, London: Unwin, pp. 17–24, 178–83.

Questions

1. Suggest the main similarities and differences between contemporary capitalism and the capitalist spirit described by Weber.
2. How is the phrase protestant or puritan ethic used today? What influence does it have on the following areas of life: (a) employment; (b) leisure; and (c) home and family life?

Reading 17

Parsons and grand theory

C. WRIGHT MILLS

Parsons is generally acknowledged as the founding figure of 'modern' functionalism, the theoretical perspective that dominated sociology in America and Britain from the late 1930s up to the 1960s. Perhaps the key aim of Parsons' wide-ranging work was to provide a theoretical structure for sociology to follow, based on the establishment of an analytical link or relationship between the action and behaviour of individuals and that of large-scale social systems. For society to function, indeed for social order to be established and maintained, individuals within the social system had to be adequately socialised and integrated. In part this integration occurred as a result of individuals holding a general agreement on values and norms. In this reading C. Wright Mills looks at Parsons' argument that functioning social systems depend on the existence of a generally agreed value orientation and attempts to offer a more 'reader friendly' summary of Parsons' theoretical position. Parsons' emphasis on the social system and its power to influence the behaviour of individuals illustrates his attempt to link macro and micro sociological theorising through a focus on socialisation and social integration. Parsons' work goes into this link or relationship between the individual and society in much greater detail than can be indicated here (for example, he developed the concept of 'pattern variables' to help explain and deal with the dilemmas of social interaction). As well as his 'grand theoretical' work, Parsons also researched and wrote a number of empirical studies on, for instance, kinship, family and medicine.

Grand Theory

Let us begin with a sample of grand theory, taken from Talcott Parsons's *The Social System* – widely regarded as a most important book by a most eminent representative of the style.

> An element of a shared symbolic system which serves as a criterion or standard for selection among the alternatives of orientation which are intrinsically open in a situation may be called a value . . . But from this motivational orientation aspect of the totality of action it is, in view of the role of symbolic systems, necessary to distinguish a 'value-orientation' aspect. This aspect concerns, not the meaning of the expected state of affairs to the actor in terms of his gratification–deprivation balance but the content of the selective standards themselves. The concept of value-orientations in this sense is thus the logical device for formulating one central aspect of the articulation of cultural traditions into the action system.
>
> It follows from the derivation of normative orientation and the role of values in action as stated above, that all values involve what may be called a social reference . . . It is inherent in an action system that action is, to use one phrase, 'normatively oriented'. This follows, as was shown, from the concept of expectations and its place in action theory, especially in the 'active' phase in which the actor pursues goals. Expectations then, in combination with the 'double contingency' of the process of interaction as it has been called, create a crucially imperative problem of order. Two aspects of this problem of order may in turn be distinguished, order in the symbolic systems which make communication possible, and order in the mutuality of motivational orientation to the normative aspect of expectations, the 'Hobbesian' problem of order.
>
> The problem of order, and thus of the nature of the integration of stable systems of social interaction, that is, of social structure, thus focuses on the integration of the motivation of actors with the normative cultural standards which integrate the action system, in our context inter-personally. These standards are, in the terms used in the preceding chapter, patterns of value-orientation, and as such are a particularly crucial part of the cultural tradition of the social system.

Perhaps some readers will now feel a desire to turn to the next chapter; I hope they will not indulge the impulse. Grand Theory – the associating and dissociating of concepts – is well worth considering . . . The fact is that it is not readily understandable; the suspicion is that it may not be altogether intelligible. This is, to be sure, a protective advantage, but it is a disadvantage in so far as its *pronunciamentos* are intended to influence the working habits of social scientists. Not to make fun but to report factually, we have to admit that its productions had been received by social scientists in one or more of the following ways:

To at least some of those who claim to understand it, and who like it, it is one of the greatest advances in the entire history of social science.

To many of those who claim to understand it, but who do not like it, it is a clumsy piece of irrelevant ponderosity. (These are rare, if only because dislike and impatience prevent many from trying to puzzle it out.)

To those who do not claim to understand it, but who like it very much – and there are many of these – it is a wondrous maze, fascinating precisely because of its often splendid lack of intelligibility.

Those who do not claim to understand it and who do not like it – if they retain the courage of their convictions – will feel that indeed the emperor has no clothes.

Of course there are also many who qualify their views, and many more who remain patiently neutral, waiting to see the professional outcome, if any. And although it is, perhaps, a dreadful thought, many social scientists do not even know about it, except as notorious hearsay.

Now all this raises a sore point – intelligibility. That point, of course, goes beyond grand theory, but grand theorists are so deeply involved in it that I fear we really must ask: Is grand theory merely a confused verbiage or is there, after all, also something there? The answer, I think, is: Something is there, buried deep to be sure, but still something is being said. So the question becomes: After all the impediments to meaning are removed from grand theory and what is intelligible becomes available, what, then, is being said?

1

There is only one way to answer such a question: we must translate a leading example of this style of thought and then consider the translation. I have already indicated my choice of example. I want now to make clear that I am not here trying to judge the value of Parsons's work as a whole. If I refer to other writings of his, it is only in order to clarify, in an economical way, some point contained in this one volume. In translating the contents of *The Social System* into English, I do not pretend that my translation is excellent, but only that in the translation no explicit meaning is lost. This – I am asserting – contains all that is intelligible in it. In particular, I shall attempt to sort out statements about something from definitions of words and of their wordy relations. Both are important; to confuse them is fatal to clarity. To make evident the sort of thing that is needed, I shall first translate several passages; then I shall offer two abbreviated translations of the book as a whole.

To translate the example quoted at the opening of this chapter: People often share standards and expect one another to stick to them. In so far as they do, their society may be orderly. (End of translation.) [. . .]

Parsons writes

> Attachment to common values means, motivationally considered, that the actors have common 'sentiments' in support of the value patterns, which may be defined as meaning that conformity with the relevant expectations is treated as a 'good thing' relatively independently of any specific instrumental 'advantage' to be gained from such conformity, e.g. in the avoidance of negative sanctions. Furthermore, this attachment to common values, while it may fit the immediate gratificational needs of the actor, always has also a 'moral' aspect in that to some degree this conformity defines the 'responsibilities' of the actor in the wider, that is, social action systems in which he participates. Obviously

> the specific focus of responsibility is the collectivity which is constituted by a particular common value-orientation.
>
> Finally, it is quite clear that the 'sentiments' which support such common values are not ordinarily in their specific structure the manifestation of constitutionally given propensities of the organism. They are in general learned or acquired. Furthermore, the part they play in the orientation of action is not predominantly that of cultural objects which are cognized and 'adapted to' but the culture patterns have come to be internalized; they constitute part of the structure of the personality system of the actor itself. Such sentiments or 'value-attitudes' as they may be called are therefore genuine need-dispositions of the personality. It is only by virtue of internalization of institutionalized values that a genuine motivational integration of behaviour in the social structure takes place, that the 'deeper' layers of motivation become harnessed to the fulfilment of role expectations. It is only when this has taken place to a high degree that it is possible to say that a social system is highly integrated, and that the interests of the collectivity and the private interests of its constituent members can be said to approach coincidence.
>
> This integration of a set of common value patterns with the internalized need-disposition structure of the constituent personalities is the core phenomenon of the dynamics of social systems. That the stability of any social system except the most evanescent interaction process is dependent on a degree of such integration may be said to be the fundamental dynamic theorem of sociology. It is the major point of reference for all analysis which may claim to be a dynamic analysis of social process.

Or in other words: When people share the same values, they tend to behave in accordance with the way they expect one another to behave. Moreover, they often treat such conformity as a very good thing – even when it seems to go against their immediate interests. That these shared values are learned rather than inherited does not make them any the less important in human motivation. On the contrary, they become part of the personality itself. As such, they bind a society together, for what is socially expected becomes individually needed. This is so important to the stability of any social system that I am going to use it as my chief point of departure if I ever analyse some society as a going concern. (End of translation.)

In a similar fashion, I suppose, one could translate the 555 pages of *The Social System* into about 150 pages of straightforward English. The result would not be very impressive. It would, however, contain the terms in which the key problem of the book, and the solution it offers to this problem, are most clearly statable. Any idea, any book can, of course, be suggested in a sentence or expounded in twenty volumes. It is a question of how full a statement is needed to make something clear and of how important that something seems to be: how many experiences it makes intelligible, how great a range of problems it enables us to solve or at least to state.

To suggest Parsons's book, for example, in two or three phrases: 'We are asked: How is social order possible? The answer we are given seems to be:

Commonly accepted values.' Is that all there is to it? Of course not, but it is the main point. But isn't this unfair? Can't any book be treated this way? Of course. Here is a book of my own treated in this way: 'Who, after all, runs America? No one runs it altogether, but in so far as any group does, the power élite.' And here is the book in your hand: 'What are the social sciences all about? They ought to be about man and society and sometimes they are. They are attempts to help us understand biography and history, and the connexions of the two in a variety of social structures.'

Here is a translation of Parsons's book in four paragraphs:
Let us imagine something we may call 'the social system', in which individuals act with reference to one another. These actions are often rather orderly, for the individuals in the system share standards of value and of appropriate and practical ways to behave. Some of these standards we may call norms; those who act in accordance with them tend to act similarly on similar occasions. In so far as this is so, there are 'social regularities', which we may observe and which are often quite durable. Such enduring and stable regularities I shall call 'structural'. It is possible to think of all these regularities within the social system as a great and intricate balance. That this is a metaphor I am now going to forget, because I want you to take as very real my Concept: the social equilibrium.

There are two major ways by which the social equilibrium is maintained, and by which – should either or both fail – disequilibrium results. The first is 'socialization', all the ways by which the newborn individual is made into a social person. Part of this social making of persons consists in their acquiring motives for taking the social actions required or expected by others. The second is 'social control', by which I mean all the ways of keeping people in line and by which they keep themselves in line. By 'line' of course, I refer to whatever action is typically expected and approved in the social system.

The first problem of maintaining social equilibrium is to make people want to do what is required and expected of them. That failing, the second problem is to adopt other means to keep them in line. The best classifications and definitions of these social controls have been given by Max Weber, and I have little to add to what he, and a few other writers since then, have said so well.

One point does puzzle me a little: given this social equilibrium, and all the socialization and control that man it, how is it possible that anyone should ever get out of line? This I cannot explain very well, that is, in the terms of my Systematic and General Theory of the social system. And there is another point that is not as clear as I should like it to be: how should I account for social change – that is, for history? About these two problems, I recommend that whenever you come upon them, you undertake empirical investigations. (End of translation.)

Perhaps that is enough. Of course we could translate more fully, but 'more fully' does not necessarily mean 'more adequately', and I invite the reader to inspect *The Social System* and find more [. . .]

2

Serious differences among social scientists occur not between those who would observe without thinking and those who would think without observing; the differences have rather to do with what kinds of thinking, what kinds of observing, and what kinds of links, if any, there are between the two.

The basic cause of grand theory is the initial choice of a level of thinking so general that its practitioners cannot logically get down to observation. They never, as grand theorists, get down from the higher generalities to problems in their historical and structural contexts. This absence of a firm sense of genuine problems, in turn, makes for the unreality so noticeable in their pages. One resulting characteristic is a seemingly arbitrary and certainly endless elaboration of distinctions, which neither enlarge our understanding nor make our experience more sensible. This in turn is revealed as a partially organized abdication of the effort to describe and explain human conduct and society plainly.

When we consider what a word stands for, we are dealing with its *semantic* aspects; when we consider it in relation to other words, we are dealing with its *syntactic* features. I introduce these shorthand terms because they provide an economical and precise way to make this point: Grand theory is drunk on syntax, blind to semantics. Its practitioners do not truly understand that when we define a word we are merely inviting others to use it as we would like it to be used; that the purpose of definition is to focus argument upon fact, and that the proper result of good definition is to transform argument over terms into disagreements about fact, and thus open arguments to further inquiry.

The grand theorists are so preoccupied by syntactic meanings and so unimaginative about semantic references, they are so rigidly confined to such high levels of abstraction that the 'typologies' they make up – and the work they do to make them up – seem more often an arid game of Concepts than an effort to define systematically – which is to say, in a clear and orderly way – the problems at hand, and to guide our efforts to solve them.

One great lesson that we can learn from its systematic absence in the work of the grand theorists is that every self-conscious thinker must at all times be aware of – and hence be able to control – the levels of abstraction on which he is working. The capacity to shuttle between levels of abstraction, with ease and with clarity, is a signal mark of the imaginative and systematic thinker.

Around such terms as 'capitalism' or 'middle class' or 'bureaucracy' or 'power élite' or 'totalitarian democracy', there are often somewhat tangled and obscured connotations, and in using these terms, such connotations must be carefully watched and controlled. Around such terms, there are often 'compounded' sets of facts and relations as well as merely guessed-at factors and observations. These too must be carefully sorted out and made clear in our definition and in our use.

To clarify the syntactic and the semantic dimensions of such conceptions, we must be aware of the hierarchy of specificity under each of them, and we must be able to consider all levels of this hierarchy. We must ask: Do we mean by 'capitalism', as we are going to use it, merely the fact that all means of production are privately owned? Or do we also want to include under the term the further idea of a free market as the determining mechanism of price, wages, profit? And to what extent are we entitled to assume that, by definition, the term implies assertions about the political order as well as economic institutions?

From C.W. Mills (1970) *The Sociological Imagination*, Harmondsworth: Penguin, pp. 32–44.

Questions

1. It is perhaps easy to 'dismiss' work because of its difficult language. Read the section of the reading from 'Parsons writes: Attachment to common values . . . a dynamic analysis of social process'. What are the strengths of Parsons' analysis of the role of common values?
2. Mills writes that 'Grand theorists (never) get down from the higher generalities to problems in their historical and structural contexts.' To what extent do you think this is a fair comment on the work of Durkheim, Marx and Weber?
   (It would be a good idea to look at Readings 11, 12 and 15 before responding to this question.)

Reading 18

The development of self

GEORGE HERBERT MEAD

George Herbert Mead's writings on the relationship between the individual and society established him as perhaps the key figure in the development of the Symbolic Interactionist perspective. Reading 18 is taken from his examination of the concept of the 'self'. The self refers to how individuals see themselves in relation to others and is, for Mead, a concept that is only meaningful in relation to other 'selfs' and to the social groups which individuals are part of. In this extract Mead describes and discusses the part played by the two basic elements of the self – the 'I' and the 'Me' (essentially the individual's inner self and their outer or public persona) – and how they interact to produce a complete self. He points out, for instance, how the 'Me', the more conventional, routine side of the individual, acts as a control, or censor, on the 'I', the impulsive side, and how both have a vital role to play: as he puts it, 'a person who cannot do a certain amount of stereotyped work is not a healthy individual'.

The Contributions of the 'Me' and the 'I'

I have been undertaking to distinguish between the 'I' and the 'me' as different phases of the self, the 'me' answering to the organized attitudes of the others which we definitely assume and which determine consequently our own conduct so far as it is of a self-conscious character. Now the 'me' may be regarded as giving the form of the 'I'. The novelty comes in the action of the 'I', but the structure, the form of the self is one which is conventional.

This conventional form may be reduced to a minimum. In the artist's attitude, where there is artistic creation, the emphasis upon the element of novelty is carried to the limit. This demand for the unconventional is especially noticeable in modern art. Here the artist is supposed to break away from convention; a part of his artistic expression is thought to be in the breakdown of convention. That attitude is, of course, not essential to the artistic function, and it probably never occurs in the extreme form in which it is often proclaimed. Take certain of the artists of the past. In the Greek world the artists were, in a certain sense, the supreme artisans. What they were to do was more or less set by the community, and accepted by themselves, as the expression of heroic figures, certain deities, the erection of temples. Definite rules were accepted as essential to the expression. And yet the artist introduced an originality into it which distinguishes one artist from another. In the case of the artist, the emphasis upon that which is unconventional, that which is not in the structure of the 'me', is carried as far, perhaps, as it can be carried.

This same emphasis also appears in certain types of conduct which are impulsive. Impulsive conduct is uncontrolled conduct. The structure of the 'me' does not there determine the expression of the 'I'. If we use a Freudian expression the 'me' is in a certain sense a censor. It determines the sort of expressions which can take place, sets the stage, and gives the cue. In the case of impulsive conduct this structure of the 'me' involved in the situation does not furnish to any such degree this control. Take the situation of self-assertion where the self simply asserts itself against others, and suppose that the emotional stress is such that the forms of polite society in the performance of legitimate conduct are overthrown, so that the person expresses himself violently. There the 'me' is determined by the situation. There are certain recognized fields within which an individual can assert himself, certain rights which he has within these limits. But let the stress become too great, these limits are not observed, and an individual asserts himself in perhaps a violent fashion. Then the 'I' is the dominant element against the 'me'. Under what we consider normal conditions, the way in which an individual acts is determined by his taking the attitude of the others in the group, but if the individual is not given the opportunity to come up against people, as a child is not who is held out of intercourse with other people, then there results a situation in which the reaction is uncontrolled.

Social control is the expression of the 'me' against the expression of the 'I'. It sets the limits, it gives the determination that enables the 'I', so to speak, to use the 'me' as the means of carrying out what is the undertaking that all are interested in. When persons are held outside or beyond that sort of organized expression, there arises a situation in which social control is absent. In the more or less fantastic psychology of the Freudian group, thinkers are dealing with the sexual life and with self-assertion in its violent form. The normal situation, however, is one which involves a reaction of the individual in a situation which is socially determined but to which he brings his own responses as an 'I'. The response is, in the experience of the individual, an expression with which the self is identified. It is such a response which raises him above the institutionalized individual.

As I have said before, an institution is, after all, nothing but an organization of attitudes which we all carry in us, the organized attitudes of the others that control and determine conduct. Now, this institutionalized individual is, or should be, the means by which the individual expresses himself in his own way, for such individual expression is that which is identified with the self in those values which are essential to the self, and which arise from the self. To speak of them as arising from the self does not attach to them the character of the selfish egoist, for under the normal conditions to which we were referring, the individual is making his contribution to a common undertaking. The baseball player who makes a brilliant play is making the play called for by the nine to which he belongs. He is playing for his side. A man may, of course, play the gallery, be more interested in making a brilliant play than in helping his team to win, just as a surgeon may carry out a brilliant operation and sacrifice the patient. But under normal conditions, the contribution of the individual gets its expression in the social processes that are involved in the act, so that the attachment of the values to the self does not involve egoism or selfishness. The other situation in which the self in its expression does in some sense exploit the group or society to which it belongs is one which sets up, so to speak, a narrow self which takes advantage of the whole group in satisfying itself. Even such a self is still a social affair. We distinguish very definitely between the selfish man and the impulsive man. The man who may lose his temper and knock another down may be a very unselfish man. He is not necessarily a person who would utilize a certain situation for the sake of his own interests. The latter case involves the narrow self that does not relate itself to the whole social group of which it is a part.

Values do definitely attach to this expression of the self which is peculiar to the self; and what is peculiar to the self is what it calls its own. And yet this value lies in the social situation and would not be apart from that social situation. It is the contribution of the individual to the situation, even though it is only in the social situation that the value is obtained.

We seek certainly for that sort of expression which is self-expression. When an individual feels himself hedged in, he recognizes the necessity of a situation in which there will be an opportunity for him to make his addition to the undertaking, and not simply to be the conventionalized 'me'. In a person who carries out the routine job, it leads to the reaction against the machine and to the demand that that type of routine work fall into its place in the whole social process. There is, of course, a certain amount of real mental and physical health, a very essential part of one's life, that is involved in doing routine work. One can very well just carry out certain processes in which his contribution is very slight, in a more or less mechanical fashion, and find himself in a better position because of it. Such men as John Stuart Mill have been able to carry on routine occupations during a certain part of the day, and then give themselves to original work for the rest of the day. A person who cannot do a certain amount of stereotyped work is not a healthy individual. Both the health of the individual and the stability of society call for a very considerable amount of such work. The reaction to machine industry simply calls for the restriction of the amount of time given to it, but it does not involve its total abolition. Nevertheless, and granting this point, there must be some way in which the individual can express himself. It is the situations in which it is possible to get this sort of expression that seem to be particularly precious, namely, those situations in which the individual is able to do something on his own, where he can take over responsibility and carry out things in his own way, with an opportunity to think his own thoughts. Those social situations in which the structure of the 'me' for the time being is one in which the individual gets an opportunity for that sort of expression of the self bring some of the most exciting and gratifying experiences.

These experiences may take place in a form which involves degradation or in a form which involves the emergence of higher values. The mob furnishes a situation in which the 'me' is one which simply supports and emphasizes the more violent sort of impulsive expression. This tendency is deeply imbedded in human nature. It is astonishing what part of the 'I' of the sick is constituted by murder stories. Of course, in the story itself, it is the tracking-down of the murderer that is the focal point of interest; but that tracking-down of the murderer takes one back to the vengeance attitude of the primitive community. In the murder story one gets a real villain, runs him down, and brings him to justice. Such expressions may involve degradation of the self. In situations involving the defense of the country a mob attitude or a very high moral attitude may prevail, depending upon the individual. The situation in which one can let himself go, in which the very structure of the 'me' opens the door for the 'I', is favorable to self-expression. I have referred to the situation in which a person can sit down with a friend and say just what he is thinking about someone else. There is a satisfaction in letting one's self go in this way. The sort of thing that under other circumstances you would not say and would not even let yourself think is now naturally uttered. Should you get in a group which thinks as you do, you can go to lengths which may surprise you. The 'me' in the above situations is definitely constituted by the social relations. Now if this situation is such that it opens the door to impulsive expression, one gets a peculiar satisfaction, high or low, the source of which is the value that attaches to the expression of the 'I' in the social process.

From G.H. Mead (1934) *Mind, Self and Society*, Chicago: University of Chicago Press, pp. 209–13.

Questions

1. To what extent is your 'I' (your impulsive side) 'censored' by your 'Me'?

Consider specific areas of your day-to-day behaviour and provide examples of when and how this control occurs. You may consider your behaviour in, for example, a lecture, a sports game, a cinema or concert and so on.

2. To what extent does the control exerted by your 'Me' reflect generally held values and standards and where does it differ from them?
3. How might Mead's notion of the self be used to explain (a) crime and deviance; (b) artistic ability; (c) a bureaucratic personality?

Reading 19

Stigma

ERVING GOFFMAN

Goffman's detailed and insightful observations of social interaction have made him one of the key figures in the development of interpretive sociology. A particular area of interest was the analysis of how individuals present themselves in everyday situations and in public life – how people establish and then defend their self-images. In spite of individual differences, people like to think of themselves as normal and in his collection of essays, Stigma, *Goffman looked at the ways in which 'normal' people respond to, and in particular stereotype and segregate, those who are seen as different. This extract starts with Goffman's categorisation of different types of stigma and his discussion of the 'information' that is of most relevance in the study of stigma, and how such information is conveyed. It can come in the form of symbols; while some symbols present essentially positive information about an individual or group, stigma symbols, by contrast, highlight negative, 'debasing' information. Goffman's early studies were written in the 1950s and 1960s and should be read with this in mind. Stigma, for instance, was first published in 1964 and, as well as the sexist language, the linking of homosexuality with a comment on 'unnatural passions', in the first paragraph of the reading, illustrate the importance of contextualising writing.*

Three types of stigma may be mentioned. First there are abominations of the body – the various physical deformities. Next there are blemishes of individual character perceived as weak will, domineering or unnatural passions, treacherous and rigid beliefs, and dishonesty, these being inferred from a known record of, for example, mental disorder, imprisonment, addiction, alcoholism, homosexuality, unemployment, suicidal attempts, and radical political behaviour. Finally there are the tribal stigma of race, nation, and religion, these being stigma that can be transmitted through lineages and equally contaminate all members of a family. In all of these various instances of stigma, however, . . . the same sociological features are found:

an individual who might have been received easily in ordinary social intercourse possesses a trait that can obtrude itself upon attention and turn those of us whom he meets away from him, breaking the claim that his other attributes have on us. He possesses a stigma, an undesired differentness from what we had anticipated. We and those who do not depart negatively from the particular expectations at issue I shall call the *normals*.

The attitudes we normals have towards a person with a stigma, and the actions we take in regard to him, are well known, since these responses are what benevolent social action is designed to soften and ameliorate. By definition, of course, we believe the person with a stigma is not quite human. On this assumption we exercise varieties of discrimination, through which we effectively, if often unthinkingly, reduce his life chances. We construct a stigma theory, an ideology to explain his inferiority and account for the danger he represents, sometimes rationalizing an animosity based on other differences, such as those of social class. We use specific stigma terms such as cripple, bastard, moron in our daily discourse as a source of metaphor and imagery, typically without giving thought to the original meaning [. . .]

Social Information

The information of most relevance in the study of stigma has certain properties. It is information about an individual. It is about his more or less abiding characteristics, as opposed to the moods, feelings, or intents that he might have at a particular moment. The information, as well as the sign through which it is conveyed, is reflexive and embodied; that is, it is conveyed by the very person it is about, and conveyed through bodily expression in the immediate presence of those who receive the expression. Information possessing all of these properties I will here call 'social'. Some signs that convey social information may be frequently and steadily available, and routinely sought and received; these signs may be called 'symbols'.

The social information conveyed by any particular symbol may merely confirm what other signs tell us about the individual, filling out our image of him in a redundant and unproblematic way. Some lapel buttons, attesting to social club membership, are examples, as are male wedding rings in some contexts. However, the social information conveyed by a symbol can establish a special claim to prestige, honour, or desirable class position – a claim that might not otherwise be presented or, if otherwise presented, then not automatically granted. Such a sign is popularly called a 'status symbol', although the term 'prestige symbol' might be more accurate, the former term being more suitably employed when a well-organized social position of some kind is the referent. Prestige symbols can be contrasted to *stigma symbols,* namely, signs which are especially effective in drawing attention to a debasing identity discrepancy, breaking up what would otherwise be a coherent overall picture, with a consequent reduction in our valuation of the individual. The shaved head of female collaborators in the Second World War is an example [. . .]

Signs conveying social information carry according to whether or not they are congenital, and, if not, whether, once employed, they become a permanent part of the person. (Skin colour is congenital; a brand mark or maiming is permanent but not congenital; a convict's head-shave is neither congenital nor permanent.) More important, impermanent signs solely employed to convey social information may or may not be employed against the will of the informant; when they are, they tend to be stigma symbols. Later it will be necessary to consider stigma symbols that are voluntarily employed.

It is possible for signs which mean one thing to one group to mean something else to another group, the same category being designated but differently characterized. For example, the shoulder patches that prison officials require escape-prone prisoners to wear can come to mean one thing to guards, in general negative, while being a mark of pride for the wearer relative to his fellow prisoners. The uniform of an officer may be a matter of pride to some, to be worn on every possible occasion; for other officers, weekends may represent a time when they can exercise their choice and wear mufti, passing as civilians. Similarly, while the obligation to wear the school cap in town may be seen as a privilege by some boys, as will the obligation to wear a uniform on leave by 'other ranks', still there will be wearers who feel that the social information conveyed thereby is a means of ensuring control and discipline over them when they are off duty and off the premises. So, too, during the eighteen hundreds in California, the absence of a pigtail (queue) on a Chinese man signified for Occidentals a degree of acculturation, but to fellow-Chinese a question would be raised as to respectability – specifically, whether or not the individual had served a term in prison where cutting off the queue was obligatory; loss of queue was for a time, then, very strongly resisted. Signs carrying social information vary of course as to their reliability. Distended capillaries on the cheek and nose, sometimes called 'venous stigmata' with more aptness than meant, can be and are taken as indicating alcoholic excess. However, teetotallers can exhibit the same symbol for other physiological reasons, thereby giving rise to suspicions about themselves which aren't justified, but with which they must deal nonetheless.

A final point about social information must be raised; it has to do with the informing character of the 'with' relationship in our society. To be 'with' someone is to arrive at a social occasion in his company, walk with him down a street, be a member of his party in a restaurant, and so forth. The issue is that in certain circumstances the social identity of those an individual is with can be used as a source of information concerning his own social identity, the assumption being that he is what the others are. The extreme, perhaps, is the situation in criminal circles: a person wanted for arrest can legally contaminate anyone he is seen with, subjecting them to arrest on suspicion. (A person for whom there is a warrant is therefore said 'to have smallpox', and his criminal disease is said to be 'catching'.) In any case, an analysis of how people manage the information they convey about themselves will have to consider how they deal with the contingencies of being seen 'with' particular others [. . .]

Visibility

Since it is through our sense of sight that the stigma of others most frequently becomes evident, the term visibility is perhaps not too misleading. Actually, the more general term 'perceptibility' would be more accurate, and 'evidentness' more accurate still. A stammer, after all, is a very 'visible' defect, but in the first instance because of sound, not sight. Before the concept of visibility can be safely used even in this corrected version, however, it must be distinguished from three other notions that are confused with it.

First, the visibility of a stigma must be distinguished from its 'known-aboutness'. When an individual's stigma is very visible, his merely contacting others will cause his stigma to be known about. But whether others know about the individual's stigma will depend on another factor in addition to its current visibility, namely, whether or not they have previous knowledge about him and this can be based on gossip about him or a previous contact with him during which his stigma was visible.

Secondly, visibility must be distinguished from one of its particular bases, namely, obtrusiveness. When a stigma is immediately perceivable, the issue still remains as to how much it interferes with the flow of interaction. For example, at a business meeting a participant in a wheelchair is certainly seen to be in a wheelchair, but around the conference table his failing can become relatively easy to disattend. On the other hand, a participant with a speech impediment, who in many ways is much less handicapped than someone in a wheelchair, can hardly open his mouth, without destroying any unconcern that may have arisen concerning his failing, and he will continue to introduce uneasiness each time thereafter that he speaks. The very mechanics of spoken encounters constantly redirect attention to the defect, constantly making demands for clear and rapid messages that must constantly be defaulted. It may be added that the same failing can have different expressions, each with a different degree of obtrusiveness. For example, a blind person with a white cane gives quite visible evidence that he is blind; but this stigma symbol, once noted, can sometimes be disattended, along with what it signifies. But the blind person's failure to direct his face to the eyes of his co-participants is an event that repeatedly violates communication etiquette and repeatedly disrupts the feedback mechanics of spoken interaction.

Thirdly, the visibility of a stigma (as well as its obstrusiveness) must be disentangled from certain possibilities of what can be called its 'perceived focus'. We normals develop conceptions, whether objectively grounded or not, as to the sphere of life-activity for which an individual's particular stigma primarily disqualifies him. Ugliness, for example, has its initial and prime effect during social situations, threatening the pleasure we might otherwise take in the company of its possessor. We perceive, however, that his condition ought to have no effect on his competency in solitary tasks, although of course we may discriminate against him here simply because of the feelings we have about looking at him. Ugliness, then, is a stigma that is focused in social situations. Other stigmas, such as a diabetic condition, are felt to have no initial effect on the individual's qualifications for face-to-face interaction; they lead us first to discriminate in such matters as job allocation, and affect immediate social interaction only, for example, because the stigmatized individual may have attempted to keep his differentness a secret and feels unsure about being able to do so, or because the others present know about his condition and are making a painful effort not to allude to it. Many other stigmas fall in between these two extremes regarding focus, being perceived to have a broad initial effect in many different areas of life. For example, a person with cerebral palsy may not only be seen as burdensome in face-to-face communication, but may also induce the feeling that he is questionable as a solitary task performer.

The question of visibility, then, must be distinguished from some other issues: the known-about-ness of the attribute, its obtrusiveness, and its perceived focus. This still leaves unconsidered the tacit assumption that somehow the public at large will be engaged in the viewing. But as we shall see, specialists at uncovering identity can be involved, and their training may allow them to be immediately struck by something that is invisible to the laity. A physician who meets on the street a man with dull red discoloration of the cornea and notched teeth is meeting someone who openly displays two of Hutchinson's signs and is likely to be syphilitic.

Others present, however, being medically blind, will see no evil. In general, then, the decoding capacity of the audience must be specified before one can speak of degree of visibility.

From E. Goffman (1970) *Stigma: Notes on the Management of Spoiled Identity*, Harmondsworth: Penguin, pp. 14–15, 58–68.

Questions

1. Think of an example of a 'prestige symbol' and a 'stigma symbol'. To what extent could these symbols be viewed differently by different people or in different situations?

2. How might Goffman's description and analysis of stigma affect the way in which 'abnormal' behaviour is responded to by (a) the general public; (b) those who work with the stigmatised, e.g. social workers, psychiatrists, prison officers?
3. Think of one example of each of the three types of stigma identified by Goffman at the start of the reading ('abominations of the body', 'blemishes of individual character', 'tribal stigma').
   (a) How evident or visible is it to outsiders?
   (b How obtrusive is it (how much does it interfere with daily interaction)?
   (c) In which social situations will it have little effect and in which a great effect?

Reading 20

Critical theory and human needs

HERBERT MARCUSE

Marcuse was an early and leading member of the Frankfurt School and one of the key exponents of critical theory. This reading provides an example of a neo-Marxist analysis of the role of ideology in perpetuating the inherently exploitative nature of modern capitalist society. In particular, Marcuse examines how powerful groups promote a false consciousness among the mass of the population through encouraging them to develop needs which are false or artificial in so far as they work in the interests of these powerful groups and, therefore, against the 'true' interests of the working classes. Although Marcuse was writing from a critical perspective, and indeed became something of a cult figure among the New Left in the 1960s, some of his language now has a dated, and even politically incorrect, feel – for instance, and in a similar vein to Simone de Beauvoir (Reading 21), he refers to 'the Negro' and, as with so many of the early theorists, he uses the male pronoun throughout his writing.

The intensity, the satisfaction and even the character of human needs, beyond the biological level, have always been preconditioned. Whether or not the possibility of doing or leaving, enjoying or destroying, possessing or rejecting something is seized as a *need* depends on whether or not it can be seen as desirable and necessary for the prevailing societal institutions and interests. In this sense, human needs are historical needs and, to the extent to which the society demands the repressive development of the individual, his needs themselves and their claim for satisfaction are subject to overriding critical standards.

We may distinguish both true and false needs. 'False' are those which are superimposed upon the individual by particular social interests in his repression: the needs which perpetuate toil, aggressiveness, misery, and injustice. Their satisfaction might be most gratifying to the individual, but this happiness is not a condition which has to be maintained and protected if it serves to arrest the development of the ability (his own and others) to recognize the disease of the whole and grasp the chances of curing the disease. The result then is euphoria in unhappiness. Most of the prevailing needs to relax, to have fun, to behave and consume in accordance with the advertisements, to love and hate what others love and hate, belong to this category of false needs.

Such needs have a societal content and function which are determined by external powers over which the individual has no control; the development and satisfaction of these needs is heteronomous. No matter how much such needs may have become the individual's own, reproduced and fortified by the conditions of his existence; no matter how much he identifies himself with them and finds himself in their satisfaction, they continue to be what they were from the beginning – products of a society whose dominant interest demands repression.

The prevalence of repressive needs is an accomplished fact, accepted in ignorance and defeat, but a fact that must be undone in the interest of the happy individual as well as all those whose misery is the price of his satisfaction. The only needs that have an unqualified claim for satisfaction are the vital ones – nourishment, clothing, lodging at the attainable level of culture. The satisfaction of these needs is the prerequisite for the realization of all needs, of the unsublimated as well as the sublimated ones [. . .]

In the last analysis, the question of what are true and false needs must be answered by the individuals themselves, but only in the last analysis; that is, if and when they are free to give their own answer. As long as they are kept incapable of being autonomous, as long as they are indoctrinated and manipulated (down to their very instincts), their answer to this question cannot be taken as their own. By the same token, however, no tribunal can justly arrogate to itself the right to decide which needs should be developed and satisfied. Any such tribunal is reprehensible, although our revulsion does not do away with the question: how can the people who have been the object of effective and productive domination by themselves create the conditions of freedom?

The more rational, productive, technical, and total the repressive administration of society becomes, the more unimaginable the means and ways by which the administered individuals might break their servitude and seize their own liberation. To be sure, to impose Reason upon an entire society is a paradoxical and scandalous idea – although one might dispute the righteousness of a society which ridicules this idea while making its own population into objects of total administration. All liberation depends on the consciousness of servitude, and the emergence of this consciousness is always hampered by the predominance of needs and satisfactions which, to a great extent, have become the individual's own. The process always replaces one system of preconditioning by another; the optimal goal is the replacement of false needs by true ones, the abandonment of repressive satisfaction.

The distinguishing feature of advanced industrial society is its effective suffocation of those needs which demand liberation – liberation also from that which is tolerable and rewarding and comfortable – while it sustains and absolves the destructive power and repressive function of the affluent society. Here, the social controls exact the overwhelming need for the production and consumption of waste; the need for stupefying work where it is no longer a real necessity; the need for modes of relaxation which soothe and prolong this stupefication; the need for maintaining such deceptive liberties as free competition at administered prices, a free press which censors itself, free choice between brands and gadgets.

Under the rule of a repressive whole, liberty can be made into a powerful instrument of domination. The range of choice open to the individual is not the decisive factor in determining the degree of human freedom, but what can be chosen and what is chosen by the individual. The criterion for free choice can never be an absolute one, but neither is it entirely relative. Free election of masters does not abolish the masters or the slaves. Free choice among a wide variety of goods and services does not signify freedom if these goods and services sustain social controls over a life of toil and fear – that is, if they sustain alienation. And the spontaneous reproduction of superimposed needs by the individual does not establish autonomy; it only testifies to the efficacy of the controls.

Our insistence on the depth and efficacy of these controls is open to the objection that we overrate greatly the indoctrinating power of the 'media', and that by themselves the people would feel and satisfy the needs which are now imposed upon them. The objection misses the point. The preconditioning does not start with the mass production of radio and television and with the centralization of their control. The people enter this stage as preconditioned receptacles of long standing; the decisive difference is in the flattening out of the contrast (or conflict) between the given and the possible, between the satisfied and the unsatisfied needs. Here, the so-called equalization of class distinctions reveals its ideological function. If the worker and his boss enjoy the same television program and visit the same resort places, if the typist is as attractively made up as the daughter of her employer, if the Negro owns a Cadillac, if they all read the same newspaper, then this assimilation indicates not the disappearance of classes, but the extent to which the needs and satisfactions that serve the preservation of the Establishment are shared by the underlying population.

Indeed, in the most highly developed areas of contemporary society, the transplantation of social into individual needs is so effective that the difference between them seems to be purely theoretical. Can one really distinguish between the mass media as instruments of information and entertainment, and as agents of manipulation and indoctrination? Between the automobile as nuisance and as convenience? Between the horrors and the comforts of functional architecture? Between the work for national defense and the work for corporate gain? Between the private pleasure and the commercial and political utility involved in increasing the birth rate?

We are again confronted with one of the most vexing aspects of advanced industrial civilization: the rational character of its irrationality. Its productivity and efficiency, its capacity to increase and spread comforts, to turn waste into need, and destruction into construction, the extent to which this civilization transforms the object world into an extension of man's mind and body makes the very notion of alienation questionable. The people recognize themselves in their commodities; they find their soul in their automobile, hi-fi set, split-level home, kitchen equipment. The very mechanism which ties the individual to his society has changed, and social control is anchored in the new needs which it has produced.

From H. Marcuse (1964) *One-Dimensional Man: Studies in the Ideology of Advanced Industrial Society*, London: Routledge & Kegan Paul, pp. 4–9.

Questions

1. What do you think Marcuse means by 'false needs'? Give some possible examples.
2. Marcuse highlights the importance of the media for the 'preservation of the Establishment'.
   (a) How difficult do you think it is to distinguish between the mass media as 'instruments of information and entertainment, and as agents of manipulation and indoctrination'?
   (b) To what extent do the mass media help to mask class distinctions?
3. Marcuse points to a number of aspects of modern society where both rational and irrational characteristics seem to be apparent – such as the spread of the automobile and 'functional architecture'. Can you suggest any other such aspects?

Reading 21

The second sex

SIMONE DE BEAUVOIR

The Second Sex is generally regarded as one of the most important books in the history of feminism. In 1949, when the book was first published, Simone de Beauvoir's argument that the subordination of women is not a fact of nature was seen as a revolutionary thesis. This reading is taken from de Beauvoir's discussion of the married woman, which makes up part of her detailed examination of the situation of women today; in other chapters she looks at the mother, social life, prostitution and old age. In this extract she describes the pressure on women to marry and argues that marriage performs distinct functions for men and women and still, in essence, involves wives becoming their husband's property. In reading this extract consider the period at which de Beauvoir was writing and the extent to which her account has relevance today.

The Married Woman

Marriage is the destiny traditionally offered to women by society. It is still true that most women are married, or have been, or plan to be, or suffer from not being. The celibate woman is to be explained and defined with reference to marriage, whether she is frustrated, rebellious, or even indifferent in regard to that institution. We must therefore continue this study by analyzing marriage.

Economic evolution in woman's situation is in process of upsetting the institution of marriage: it is becoming a union freely entered upon by the consent of two independent persons; the obligations of the two contracting parties are personal and reciprocal; adultery is for both a breach of contract; divorce is obtainable by the one or other on the same conditions. Woman is no longer limited to the reproductive function, which has lost in large part its character as natural servitude and has come to be regarded as a function to be voluntarily assumed; and it is compatible with productive labor, since, in many cases, the time off required by pregnancy is taken by the mother at the expense of the State or the employer. In the Soviet Union marriage was for some years a contract between individuals based upon the complete liberty of husband and wife; but it would seem that it is now a duty that the State imposes upon them both. Which of these tendencies will prevail in the world of tomorrow will depend upon the general structure of society. Nevertheless, the epoch in which we are living is still, from the feminist point of view, a period of transition. Only a part of the female population is engaged in production, and even those who are belong to a society in which ancient forms and antique values survive. Modern marriage can be understood only in the light of a past that it tends to perpetuate in part.

Marriage has always been a very different thing for man and for woman. The two sexes are necessary to each other, but this necessity has never brought about a condition of reciprocity between them; women, as we have seen, have never constituted a caste making exchanges and contracts with the male caste upon a footing of equality. A man is socially an independent and complete individual; he is regarded first of all as a producer whose existence is justified by the work he does for the group; we have seen why it is that the reproductive and domestic role to which woman is confined has not guaranteed her an equal dignity. Certainly the male needs her; in some primitive groups it may happen that the bachelor, unable to manage his existence by himself, becomes a kind of outcast; in agricultural societies a woman coworker is essential to the peasant; and for most men it is of advantage to unload certain drudgery upon a mate; the individual wants a regular sexual life and posterity, and the State requires him to contribute to its perpetuation. But man does not make his appeal directly to woman herself, it is the men's group that allows each of its members to find self-fulfilment as husband and father; woman, as slave or vassal, is integrated within families dominated by fathers and brothers, and she has always been given in marriage by certain males to other males. In primitive societies the paternal clan, the gens, disposed of woman almost like a thing: she was included in deals agreed upon by two groups. The situation is not much modified when marriage assumes a contractual form in the course of its evolution; when dowered or having her share in inheritance, woman would seem to have civil standing as a person, but dowry and inheritance, still enslave her to her family. During a long period the contracts were made between father-in-law and son-in-law, not between wife and husband; only widows then enjoyed economic independence. The young girl's freedom of choice has always been much restricted; and celibacy – apart from the rare cases in which it bears a sacred character – reduced her to the rank of parasite and pariah; marriage is her only means of support and the sole justification of her existence. It is enjoined upon her for two reasons.

The first reason is that she must provide the society with children; only rarely – as in Sparta and to some extent under the Nazi regime – does the

State take woman under direct guardianship and ask only that she be a mother. But even the primitive societies that are not aware of the paternal generative role demand that woman have a husband, for the second reason why marriage is enjoined is that woman's function is also to satisfy a male's sexual needs and to take care of his household. These duties placed upon woman by society are regarded as a *service* rendered to her spouse: in return he is supposed to give her presents, or a marriage settlement, and to support her. Through him as intermediary, society discharges its debt to the woman it turns over to him. The rights obtained by the wife in fulfilling her duties are represented in obligations that the male must assume. He cannot break the conjugal bond at his pleasure; he can repudiate or divorce his wife only when the public authorities so decide, and even then the husband sometimes owes her compensation in money: the practice even becomes an abuse in Egypt under Bocchoris or, as the demand for alimony, in the United States today. Polygamy has always been more or less openly tolerated: man may bed with slaves, concubines, mistresses, prostitutes, but he is required to respect certain privileges of his legitimate wife. If she is maltreated or wronged, she has the right more or less definitely guaranteed – of going back to her family and herself obtaining a separation or divorce.

Thus for both parties marriage is at the same time a burden and a benefit; but there is no symmetry in the situations of the two sexes; for girls marriage is the only means of integration in the community, and if they remain unwanted, they are, socially viewed, so much wastage. This is why mothers have always eagerly sought to arrange marriages for them. In the last century they were hardly consulted among middle-class people. They were offered to possible suitors by means of 'interviews' arranged in advance [. . .]

In such circumstances the girl seems absolutely passive; she *is* married, *given* in marriage by her parents. Boys get married, they *take* a wife. They look in marriage for an enlargement, a confirmation of their existence, but not the mere right to exist; it is a charge they assume voluntarily. Thus they can inquire concerning its advantages and disadvantages, as did the Greek and medieval satirists; for them it is one mode of living, not a preordained lot. They have a perfect right to prefer celibate solitude; some marry late, or not at all.

In marrying, woman gets some share in the world as her own; legal guarantees protect her against capricious action by man; but she becomes his vassal. He is the economic head of the joint enterprise, and hence he represents it in the view of society. She takes his name; she belongs to his religion, his class, his circle; she joins his family, she becomes his 'half'. She follows wherever his work calls him and determines their place of residence; she breaks more or less decisively with her past, becoming attached to her husband's universe; she gives him her person, virginity and a rigorous fidelity being required. She loses some of the rights legally belonging to the unmarried woman. Roman law placed the wife in the husband's hands *loco filia*, in the position of a daughter; early in the nineteenth century the conservative writer Bonald pronounced the wife to be to her husband as the child is to its mother; before 1942 French law demanded the wife's obedience to her husband; law and custom still give him great authority, as implied in the conjugal situation itself [. . .]

Marriage today still retains, for the most part, this traditional form. And, first of all, it is forced much more tyrannically upon the young girl than upon the young man. There are still important social strata in which no other vista opens before her; among the workers of the land the unmarried woman is a pariah; she remains a servant of her father, of her brothers, or of her brother-in-law; she can hardly join the exodus to the cities; marriage enslaves her to a man, but it makes her mistress of a home. In certain middle-class circles, the young girl is still left incapable of making a living; she can only vegetate as a parasite in her father's home or take some menial position in the home of a stranger. Even when she is more emancipated, she is led to prefer marriage to a career because of the economic advantages held by men: she tends to look for a husband who is above her in status or who she hopes will make a quicker or greater success than she could.

It is still agreed that the act of love is, as we have seen, a *service* rendered to the man; he *takes* his pleasure and owes her some payment. The woman's body is something he buys; to her he represents capital she is authorized to exploit. Sometimes she may bring a dowry; or, often, she undertakes to do certain domestic work: keeping house, rearing children. In any case she has the right to accept support and is even urged to do so by traditional morality. She is naturally tempted by this relatively easy way, the more so because occupations open to women are often disagreeable and poorly paid; marriage, in a word, is a more advantageous career than many others.

The attainment of sexual freedom by the unmarried woman, further, is still made difficult by social customs. In France adultery committed by a wife has been considered, up to the present time, to be a legal offense, whereas no law forbids a woman free love; nevertheless, if she wishes to take a lover, she must first get married. Even at the present time many young middle-class women of strict behavior marry 'so as to be free'. A good many American young women have gained sexual freedom; but their actual experiences are rather like those of the young girls described by Malinowski in *The Sexual Life of Savages*, who practice inconsequential love-making in the 'bachelors' house'; it is understood that they will marry later, when they will be regarded as fully adult. A single woman in America, still more than in France, is a socially incomplete being even if she makes her own living; if she is to attain the whole dignity of a person and gain her full rights, she must wear a wedding ring. Maternity in particular is respectable only for a married woman; the unwed mother remains an offense to public opinion, and her child is a severe handicap for her in life.

For all these reasons a great many adolescent girls – in the New World as in the Old – when asked about their plans for the future, reply today as formerly: 'I want to get married'. But no young man considers marriage as his fundamental project. Economic success is what will bring him adult standing; such success may imply marriage – especially for the peasant – but it can also preclude it. The conditions of modern life – less stable, more uncertain than in the past – make the responsibilities of marriage especially heavy for the young man. Its benefits, on the other hand, have decreased, since it is easily possible for him to obtain board and room and since sexual satisfaction is generally available. No doubt marriage can afford certain material and sexual conveniences: it frees the individual from loneliness, it establishes him securely in space and time by giving him a home and children; it is a definitive fulfilment of his existence. But, for all that, the masculine demand is on the whole less than the feminine supply. A father can be said less to give his daughter than to get rid of her; the girl in search of a husband is not responding to a masculine demand, she is trying to create one.

The arranged marriage is not a thing of the past; there is a whole bourgeois class of solid substance which is keeping it alive. Around Napoleon's tomb, at the Opera, at a ball, on the beach, at a tea, the fair aspirant, with every hair in place and wearing a new gown timidly exhibits her physical graces and her modest conversation; her parents keep at her: 'You have already cost me enough in meeting different ones; make up your mind. The next time it will be your sister's turn.' The unhappy candidate knows that her chances become fewer and fewer as she approaches nearer and nearer to being an old maid; claimants to her hand are few: she has scarcely more freedom of choice than the Bedouin girl given in exchange for a flock of sheep [. . .]

Arranged marriages have always been more numerous in France than elsewhere, and clubs devoted to such matters still flourish. Matrimonial notices occupy much space in newspapers. In France, as in America, mothers, older friends, and women's magazines cynically teach young women the art of 'catching' husbands, as flypaper catches flies; it is a kind of 'fishing' or 'hunting' that requires great skill: 'Don't aim too high or too low; be realistic, not romantic; mix coquettishness with modesty; don't demand too much or too little.' Young men mistrust women who 'want to get married'. Mme Leplae reports a young Belgian's remark: 'Nothing is more disagreeable to a man than to feel himself pursued, to realize that a woman is trying to hook him.' And men endeavor to avoid such efforts to ensnare them. The girl's choice is usually quite limited; and it could not be really free unless she felt free also not to marry. Her decision is ordinarily marked by calculation, disgust, resignation, rather than by enthusiasm. If the man is reasonably eligible in such matters as health and position, she accepts him, love or no love.

While desiring marriage, however, the girl frequently fears it. It is of greater benefit to her than to the man, and hence she is more eager for it than he is; but it also means greater sacrifices for her, in particular because it implies a more drastic rupture with the past. We have seen that many adolescent girls feel anguish at the thought of leaving the paternal home; this anxiety increases as the event draws near. Here is the moment when many neuroses originate; the same thing may happen with young men who fear the new responsibilities they are about to assume; but it is much commoner with young girls for reasons already discussed, reasons that are most weighty at this critical time [. . .]

Marriages, then, are not generally founded upon love. As Freud put it: 'The husband is, so to speak, never more than a substitute for the beloved man, not that man himself.' And this dissociation is in no way accidental. It is implied in the very nature of the institution, the aim of which is to make the economic and sexual union of man and woman serve the interest of society, not assure their personal happiness. In patriarchal regimes – as today among certain Mohammedans – it may happen that engaged persons chosen by parental authority have not even seen each other's faces before the wedding day [. . .]

Because it is the man who 'takes' the woman, he has somewhat more possibility of choosing – especially when feminine offers are numerous. But since the sexual act is regarded as a *service* assigned to woman, on which are based the advantages conceded to her, it is logical to ignore her personal preferences. Marriage is intended to deny her a man's liberty; but as there is neither love nor individuality without liberty, she must renounce loving a specific individual in order to assure herself the lifelong protection of some male. I have heard a pious mother of a family inform her daughters that 'love is a coarse sentiment reserved for men and unknown to women of propriety.' In naïve form, this is the very doctrine enunciated by Hegel when he maintains that woman's relations as mother and wife are basically general and not individual. He maintains, therefore, that for her it is not a question of *this husband* but of *a husband* in general, of children in general.

From S. de Beauvoir (1993) (1949) *The Second Sex*, London: Everyman Library, pp. 446–57.

Questions

1. Bearing in mind that de Beauvoir's study was first published in 1949, which elements of her description of the married woman's position (a) still have relevance in today's society; and (b) do you feel no longer apply to contemporary marriage?
2. What do you think de Beauvoir means when she says that 'the aim (of marriage) is to make the economic and sexual union of man and woman serve the interest of society, not assure their personal happiness'?

Reading 22

The theory of sexual politics

KATE MILLETT

In her now classic feminist study, Sexual Politics, *Kate Millett emphasised the systematic oppression of women by men and the overarching patriarchal influences on all aspects of contemporary society. In this extract Millett points out that while traditional patriarchy may have involved the use of more open force and physical abuse, in the contemporary context patriarchy manifests itself in a perhaps less obvious but no less intrusive manner – 'so perfect is its (patriarchy's) system of socialization, so complete the general assent to its values . . . that it scarcely seems to require violent implementation'. Millett is aware, however, of the continued use of sexual violence, including rape, to support contemporary patriarchal relations. As an illustration of the extent to which modern society, as with all historical civilisations, is a patriarchy, the last section of this reading looks at the way in which the socialisation of both sexes – into, for example, domestic roles – supports basic patriarchal principles.*

As co-operation between the family and the larger society is essential, else both would fall apart, the fate of three patriarchal institutions, the family, society and the state are interrelated. In most forms of patriarchy this has lead to the granting of religious support in statements such as the Catholic precept that the father is the head of the family, or Judaism's delegation of quasi-priestly authority to the male parent. Secular governments also confirm this, as in the census practices of designating the male as head of household, taxation, passports etc. Female heads of household tend to be regarded as undesirable; the phenomenon is a trait of poverty or misfortune. The Confucian prescription that the relationship between ruler and subject is parallel to that of father and children points to the essentially feudal character of the patriarchal family (and conversely, the familial character of feudalism) even in modern democracies.

Traditionally, patriarchy granted the father nearly total ownership over wife or wives and children, including the powers of physical abuse and often even those of murder or sale. Classically, as head of the family the father is both begetter and owner in a system in which kinship is property . . . In contemporary patriarchies the male's *de jure* priority has recently been modified through the granting of divorce protection and citizenship, and property to women. Their chattel status continues in their loss of name, their obligation to adopt their husband's domicile, and the general legal assumption that marriage involves an exchange of the female's domestic service and (sexual) consortium in return for financial support [. . .]

We are not accustomed to associate patriarchy with force. So perfect is its system of socialization, so complete the general assent to its values, so long and so universally has it prevailed in human society, that it scarcely seems to require violent implementation. Customarily, we view its brutalities in the past as exotic or 'primitive' customs. Those of the present are regarded as the product of individual deviance, confined to the pathological or exceptional behavior, and without general import. And yet, just as under other total ideologies (racism and colonialism are somewhat analogous in this respect) control in patriarchal society would be imperfect, even inoperable, unless it had the rule of force to rely upon, both in emergencies and as an ever-present instrument of intimidation.

Historically, most patriarchies have institutionalized force through their legal systems. For example strict patriarchies such as that of Islam, have implemented the prohibition against illegitimacy or sexual autonomy with a death sentence. In Afghanistan and Saudi Arabia the adulteress is still stoned to death with a mullah presiding at the execution.

Patriarchal force also relies on a form of violence particularly sexual in character and realized most completely in the act of rape. The figures of rapes reported represent only a fraction of those which occur, as the 'shame' of the event is sufficient to deter women from the notion of civil prosecution under the public circumstances of trial. Traditionally rape has been viewed as an offense one male commits against another – a matter of abusing 'his woman'. Vendetta, such as occurs in the American south, is carried out for masculine satisfaction, the exhilarations of race hatred, and the interests of property and vanity (honor). In rape the emotions of aggression, hatred, contempt and the desire to break or violate personality, take a form consummately appropriate to sexual politics.

What goes largely unexamined, often even unacknowledged (yet is institutionalized nonetheless) in our social order, is the birthright priority whereby males rule females. Through this system a most ingenious form of 'interior colonization' has been achieved. It is one moreover to be sturdier than any form of segregation, and more rigorous than class stratification, more uniform, certainly more enduring. However muted its present appearance may be, sexual dominion obtains nevertheless as perhaps the most pervasive ideology of our culture and provides its most fundamental concept of power.

This is so because our society, like all other historical civilizations is a patriarchy. The fact is evident at once if one recalls that the military, industry, technology, universities, science, political office, and finance – in short every avenue of power within the society, including the coercive force of the police – is entirely in male hands. As the essence of the politics is power, such realization cannot fail to carry impact. What lingers of supernatural authority, the Deity, 'His' ministry, together with the ethics and values, the philosophy and art of our culture – its very civilization – as T.S. Eliot once observed, is of male manufacture [. . .]

Sexual politics obtains consent through the 'socialization' of both sexes to the basic patriarchal polities with regard to temperament, role and status. As to status, a pervasive assent to the prejudice of male superiority guarantees superior status in the male, inferior in the female. The first item, temperament, involves the formation of human personality along stereotyped lines of sex category ('masculine' and 'feminine'), based on the needs and values of the dominant group and dictated by what its members cherish in themselves and find convenient in subordinates: aggression, intelligence, force and efficacy in the male; passivity, ignorance, docility, 'virtue' and ineffectuality in the female. This is complemented by a second factor, sex role, which decrees a consonant and highly elaborate code of conduct and attitude for each sex. In terms of activity, sex role assigns domestic service and attendance upon infants to the female, the rest of human achievement, interest and ambition to the male. The limited role allotted the female tends to arrest her at the level of biological experience. Therefore, nearly all that can be described as distinctly human rather than animal activity (in their own way animals also give birth and care for young) is largely reserved for the male. Of course, status again follows from such assignment [. . .]

Patriarchy's chief institution is the family. It is both a mirror of and a connection with larger society; a patriarchal until in a patriarchal whole. Mediating between the individual and the social structure, the family effects control and conformity where political and other authorities are insufficient. As the fundamental instrument and foundation unit of patriarchal society the family and its roles are prototypical. Serving as an agent of the larger society, the family not only encourages its own members to adjust and conform, but acts as a unit in the government of the patriarchal state which rules its citizens through its family heads. Even in the patriarchal societies where they are granted legal citizenship, women tend to be ruled through the family alone and have little or no formal relation to the state.

From K. Millett (1977) (1971) *Sexual Politics*, London: Virago, pp. 25–44.

Questions

1. How does Millett suggest that gender socialisation and the ideology of sex differences are used to justify women's subordination?
2. What role does violence in the family play in reinforcing oppressive gender relations?
3. To what degree do you think that Millett's arguments still apply to contemporary British family life?

Reading 23

Black women and feminist theory

bell hooks

Feminism is not a unified body of thought but contains a number of different strands. Black feminism, in particular, has criticised much of feminist theory for its White, middle-class bias. bell hooks' (hooks herself routinely uses the lower case letters for her name) work has developed this criticism of feminist theory and in this reading she highlights the interrelationship of different forms of inequality and how these particularly disadvantage Black women. In contrast to Black women, 'White women and black men have it both ways. They can act as oppressor or oppressed.' hooks argues that middle-class, White feminism has tended to take a somewhat patronising approach to the contribution of Black women to the development of feminist theory.

Privileged feminists have largely been unable to speak to, with, and for diverse groups of women because they either do not understand fully the inter-relatedness of sex, race, and class oppression or refuse to take this inter-relatedness seriously. Feminist analyses of woman's lot tend to focus exclusively on gender and do not provide a solid foundation on which to construct feminist theory. They reflect the dominant tendency in Western patriarchal minds to mystify woman's reality by insisting that gender is the sole determinant of woman's fate. Certainly it has been easier for women who do not experience race or class oppression to focus exclusively on gender. Although socialist feminists focus on class and gender, they tend to dismiss race or they make a point of acknowledging that race is important and then proceed to offer an analysis in which race is not considered.

As a group, black women are in an unusual position in this society, for not only are we collectively at the bottom of the occupational ladder, but our overall social status is lower than that of any other group. Occupying such a position, we bear the brunt of sexist, racist, and classist oppression. At the same time, we are the group that has not been socialized to assume the role of exploiter/oppressor in that we are allowed no institutionalized 'other' that we can exploit or oppress. (Children do not represent an institutionalized other even though they may be oppressed by parents.) White women and black men have it both ways. They can act as oppressor or be oppressed. Black men may be victimized by racism, but sexism allows them to act as exploiters and oppressors of women. White women may be victimized by sexism, but racism enables them to act as exploiters and oppressors of black people. Both groups have led liberation movements that favor their interests and support the continued oppression of other groups. Black male sexism has undermined struggles to eradicate racism just as white female racism undermines feminist struggle. As long as these two groups or any group defines liberation as gaining social equality with ruling class white men, they have a vested interest in the continued exploitation and oppression of others.

Black women with no other institutionalized 'other' that we may discriminate against, exploit, or oppress often have a lived experience that directly challenges the prevailing classist, sexist, racist social structure and its concomitant ideology. This lived experience may shape our consciousness in such a way that our world view differs from those who have a degree of privilege (however relative within the existing system). It is essential for continued feminist struggle that black women recognize the special vantage point our marginality gives us and make use of this perspective to criticize the dominant racist, classist, sexist hegemony as well as to envision and create a counter-hegemony. I am suggesting that we have a central role to play in the making of feminist theory and a contribution to offer that is unique and valuable. The formation of a liberatory feminist theory and praxis is a collective responsibility, one that must be shared. Though I criticize aspects of feminist movement as we have known it so far, a critique which is sometimes harsh and unrelenting, I do so not in an attempt to diminish feminist struggle but to enrich, to share in the work of making a liberatory ideology and a liberatory movement.

As a black woman interested in feminist movement, I am often asked whether being black is more important than being a woman; whether feminist struggle to end sexist oppression is more important than the struggle to end racism and vice-versa. All such questions are rooted in competitive either/or thinking, the belief that the self is formed in opposition to an other. Therefore one is a feminist because you are not something else. Most people are socialized to think in terms of opposition rather than compatibility. Rather than see anti-racist work as totally compatible with working to end sexist oppression, they are often seen as two movements competing for first place. When asked 'Are you a feminist?' it appears that an affirmative answer is translated to mean that one is concerned with no political issues other than feminism. When one is black, an affirmative response is likely to be heard as a devaluation of struggle to end racism. Given the fear of being misunderstood, it has been difficult for black women and women in exploited and oppressed ethnic groups to give expression to their interest in feminist concerns. They have been wary of saying 'I am a feminist.' The shift in expression from 'I am a feminist' to 'I advocate feminism' could serve as a useful strategy for eliminating the focus on identity and lifestyle. It could serve as a way women who are concerned about feminism as well as other political movements could express their support while avoiding linguistic structures that give primacy to one particular group. It would also encourage greater exploration in feminist theory.

The shift in definition away from notions of social equality towards an emphasis on ending sexist oppression leads to a shift in attitudes in regard to the development of theory. Given the class nature of feminist movement so far, as well as racial hierarchies, developing theory (the guiding set of beliefs and principles that become the basis for action) has been a task particularly subject to the hegemonic dominance of white academic women. This has led many women outside the privileged race/class group to see the focus on developing theory, even the very use of the term, as a concern that functions only to reinforce the power of the élite group. Such reactions reinforce the sexist/racist/classist notion that developing theory is the domain of the white intellectual. Privileged white women active in feminist movement, whether liberal or radical in perspective, encourage black women to contribute 'experiential' work, personal life stories. Personal experiences are important to feminist movement but they cannot take the place of theory [. . .]

Since bourgeois white women had defined feminism in such a way as to make it appear that it had no real significance for black women, they could then conclude that black women need not contribute to developing theory. We were to provide the colorful life stories to document and validate the prevailing set of theoretical assumptions. Focus on social equality with men as a definition of feminism led to an emphasis on discrimination, male attitudes, and legalistic reforms. Feminism as a movement to end sexist oppression directs our attention to systems of domination and the interrelatedness of sex, race, and class oppression. Therefore, it compels us to centralize the experiences and the social predicaments of women who bear the brunt of sexist oppression as a way to understand the collective social status of women in the United States. Defining feminism as a movement to end sexist oppression is crucial for the development of theory because it is a starting point indicating the direction of exploration and analysis.

The foundation of future feminist struggle must be solidly based on a recognition of the need to eradicate the underlying cultural basis and causes of sexism and other forms of group oppression. Without challenging and changing these philosophical structures, no feminist reforms will have a long-range impact. Consequently, it is now necessary for advocates of feminism to collectively acknowledge that our struggle cannot be defined as a movement to gain social equality with men; that terms like 'liberal feminist' and 'bourgeois feminist' represent contradictions that must be resolved so that feminism will not be continually co-opted to serve the opportunistic ends of special interest groups.

From bell hooks (1984) *Feminist Theory: from Margin to Center*, Boston: South End Press, pp. 14–15, 29–31.

Questions

1. What sort of people do you think hooks is talking about when she uses the term 'privileged feminist'? Why do you think that feminist theory has tended to be associated with privileged women?
2. As well as gender inequality, what other forms of inequality and oppression does hooks suggest that feminists should recognise?
3. What evidence is there to (a) confirm and (b) question hooks' contention that the status of black women is 'lower than that of any other group'?

Reading 24

City cultures and postmodern lifestyles

MIKE FEATHERSTONE

In this reading Mike Featherstone considers the extent to which changes in lifestyles and city cultures amount to what could be termed a postmodern shift. The postmodern city is seen as both a centre of cultural consumption and an arena of play and entertainment. In such a context, it is possible to find common features in a wide range of areas and activities. As Featherstone puts it, 'There are therefore common features emerging between shopping centres, malls, museums, theme parks and tourist experiences in the contemporary city.' As examples of the 'convergence of cultures' and of the blurring of the distinction between high and low culture and between commerce and culture he refers to Japanese department stores that regularly display art treasures and hold art exhibitions and to the Metrocentre in Gateshead in north-east England promoting itself as a tourist attraction with its 'Antiques Village and Ancient Roman Forum gallery'. In this extract, Featherstone points out how, in spite of these cultural changes and the move away from strong neighbourhood identifications, there remains a persistence of hierarchy and segregation in the city – evidenced by the 'gentrification' of and investment in certain areas which become highly exclusive.

The proponents of postmodernism detect a major shift in culture taking place in which existing symbolic hierarchies are deconstructed and a more playful, popular democratic impulse becomes manifest. Here we have spatialization out of the previous more firmly structured symbolic hierarchies which became dominant motifs within Western modernity and established particular notions of universal history, progress, the cultivated person, state political structures and aesthetic ideals. With respect to the contemporary Western city it has been argued that postmodern and postmodernizing tendencies can be observed in the new urban spaces which point to a greater aestheticization of the urban fabric and the daily lives of people, the development of new consumption and leisure enclaves (such as shopping centres, theme parks, museums) and the drawing back of new middle-class gentrifying populations into the inner city. These postmodern impulses suggest less strong neighbourhood identifications and a less fixed habitus or rigid set of dispositions and classifications into which encounters are framed. Some of the new urban lifestyles point to a decentring of identity and a greater capacity to engage in a decontrol of the emotions and aestheticized play. It can also be argued that on the global level we are witnessing the end of the dominance of a few metropolitan centres over artistic and intellectual life (Williams 1983). Paris and New York as centres of culture, the arts, fashion, culture and entertainment industries, television, publishing and music, now face greater competition from a variety of directions. New forms of cultural capital and a wider range of symbolic experiences are on offer within an increasingly globalized – that is, more easily accessible via financial (money) communications (travel), and information (broadcasting, publishing, media) – field of world cities.

Hence it could be argued by those who emphasize the novelty and historical events which postmodernism is purported to bring, that we are entering a phase in which the old cultural hierarchies are becoming obsolete. The dehierarchizing impulse suggests that high/low, élite/popular, minority/mass, taste/tasteless, art/life, vertical classificational hierarchies (Schwartz 1983; Goudsblom 1987) which are held to be endemic features of social life, no longer apply.

Against this seductively oversimplified postmodern story of the end of history we have to point to the persistence of classification, hierarchy and segregation within the city. As we mentioned, the new middle class and new rich live in enclaved areas of gentrification and redevelopment which are designed to exclude outsiders. These enclaves are areas of high investment in designed environments, stylized form and the aestheticization of everyday life. Such groups expect to be entertained while they shop and shop at places of entertainment. They seek to cultivate a style of life and have an interest in the arts and a pleasurable aestheticized living environment (Boyer 1988). For certain fractions of the new middle class this style of life certainly has affinities with the range of characteristics and experience designated postmodern. There are tendencies which point to an overload of information and signs, which make the ordered reading of bodily presentation, fashion, lifestyle and leisure pursuits much more difficult. People are able to draw from a much wider repertoire of instantly accessible symbolic goods and styles from the 'global showcase' and it is more difficult to make a judgement of class from taste and lifestyle. Since the 1960s there has been a more general informalization and elaboration of previously restricted codes of behaviour. Notions of beauty prominent in consumer culture, for example, widened beyond the classic Western one in the 1960s to take into account standards of other cultures (Marwick 1988). Yet for all the democratizing tendencies there are status differences. As Douglas and Isherwood (1980) point out, the informational component of consumer goods rises as one moves up the class scale. Those in the middle and upper reaches continue to use information about consumption goods to build bridges with like-minded people and close doors to exclude outsiders. This is very much the case with knowledge of the arts.

If, then, we are arguing that it is still possible to read bodily presentation and lifestyles as indicators of social status it is clear that the game is much more complex now. If postmodern points to something it is the eclipse of a particular coherent sense of culture and associated way of life which was dominant in the Western upper and middle classes which set the tone for the culture as a whole. This happens as the historical generations which carried them slowly recede in numbers and influence. Here one thinks of the notion of a common culture as a goal; as based on an educational formative project, as something unified, a totality of knowledge (the classics in literature, music and the arts), which had to be struggled through to improve the person. Along with it went the notion of a cultured or cultivated person, the ideal of a gentleman, the product of a civilizing process (Elias, 1978, 1982). The middle and upper classes in the second half of the nineteenth century were prime carriers of this cultural ideal and sought to extend it through museums and educational institutions.

Since the 1960s the process of cultural declassification has seen the decline and relativization of this ideal. The question is whether these tendencies, which have been labelled postmodern, merely point to a collapse of an established hierarchy, a temporary phase, a cultural intermezzo of intensified competition, varied standards and value complexes, before a remonopolization by a new establishment. Or should we see the extension of the current tendencies *ad infinitum* – the end of history? In this context it is salutary to refer to similar historical ages of cultural turmoil and incoherence. If it is proclaimed today that there is no fashion, only fashions, then we should bear in mind that Simmel discovered similar tendencies in Florence around 1390 when the styles of the social élite were not met with imitation and each individual sought to create his own style. Fashion and other lifestyle pursuits, to use Simmel's metaphor, are used as 'bridges and doors' to unite and exclude. If these functions appear to decline does it mean that we are merely in a temporary intermezzo? Or does the extension of the game to draw more groups, cultures and nations into a widened global system mean that the conditions for particular dominant élites to exercise global hegemony over taste and culture are destroyed with the unlikelihood of foreseeable remonopolization, thus pointing us towards a historical development in which some of the impulses detected and labelled postmodern may become more widespread?

From M. Featherstone (1991) *Consumer Culture and Postmodernism*, London: Sage, pp. 109–11.

Questions

1. To what extent do you think that 'old cultural hierarchies' are becoming obsolete? You might consider whether current examples of the following cultural hierarchies still exist: high/low culture; élite/popular culture; minority/mass culture.
2. Can you think of areas in cities with which you are familiar that might fit Featherstone's description of 'enclaved areas of gentrification and redevelopment which are designed to exclude outsiders'?

Reading 25

Disciplinary control

MICHEL FOUCAULT

In this extract, Foucault analyses how 'disciplinary power' works. It starts with a discussion of how disciplinary power can 'train' a multitude of individuals to accept the rule of sovereignty and the state. Disciplinary power 'succeeds' by using a series of simple instruments, including hierarchical observation, Foucault's discussion of which is the focus of this reading. Coercion, Foucault argues, can be exercised through the detailed and exact observation of the 'human multiplicity'. He describes how architectural planning can be used to ease the surveillance of individuals in a range of social institutions, including hospitals, schools and working-class housing estates as well as the more obvious examples such as prisons. The school building provides an example of how architectural planning can permit detailed control: rooms are 'distributed along a corridor like a series of small cells'; and toilets have 'half doors, so that the supervisor on duty could see the head and legs of the pupils'. This power of observation works in a more insidious and subtle manner than conventional means of exercising power, such as the use of force or violence. It is more effective because of this discretion, because, as Foucault puts it, it 'functions permanently and largely in silence'.

At the beginning of the seventeenth century, Walhausen spoke of 'strict discipline' as an art of correct training. The chief function of the disciplinary power is to 'train', rather than to select and to levy; or, no doubt, to train in order to levy and select all the more. It does not link forces together in order to reduce them; it seeks to bind them together in such a way as to multiply and use them. Instead of bending all its subjects into a single, uniform mass, it separates, analyzes, differentiates, carries its procedures of decomposition to the point of necessary and sufficient single units. It 'trains' the moving, confused, useless multitudes of bodies and forces them into a multiplicity of individual elements – small, separate cells; organic autonomies; genetic identities and continuities; combinatory segments.

Discipline 'makes' individuals; it is the specific technique of a power that regards individuals both as objects and as instruments of its exercise. It is not a triumphant power, which because of its own excess can pride itself on its omnipotence; it is a modest, suspicious power, which functions as a calculated but permanent economy. These are humble modalities, minor procedures, compared with the majestic rituals of sovereignty or the great apparatuses of the state. And it is precisely they that were gradually to invade the major forms, altering their mechanisms and imposing their procedures. The legal apparatus was not to escape this scarcely secret invasion. The success of disciplinary power derives no doubt from the use of simple instruments: hierarchical observation, normalizing judgement, and their combination in a procedure that is specific to it – the examination.

Hierarchical Observation

The exercise of discipline presupposes a mechanism that coerces by means of observation; an apparatus in which the techniques that make it possible to see induce effects of power and in which, conversely, the means of coercion make those on whom they are applied clearly visible. Slowly, in the course of the classical age, we see the construction of those 'observatories' of human multiplicity for which the history of the sciences has so little good to say. Side by side with the major technology of the telescope, the lens, and the light beam, which were an integral part of the new physics and cosmology, there were the minor techniques of multiple and intersecting observations, of eyes that must see without being seen; using techniques of subjection and methods of exploitation, an obscure art of light and the visible was secretly preparing a new knowledge of man.

These 'observatories' had an almost ideal model: the military camp – the short-lived, artificial city, built and reshaped almost at will; the seat of a power that must be all the stronger, but also all the more discreet, all the more effective and on the alert in that it is exercised over armed men. In the perfect camp, all power would be exercised solely through exact observation; each gaze would form a part of the overall functioning of power. The old, traditional square plan was considerably refined in innumerable new projects. The geometry of the paths, the number and distribution of the tents, the orientation of their entrances, the disposition of files and ranks were exactly defined; the network of gazes that supervised one another was laid down: 'In the parade ground, five lines are drawn up; the first is sixteen feet from the second; the others are eight feet from one another; and the last is eight feet from the arms depots. The arms depots are ten feet from the tents of the junior officers, immediately opposite the first tentpole. A company street is fifty-one feet wide . . . All tents are two feet from one another. The tents of the subalterns are opposite the alleys of their companies. The rear tentpole is eight feet from the last soldiers' tent and the gate is opposite the captains' tent . . . The captains' tents are erected opposite the streets of their companies. The entrance is opposite the companies themselves.' The camp is the diagram of a power that acts by means of general visibility. For a long time this model of the camp, or at least its underlying principle, was found in urban development, in the construction of working-class housing estates, hospitals, asylums, prisons, schools: the spatial 'nesting' of hierarchized surveillance. The principle was one of 'embedding' (*encastrement*). The camp was to the rather shameful art of surveillance what the dark room was to the great science of optics.

A whole problematic then develops: that of an architecture that is no longer built simply to be seen (as with the ostentation of palaces), or to observe the external space (cf. the geometry of fortresses), but to permit an internal, articulated and detailed control – to render visible those who are inside it; in more general terms, an architecture that would operate to transform individuals: to act on those it shelters, to provide a hold on their conduct, to carry the effects of power right to them, to make it possible to know them, to alter them. Stones can make people docile and knowable. The old simple schema of confinement and enclosure – thick walls, a heavy gate that prevents entering or leaving – began to be replaced by calculations of openings, of filled and empty spaces, passages and transparencies. In this way the hospital building was gradually organized as an instrument of medical action: it was to allow a better observation of patients, and therefore a better calibration of their treatment; the form of the buildings, by the careful separation of the patients, was to prevent contagions; lastly, the ventilation and the air that circulated around each bed were to prevent the deleterious vapors from stagnating around the patient, breaking down his humors and spreading the disease by their immediate effects. The hospital – which was to be built in the second half of the century and for which so many plans were drawn up after the Hotel-Dieu burnt down for the second time – was no longer simply the roof under which penury and imminent death took shelter; it was, in its very materiality, a therapeutic operator.

Similarly, the school building was to be a mechanism for training. It was as a pedagogical machine that Paris-Duverney conceived the Ecole Militaire, right down to the minute details that he had imposed on the architect, Gabriel. Train vigorous bodies, the imperative of health; obtain competent officers, the imperative of qualification; create obedient soldiers, the imperative of politics; prevent debauchery and homosexuality, the imperative of morality. A fourfold reason for establishing sealed compartments between individuals, but also apertures for continuous surveillance. The very building of the Ecole was to be an apparatus for observation; the rooms were distributed along a corridor like a series of small cells; at regular intervals, an officer's quarters was situated, so that 'every ten pupils had an officer on each side'; the pupils were confined to their cells throughout the night; and Paris had insisted that 'a window be placed on the corridor wall of each room from chest level to within one or two feet of the ceiling. Not only is it pleasant to have such windows, but one would venture to say that it is useful, in several respects, not to mention the disciplinary reasons that may determine this arrangement.' In the dining rooms was 'a slightly raised platform for the tables of the inspectors of studies, so that they may see all the tables of the pupils of their divisions during meals'; latrines had been installed with half-doors, so that the supervisor on duty could see the head and legs of the pupils, and also with side walls sufficiently high 'that those inside cannot see one another'. This infinitely scrupulous concern with surveillance is expressed in the architecture by innumerable petty mechanisms. These mechanisms can only be seen as unimportant if one forgets the role of this instrumentation, minor but flawless, in the progressive objectification and the ever more subtle partitioning of individual behaviour. The disciplinary institutions secreted a machinery of control that functioned like a microscope of conduct; the fine, analytical divisions that they created formed around men an apparatus of observation, recording, and training. How was one to subdivide the gaze in these observation machines? How was one to establish a network of communications between them? How was one so to arrange things that a homogeneous, continuous power would result from their calculated multiplicity?

The perfect disciplinary apparatus would make it possible for a single gaze to see everything constantly. A central point would be both the source of light illuminating everything and a locus of convergence for everything that must be known: a perfect eye that nothing would escape and a center toward which all gazes would be turned [. . .]

Hierarchized, continuous, and functional surveillance may not be one of the great technical 'inventions' of the eighteenth century, but its insidious extension owed its importance to the mechanisms of power that it brought with it. By means of such surveillance, disciplinary power became an 'integrated' system, linked from the inside to the economy and to the aims of the mechanism in which it was practiced. It was also organized as a multiple, automatic, and anonymous power; for although surveillance rests on individuals, its functioning is that of a network of relations from top to bottom, but also to a certain extent from bottom to top and laterally; this network 'holds' the whole together and traverses it in its entirety with effects of power that derive from one another: supervisors, perpetually supervised. The power in the hierarchized surveillance of the disciplines is not possessed as a thing, or transferred as a property; it functions like a piece of machinery. And, although it is true that its pyramidal organization gives it a 'head', it is the apparatus as a whole that produces 'power' and distributes individuals in this permanent and continuous field. This enables the disciplinary power to be both absolutely indiscreet, since it is everywhere and always alert, since by its very principle it leaves no zone of shade and constantly supervises the very individuals who are entrusted with the task of supervising; and absolutely 'discreet', for it functions permanently and largely in silence.

Discipline makes possible the operation of a relational power that sustains itself by its own mechanism and which, for the spectacle of public events, substitutes the uninterrupted play of calculated gazes. Thanks to the techniques of surveillance, the 'physics' of power, the hold over the body, operates according to the laws of optics and mechanics, according to a whole play of spaces, lines, screens, beams, degrees, and without recourse, in principle at least, to excess, force, or violence. It is a power that seems all the less 'corporal' in that it is more subtly 'physical'.

From M. Foucault (1977) *Discipline and Punish: The Birth of the Prison*, London: Allen Lane, pp. 170–7.

Questions

1. Consider a range of institutions which you have attended – such as schools/colleges, places of work, leisure centres, hospitals, etc. To what extent does their design and architecture help to impose discipline and control?
2. What do you think are the main strengths and weaknesses of Foucault's argument that observation can be used as a means of regulation and control?

Part II Sociological Theories

Further Reading

The readings in this section have been selected to illustrate the history, range and style of sociological theorising. Any selection, though, can only present a very partial picture. There are many famous social theorists whose work is not introduced here and there are numerous different extracts that we could have chosen from the writers we have included. Here we will highlight some of the general introductions to sociological theorising that would complement these readings.

There are many selections and summaries of the writings of the major founding writers in sociology, including:

Giddens, A. (1971) *Capitalism and Modern Social Theory: An Analysis of the Writings of Marx, Durkheim and Max Weber*, Cambridge: Cambridge University Press.

Hughes, J.A., Martin, P.J. and Sharrock, W.W. (1995) *Understanding Classical Sociology: Marx, Weber, Durkheim*, London: Sage.

McIntosh, I. (1997) *Classical Sociological Theory: A Reader*, Edinburgh: Edinburgh University Press.

These three titles focus on the 'holy trinity' of Durkheim, Marx and Weber. The first two provide detailed accounts of the main ideas of each writer and discuss how they connect with more recent sociological theories. The third is a reader that brings together a selection of readings from the original texts of each writer.

Of the many theoretical studies which examine both classic and more contemporary theories, the following are particularly recommended:

Craib, I. (1992) *Modern Social Theory*, London: Harvester Wheatsheaf.

Layder, D. (1994) *Understanding Social Theory*, London: Sage.

Ritzer, G. (1992) *Sociological Theory*, 3rd edn, New York: McGraw-Hill.

Scott, J. (1995) *Sociological Theory: Contemporary Debates*, Aldershot: Edward Elgar.

Each of these studies provide detailed yet accessible discussions of contemporary theories, including postmodernism, and their relationship to classic theorising.

Two edited collections that include readings from both classic and contemporary sociological theorists are:

Lemert, C. (ed.) (1993) *Social Theory: The Multicultural and Classic Readings*, Oxford: Westview.

The Polity Reader in Social Theory (1994), Cambridge: Polity Press.

Lemert's reader adopts a chronological approach starting from the mid-nineteenth century and Marx and ending with a wide selection of writing since 1979, both postmodernist and 'post' postmodern. The emphasis of the Polity text is on current social theory and some of the dominant areas of controversy and advance; the majority of contributions are concerned with the theoretical interpretation of modern social institutions.

On feminist theory, the following readers are excellent starting points and include examples of the various theoretical strands of feminism:

Humm, M. (ed.) (1992) *Feminisms: A Reader*, London: Harvester Wheatsheaf.

Whelehan, I. (ed.) (1995) *Modern Feminist Thought: From Second Wave to 'Post Feminism'*, Edinburgh: Edinburgh University Press.

Two clear and short critical introductions to postmodernism are provided by Smart's introduction to the debate about modernity and postmodernity and Gellner's discussion of what he terms the postmodernist indulgence in relativism and subjectivism:

Gellner, E. (1992) *Postmodernism, Reason and Religion*, London: Routledge.

Smart, B. (1993) *Postmodernity*, London: Routledge.

Activity

This activity requires you to adopt C. Wright Mills' strategy of translating an example of a social theorist's work into 'straightforward English'.

Choose (up to) three of the readings from this section – including at least one from Durkheim, Marx or Weber and one from the feminist writers – de Beauvoir, Millett or bell hooks.

Read it carefully and summarise in not more than 400 words.

After you have done this try to make a numerical list of the key points being made by the writer.

- What difficulties did you find in 'translating' each of the pieces?
- Which of the readings did you find easiest to summarise?
- Why do you think you found this easiest: was it because of the language or style of writing or because the ideas being expressed were simpler?
- How much 'meaning' has been lost by your summary translation?

After doing this find two other examples of theoretical writing from writers not included in this book and do the same exercise. See Further Reading suggestions for possible sources.

This activity could be done individually or as a group activity, with students being given particular readings to summarise and the tutor ensuring that all the readings in this section of the book are covered.

Part III

Differences and Inequalities

26

Introduction

Examination of inequalities and differences has been arguably the major area of sociological inquiry: issues of inequality have been central to both classic and contemporary sociological theorising and research. Sociological work has shown that the social opportunities available to and the achievement of different individuals and social groups are clearly related to inequalities in various areas of social life, including housing, family background and educational provision.

Although there is no disputing the obvious differences that exist between people – some are born with physical or mental impairment, for instance – nor that these differences are likely to affect an individual's life chances, the sociological study of inequality has focused on how social structure and culture create and maintain individual and group inequalities.

One of the difficulties faced by the sociological study of inequality (and by the attempt to look at differences and inequalities in one section of a book of readings such as this) is the overlap between different forms of inequality: ethnic background can influence educational attainment which is liable to affect occupational opportunities and so on. However, until the last thirty or so years, much of the work on inequality in sociology was based around social class. The first readings in this section illustrate the debate in postwar and contemporary sociology over the extent to which social class should be a central concept in sociological analysis. In spite of Marx's prediction of a proletarian revolution, the failure of the working class in Western industrial societies to develop a class consciousness led many sociologists to examine working-class attitudes and to question the importance of social class. The readings from Ralph Dahrendorf and Tom Bottomore illustrate this concern. Dahrendorf and Bottomore were two of the most influential theorists who analysed the role of social class in the supposedly affluent, 'never had it so good' period of the late 1950s and 1960s. Dahrendorf (Reading 27) argues that modern industrial societies are highly differentiated by grades of status rather than class differences so that the class conflict of the nineteenth century has evaporated to be replaced by conflicts between various competing interest groups over the exercise of authority. While accepting that many of the social changes referred to by Dahrendorf and other critics of Marx have taken place, Bottomore (Reading 28) disputes the implication that these changes have reduced the importance of class and class conflict in industrial societies. Instead he argues that changes in the distribution of reward, social welfare, social mobility and education have simply blurred class boundaries and created an illusion of equality. Despite the apparent changes in lifestyle and opportunity he argues that Dahrendorf's conclusions simply reinforce the ideological myth of 'classlessness'. As he puts it, 'In so far as social mobility has increased, and the middle class has grown in numbers, the image of society as divided between two great contending classes has become blurred by the superimposition of another image, in which society appears as an indefinite and changing hierarchy of status positions, which merge into each other, and between which individuals and families are able to move with much greater facility than in the past.'

The studies from which these two readings are taken were seen as seminal texts at the time and they still have great resonance for current social analysis. The debate Dahrendorf, Bottomore and others, including Goldthorpe and Lockwood and their famous critique of the embourgeoisiement thesis, engaged in did not end in the 1960s and the next two readings reflect the contemporary debate in sociology. Clark and Lipset (Reading 29) suggest that there has been a decline in the importance of social class as a determinant of lifestyle and life chances. Hout and colleagues (Reading 30) attack this argument and the conclusion that social class has become an almost redundant concept in advanced industrial societies and highlight the persistence of social class-based inequalities. Peter Saunders has long held a reputation for challenging sociological orthodoxy on social class and inequality. In his recent study for the Institute of Economic Affairs, *Unequal but Fair?* (1996) he argues that although Britain is unequal it is also a meritocracy in which the link between social disadvantage and social class is a thing of the past. According to this view, personal achievement is open to people from the poorest backgrounds so long as they possess 'the ability and the will to start climbing'. The myth that social class still creates barriers to achievement is, according to Saunders, part of the 'British obsession' with social class and is largely perpetuated by the British intelligentsia, particularly those playwrights and television producers who have 'made it' from working-class backgrounds but persist in developing a 'bitter critique' of what they see as a self-perpetuating establishment. Within this group, the 'great and good of British Sociology' are singled out for particular ridicule as the source of the widespread belief that 'British society remains relatively closed and that the system is unjust' (p. 5). In particular, Saunders develops and sustains his argument by critically examining the work of fellow sociologists such as Glass (1954), Heath (1981), Goldthorpe (1987) and Marshall *et al.* (1988).

His review leads him to the conclusion that 'ability correlates more strongly with class of destination than with class of origin . . . that ability and motivation are the key predictions of, lower working-class success and of middle-class failure . . . [and] that class destinations reflect individual merit (ability and motivation) much more than class background' (p. 57). Reading 31 is taken from Saunders' examination of the principles of meritocracy and the difficulties with and alternatives to a meritocratic system.

Social inequality and social class differences are not, of course, unique to Britain. In Reading 32, Howard Davis examines social stratification in Europe. He considers whether some European countries are more equal than others and explores what characteristics they share and what differences arise when they follow alternative social processes. As Bailey (1998) points out, 'making sense of the differences between countries and what they simultaneously share as advanced industrial societies is the most difficult and most important task of any social science with Europe as its focus'. As well as explaining the differences and inequalities between people and social groups, Davis suggests that structural social inequality provides the key to discovering why particular societies take the form they do and how they can change.

With the supposed affluence of postwar Western society it is sometimes assumed that poverty, squalor and associated epidemic illnesses have become things of the past. However, while working-class people do, on the whole, live in better conditions than the back-to-back housing of the Victorian industrial cities, there are still massive inequalities in health across different social groupings. Reading 33 is taken from *The Black Report*, which found and catalogued a mass of evidence on the persistence of inequalities of health. The Report's findings, published in 1980, demonstrated that in spite of the introduction of the NHS after the Second World War, clear inequalities in health remained. *The Black Report* had a considerable influence on research in the area of health, and in particular the health and well-being of socially marginalised groups and their experiences of health-care provision. The relationship between socioeconomic inequality and health has become a central area of interest within Health Studies and the Sociology of Health and research evidence has shown that inequalities in health have continued into the 1980s and 1990s. In 1986 Margaret Whitehead was commissioned by the Health Education Council to undertake research to update the evidence on inequalities in health and to assess the progress made since *The Black Report*. Her findings, published in 1987 in *The Health Divide*, again highlighted the persistence of health inequalities throughout Britain.

The first six readings in this section demonstrate the continuing relevance of class analysis for contemporary sociology. However, social class is not the only means by which social inequalities and differences are transmitted. Since the early 1970s sociologists have become more aware of the relative importance of gender and race as the bases of inequality. The readings we have selected aim to demonstrate the significance of gender and race in a number of areas of social life (including the family, education, the criminal justice system and health) and also to show the ways in which gender, race and class overlap with each other and with other social characteristics, such as age.

Feminist theorists and researchers have examined women's historical and contemporary experiences and tried to make sense of these in the context of a society which they argued is male dominated. A wide range of mechanisms which controlled women and perpetuated their social and economic subordination to men have been identified; one of the most dramatic of these is the use of violence against women. It has been argued that violence against women could only be understood in the context of unequal power relations between men and women. Indeed, violence against women has been identified by some feminists as one of the major reasons for women's continued oppression, both a product of and means for ensuring the replication of patriarchy and male power. A key text making this case was *Violence Against Wives* by Dobash and Dobash (1979), which provided a comprehensive and rigorous feminist analysis of the phenomenon commonly referred to as domestic violence. This study was not purely a theoretical work, but was based on interviews which the Dobashes carried out in Scotland with women who had lived through violence in marriage. The Dobashes argued that patriarchal culture and institutions legitimate violence against women generally and wives specifically. Reading 34 is taken from their historical overview of evidence which shows that violence against wives has often been culturally condoned and that the right to exert physical force over them has often been enshrined within law. In their book, the Dobashes document how violence against wives is widespread and often involves serious physical assaults. They also stressed that the socioeconomic subordination of women presented barriers to their leaving violent relationships. In their more recent text, *Women, Violence and Social Change* (1992), the Dobashes argue that although attitudes towards gender relations and violence against wives are changing, such violence is far from a thing of the past.

Research in the Sociology of Education has examined the influence of social class, gender and race on educational outcomes and has demonstrated that individual 'failures' and 'successes' are socially as well as personally constructed. Before the Second World War the sort of educational provision that individuals received was heavily dependent on their social class background. Concern over the strong, and often negative, effect of social background encouraged an emphasis on equal opportunities in the postwar years. This was reflected in the changes in secondary education – initially the tripartite system based on the assessment of children's intelligence at the age of eleven and then, in response to criticisms of this selective system, the development of comprehensive secondary schools. In spite of these concerns and developments there is little evidence of a weakening of the relationship between social background and education; social class, gender and racial identity continue to influence educational achievement. It has been commonplace for explanations of this relationship to focus on one major social characteristic – such as class, gender or race – and, despite the obvious overlaps between them, for discussions of educational opportunity and achievement to be grouped under those three headings. In her study *Young, Female and Black,* Heidi Mirza has tried to avoid this difficulty by looking at the interaction between gender, ethnicity and other social characteristic. Reading 35 is taken from this study and considers how the education system, and classroom relationships in particular, can effect the lives of young Black women.

As well as inequalities in key areas of socialisation such as the family and education, women can also face disadvantage and discrimination in the more formal agencies of society. In spite of the belief that the British legal system is based on the principle of everyone being equal before the law, there is plenty of evidence to demonstrate that males and females are treated differently by different elements of the criminal justice system, including the police, the courts and institutions of punishment such as prisons. Perhaps the most obvious gender disparities within the criminal justice system are numerical: there are far fewer women police officers than men (and particularly higher ranking police officers); women make up just over 10 per cent of those who are convicted for more serious, indictable crimes and only 3 to 4 per cent of the prison population of this country. Reading 36 from Ann Lloyd's book *Doubly Deviant, Doubly Damned* looks at the way in which the criminal justice system treats those women with whom it has to deal and considers, in particular, two basic and apparently contradictory theoretical models: the 'chivalry' notion that women are treated more favourably as the 'weaker sex' and the 'evil woman' theory that women receive more severe and intrusive treatment.

The proliferation of the area of Women's Studies within and outside Sociology has meant the growth of studies of women's experiences in many areas of society. This body of predominantly feminist research has aimed to make women's experiences visible after their protracted marginalisation as subjects in social research, and to consider how men's and women's experiences differ and how they are in turn linked to gender inequality and women's subordination. In her book *What Makes Women Sick* Lesley Doyal focuses on women's experiences of health. Her underlying thesis is that in the 1990s structured and institutionalised gender inequality has serious implications for women's health and the health care they receive. Doyal approaches health and well-being holistically, as something that is not only shaped by biological factors but also by social, economic and cultural forces. Indeed, she argues that the socioeconomic system that frames women's lives can make women sick: the social, economic and cultural conditions of women's subordination creates barriers to their optimum health. Doyal's work reflects a growing awareness among feminist researchers and theorists that women are not a unified group. A theme throughout this study is that a key disparity among women is between those in affluent, Western countries and those living in the poorer countries. Although she acknowledges the need to avoid making universal claims about women's experiences of health, she argues that women as a group do still have certain things in common. Across different cultures, women share the reality of having to struggle with and resist similar processes of gender discrimination which act as barriers to good health.

In her study *Black Feminist Thought* Pat Hill-Collins shows how the experience of being Black can provide an illuminating picture of social structures in contemporary society. The basic theme of the book is on what Hill-Collins terms the 'matrix of oppression' – the interaction of factors including class, religion, sexual identity and race – and how it produces a different experience for Black women compared to White women. Reading 38 illustrates this argument by exploring how standards of female 'beauty' are constructed in White-centred terms. As with Mirza's work (Reading 35), Hill-Collins demonstrates how different aspects of social background do not exist in isolation from one another; in particular how race and gender combine to influence the experiences and life chances of individuals.

It is clear, then, that when examining differences and inequalities in modern industrial societies it is not always possible to separate out the effects of particular aspects of social background. As well as the interaction of gender and race highlighted above, there is a clear overlap between race and social class in that ethnic minority groups in Britain are disproportionately represented in the 'lower' social class groupings. However, there is also plenty of evidence that race has a specific and very strong influence across many areas of social life and, therefore, on an individual's life chances. The issues of race and racism are often associated in Britain with the arrival of Black and Asian immigrants from the Commonwealth after the Second World War. However, Black people have played a part in British history for centuries. This presence, which predates colonialism and slavery, can be traced back to the Roman invasion when African soldiers and slaves were part of the conquering force. Some writers have suggested an even earlier presence through links between African traders and the Celts of Ireland and Scotland (see Edwards 1992, for example). These early settlers may have made little impact upon our history but it seems fair to conclude that Black Africans certainly arrived in the British Isles before the English. In *Staying Power: The History of Black People in Britain* (from which Reading 39 is taken), Peter Fryer shows that Black settlement and racism preceded British colonialism and the slave trade and implies that we need to rethink our ideas about history and the origins of racial prejudice. He argues that the fantastic, and very negative, 'folk myths' surrounding Black Africans enabled the creation of 'coherent racist ideology' to justify the trade in Black slaves which became commercially organised from about the mid-sixteenth century.

After this account of the early history of Black people and other immigrant groups in Britain and the ways in which they have been responded to, Reading 40 focuses on the position and experiences of ethnic minorities in contemporary Britain. It is taken from the Fourth National Survey of Ethnic Minorities in Britain undertaken by the Policy Studies Institute (called

Political and Economic Planning (PEP) until 1978) into the opportunities and experiences of ethnic minorities. These studies have provided invaluable data and analysis on the economic and social situation of ethnic minorities. The first study (Daniel 1968) showed a depressing pattern of racial prejudice and open discrimination in housing and employment. Amid further evidence of inequality, the second report (Smith 1977) found some grounds for optimism, discovering that there was a growing degree of diversity among ethnic minority groups with some creating opportunities through self-employment and educational attainment. However, there were still very few ethnic minority people in professional and managerial jobs and although many had penetrated into skilled manual jobs, all the minority groups were disproportionately concentrated in semi-skilled and unskilled manual work. By the time the third report emerged in 1984 (Brown) some groups were clearly doing better than others in employment, housing and education, although the economic climate of recession and declining manual industries made the outlook generally pessimistic. The fourth report, subtitled 'Diversity and Disadvantage', was published in 1997 and was based on a survey of over 5000 people of Caribbean and Asian origin and almost 3000 White people. It covered the conventional areas of employment, housing and education but also examined new areas such as income, health and cultural identity. Our reading is taken from the final chapter of the report which provides an overview of the position of ethnic minority groups. Essentially it shows that some ethnic minority groups, for instance Pakistanis and Bangladeshis, continue to face severe disadvantages in British society, while others groups, such as African Asians and Chinese, have reached a position of broad parity with the White population.

Discussions of race and ethnicity very quickly focus on the physical characteristics which are used to distinguish between people – such as skin colour, facial shape and body size – and whether or not such 'racial' differences are responsible for perceived differences in behaviour and ability. However, issues of race and racism do not just revolve around such factors and a wide range of ethnic minority and immigrant groups have been and are still subject to discrimination and prejudice. Reading 41 is taken from the philosopher and broadcaster Michael Ignatieff's book *Blood and Belonging*, in which he examines the ways in which nationalism exaggerates the ethnic differences between people. The reading illustrates his concern at how a sense of nationalist loyalty can so quickly and easily be translated into feelings of bitter hatred and vengeance. In the struggle to shape a national identity and establish the right to self-determination, violence is regularly turned against those who do not share the same cultural roots in orgies of ethnic 'blood loyalty' and 'blood sacrifice' which become the excuse for future nationalist atrocities. In a journey which took him to Yugoslavia, Germany, Ukraine, Quebec, Kurdistan and finally Northern Ireland, Ignatieff explores the themes of nationalism and ethnic violence. He starts his account in the 1990s because the optimism following the end of the Cold War and the dreams of a democratic 'new world order' have resulted in the nightmare of 'ethnic cleansing'. As Ignatieff puts it: 'When the Berlin Wall came down, when Vaclav Havel stood on the balcony in Prague's Wenceslas Square and crowds cheered the collapse of the Communist regimes across Europe, I thought, like many people, that we were about to witness a new era of liberal democracy . . . We soon found out how wrong we were. For what has succeeded the last age of empire is a new age of violence. They key narrative of the new world order is the disintegration of nation states into ethnic civil war; the key architects of that order are warlords; and the key language of our age is ethnic nationalism' (p. 2).

Although the focus on this section is on differences and inequalities in modern industrial societies and Britain in particular, it is also important not to forget the massive and perhaps more obvious nature of global inequalities. In her now classic study *How the Other Half Dies,* Susan George examined and dispelled some of the myths about the causes of poverty and hunger in the Third World – that they are caused by overpopulation or drought, for instance. Instead George contends that the roots of world hunger are based in exploitation by powerful Western institutions, such as the World Bank and multinational agribusiness corporations, and national governments as well as the consumerism and overconsumption of the wealthy, 'First World' nations. George argues that international capitalism leads to the inequitable distribution of the world's resources and exacerbates hunger in the poorer countries. Powerful international bodies co-opt the support of local élites who benefit and remain protected while large numbers of the local populations live in poverty. She suggests that radical social change, rather than more aid, is the only solution. This analysis reflects a trend in the Sociology of Development away from a focus on internal factors in Third World nations, such as drought, natural disasters, war and poor education, to an examination of structural factors within the international relations of capitalism. From this perspective, Third World poverty is seen as an outcome of complex historical processes of economic and cultural imperialism, domination and exploitation which has left many Third World countries dependent on trade and aid from the rich countries, within an inequitable global economic system which perpetuates dependency.

The section concludes with a reading on disability. Although clearly an area which raises issues of inequality and prejudice, disability has been a little studied area for sociology and has largely been the preserve of medical and psychological work. Disability is unlikely to be mentioned in introductory textbooks or chapters on inequality and stratification. Len Barton's work shows how the sociological approach can help provide a fuller understanding of the position of the disabled in contemporary society and Reading 43, taken from his paper *Sociology and Disability: Some Emerging Issues,* considers the limited sociological contributions to the study of disability before arguing for the development of a sociology of disability that engages with key issues such as power, social justice, citizenship and human rights.

Reading 27

Changes in the structure of industrial societies since Marx

RALPH DAHRENDORF

One of the best-known critics of Marx's notions of class and class conflict is Ralph Dahrendorf. Although a conflict theorist, Dahrendorf argues that changes in the nature of work, organisations and society in general have transformed capitalist societies into a new type of industrial society known as 'post-capitalist'. This new social formation retains a hierarchy of status by occupation, characterised by relations of domination and subordination. However, these are relations of power and authority and are no longer based on class. This extract, which is taken from Dahrendorf's renowned text Class and Class Conflict in an Industrial Society, *first published in 1959, starts with a comment on the changing nature of industrial capitalism – in particular the move away from the 'classical capitalist enterprise' discussed by Marx and the changing roles of owners and managers as a consequence of the rise of joint-stock companies. Dahrendorf then examines the effects of this on the working class, the extent to which it is feasible to talk about a new middle class and the extent of social mobility in modern industrial societies, before reflecting on the changing nature of class conflict.*

Ownership and Control, or the Decomposition of Capital

[. . .]

The crucial effect of the separation of ownership and control in industry [is] that it produces two sets of roles the incumbents of which increasingly move apart in their outlook on and attitudes toward society in general and toward the enterprise in particular. Their reference groups differ, and different reference groups make for different values. Among classical capitalists, the 'organization man' is an unthinkable absurdity. Yet the manager is 'not the individualist but the man who works through others for others' (Whyte 1957). Never has the imputation of a profit motive been further from the real motives of men than it is for modern bureaucratic managers. Economically, managers are interested in such things as rentability, efficiency, and productivity. But all these are indissolubly linked with the imponderables of what has been called the social 'climate of enterprise'. The manager shares with the capitalist two important social reference groups: his peers and his subordinates. But his attitude toward these differs considerably from that of the capitalist (as does consequently, the attitude expected from him by his peers). For him, to be successful means to be liked, and to be liked means, in many ways, to be alike. The manager is an involuntary ruler, and his attitudes betray his feelings [. . .]

The separation of ownership and control has replaced one group by two whose positions, roles, and outlooks are far from identical. In taking this view, one does of course agree with Marx against himself. For it follows from this that the homogenous capitalist class predicted by Marx has in fact not developed. Capital – and thereby capitalism – has dissolved and given way, in the economic sphere, to a plurality of partly agreed, partly competing, and partly simply different groups. The effect of this development on class conflict is threefold: first, the replacement of capitalists by managers involves a change in the composition of the groups participating in conflict; second, and as a consequence of this change in recruitment and composition, there is a change in the nature of the issues that cause conflicts, for the interests of the functionaries without capital differ from those of full-blown capitalists, and so therefore do the interests of labor *vis-à-vis* their new opponents; and third, the decomposition of capital involves a change in the patterns of conflict. One might question whether this new conflict, in which labor is no longer opposed to a homogenous capitalist class, can still be described as a class conflict at all. In any case, it is different from the division of the whole society into two great and homogenous hostile camps with which Marx was concerned [. . .]

Skill and Stratification, or the Decomposition of Labor

While Marx had at least a premonition of things to come with respect to capital, he remained unaware of developments affecting the unity and homogeneity of labor. Yet in this respect, too, the sphere of production which loomed so large in Marx's analysis became the starting point of changes that clearly refute his predictions. The working class of today, far from being a homogenous group of equally unskilled and impoverished people, is in fact a stratum differentiated by numerous subtle and not-so-subtle distinctions. Here, too, history has dissolved one position, or role, and has substituted for it a plurality of roles that are endowed with diverging and often conflicting expectations.

In trying to derive his prediction of the growing homogeneity of labor from the assumption that the technical development of industry would tend to abolish all differences of skill and qualification, Marx was a genuine child of his century [. . .]

Indeed, so far as we can tell from available evidence, there was, up to the end of the nineteenth century, a tendency for most industrial workers to become unskilled, i.e. to be reduced to the same low level of skill. But since then, two new patterns have emerged which are closely related on the one hand to technical innovations in production, on the other to a new philosophy of industrial organization as symbolized by the works of F.W. Taylor (1947) and H. Fayol (1916). First, there emerged, around the turn of the century, a new category of workers which today is usually described as semi-skilled. As early as 1905, Max Weber referred to the growing importance of 'the semi-skilled workers trained directly on the job' . . . Apart from the semi-skilled, there appeared, more recently, a new and ever-growing demand for highly skilled workers of the engineer type in industry . . . Increasingly complex machines require increasingly qualified designers, builders, maintenance and repair men, and even minders, so that Drucker (1950) extrapolates only slightly when he says: 'Within the working class a new shift from unskilled to skilled labor has begun – reversing the trend of the last fifty years. The unskilled worker is actually an engineering imperfection, as unskilled work, at least in theory, can always be done better, faster and cheaper by machines.' [. . .]

Analysis of industrial conditions suggests quite clearly that within the labour force of advanced industry we have to distinguish at least three skill groups: a growing stratum of highly skilled workmen who increasingly merge with both engineers and white-collar employees, a relatively stable stratum of semi-skilled workers with a high degree of diffuse as well as specific industrial experience, and a dwindling stream of totally unskilled labourers who are characteristically either newcomers to industry (beginners, former agricultural labourers, immigrants) or semi-unemployables. It appears, furthermore, that the three groups differ not only in their level of skill, but also in other attributes and determinants of social status. The semi-skilled almost invariably earn a higher wage than the unskilled, whereas the skilled are often salaried and thereby participate in white-collar status. The hierarchy of skill corresponds exactly to the hierarchy of responsibility and delegated authority within the working class. From numerous studies it would seem beyond doubt that it also correlates with the hierarchy of prestige, at the top of which we find the skilled man whose prolonged training, salary, and security convey special status, and at the bottom of which stands the unskilled man who is, according to a recent German investigation into workers' opinions, merely 'working' without having an 'occupation' proper (see Kluth 1955). Here as elsewhere Marx was evidently mistaken. 'Everywhere, the working class differentiates itself more and more, on the one hand into occupational groups, on the other into three large categories with different, if not contradictory, interests: the skilled craftsmen, the unskilled labourers, and the semi-skilled specialist workers' (Philip 1955).

In trying to assess the consequences of this development, it is well to remember that, for Marx, the increasing uniformity of the working class was an indispensable condition of that intensification of the class struggle which was to lead, eventually, to its climax in a revolution. The underlying argument of what for Marx became a prediction appears quite plausible. For there to be a revolution, the conflicts within society have to become extremely intense. For conflicts to be intense, one would indeed expect its participants to be highly unified and homogenous groups. But neither capital nor labour have developed along these lines. Capital has dissolved into at least two, in many ways distinct, elements, and so has labour. The proletarian, the impoverished slave of industry who is indistinguishable from his peers in terms of his work, his skill, his wage and his prestige, has left the scene. What is more, it appears that by now he has been followed by his less depraved, but equally alienated, successor, the worker. In modern industry, 'the worker' has become precisely the kind of abstraction which Marx quite justly resented so much. In his place, we find a plurality of status and skill groups whose interests often diverge. Demands of the skilled for security may injure the semi-skilled; wage claims of the semi-skilled may raise objections by the skilled; and any interest on the part of the unskilled is bound to set their more highly skilled fellow workmen worrying about differentials.

Again, as in the case of capital, it does not follow from the decomposition of labour that there is no bond left that unites most workers – at least for specific goals; nor does it follow that industrial conflict has lost its edge. But here, too, a change of the issues and, above all, of the patterns of conflict is indicated. As with the capitalist class, it has become doubtful whether speaking of the working class still makes much sense [. . .]

The 'New Middle Class'

Along with the decomposition of both capital and labour a new stratum emerged within, as well as outside, the industry of modern societies, which was, so to speak, born decomposed. Since Lederer and Marschak first published their essay on this group, and coined for it the name 'new middle class' (*neuer Mittelstand*), so much has been written by sociologists about the origin, development, position, and function of white-collar or black-coated employees that whatever one says is bound to be repetitive. However, only one conclusion is borne out quite clearly by all these studies of salaried employees in industry, trade, commerce, and public administration: that there is no word in any modern language to describe this group that is no group, class that is no class, and stratum that is no stratum [. . .]

If one is, as we are, concerned not with patterns of social stratification but with lines of conflict, then one thing is certain: however we may choose to delimit the aggregate of salaried employees, they are not a 'middle class', because from the point of view of a theory of conflict there can be no such entity as a middle class. Evident as it is, this statement is bound to be misunderstood – but, then, much of this study is an attempt to elucidate it. It is true that in terms of prestige and income many salaried employees occupy a position somewhere between the very wealthy and the very poor, somewhere in the middle of the scale of social stratification. But in a situation of conflict, whether defined in a Marxian way or in some other way, this kind of intermediate position just does not exist, or, at least, exists only as a negative position of nonparticipation [. . .]

It seems to me that a fairly clear as well as significant line can be drawn between salaried employees who occupy positions that are part of a bureaucratic hierarchy and salaried employees in positions that are not. The occupations of the post-office clerk, the accountant, and, of course, the senior executive are rungs on a ladder of bureaucratic positions; those of the salesgirl and the craftsman are not. There may be barriers in bureaucratic hierarchies which are insurmountable for people who started in low positions; salaried employees outside such hierarchies may earn more than those within, and they may also change occupations and enter upon a bureaucratic career; but these and similar facts are irrelevant to the distinction between bureaucrats and white-collar workers proposed here. Despite these facts I suggest that the ruling-class theory applies without exception to the social position of bureaucrats, and the working-class theory equally generally to the social position of white-collar workers.

There is, in other words, one section of the 'new middle class' the condition of which, from the point of view of class conflict, closely resembles that of industrial workers. This section includes many of the salaried employees in the tertiary industries, in shops and restaurants, in cinemas, and in commercial firms, as well as those highly skilled workers and foremen who have acquired salaried status. It is hard to estimate, from available evidence, the numerical size of this group, but it probably does not at present exceed one-third of the whole 'new middle class' – although it may do so in future, since the introduction of office machinery tends to reduce the number of bureaucrats while increasing the demand for salaried office technicians. Although some white-collar workers earn rather more than industrial workers, and most of them enjoy a somewhat higher prestige, their class situation appears sufficiently similar to that of workers to expect them to act alike. In general, it is among white-collar workers that one would expect trade unions as well as radical political parties to be successful.

The bureaucrats, on the other hand, share, if often in a minor way, the requisites of a ruling class. Although many of them earn less than white-collar and even industrial workers, they participate in the exercise of authority and thereby occupy a position *vis-à-vis* rather than inside the working class. The otherwise surprising fact that many salaried employees identify themselves with the interests, attitudes, and styles of life of the higher-ups can be accounted for in these terms. For the bureaucrats, the supreme social reality is their career that provides, at least in theory, a direct link between every one of them and the top positions which may be described as the ultimate seat of authority. It would be false to say that the bureaucrats are a ruling class, but in any case they are part of it, and one would therefore expect them to act accordingly in industrial, social, and political conflicts.

The decomposition of labour and capital has been the result of social developments that have occurred since Marx, but the 'new middle class' was born decomposed. It neither has been nor is it ever likely to be a class in any sense of this term. But while there is no 'new middle class', there are, of course, white-collar workers and bureaucrats, and the growth of these groups is one of the striking features of historical development in the past century. What is their effect on class structure and class conflict, if it is not that of adding a new class to the older ones Marx described? It follows from our analysis that the emergence of salaried employees means in the first place an extension of the older classes of bourgeoisie and proletariat. The bureaucrats add to the bourgeoisie, as the white-collar workers add to the proletariat. Both classes have become, by these extensions, even more complex and heterogeneous than their decomposition has made them in any case. By gaining new elements, their unity has become a highly doubtful and precarious feature. White-collar workers, like industrial workers, have neither property nor authority, yet they display many social characteristics that are quite unlike those of the old working class. Similarly, bureaucrats differ from the older ruling class despite their share in the exercise of authority. Even more than the decomposition of capital and labour, these facts make it highly doubtful whether the concept of class is still applicable to the conflict groups of post-capitalist societies. In any case, the participants, issues, and patterns of conflict have changed, and the pleasing simplicity of Marx's view of society has become a nonsensical construction. If ever there have been two large, homogenous, polarized, and identically situated social classes, these have certainly ceased to exist today, so that an unmodified Marxian theory is bound to fail in explaining the structure and conflicts of advanced industrial societies.

Social Mobility

The decomposition of capital and labour as well as their extension by sections of the 'new middle class' are phenomena which have an obvious and direct bearing on class structure. But they are neither the only changes that have occurred since Marx nor, perhaps, the most significant ones from the point of view of class. Apart from such political and economic forces as totalitarianism and socialism, it was in particular the institutionalization of the two great social forces of mobility and equality that has steered class structures and conflicts in directions unforeseen by Marx. Marx was not, in fact, unaware of the importance of these forces. In explaining the absence of stable classes in the United States in terms of what he called the 'exchange between classes', he anticipated the cardinal thesis of Sombart's brilliant essay, *Why is there no Socialism in the United States?* But for Marx, mobility was a symptom of short-lived transitional periods of history, i.e., of either the emergence or the impending breakdown of a society. Today, we would tend to take the opposite view. Social mobility has become one of the crucial elements of the structure of industrial societies, and one would be tempted to predict its 'breakdown' if the process of mobility were ever seriously impeded. Marx believed that the strength of a ruling class documents itself in its ability to absorb the ablest elements of other classes. In a manner of speaking, this is permanently the case in advanced industrial societies, yet we should hesitate to infer from a steady increase in the upward mobility of the talented that the present ruling class is particularly strong or homogeneous [. . .]

When Marx wrote his books, he assumed that the position an individual occupies in society is determined by his family origin and the position of his parents. The sons of workers have no other choice but to become workers themselves, and the sons of capitalists stay in the class of their fathers. At the time, this assumption was probably not far from the truth. But since then a new pattern of role allocation has become institutionalized in industrial societies. Today, the allocation of social positions is increasingly the task of the educational system . . . In post-capitalist society, it is 'the process of socialization itself, especially as found in the educational system, that is serving as the proving ground for ability and hence the selective agency for placing people in different statuses according to their capacities' (Davis 1949).

To be sure, there are still numerous obstacles and barriers in the way of complete equality of educational opportunity, but it is the stubborn tendency of modern societies to institutionalize intergeneration mobility by making a person's social position dependent on his educational achievement. Where this is the case, no social stratum, group, or class can remain completely stable for more than one generation. Social mobility, which, for Marx, was the exception that confirmed the rule of class closure, is built into the structure of post-capitalist society and has therefore become a factor to be reckoned with in all analyses of conflict and change [. . .]

Equality in Theory and Practice

In the preceding sections two of the three predictions that Marx made about the future development of classes in capitalist society have been discussed in the light of the social history of the last decades. We have seen that neither of them has come true. Contrary to Marx's expectations, the increasing differentiation as well as homogeneity of classes was checked by the decomposition of labour and capital, the emergence of white-collar workers and bureaucrats, and the institutionalization of social mobility. But none of Marx's hopes – for such they were – has been refuted more dramatically in social development than his prediction that the class situations of bourgeoisie and proletariat would tend toward extremes of wealth and poverty, possession and deprivation. Here, too, Marx had a simple theory. He believed in a direct and unfailing correlation between the extremity of class situations and the intensity of class conflict. It is quite possible that this theory contains an element of truth, but if it does, then the remarkable spread of social equality in the past century has rendered class struggles and revolutionary changes utterly impossible [. . .]

Along with the spread of citizenship rights, the social situation of people became increasingly similar. The completeness of this levelling tendency can be, and has been, exaggerated. There are of course even today considerable differences in income, prestige, spending habits, and styles of life. But as a tendency the process of levelling social differences cannot be denied. By the simultaneous rise of the real wages of workers and the taxation of top earnings, a redistribution of incomes has taken place – a redistribution that some believe today has gone so far as to remove every incentive for work requiring special training or skill. Many of the technical comforts and status symbols of modern life are increasingly available to everybody. The 'mass-produced commodities of the culture industry' (Horkheimer and Adorno 1947) unite distant people and areas in nearly identical leisure-time activities. Schelsky gives voice to the impression of many when he summarizes this development as a process of 'social levelling with predominantly petty-bourgeois or middle-class patterns of behaviour and ideals' (1955).

Social stratification and class structure are two distinct aspects of social organization, but they both refer to inequalities in the social life of individuals. If, therefore, the legal and social status of people undergoes a process of levelling which apparently tends towards complete equality of status, the concepts of social stratification and class structure tend to lose their meaning . . . With respect to class structure . . . there can be little doubt that the equalization of status resulting from social developments of the past century has contributed greatly to changing the issues and diminishing the intensity of class conflict. By way of extrapolation – fairly wild extrapolation, I may say – some authors have visualized a state in which there are no classes and no class conflicts, because there is simply nothing to quarrel about. I do not think that such a state is ever likely to occur. But in order to substantiate this opinion, it is necessary to explore the structural limits equality, i.e., to find the points at which even the most fanatic egalitarian comes up against insurmountable realities of social structure . . . In so far as the theory and practice of equality in post-capitalist societies are concerned, it seems certain that they have changed the issues and patterns of class conflict, and possible that they have rendered the concept of class inapplicable, but they have not removed all significant inequalities, and they have not, therefore, eliminated the causes of social conflict.

From R. Dahrendorf (1959) *Class and Class Conflict in an Industrial Society*, London: Routledge & Kegan Paul, pp. 46–64.

Questions

1. Summarise in your own words the key changes in social conditions which Dahrendorf believes characterise post-capitalist industrial societies.
2. How does Dahrendorf's argument challenge Marx's predictions about class and class conflict?
3. What clues are there in the text to suggest that Dahrendorf is a conflict theorist?

Reading 28

Classes in the industrial societies

TOM BOTTOMORE

In this extract from Classes in Modern Society, *Bottomore examines and discusses the extent to which social mobility has increased and whether this has led to embourgeoisement. In arguing that social classes continue to play a key role in modern society, he takes issue with Dahrendorf, concluding that 'there is no general sense of greater "classlessness", nor of great opportunities for the individual to choose and create his way of life regardless of inherited wealth or social position'. In his discussion of social mobility and education, Bottomore refers to grammar schools as providing an opportunity for upward mobility, which reminds us that, as with all the readings in this collection, it is important to consider the social and historical context of the writing – in this case the early 1960s when selective secondary education was the norm.*

The improvement in the conditions of life for the working class in post-war Britain obviously owes much to the maintenance of full employment and to the development of the health services. Full employment, besides raising the level of income of the working class and providing a degree of that economic security which the upper class has always taken for granted, has almost entirely eliminated the class of domestic servants; and this is one of the greatest gains which the working class has made in the twentieth century, in escaping from one particularly onerous form of subjection to another class [. . .]

The social services do not only help to create an equality in the vital conditions of life for all citizens; so far as they are used by everyone the standard of the service tends to rise. It may well be true, as some have argued, that the middle classes have benefited at least as much as the working class from the expansion of the social services, but one important consequence has been that, for example, the standards of free medical care have been vastly improved as compared with the time when such care was provided only for the poor and needy. In the field of education a similar progress is evident since the Education Act of 1944, although here class differences have proved more tenacious and difficult to overcome, while the existence of a large private sector of education has meant that there has been less vigour in the drive to improve the standard of the public service.

We must conclude that the general advance in the material conditions of the British working class, in recent decades, has been due overwhelmingly to the rapid growth of national income, which has also made possible the expansion of the social services, and not to any radical redistribution of wealth or income between classes. Moreover, even in this more affluent society a great deal of poverty remains. Its significance for the relations between classes is, however, very different from that which it had in the nineteenth century. Then, poverty was the lot of a whole class, and there was no expectation that it could be quickly alleviated within the limits of the capitalist economic system. It separated one class in society distinctly from others, and at the same time engendered a movement of revolt. In present day Britain, as in other advanced industrial countries, poverty has ceased to be of this kind; it is now less extensive, and is confined to particular groups in the population – mainly old people and workers in certain occupations or regions which have been left behind as a result of technological progress – which are too isolated or heterogeneous to form the basis of a radical social movement. These impoverished groups stand in marked contrast with the majority of the working class which enjoys a high level of living in relation both to past societies and to some middle class groups in present day society.

The thesis of *embourgeoisement* . . . relies in the main for its factual basis upon this improvement in levels of living and the changes in the relative economic position of manual workers and some sections of white-collar workers, but it also brings in the effects of social mobility in modifying the class system. Since the war, sociologists have studied social mobility much more intensively than they have studied the changes within classes themselves, and they have attributed much importance to it as a solvent of class divisions. The finds of recent studies may be summarized in the following way. Social mobility has generally increased with the economic development of the industrial societies, but the increase has been due very largely to changes in the occupational structure; that is, to the expansion of white collar and professional occupations and the contraction of manual occupations [. . .]

A second important feature is that most social mobility takes place between social levels which are close together; for example, between the upper levels of the working class and the lower levels of the middle class. Movement from the working class into the upper class is very limited in any society, and notably so in Britain. This characteristic can be shown more clearly by studies of recruitment to particular élite occupations such as the higher civil service, business management, and the older professions. In Britain, a study of the directors of large public companies reveals that more than half of them began their careers with the advantage of having business connections in the family, while another 40 per cent came from families of landowners, professional men and others of similar social position. A study of higher civil servants in the administrative class shows that 30 per cent came from families of the upper and upper middle classes, and another 40 per cent from the intermediate levels of the middle class, while only 3 per cent were recruited from families of semi-skilled and unskilled manual workers. Nevertheless, the same study indicates that the area of recruitment of high civil servants has been extended somewhat during the past 30 years, and the same may well be true in the case of other professions.

The main influence here has been the extension of educational opportunities; and the view that social mobility has increased substantially in post-war Britain derives very largely from the belief that educational reforms have provided vast new opportunities for upward movement. It is certainly true that before the war social mobility was restricted especially by financial and other obstacles in the way of access to secondary and higher education. The Education Act of 1944 established for the first time a national system of secondary education and greatly increased the opportunities for working-class children to obtain a grammar school education. Also in the post-war period the access of working-class children to university has been made somewhat easier by the increase of student numbers and the more lavish provision of the maintenance grants. Nevertheless, Britain is still very far from having equality of opportunity in education. The existence of a private sector of school education, misleadingly called the 'public schools', maintains the educational and occupational advantages of upper-class families, while in the state system of education, although the opportunities for working-class children have increased, it is probable that middle-class families have actually made greater use of the new opportunities for grammar school and university education. Even if we add to the social mobility which takes place through the educational system, that which may be assumed to occur as a result of the growth of new middle-class occupations – for example, in the entertainments industry – where educational qualifications are less important, it can still not be said that the movement of individuals in the social hierarchy is very considerable or is increasing rapidly. The vast majority of people still remain in their class of origin.

It may be questioned, too, whether even a much higher rate of social mobility, involving an interchange between classes in which downward mobility was roughly equal to upward mobility, would have much effect upon the class system, in the sense of reducing the barriers or the antagonism between classes. On the contrary, in such a situation of high mobility, the working class would come to comprise those who had failed to rise in the social hierarchy in spite of the opportunities available to them, and those who had descended, through personal failure, from higher social levels; and such a class, made up of particularly embittered and frustrated individuals, might be expected to be very sharply distinguished from, and in conflict with, the rest of society. There are apparent, indeed, in Britain and in other industrial societies, some elements of such a condition among the younger generations in the population.

The most important aspect of social mobility is perhaps the impression which it makes upon the public consciousness. According to the type and degree of social mobility a society may appear to its members to be 'open' and fluid, presenting manifold opportunities to talent and energy, or it may appear to be rigid and 'closed'. In Britain, all manner of ancient institutions and modes of behaviour – the aristocracy, the public schools, Oxbridge, differences of speech and accent, the relationships of the 'old boy' network – frustrate mobility and buttress the public conception of a rigidly hierarchical society. Any increase in social mobility, even in the past two decades, has been too modest, gradual and discreet to create a new outlook. The boundaries of class may have become more blurred, chiefly at the lower levels of the social hierarchy and there may have been some expansion of opportunities, especially in the sphere of consumption, for large sections of the population. But there is no general sense of greater 'classlessness', nor of great opportunities for the individual to choose and create his way of life regardless of inherited wealth or social position [. . .]

[He concludes] The principal fault in many recent studies of social classes has been that they lack an historical sense. Like the economists of whom Marx said that they believed there had been history, because feudalism had disappeared, but there was no longer any history, because capitalism was a natural and eternal social order, some sociologists have accepted that there was an historical development of classes and class conflicts in the early period of industrial capitalism, but that this has ceased in the fully evolved industrial societies in which the working class has escaped from poverty and has attained industrial and political citizenship. But this assumption is made without any real study of the evolution of social classes in recent times, or of the social movements at the present time which reveal the possibilities of future social change. An historical analysis of the changing class structure in modern societies, such as I have merely outlined here, remains one of the most important unfulfilled tasks of sociology today.

From T. Bottomore (1965) *Classes in Modern Society*, London: Allen & Unwin, pp. 36–41, 77.

Questions

1. Bottomore's study was written in the 1960s. What evidence can you suggest to illustrate the argument that social mobility has increased in the last 30 years? What factors continue to work against social mobility?

2. Given the changes which have occurred in the distribution of wealth and income, the increase in social mobility and the increase in social rights, how does Bottomore arrive at the conclusion that 'there is no general sense of greater "classlessness" '?

Reading 29

Are social classes dying?

TERRY CLARK AND SEYMOUR LIPSET

In this article Clark and Lipset concentrate on the concept of class and its application beyond workplace differences to distinct sectors of social organisation, or 'situses' as the authors call them. They tackle the debate about class on an international level rather than focusing exclusively on British society and the broad sweep of their approach takes in America, Western Europe and the changes that have taken place in Eastern Europe. According to Clark and Lipset, class distinctions are directly related to hierarchy and as hierarchical structures decline so do class differences. In short they argue that in post-industrial societies the fragmentation of hierarchy has led to the decline of class as a determinant of lifestyle and life chances and its replacement by new patterns of social stratification.

New forms of social stratification are emerging. Much of our thinking about stratification – from Marx, Weber and others – must be recast to capture these new developments. Social class was the key theme of past stratification work. Yet class is an increasingly outmoded concept, although it is sometimes appropriate to earlier historical periods. Class stratification implies that people can be differentiated on one or more criteria into distinct layers, classes. Class analysis has grown increasingly inadequate in recent decades as traditional hierarchies have declined and new social differences have emerged. The cumulative impact of these changes is fundamentally altering the nature of social stratification – placing past theories in need of substantial modification [. . .]

If one looks closely at class theories in recent decades, it is striking how much class has changed. This is not immediately obvious since most theorists claim direct descendance from Marx and Weber. But many have in fact fundamentally altered the concept of class towards what we term *the fragmentation of stratification.* Consider some examples of class theory and social stratification. Dahrendorf (1959:157–206) stressed that many lines of social cleavage have not erupted into class conflict. For a Marxian revolution, the working class should suffer immiseration and grow more homogenous; capitalists should join in combat against them. But Dahrendorf points instead to the 'decomposition of labour': workers have become more differentiated by skill level – into skilled, semi-skilled and unskilled. Unions often separate more than join these groups. Perhaps even more important is the expansion of the 'middle class' of white-collar non-manual workers. Such a middle class was largely ignored by Marx; it was expected to join the capitalists or workers. Instead it has grown substantially, and differentiated internally, especially between lower-level salaried employees and managers. Dahrendorf might have abandoned the concept of class, but instead retained the term while redefining it to include all sorts of groups in political or social conflict: '"class" signifies conflict groups that are generated by the differential distribution of authority in imperatively coordinated associations' (Dahrendorf 1959: 204) [. . .]

[This analysis stresses] changes in work-place relations. Yet social relations outside the work-place are increasingly important for social stratification. If proletarians are visibly distinct in dress, food and life style, they are more likely to think of themselves, and act as a politically distinct class. In the nineteenth and early twentieth centuries, this was often the case, as novels and sociologists report. The decreasing distinctiveness of social classes is stressed by Parkin (1979:69), who holds that this brings the 'progressive erosion of the communal components of proletarian status'. Specifically, 'the absence of clearly visible and unambiguous marks of inferior status has made the enforcement of an all-pervasive deference system almost impossible to sustain outside the immediate work situation. It would take an unusually sharp eye to detect the social class of Saturday morning shoppers in the High Street, whereas to any earlier generation it would have been the most elementary task.' [. . .]

Should the social class concept be abandoned? In a 1959 exchange, Nisbet suggested that class 'is nearly valueless for the clarification of the data of wealth, power and social status in the contemporary United States' (1959:11). Commenting on Nisbet in the same journal, Bernard Barber and O.D. Duncan both argued that his position had not been substantiated, and that a sharper analysis and evidence were necessary. This was over 30 years ago. Yet today class remains salient in sociologists' theories, and commentaries. We do not suggest it be altogether abandoned, but complemented by other factors [. . .]

Many stratification analysts used class analysis longer and more extensively than empirically warranted due to their focus on Europe. Analysts of American society are often defensive, suggesting that America is somehow 'behind' Europe. Marxists were among the most outspoken in this regard, but not unique (e.g. Wilson 1978). However, things changed as new social movements emerged in the 1970s and 1980s. The United States then often seemed more a leader than a laggard. This seemed even more true in the dramatic changes of the late 1980s as the former communist societies, led by Eastern Europe, sought to throw off their central hierarchical planning and move toward free economic markets and political democracy.

What do these changes imply for theories of stratification? A critical point is that traditional hierarchies are declining; economic and family hierarchies determine much less than just a generation or two ago. Three general propositions state this argument:

1. *Hierarchy generates and maintains rigid class relations. The greater the hierarchical (vertical) differentiation among persons in a social unit, the deeper its class divisions tend to become.*

Since the degree of hierarchy will vary with a society, we add:

2. *The greater the hierarchical differentiation in each separate situs (or separate vertical dimension, e.g. economic institutions, government organisations, and families), the most salient are class-defined patterns in informed social relations, cultural outlooks, and support for social change, such as support for social movements and political behaviour.*
3. *Conversely, however, the more the hierarchy declines, the more structured social class relations diminish in salience.*

[. . .]

We now consider separate situses of social stratification in terms of our three general propositions. In each situs we consider some of the specific dynamics by which social classes have declined. The cumulative effect, across situses, is the emergence of a new system of social stratification.

Politics: Less Class, More Fragmentation

Political behaviour is an ideal area to assess changes in stratification. It was central to Marx and Weber, it is highly visible today; it has been studied in detail; it permits tests of competing, hypotheses, Lipset's *Political Man* stressed class politics in its first edition (1960). But the second edition (1981, especially pp. 459 ff.) focused on the declines in class voting. A striking illustration of this change is in the results from the 1940s to 1980s on the Alford Index of Class Voting. This index is based on the percentage of persons by social class who vote for left or right parties. For instance, if 75 per cent of the working class votes for the left, and only 25 per cent of the middle class does so, the Alford index score is 50 (the difference between these two figures). The Alford Index has declined in every country for which data are available (see Lipset 1981, updated in Clark and Inglehart 1991) [. . .]

What is replacing class? The classical left-right dimension has been transformed. People still speak of left and right, but definitions are changing. There are now two lefts, with distinct social bases. The traditional left is blue-collar based and stresses class-related issues. But a second left is emerging in Western societies (sometimes termed New Politics, New Left, Post-Bourgeois, or Post-Materialist), which increasingly stresses social issues rather than traditional political issues. The most intensely disputed issues for them no longer deal with ownership and control of the means of production. And in many socialist and even communist parties (in the 1970s in Italy, in the 1990s in Eastern Europe) supporters of these new issues are supplanting the old.

Political issues shift with more affluence: as wealth increases, people take the basics for granted; they grow more concerned with life style and amenities. Younger, more educated and more affluent persons in more affluent and less hierarchical societies should move furthest from traditional class politics [. . .]

Economic Organisation Changes: Sources of a New Market Individualism

One simple, powerful change has affected the economy: growth. And economic growth undermines hierarchical class stratification. Affluence weakens hierarchies and collectivism; but it heightens individualism. With more income, the poor depend less on the rich. And all can indulge progressively more elaborate and varied tastes. *Markets, ceteris paribus, grow in relevance as income rises.* But as such complexity increases, it grows harder to plan centrally; decentralised, demand-sensitive decision-making becomes necessary. These contrasts particularly affect(ed) centrally planned societies like the Soviet Union. But they operate too for firms like General Motors or US Steel.

Many private goods come increasingly from more differentiated and sub-market-oriented small firms, especially in such service-intensive fields as 'thoughtware', finance and office activities. By contrast huge firms are in relative decline, especially for traditional manufacturing products like steel and automobiles. Some 2/3 of all new jobs are in firms with 20 or fewer employees, in many countries (Birch 1979). These small firms emerge because they out-compete larger firms. Why? Technology and management style are critical factors.

The more advanced the technology and knowledge base, the harder it is to plan in advance and control administratively, both within a large firm and still more by central government planners. Technological changes illustrate how new economic patterns are no longer an issue of public versus private sector control, but bring inevitable frustrations for hierarchical control by anyone. As research and development grow increasingly important for new products and technologies, they are harder to direct or define in advance for distant administrators of that firm, and even harder for outsider regulators or political officials seeking to plan centrally (as in a Soviet five-year plan, to use an extreme case). Certain plastics firms have as much as one-third of staff developing the chemistry for new products. Computers, biological engineering and robotics illustrate the dozens of areas that are only vaguely amenable to forecast and hence central control.

A major implication for social stratification of these economic changes is the decline in traditional authority, hierarchy and class relations. Current technologies require fewer unskilled workers performing routine tasks, or a large middle-management to coordinate them, than did traditional manufacturing of steel, automobiles, etc. High tech means increasing automation of routine tasks. It also demands more professional autonomous decisions. More egalitarian, collegial decision-making is thus increasingly seen as a hallmark of modern society, by analysts from Habermas and Parsons to Daniel Bell and Zbigniew Brzezinski, and to consultants in business schools who teach the importance of new 'corporate culture' – as illustrated by *In Search of Excellence* (Peters and Waterman 1982), the number one non-fiction best-seller in the United States for some time, and widely read by business leaders in the United States and Europe. Even Soviet scholars as early as 1969 noted 'a sweeping qualitative transformation of productive forces as a result of science being made the principal factor in the development of social production' (Richta *et al.* 1969:39). The occupations that are expanding are white-collar, technical, professional and service-oriented. The class structure increasingly resembles a diamond bulging at the middle rather than a pyramid. Higher levels of education are needed in such occupations; the numbers of students pursuing more advanced studies has rapidly increased in the past few decades [. . .]

A Slimmer Family

Major trends here parallel those in the economy. The traditional family has been slimmed and hierarchical stratification has weakened. Family and intimate personal relations have increasingly become characterised by more egalitarian relations, more flexible roles, and more tolerance for a wider range of behaviour. The authoritarian paternalistic family is decreasingly the model for stratification in the rest of society. Fewer young people marry, they wed later, have fewer children, far more women work outside the home, divorce rates have risen, parents and grandparents live less often with children (e.g. Cherlin 1981; Forse 1986). Paralleling these sociodemographic changes are changes in attitudes and roles concerning the family. Children and wives have grown substantially more egalitarian in a very short period of time. Indeed attitudes towards the family have changed more than almost any other social or political factor in the past 20–30 years, especially to questions like

'Should women work outside the home?' The proportions of wives and mothers working in jobs outside the home have grown dramatically, first and especially in the United States, but in many European countries too.

The family has also grown less important as a basis of stratification in relation to education and jobs. Increased wealth and government-support programmes have expanded choice to individuals, and cumulatively transferred more functions than ever away from the family. Families are thus decreasingly responsible for raising children and placing them in jobs. Fewer children work in family firms (farms, shops, etc.). US mobility studies from the late nineteenth century onward report few changes until the 1960s (Lipset and Bendix 1991) but major changes since: Hout's (1988) replication of Featherman and Hauser (1978) showed that the effect of origin status on destination status declined by 28 per cent from 1962 to 1973 and by one-third from 1972 to 1985. Social mobility studies also show decreasing effects of parents' education and income in explaining children's occupational success. At the same time the independent effects of education have increased.

Conclusion

New patterns of social stratification are emerging. The key trend could be described as one of 'fragmentation of stratification': the weakening of class stratification, especially as shown in distinct class-differentiated life styles; the decline of economic determinism, and the increased importance of social and cultural factors; politics less organised by class and more by other loyalties; social mobility less family-determined, more ability and educational-determined.

From T.N. Clark and S.M. Lipset (1996) 'Are social classes dying?', in D.J. Lee and B.S. Turner (eds) *Conflicts About Class: Debating Inequality in Late Industrialism*, Harlow: Longman, pp. 42–8.

Questions

1. What 'clearly visible and unambiguous marks of inferior status' allowed early writers to identify members of the proletariat? Do they still exist? If so, how have they changed?
2. Summarise the argument for the fragmentation of class in each of the 'situses' mentioned in the extract: (a) politics; (b) the economy; and (c) the family.

Reading 30

The persistence of classes in post-industrial societies

MIKE HOUT, CLEM BROOKS AND JEFF MANZA

Hout, Brooks and Manza attack the conclusion of Clark and Lipset (Reading 29) that social classes are dying and that the concept of social class has been rendered redundant by changes in the hierarchical nature of society. They complain that Clark and Lipset confuse social class with social status (hierarchy) and have produced an argument which is conceptually vague and misleading. As a result the reader is diverted from examining enduring inequalities by references to democratisation elsewhere in society. In this extract, Hout and colleagues examine the three 'situses' of politics, the economy and the family and, as a result, reject Clark and Lipset's conclusion. They assert that despite change in advanced capitalist societies, class-based inequalities persist.

Clark and Lipset have joined with other writers past and present who leap from data on trends to conjectures about the future. The death and dying metaphors suggest more finality than the data will support. For, while we would be contradicting our own results if we were to deny that there have been trends towards a diminished effect of class on important social indicators, e.g., the openness in mobility (Hout 1988), we see those trends as the outcome of a class-political process that is neither immutable nor irreversible. The past 25 years of class research reveal a mix of upward and downward trends in the effects of class [. . .]

Coming from Seymour Martin Lipset, whose earlier work taught us much about the link between class and political life, this latest challenge to class analysis should not be ignored. Unlike Nisbet, who explicitly dismissed empirical research, arguing that 'statistical techniques have had to become ever more ingenious to keep the vision of class from fading away altogether' (1959: 12), Clark and Lipset summarise a wealth of empirical data to make their case. On closer examination, however, we find that much of the evidence they cite is highly selective and cannot withstand critical scrutiny. We are especially troubled by their complete neglect of other evidence which shows the continuing – and even rising – importance of class. Altogether, we believe it is impossible to sustain their conclusion, and in the discussion which follows we seek to show that, while class may be defined and used by social scientists in a number of different ways, the concept remains indispensable. Be it as an independent or dependent variable, sociologists will turn away from class at their own peril.

The Persistence of Classes

Sociologists did not invent the concept of class. But we have made more out of it than others have, mainly by emphasising the point that it is how one makes a living that determines life chances and material interests. We differ from economists' nearly exclusive focus on the quantity of income or wealth and commonsense conceptions that blend life style and morality with economic and sociological considerations (Jencks and Petersen 1991). The part-time school teacher, the semi-skilled factory worker and the struggling shopkeeper may all report the same income on their tax returns, but we recognise that as salaried, hourly and self-employed workers they have different sources of income and, consequently, different life chances. Clark and Lipset, however, put great stock in life style, citing Parkin's contention that 'the absence of clearly visible and unambiguous marks of inferior *status* has made the enforcement of an all-pervasive deference system almost impossible to sustain outside the immediate work situation' (Parkin 1979: 69; our emphasis). To our mind this counters Clark and Lipset's general point that status distinctions are on the rise as class is on the wane.

At various points in their paper, Clark and Lipset seem to equate class and hierarchy, but they are separate dimensions. Hierarchy, in sociological usage, could refer to any rankable distinctions. Class refers to a person's relationship to the means of production and/or labour markets, and it is an important determinant of an individual's income, wealth and social standing. We thus adopt a generic definition of class that we hope is compatible with the contemporary versions of both neo-Marxist and neo-Weberian concepts [. . .]

Class is an indispensable concept for sociology because: (1) class is a key determinate of material interests; (2) structurally defined classes give rise to – or influence the formation of – collective actors seeking to bring about social change; and (3) class membership affects the life chances and behaviour of individuals. The first concern refers to the intrinsic importance of class. The other two are relevant for 'class analysis' – the investigation of how class affects other aspects of social life. Clark and Lipset state their case – which refers to all three of these concerns – without acknowledging that each raises different sets of issues. As a result of these confusions, Clark and Lipset's argument collapses analytically distinct processes.

Clark and Lipset also confuse trends in society with trends in writing about society. To be sure, our conceptions of class have grown more complex over the years. Marx's initial codification of the importance of whether one works for a living or expropriates a profit from the sale of goods produced by others has been supplemented over the years by additional distinctions, most of which are ignored by Clark and Lipset. In addition to workers and capitalists, contemporary Marxist accounts of class structure recognise professionals and crafts persons, who extract rents on their expertise, and managers and supervisors, who extract rents on their organisational assets (Wright 1985). These are not mere status distinctions, as Clark and Lipset would have it. They are class distinctions because they specify economic roles with respect to labour markets and material interests . . . While sociologists' models of class are a lot more complicated than they used to be, complexity alone does not imply that class is dead or dying.

Clark and Lipset's conclusions about the decline of class in post-industrial societies hinge on the claim that 'traditional hierarchies are declining; economic and family hierarchies determine much less than just a generation or two ago' [see p. 171]. However, hierarchy is never defined and the assumed link between hierarchy and class in their formulation is at best vague. In moving back and forth between a materialist analysis of class to the vaguer concept of 'hierarchy', Clark and Lipset are tacitly shifting the terrain of debate away from class *per se*. This conceptual slippage makes it easier for them to conclude that classes are dying. Their emphasis on hierarchy is also potentially misleading in that forms of hierarchy could decline without any change in class structure or the general importance of class for systems of stratification or political behaviour. They persistently conflate class-based inequalities with non-class forms of stratification. Perhaps as a consequence, Clark and Lipset conveniently ignore some of the most salient aspects of class inequalities in contemporary capitalist societies. First, they completely ignore the remarkable persistence in the high levels of wealth controlled by the bourgeoisie in these societies. The pattern of the amount of wealth controlled by the richest 1 per cent of the populations of different capitalist societies seems to be remarkably consistent and seems to hold across different societies . . . Secondly, they ignore the capacity of wealth-holders to influence political processes, either directly through financial contributions, intra-class organisational and political networks and government agencies, or indirectly through control over investment decisions . . . Lastly, educational institutions play an important role in transmitting privilege from one generation to another [. . .]

Private fortunes are still predicated on ownership of the means of production. During the 1930s when inequality of wealth and earnings was growing in the United States and elsewhere, the private fortunes at the forefront of resurgent inequality were in almost all cases built through ownership. High-tech champions like Gates, merchandisers like Walton and developers like Trump got rich because they owned the means of production. Arbitragers collected high fees and executives were 'overcompensated', but they gained more from ownership of shares of stock than from their wages and salaries (Crystal 1991) [. . .]

The growth of the proportion of the population that is middle class and the proliferation of middle classes has also not negated the persistence of income inequality (Smeeding 1991) and the growing proportions of the populations of industrial societies that are living in extreme poverty. The broad outlines of this 'new poverty' (Markland 1990) are becoming increasingly clear (Wacquant 1993; cf. Jencks and Petersen 1991; Townsend *et al.* 1987; Mingione 1991; Engbersen 1989). The existence of long-term joblessness or occupational marginality among sectors of the populations of these societies, and the growth of low-income areas characterised by multiple sources of deprivation for residents (Massey 1990) does not fit very well with Clark and Lipset's claims about the decline of 'traditional hierarchies'.

In general, the persistence of wealth and power at the top and growing poverty and degradation at the bottom of contemporary class structures suggests that Clark and Lipset's conclusions about the impending death of classes is premature. In the United States, the country which we know best, it is becoming increasingly common in urban communities for privileged professionals and managers to live in secluded enclaves and suburbs (often behind locked gates) or in secured high-rise condominiums, while marginalised sectors of the population are crowded into increasingly dangerous inner-city areas (a trend discussed at length by the new Secretary of Labor in the United States, Robert Reich, in a recent book: Reich 1991; Davis 1991). As long as such conditions prevail, we are sceptical that sociologists would be wise to abandon the concept of class, whatever other evidence might be adduced to show that the importance of class is declining.

Are Social Classes Dying? No

The evidence presented above should be enough to sustain our thesis that class divisions persist in post-industrial societies. But Clark and Lipset base their critique less on the existence of class divisions than on the supposed decline in the effects of class in three 'situses' (politics, the economy and the family) in these societies. We shall show that, even on their own terms, Clark and Lipset's empirical evidence cannot support their conclusions about the declining significance of class.

Politics

To demonstrate the declining significance of class in the political arena, Clark and Lipset attempt to show that class voting has declined [. . .]

Clark and Lipset seem to assume an unmediated connection between class and voting, ignoring completely the decisive role of unions, social movement organisations and political parties in shaping the conditions under which voters make choices. When parties and other political organisations are organised around class, high levels of class voting can be expected. Przeworski and Sprague's (1986) analysis of the dynamics of social democratic parties based originally on working-class votes suggests that the strategic decision of these parties to weaken their class-based appeals to seek middle-class votes – a trend celebrated in Lipset (1990) – has had a profound effect on the social bases of their political support. If workers' parties abandon or compromise their specific interests, does it mean those interests no longer exist? We say 'no'. Class interests may remain latent in the political arena, but this does not mean they do not exist.

Clark and Lipset flesh out their case for the declining significance of class for politics by arguing that the traditional left/right cleavages characteristic of democratic capitalist societies have increasingly given way to more complex, multidimensional political ideologies. Such a claim shifts the focus from class as a determinant of political views to class or class inequalities as an object of public opinion. Clark and Lipset repeat the assertion that there are now 'two lefts', one based on the economic demands of subordinates classes, the other stressing 'social issues' (see pp. 171–2; Lipset 1981). From this disjuncture of economy and society, they wish to infer that the class content of political struggles and public debate is declining. However, this contention is not supported by either the data they cite or by the existing research literature. For example, Weakliem's (1991) research on the dimensionality of class and voting casts doubt on the empirical adequacy of Clark and Lipset's interpretation of political trends. Weakliem finds that, while a second (plausibly post-materialist) dimension of politics is necessary to explain the relationship between class and party identification, it applies equally well to older and younger cohorts. The similarity of cohorts contradicts the claim that complexity is new, and Weakliem's crucial finding that 'all classes have been moving towards the post-materialist left' in his analysis of voting trends in Italy, the Netherlands and France (1991: 1350) leads us to reject Clark and Lipset's assertions about the 'two lefts'. In any case, the emergence or re-emergence of 'new' political issues, such as gender or the environment, does not mean that they are sufficient to displace or reconstitute fundamental dimensions such as the left–right split in politics [. . .]

In short, Clark and Lipset's evidence on class politics is incomplete and unconvincing. They have failed to make the case that class is declining in importance for politics. Class never was the all-powerful explanatory variable that some intellectual traditions assumed in earlier periods; class was always only one source of political identity and action alongside race, religion, nationality, gender and others. To say that class matters less now than it used to requires that one exaggerate its importance in the past and understate its importance at present. Class is important for politics to the extent that political organisations actively organise around class themes. Hence, in some periods the political consequences of class may appear latent, even if the underlying logic of class is unchanged. We would suggest that the same is true of other sources of social inequality. Race and gender, for example, have always been important to the social fabric of American society, but they have not always been central loci of political organisation and struggle. We believe that on balance, however, the evidence shows that class remains important, and that Clark and Lipset fail to demonstrate that class voting and traditional political values have declined.

Post-Industrial Economic Trends

Clark and Lipset argue that 'economic growth undermines hierarchical class stratification' (see p. 172). They argue markets are growing in relevance as a consequence of rising incomes, and that 'decentralised, demand-sensitive decision-making' is growing to meet ever more complex consumer demand (ibid.). While huge firms are in relative decline and smaller niche-oriented ventures are increasing in at least some countries (Sabel 1982), we question whether any of the other claims they make in this section can stand up to critical scrutiny.

We first note that Clark and Lipset's claims about the growing 'marketness' of capitalist societies in comparison to earlier periods is very difficult to sustain empirically (Block 1990: 56–66), and no substantial evidence is provided by these authors. Further, it ignores completely the steady and spectacular growth of the state throughout the course of the twentieth century in all industrial societies (Esping-Anderson 1990).

Even if Clark and Lipset's claims about growing marketness were true, there is good reason to question their analysis of how this affects class-based stratification. For example, they note that most good job growth in recent years has taken place in small firms. But they fail to point out that smaller firms are rarely able to offer their employees all of the income, benefits and job security of larger firms and that most unstable, low-paying jobs are located in small firms.

Clark and Lipset then argue that more advanced technologies make it 'harder . . . to plan in advance and control administratively' and that these economic changes are leading to a '*decline in traditional authority, hierarchy and class relations*' (see p. 173; emphasis in the original). Their discussion of technology takes the most optimistic conceivable scenarios as reality, ignoring the more complex institutional patterns actually emerging in post-industrial societies. The use of new management styles in response to the appearance of high technology is heavily dependent on the context in which it is embedded (Zuboff 1988; Shaiken 1984). In many firms, managers resist any transfer of authority to lower-level employees, even if the new, smart machines make possible a democratisation of decision-making within firms (Zuboff 1988). Far from eliminating class struggle, the introduction of new technology and management styles often creates new forms of class conflict. The jury is still out on the fate of hierarchy in post-industrial firms.

Finally, Clark and Lipset argue that economic growth is undermining 'local stratification hierarchies as markets grow – regionally, nationally, internationally'. Mills (1946) effectively countered such observations half a century ago by arguing that the gulf between decision centres in metropolitan skyscrapers and the dispersed loci of production and consumption was yet another layer of stratification, not a pattern that 'combines to undermine the familistic-quasi-monopolistic tradition of business hierarchy and class stratification patterns', as Clark and Lipset would have it.

Family

Clark and Lipset argue that the 'slimmed' family in post-industrial society has 'increasingly become characterised by more egalitarian relations . . . [as] hierarchical stratification has weakened' (see p. 173). While the patterns they refer to in support of these arguments (greater freedom of marriage and divorce, greater opportunities for women to work in the paid labour force, and the decline of extended family arrangements) are clearly important, they provide no evidence that the 'slimmed' family is a more egalitarian one. The modern family is a good deal more complex than Clark and Lipset imply (Connell 1987: 120–5). Research on contemporary family life suggests that while egalitarian beliefs are more widespread than in earlier periods, a clear gender division of labour remains in place in most families (Hochschild 1989). In the United States, for example, the evidence overwhelmingly suggests that the rise in female-headed 'slimmed' families with the liberalisation of divorce law has led to rising rates of poverty in female-headed families (Thistle 1992: Ch. 4; Weizman 1985). For the urban poor, the 'slimmed family' celebrated by Clark and Lipset is a major source of poverty and inequality (Wilson 1987). This is attributable in part to the positive association between husbands' and wives' occupations that increases differences among families even as differences within families decrease (Bianchi 1981; Hout 1982).

Under 'family', Clark and Lipset also address recent changes in social mobility, arguing that 'the slimmer family determines less the education and jobs of individual family members' and that 'social mobility studies show decreasing effects of parents' education and income in explaining children's occupational success' (citing Featherman and Hauser 1978; Hout 1988). However, Clark and Lipset fail to take due note of the sources of those changes. It is true that class origin affects students' progress through the educational systems of most industrial societies less than it used to, but the cause of diminished educational stratification is not less class-based selection but less selection of any kind at the early transitions where class matters most (Mare 1980, 1981). Replications of Mare's results for the United States in 15 industrial societies show that only Sweden, Hungary and the former Czechoslovakia had real declines in class-based selection (Shavit and Blossfeld 1992; Raftery and Hout 1993). In Hungary and Czechoslovakia political party tests replaced class selection; only Sweden saw a real growth in the openness of the educational stratification process [. . .]

Conclusion: Classes are not Dying

Class structures have undergone important changes in recent decades, with the rise of post-industrial societies. The birth of new sources of inequality does not imply the death of the old ones. In arguing that Clark and Lipset have failed to show that social classes are dying, we do not wish to imply that there have been no changes in the class structure of advanced capitalist societies, or in the association between class and other social phenomena. The manual working class has declined in recent decades in most countries, while the proportion of the labour force working in the service sector has increased. Such changes are important; they tell us that the nineteenth-century models of class are no longer adequate. Yet moving to more complex, multidimensional models of class does not imply that classes are dying. The persistence of class-based inequalities in capitalist societies suggest that in the foreseeable future the concept of class will – and should – play an important role in sociological research.

While the research evidence on the persistence of class as a factor in life chances and politics is abundant and convincing, explanations for that persistence are not. As a profession we have documented the parameters of class relations to a high degree of precision, while simultaneously demolishing the older theories that framed our work. We have discovered that class structures are more complex than Marxist and other theories that assign class structure a causal role in the evolution of societies and less subject to the calming effects of affluence that modernisation theories posit. The theoretical question for the next decade is 'Why is class so complex and why is it dependent on politics instead of determinative of politics?' As citizens and sociologists we would very much like to live in a world in which class inequalities have disappeared. But – to paraphrase Gramsci – class society is not yet dying, and truly classless societies have not yet been born.

From M. Hout, C. Brooks and J. Manza (1996) 'The persistence of classes in post-industrial societies', in D.J. Lee and B.S. Turner (eds) *Conflicts About Class: Debating Inequality in Late Industrialism*, Harlow: Addison Wesley Longman, pp. 49–59.

Questions

1. What do you understand by the criticism that Clark and Lipset 'persistently conflate class-based with non-class forms of stratification'.
2. Refer back to your summary of the three 'situses' outlined by Clark and Lipset (see Reading 29, Question 2).
   (a) How do Hout and colleagues criticise their arguments?
   (b) From your own experience of these situses, which position do you find most persuasive? Why?

Reading 31

The meritocratic ideal – unequal but fair?

PETER SAUNDERS

In his recent study Unequal but Fair? *Peter Saunders argues that while there are clear inequalities in contemporary British society, this does not mean it is necessarily unfair. He draws on a range of evidence to support his case that Britain is much more open than most people (and especially sociologists!) realise. This extract is taken from his discussion of the concept of meritocracy and, in particular, the difficulties inherent to it. After considering some of the early functionalist writers who assumed that modern advanced societies would need to operate according to meritocratic principles in order to sustain moral cohesion, Saunders looks at the criticisms of these assumptions through the work of Michael Young (1958) and Herrnstein and Murray (1994). He then considers the alternatives offered by egalitarianism and libertarianism. Despite these attacks the meritocratic 'ideal' has a far greater degree of general support from the British people than either the egalitarian or libertarian oppositions and he concludes that 'in modern society . . . there is a strong and shared sense of fairness and justice which demands that there be some link between individual talent and effort on the one hand and reward through occupational success on the other'.*

De We *Really* Want to Live in a Meritocratic Society?

The essence of a meritocratic society is that it offers individuals equal opportunities to become unequal. There is open competition for the most desirable, responsible and well-rewarded positions, and the most able and committed people generally succeed in attaining these positions.

It might be assumed that meritocracy is an ideal which is shared by virtually everybody. It seems to be a 'good thing', both for the society (for it ensures that the most talented people get into the key leadership positions) and for individuals themselves (for it respects and justly rewards individual achievement). Against this, however, a meritocracy can be an uncomfortable place in which to live, for it is inherently competitive, and it produces losers as well as winners. For this reason, the meritocracy ideal has many enemies, not least among egalitarians . . . I shall therefore move beyond discussion of the evidence about whether Britain is meritocratic to consider the broader question of whether meritocracy as an ideal can be defended against its critics.

The meritocracy ideal is an individualistic ideal in that it celebrates individual achievement. The notion that individuals should be allocated to social positions on the basis of their talents and hard work, rather than according to their station at birth, is a relatively recent development with its origins in the development of political liberalism in Europe [. . .]

Durkheim's analysis (of social solidarity, addressed in his book *The Division of Labour in Society*, 1960) represents a classic statement of the meritocracy ideal: class inequalities need not generate class antagonisms provided recruitment is open and the competition is fair, for it is in everybody's interest that the best people fill the top positions and that all individuals occupy the social roles to which they are naturally best suited.

This argument was subsequently further elaborated by sociologists in the USA in the 1950s who developed what they called a *functional theory of stratification*. Following Talcott Parsons, who saw that social stratification might contribute to social integration rather than tearing a society asunder, theorists like Kingsley Davis and Wilbert Moore proposed that societies need to recruit the most talented and able individuals to fill the most important positions, and that the only way of achieving this, short of physical coercion, is by means of some system of social inequality. They sought to demonstrate that the social positions of greatest functional importance (judged in terms of the number of other positions which depend upon them) tend in modern societies to be the most highly rewarded, and that a system of unequal financial rewards is necessary to encourage the most talented individuals to undergo the sacrifice of long-term training required by positions of high responsibility. Like Durkheim, therefore, the functionalist theorists of the 1950s believed that social stratification could represent part of the solution to the problem of social cohesion, rather than (as in Marx's theory) part of the cause. For this to happen, however, it was necessary that talent be recognised and rewarded appropriately.

How plausible is all this? Is meritocracy consistent with, even necessary for, social cohesion in modern societies? There is an altogether opposite view which suggests that a meritocratic society will end up tearing itself apart.

Michael Young, the sociologist who first coined the term 'meritocracy' in the 1950s, provides a clear and provocative statement of this second position. In *The Rise of the Meritocracy*, published in 1958, he developed a futuristic fable (a sort of 'social science fiction') purporting to be a social history of Britain written in the year 2034. His story tells of how an increasing premium had come to be placed on talent such that, by 1990, all individuals with high IQs were being recruited into the leading positions in society irrespective of their social backgrounds. This meant that the lower social strata were progressively stripped of their 'natural leaders' as talented individuals were selected out. Far from fostering social cohesion, as Durkheim would have predicted, this generated a festering resentment at the base of the society, for those individuals who remained in the lower strata were left to contemplate their own personal failure and could find nobody to blame but themselves. Residualised and marginalised by the stigma of failure, they were gradually attracted to a new form of radical populism aimed at replacing élitism based on intelligence with an egalitarian, classless society in which every individual was held in equal social esteem. Young's fable ends in the year 2033 when the Meritocracy was overthrown by a Populist revolt.

Young's thesis has recently been given credence from what might seem a very unlikely source. Richard Herrnstein and Charles Murray's *The Bell Curve* has attracted most attention for its claim that race and intelligence are related. The core thesis of the book, however, does not revolve around the issue of race. It is rather that meritocracy in the United States is generating a system of social stratification based upon 'cognitive classes', and that this threatens to undermine social cohesion.

Herrnstein and Murray base their analysis on two key propositions. First, class recruitment in the United States has become more open during the course of the twentieth century, and for the first time in its history, the most intelligent individuals are now being selected for élite membership irrespective of their social origins. The change has come about mainly through the expansion of higher education with college access now determined solely on the basis of ability. Secondly, the development of a high technology, knowledge-based society has meant that the number of jobs requiring high levels of intelligence and training has expanded, and that the market value of high intelligence has been rising. This means that the talented individuals from different social origins who get recruited into the 'cognitive élite' have been growing increasingly affluent.

As the brightest individuals are sucked out of the lower social strata, they come to form a relatively exclusive stratum based on membership of about a dozen main professions plus senior business executive positions. These people interact professionally and socially more or less exclusively with each other and have little realistic understanding of what is going on elsewhere in the society. Meanwhile, at the opposite end of the spectrum, those of low intelligence are left in an increasingly homogenous lower class, and the least intelligent are now congregating in a burgeoning underclass which is associated with the rise of many linked social problems [. . .]

The most likely outcome of all of this, according to the authors, is the strengthening of a 'custodial state' designed to maintain order through intensified intervention and surveillance while leaving the 'cognitive élite' free to go about its business. In short, meritocracy is producing social fragmentation and polarisation.

Both Young and Herrnstein and Murray are pointing in their different ways to a problem which Durkheim and the functionalist sociologists of the 1950s completely overlooked. Meritocracy might work for those who have 'merit', but it seems to offer little to those who do not. Why should those at the bottom, those who fail, accept the results of meritocratic selection as binding upon them? Why should they accept that their intellectual 'superiors' should become their economic, social and political superiors?

This question raises three related issues associated with the growth of meritocracy. First, how can a meritocracy secure legitimacy in the eyes of those who fail (the problem of legitimation)? Second, how can it meet the expectations of those who succeed (the problem of 'positional goods')? And third, how can it avoid the paradox that human dissatisfaction often increases as opportunities expand (the problem of 'relative deprivation')? As society becomes more genuinely open, more genuinely meritocratic, so these three issues are likely to become ever more acute.

The problem of *legitimation* turns on the question of effective socialisation. If social position is determined at birth (as in a caste system), it is possible to prepare each generation for its fate. No false hopes are raised, no possibility of improving one's situation can be entertained. If social position is determined by a long-running talent contest, however, each generation spends its formative years anticipating the possibility of success, and the problem then arises of how to placate the eventual losers. Given that a meritocracy must be an open system, there is always likely to be a problem in educating the eventual losers to accept their fate [. . .]

This brings us to the second issue, the problem of *positional goods.* Put simply, the problem here is that, the more people who are enabled to succeed, the less value attaches to success and the more severe are the penalties of failure. Higher education is a classic 'positional good' – the more people who have it, the less valuable it becomes as a means of entering top positions, but the greater is the penalty for those who fail to get access to it at all, for a higher qualification becomes the prerequisite for entry to all sorts of jobs which previously did not demand it.

Applied specifically to the phenomenon of social mobility and occupational selection, this means that membership of the middle-class is likely to be less advantageous the bigger that class becomes. When everybody else is working-class, it is a huge bonus to achieve upward mobility into the middle-class, but when such movement becomes common, the advantages decline. The more the opportunities for social mobility open up, therefore, the less they seem to offer. In such a situation, it is easy to see how a more open and fluid society may become a less cohesive and contented one.

This in turn leads us to the third issue, the problem of *relative deprivation.* There is a long and fascinating history of sociological research which demonstrates that individual dissatisfaction has more to do with relative than with absolute deprivation, and that the most acute resentment is often felt in situations of widening opportunity. In his classic analysis of data on satisfaction with promotion prospects in the American military, for example, Robert Merton found that those units with the highest promotion rates recorded the lowest levels of satisfaction, and vice versa. He reasoned that this was because high rates of promotion encouraged those in the ranks to compare themselves with those who had been elevated, with the result that they felt aggrieved at being passed over. Low promotion rates, on the other hand, encouraged identification with others remaining in the same position as oneself, and therefore fostered greater contentment.

The implications of this for social mobility in society as a whole are obvious. With limited rates of social mobility, nobody expects to move up, and everybody is fairly contented with their lot. With extensive social mobility, many people move up, and those who are left behind begin to compare their situation unfavourably with that of their more successful peers. It is in this sense that a move to greater meritocracy is likely to generate increased frustration and resentment in society.

It seems that the ideology of meritocracy can be almost self-defeating. The more opportunities are held open for people, the more difficult it is likely to become to get those who fail to accept the result as legitimate, the less likely it is that those who succeed will feel any great sense of benefit, and the more resentful people are likely to become when they fail to emulate the success of their neighbours. These problems do not necessarily threaten social breakdown and fragmentation, but they can generate widespread disillusionment among successes and failures alike.

If meritocracy turns out to be so problematic, what are the alternatives? Assuming that we do not wish to return to the pre-modern system of social placement based on birth and inherited privilege (and even if we did, it is difficult to see, realistically, how we could), there are two major contenders.

The first, egalitarianism, is favoured by most contemporary critics of meritocracy. It would mean rejecting individual ability and effort as legitimate means by which people may strive to improve their situation relative to others, and moving increasingly to a system where status hierarchies are flattened and rewards are distributed with reference to some principle of a common citizenship entitlement. The second, libertarianism, favours abandoning altogether any attempt to link the allocation of social rewards to some principle of just or 'fair' allocation, and accepting as legitimate any outcome provided it has not arisen from the explicit application of physical force.

The *egalitarian* case against meritocracy is essentially that it is morally wrong to reward people on the basis of their talents (and, perhaps, also their effort).

Where meritocracy requires only equality of opportunity as the criterion of 'social justice', egalitarianism requires equality of outcomes ('end-state' equality).

There are two variants to the egalitarian critique of meritocracy. The first is already familiar to us, for it holds that there are no innate differences of ability between people and that talent, like effort, is merely the product of a privileged environment. Rewarding ability is thus tantamount to rewarding the children of the more privileged classes, which means that meritocracy turns out to be just another way in which dominant classes try to justify their continuing hold on top positions in society.

[. . .] Many sociologists have adopted this line of attack, and it is one which remains common within so-called 'progressive' circles to this day. Egalitarians basically dislike the idea of selection and competition and they would prefer a situation where there are no losers. They particularly dislike meritocratic selection because it seems to justify inequalities which they would prefer did not exist [. . .]

This kind of argument is clearly vulnerable to the growing weight of evidence that there are natural differences between people, and this has given rise to the second variant of the egalitarian critique of meritocracy. This grudgingly accepts that there may be some innate differences between people, but denies that this is any reason to reward them differently. This is a much more interesting and challenging version of the argument, for it poses the pertinent question of why individuals should expect to be rewarded for talents which they were lucky enough to be born with and which they have themselves done nothing to deserve.

This is the position adopted by A.H. Halsey, John Goldthorpe's principal collaborator on the Nuffield College social mobility project, for he explicitly denies that what he calls the 'liberal principle of "justice as desert"' should be accepted as the criterion of social fairness. The argument has recently been reiterated by Gordon Marshall and Adam Swift in a critique of my work on social mobility. Even if it were the case, they say, that ability alone determined class destinations, why should we equate ability with individual 'merit'? As they put it:

> It [is] particularly apt to ask whether an inherited characteristic – genetically determined intelligence – is an appropriate basis for reward at all. A crucial issue here would seem to be the distinction between those attributes for which the individual can claim responsibility and those which are his or hers merely by chance. If someone possesses particular talents or skills merely as a result of the natural lottery then it is not clear how justice is served by rewarding such possession.

[. . .]

[With regard to the] libertarian conception of fairness based in a theory of just entitlement. Robert Nozick has outlined such an approach with great clarity. He argues that rewards follow entitlement and that entitlement can be established through three principles – just acquisition (established by producing resources oneself or through the freely contracted help of others), just transfer (through voluntary gifts or exchange), and rectification of past injustices (i.e. reallocation of resources in those cases where either of the first two principles has been violated). Put into practice, this means that individuals have a right to the money they have earned and to the money which others have freely given them.

Nozick's theory seems to pose a problem for the meritocracy ideal, however, for it is a theory of entitlement, not a theory of just deserts. It has nothing to say about rewarding talent or effort as such. It will often be the case, of course, that talented and hard working people end up establishing entitlement to substantial rewards, but this is in a sense incidental. Lazy people with little ability might also end up rich or successful – they might simply happen to find themselves in the right place at the right time, or they might inherit a company from their parents, or they might scoop the jackpot on the National Lottery. Luck, caprice, fluke, effort, all are equally legitimate as a basis for reward provided they involve no direct coercion of other people. The question of whether people deserve their good fortune is, for Nozick, irrelevant.

A similar argument is found in the work of Friedrich Hayek. With disarming frankness, he accepts that market capitalism can sometimes reward those whom we tend to think of as undeserving while meting out harsh treatment to those who display genuine merit. The talented individual who works hard but fails to find a market for his or her services will fail, just as the rogue who manages to convince others that they want what he or she is offering will succeed. For Hayek, there is nothing wrong with this, and nothing to be done about it. He assures us that in a free society, it will normally be the case that rewards flow to those individuals who put their talents to good use in providing a genuine service of value to other people, but he resists the idea that such an outcome should be engineered or enforced simply because we think of it as desirable:

> However able a man may be in a particular field, the value of his services is necessarily low in a free society unless he also possesses the capacity of making his ability known to those who can derive the greatest benefit from it. Though it may offend our sense of justice to find that of two men who by equal effort have acquired the same specialized skill and knowledge, one may be a success and the other a failure, we must recognize that in a free society it is the use of particular opportunities that determines usefulness . . . In a free society we are remunerated not for our skill but for using it rightly.

This is a hard-nosed position which makes no compromises. Hayek is, of course, critical of the egalitarian position, arguing that the inherent differences between individuals mean that end-state equality could only be achieved by treating them unequally (i.e. unfairly). But, in the end, he is just as critical of the meritocratic position, arguing (like Marshall and Swift) that there is no credit to be claimed for talents which one happens to have acquired by accident of genetics, and that a meritocratic society would undermine liberty by fixing rewards according to people's attributes rather than according to their entitlements. For Hayek, as for Nozick, all that matters is that we should come by our success without coercing others, not that we should 'deserve' it.

It seems that having saved the meritocratic ideal from the egalitarian critique, we have ended up losing it again through a retreat into libertarianism. Neither egalitarians nor libertarians have any reason to be particularly interested in the kind of analysis of social mobility developed in this book, for neither sees any good reason why we should be concerned about rewarding talent and hard work. For egalitarians, what matters is that people should get the same at the end of the day, so if I end up in a low-paid, low status job because I have no aptitude for anything better, and you end up in a well-paid high status job because you work every hour of the day and pursue your ambition to its limits, the results are deemed unjust because they are unequal. For libertarians, what matters is that people should be able to keep whatever they happen to have freely acquired, so if I have no talent but am given a good job because my brother is on the Board, and if you are bright and committed but are denied an appointment because my brother happens to dislike the look of your face, no injustice has been done. Starting from opposite extremes, these two critiques of meritocracy meet, absurdly, in the middle.

Against both of these positions, the underlying premise of this book has been that it does matter why people end up in the positions they do. Both the egalitarian and libertarian positions have some intuitive sense to them, but in the end, they both founder on the fact that, in a modern society like contemporary Britain, there is a strong and shared sense of fairness and justice which demands that there be some link between individual talent and effort on the one hand, and reward through occupational success on the other.

Consistently with the egalitarian position, most of us do feel some sympathy for those who fail, but we also generally demand to know whether this has followed from their own stupidity or recklessness or was a result of circumstances largely beyond their control. This is precisely why the social welfare system for so many centuries attempted to distinguish the 'deserving' poor from the 'undeserving' and to treat them differently, and it is why so many people today feel angry at the thought egalitarianism is always qualified by the question of just desert.

The same is true of support for libertarianism. Consistently with the libertarian position, few of *us* feel genuinely aggrieved by those who make good simply because they are 'lucky'. National Lottery jackpot winners are not widely resented for their good fortune, and although we may feel some envy when we hear of somebody who has come into an inheritance or has stumbled upon a new invention which makes them a millionaire, most of us simply shrug, smile, and mutter 'Good luck to them!' We do, however, resent those who get to positions of wealth and influence through nepotism or the mobilisation of privileged social networks rather than through open competition, and we get justifiably angry about the allocation of positions on the basis of ascribed rather than achieved characteristics (e.g. allocation of jobs by race or gender rather than by talent or effort is widely held to be offensive).

Why are we generally happy to help out people who fall on hard times but not those who are feckless? Why are we happy to let lucky people enjoy their good fortune but not those who have gained success by virtue of their family connections? The common factor in all of this is a sense of fairness which holds that we should all be treated according to the same criteria. If I have to work in order to gain a living, then others who are also capable of working should not expect to live off my earnings. If I have to compete on the basis of my talent and effort in order to get a good job, then others should not be able to walk into top positions simply because they play golf with the boss's son. The lottery winner does not offend us because the rules are clear and we can all buy a ticket, and the beneficiary of a will does not offend us because we can all transfer money to anybody we wish. It is when the rules are bent such as to favour one party over another that the collective sense of justice gets badly bruised [. . .]

There is, in the end, something unsatisfactory about a libertarian ethic which allows the 'deserving' to be disadvantaged without even trying to do anything about it, just as there is something unsatisfactory about an egalitarian ethic which allows the 'undeserving' to be advantaged without even trying to prevent it. Libertarians do have a problem in justifying caprice or bigotry as the basis for rewarding one individual while denying another, just as egalitarians do have a problem in justifying laziness or stupidity as legitimate grounds for doling out resources which other people have earned. Because both positions refuse to be drawn on the issue of merit, neither finally satisfies that generalised sense of fair competition on which the legitimacy of modern capitalist societies ultimately depends.

A few years ago, I organised a survey in which a sample of the British population was asked to respond to three different statements about the 'fairest' way to establish individual entitlement to material resources. One of these statements represented the egalitarian ideal that 'people's incomes should be made more equal by taxing higher earners'. Just over half of the sample agreed with this while around one-third disagreed. A second statement expressed the free market, libertarian position that 'people's incomes should depend on market demand for their services'. Again, something more than a half of respondents agreed and around one-third disagreed. The final statement reflected the meritocratic ideal that 'people's incomes should depend on hard work and ability'. Fully 90 per cent of respondents agreed with this with fewer than 10 per cent disagreeing. Few moral principles can command universal assent in a modern, pluralistic, individualistic society, but meritocracy clearly comes pretty close.

This strong support for meritocracy relative to the other two positions reflects the fact that most of us understand that inequality is not necessarily 'unfair' – it depends on whether it is justifiable with reference to individual talent and individual effort. If we are convinced that, by and large, those who have the ability and who make an effort can usually find success, and that those who do not will not generally prosper, then the basis is laid for a society which should be able to function reasonably harmoniously. Meritocracy does have a problem in dealing with the social consequences of failure, but this need not be catastrophic as regards social cohesion provided the competition is known to have been fair. Ninety per cent agreement is not a bad basis on which to build and sustain a moral social order.

From P. Saunders (1996) *Unequal but Fair? A Study of Class Barriers in Britain*, London: Institute of Economic Affairs, pp. 76–90.

Questions

1. According to Young and Herrnstein and Murray, what are the social and political consequences of genuine meritocracy?
2. Summarise the egalitarian and libertarian objections to a society which rewards merit.
3. To what extent do you agree with Saunders' conclusion that a meritocratic system is essentially a fair one?
4. Using your sociology course textbooks carry out a simple content analysis to examine Saunders' claim that sociology encourages an 'obsession' with social class and class barriers. You could carry out a follow-up analysis of television drama and soap operas to see if they too reflect a British obsession with class.

Reading 32

Social stratification in Europe

HOWARD DAVIS

In this reading, Davis takes a European perspective on social stratification and examines the differences between countries and the structural features they share. He starts with a brief review of the changing patterns of distribution of income, wealth and poverty in various European countries. On the basis of this evidence, Davis then suggests that it is possible to distinguish four basic occupational categories that are relevant across most European societies. The rest of the extract includes his discussion of this 'composite classification' as he puts it.

The division of societies into social strata defined by differences of wealth, income, power and prestige is one of the most complex and fascinating problems of social and political analysis. Structured social inequalities are the key to answering the fundamental question: what kind of society is this and how is it changing? From a European perspective, the question concerns both the differences between countries and the structural features which they have in common. Are some more equal than others? Do they share similar characteristics because they have market economies? Do differences arise when they pursue alternative social policies? [This extract] addresses these topics through a broadly comparative approach, beginning with a discussion of some of the concepts which are necessary for the analysis of social stratification. It then considers the patterns in a range of European countries using available economic and social data to show how these patterns are changing.

[. . .]

The Distribution of Income, Wealth and Poverty

[. . .]

Studies spanning several decades have shown that there is a very skewed pattern of income distribution in the European countries, which, for most

Table 1 *Poverty in the EC, 1985, defined as households or persons receiving 50 per cent or less of the respective national average*

	% households	% persons
Belgium	6.3	7.1
Denmark	8.0	7.9
FR Germany	10.3	10.5
Greece	20.5	21.5
Spain	20.3	20.9
France	18.0	19.1
Ireland	18.5	18.4
Italy	12.0	14.1
Netherlands	6.9	9.6
Portugal	31.4	32.4
UK	14.1	14.6
EUR 12	14.1	15.5

Source: Eurostat 1990; figures for Luxembourg unavailable

of the postwar period, has been moving slowly towards more equality. However, the late 1970s saw a reversal in this trend in the United Kingdom and probably in many other European countries as a result of economic recession and the rightward shift in economic policy. In order to make comparisons across time and between countries, the total income at a particular time is divided up into the 'shares' which various sections of the population receive. Thus, in the 1960s, the share of the top 20 per cent was 44.2 per cent of total income in the United Kingdom, 52.9 per cent in West Germany and 53.7 per cent in France. The proportion in Sweden was 44.0 per cent (Atkinson 1983: 26). A decade later, the same differences could be found between these countries, but at somewhat lower levels.

[. . .]

According to these general comparisions, the postwar trend has therefore been in the direction of more equality, but a closer inspection of the effects of taxation and welfare shows that the benefits of redistribution have not been evenly spread throughout society. The Royal Commission on the Distribution of Income and Wealth examined this issue closely in the United Kingdom and found that, although the wealth of the top 1 per cent was much reduced by the 1970s, much of the redistribution occurred within the top 10 per cent. The intermediate groups have received a larger share of the redistribution than the poorest, whose position, according to a comparative study by Lawson and George (1980), improved only very slightly or not at all in the period up to 1980. In 1985 the top 1 per cent still owned 20 per cent of net personal wealth and the top 10 per cent more than half. The overall effect of economic growth on social inequality is, to use a familiar illustration, like the effect of a marching column: the column advances and the last rank (or most of it, at least) eventually passes the point which was reached by the vanguard some time before. The distance between the front and the rear does not change as the column moves forward. Although the rich have stayed rich or become richer, the position of the poor remains relatively unchanged. However they are defined, the poor continue to make up a large proportion of the European population, largely because of low incomes and unemployment. The 'poverty line' according to an EC definition, is an income half or less than half of the country's national average income per person. The countries which have levels of poverty above 15 per cent of the population include Portugal, Greece, Spain and Ireland, which are on the periphery of Europe and less developed. The lowest levels of poverty (below 10 per cent) are in Belgium, Denmark and The Netherlands. Italy and the United Kingdom are near average in the intermediate category. The United Kingdom has been moving in the direction of the 'peripheral' countries with a high level of poverty (18 per cent in 1990) through a combination of economic recession and rigid government policies on transfer payments.

[. . .]

Stratification and Social Consciousness

[. . .]

We can now integrate the analysis of the market situation of each stratum (defined by the source and amount of wealth and income) with their social situation (defined by their occupation or position within the division of labour and system of authority relations). These are connected in turn with differences of status and lifestyle. A composite classification which is relevant to most European societies will include the following categories:[1]

1. a capitalist class, comprising business proprietors, and owners of large-scale shareholdings, land and property
2. a service class, comprising two strata: directors, managers and higher-grade professional employees; and lower-grade professionals, managers and technical workers
3. a working class, comprising two strata: clerical, secretarial and routine non-manual workers; and skilled manual workers
4. a lower working class: comprising semi- and unskilled manual workers and those who regularly depend on state benefits because of low wages or unemployment.

The 'capitalist class' is the smallest but the most powerful of the categories. In modern industrial societies this stratum, which includes members of the economic, political and cultural élites, forms about 1 per cent of the total population. Although much of their wealth and power is hidden from general view, their importance is not diminished by their lack of conspicuous consumption. The character of this stratum varies between countries according to their patterns of history and social development. In Britain, the term 'establishment' is often used to describe the typical relationships and patterns of influence which operate within the ruling group. The oldest of the industrial societies, Britain has long since combined the features of the old aristocracy with the capitalist class to form a relatively cohesive ruling group defined by its control over the industrial firms and banks which dominate the economy, its monopoly of social privilege, and its capacity to steer the political system. Although it is no longer entirely based on leading families, there are closely interlocking social networks which are reinforced from one generation to the next by the exclusive mechanisms of private education. It has a cohesive culture which is based on a shared conception of the 'nation' and the identification of the national interest with its own interests. It exercises its power in subtle ways, as Coates says, protecting itself through 'its own exclusivity, low public profile, and astute public orchestration of the pre-capitalist institutions of monarchy and aristocracy' (in Bottomore and Brym 1989: 43).

The character of the capitalist class in France derives from the structure of capital and the distinctive role of the state in promoting a technocracy in public administration. The relatively late arrival of industrialisation in France meant that even as late as the 1970s, half of the 200 largest companies were still family-controlled. Marceau (1989) has described how the restructuring of capital in the subsequent decades brought about a convergence between owners and controllers of capital so that, through family ties, similarities of education, and parallel career paths in public administration or industry, the distinction between ownership and control has become relatively unimportant. The *grandes écoles*, the élite institutions of higher education, are the proving grounds for talent and sustain a modern form of legitimacy for the ruling class, namely 'technocracy', which is sufficiently broad to include the exercise of power through both private and public institutions. The Paris-based élitist technocracy of France complements the inegalitarian social system and has at least as much social and political homogeneity as its parallel stratum in Britain. It retains its legitimacy not through the acceptance of tradition but because the mechanisms of exclusion are ostensibly designed to create professional rulers rather than privilege for its own sake.

In contrast to both Britain and France, which have distinctive capitalist classes, Germany has no easily identifiable ruling group. There are several reasons for this, including the discontinuities resulting from the Second World War, the enhanced opportunities for mobility into the economic élite during the postwar boom period, and the attempt systematically to integrate all social strata into the social market economy. This does not mean that there is no capitalist class in Germany, only that it has greater fluidity and less social and political cohesion than in Britain and France. As Ardagh observes, its prosperity and lack of inherited privilege makes the stratification of German society more like that of the United States than any other country in Europe (1988: 146).

This comparison between the capitalist classes in three European countries illustrates the fact that countries with a broadly similar range of social inequality may exhibit varying degrees of permeability across their social boundaries. In an extreme case, a highly unequal and élitist social system could nevertheless be called 'open' if it encouraged a high rate of social mobility. In contrast, a relatively egalitarian society could be called 'closed' if it had powerful exclusionary mechanisms to discourage movement between strata. Studies of social mobility have to contend with some of the most intractable problems of international data comparison, and it is impossible to do justice to this question here.

[. . .]

The most striking development in the stratification system in recent decades has been the growth of the professional and managerial strata and the corresponding decrease in manual occupations in manufacturing industry. The rise of what is often called the 'service class', with a vast array of new occupations, creates problems of definition as well as difficulties in interpreting its political significance. It is not simply a question of the expansion of the 'middle classes' or white-collar employment generally, although on average nearly two-thirds of all workers in Western European economies are in service occupations (that is, not in agricultural or industrial occupations). It concerns the emergence of a new and powerful stratum within the broad category of services with its own distinctive economic position and social identity. According to Goldthorpe's definition, the service class includes professionals, administrators and managers whose positions involve the application of specialised knowledge within the framework of bureaucratic organisations, whether public or private (Goldthorpe 1982). The increasing scale, complexity and rationalisation of the capitalist productive system has created the need for this stratum to control and coordinate the functions of capital on behalf of the capitalist class. It typically accounts for between 10 and 25 per cent of all employees. Their distinctiveness comes from a strong market situation owing to their professional expertise, combined with a work situation which allows a high degree of autonomy and discretion.

Previous arguments about the service class (for example, Dahrendorf 1963) were naturally concerned with its political orientation, yet they found it difficult to reach a conclusion. The service relationship to capital implied that their chief loyalty would be to the ruling group but the influence of advanced education, the experience of mobility and the ideology of rationality and progress appeared to give the service class a certain independence from the conservative culture and politics of the superordinate stratum. More recent evidence of service-class formation in three European countries (Erikson, Goldthorpe and Portocarero 1979) points to other reasons for divided loyalties. The very rapid growth of the service class has encouraged recruitment from a wide range of social strata, including the working class. Their closeness to working-class origins and social heterogeneity suggests that a new class identity has not had sufficient time to develop. The 'demographic' and 'sociocultural' identity of the stratum has so far been inhibited (Goldthorpe 1982: 174–5). This tends to be confirmed by studies carried out in individual countries. In France, for example, Boltanski (1987) made a study of *cadres* but found it impossible to identify precise boundaries or collective action based on common attributes and shared interests. What is likely, as the service class matures, is that it will find a place which is more than simply an appendage of the capitalist class but one which is unlikely to bring it into conflict with the class above. As the process of economic and political integration in Europe develops, the role of the service class will be enhanced through its characteristics of expertise, mobility and relative lack of commitment to traditional or national culture.

The fate of the working class across Europe has provoked writers in many countries to pronounce on its demise, its transformation or even its reincarnation. The universal and incontrovertible facts are these: that the mass-employment manufacturing industries which were the backbone of working-class communities and labour organisations have either been eliminated through global competition or altered out of recognition by the application of new technologies; that there has been a numerical decline in the main categories of working-class occupations; and trade unions have suffered a significant decline in membership. This has radically altered the framework for the interpretation for the sociology of this stratum. In the 1950s and 1960s the participation of workers in the new prosperity seemed to be a part of the process of integration of the formerly dichotomous and conflictual class structure. For more than a decade, research focused on the evidence for '*embourgeoisement*' and indicators of change or decline in the patterns of industrial and class conflict (Goldthorpe *et al.* 1969). Today, the themes of fragmentation and even destruction of the working class are ascendant, as economic recession, technological change and the collapse of socialism in Eastern Europe have created a radically different set of conditions.

[. . .]

One of the advantages for the employer is that job demarcations are removed and working practices are made more flexible. The position of the employee is likely to deteriorate into one of low security, low wages and low opportunity.

There is no sharp boundary between relatively disadvantaged workers and the unemployed. There is a case for describing the latter (and the poor generally) as an 'underclass' because they are not fully integrated into the class structure (Dahrendorf 1987). The case against describing them in this way is that the condition of unemployment is, for the majority who escape long-term unemployment, intermittent, and there is constant movement up and down the lower ranks of the working class. The fact that poverty may be a result of low wages, stage in the lifecycle or single-parent status as well as unemployment suggests that the new poor are part of a working class which has become increasingly fragmented. Dependency on income from employment may be exchanged for dependency on the state, but this does not always involve a radical transition in income or status.

[. . .]

The detailed study of social stratification in European societies has usually been carried out in the context of single societies. Some studies compare two, or not usually more than three, countries. There are certainly no equivalent social data to match the continuous and detailed monitoring of economic performance throughout Europe. This makes it difficult to draw general conclusion. However, there is a family resemblance between the systems of social stratification in the European countries because they have in common the same, and increasingly internationalised, capitalist production and market system. They also have in common the features of state welfare. These two aspects of contemporary society create the framework for social differentiation. We have seen that within this framework there is considerable room for variation both in the objective features which divide the strata and in the subjective responses and collective action which they may inspire. In thinking about comparative stratification it is prudent to bear in mind the following advice from a discussion of the do's and don't's of class analysis (Giddens 1982: 164–6).

The first rule is not to extrapolate from short-term trends. Each decade of the postwar period has brought its own style of sociological analysis and interpretation: from the promise of 'classlessness' in the years of the economic miracle to the resurgence of class and class conflict in the 1970s, and the 'recomposition of class' in the 1980s. Too much emphasis on the short term leads to perceptions of change which overlook the continuities of social structure and exaggerate the speed of current developments.

The second rule is not to generalise from a single society. The United States can hardly be used today, as it was in the past, as the prototype of industrialism, and as a symbol of the European future, because Japan and the European societies themselves show the possibility of viable alternative paths of development. Perhaps the contemporary illusion for Europeans is the idea of an integrated 'European society' to which all the individual countries will converge. Whether this is seen in a positive or a negative light, the evidence does not support the idea that national societies will be rapidly subsumed into a common type.

The third rule is to accept the contingent character of social change, not to assume that there is a single force or tendency causing societies to develop along a predetermined path. The interaction between the class dynamic of the economic system and the citizenship dynamic of the state welfare system best illustrates this point in the European societies. The interplay of similar structures and processes can lead to a variety of outcomes.

Finally, there is an increasingly important rule, which is to recognise the international context of social change and to use comparative evidence as far as possible. Social analysis has been no less insular and national in its concern than most other aspects of society. The dearth of good comparative social data is an obstacle which will have to be removed if we are to gain a better understanding of the divisions and conflicts within social Europe.

Note

1. This is applicable to the capitalist societies of western Europe, not to state socialism in eastern Europe, where the boundaries of stratification were defined by the party-state system and not by the market. Recent changes in these countries are likely to bring about some convergence towards the western types of stratification. For a discussion of the contrasts between the capitalist and state socialist forms of stratification, see Davis and Scase (1985).

From H.H. Davis (1998) 'Social stratification in Europe', in J. Bailey (ed.) *Social Europe*, Harlow: Addison Wesley Longman, pp. 17–35.

Questions

1. What problems might a researcher find in trying to compare patterns of income, wealth and poverty across different countries?
2. Take each of the four class grouping suggested by Davis and summarise (a) the basic similarities; and (b) any differences that exist within each.

Reading 33

Inequalities in health

PETER TOWNSEND AND NICK DAVIDSON

In 1980 the British government published a report, Inequalities in Health, *more generally known as* The Black Report, *after Sir Douglas Black, the chair of the working party who produced the report. It was widely seen as one of the most significant pieces of research into the nation's health and it has become a key study in the Sociology of Health. This extract starts by detailing some of the Report's findings on the pattern of health inequalities, in particular the relationship between mortality and occupational class, gender, regional background and race. It then highlights the extent of inequalities in the use of Health Service facilities: for instance, the tendency for women from non-manual backgrounds to make much greater use of antenatal care and cervical screening services than those from manual backgrounds. The findings of* The Black Report, *such as the recommendation for further investment in the NHS and the need to tackle socioeconomic inequality in order for health inequality to be eroded, had serious political implications. The response to the Report from the British government at the time – a new Conservative administration led by Margaret Thatcher – has become almost as notorious as the findings. The Secretary of State for Health stated that he could not endorse the recommendations; and the authors of the report described how the Report itself was suppressed: 'Instead of being properly printed and published . . . only 260 duplicated copies of the typescript were made available in the week of the August Bank Holiday.'*

The Pattern of Present Health Inequalities

Inequalities in health take a number of distinctive forms in Britain today . . . But undoubtedly the clearest and most unequivocal – if only because there is more evidence to go on – is the relationship between occupational class and mortality [. . .]

Occupational class and mortality

Every death in Britain is a registered and certified event in which both the cause and the occupation of the deceased or his or her next of kin are recorded. By taking the actual incidence of death among members of the Registrar General's occupational classes and dividing this by the total in each occupational class it is possible to derive an estimate of class differences in mortality. This shows that on the basis of figures drawn from the early 1970s, when the most recent decennial survey was conducted, men and women in occupational class V had a two-and-a-half times greater chance of dying before reaching retirement age than their professional counterparts in occupational class I (Table 1). Even when allowance is made for the fact that there are more older people in unskilled than professional work, the probability of death before retirement is still double.

What lies behind this gross statistic? Where do we begin to look for an explanation? If we break it down by age we find that class differences in mortality are a constant feature of the entire human life-span. They are found at birth, during the first year of life, in childhood, adolescence and adult life. At *any* age people in occupational class V have a higher rate of death than their better-off counterparts. This is not to say that the differences are uniform; in general they are more marked at the start of life and, less obviously, in early adulthood.

At birth and during the first month of life the risk of death in families of unskilled workers is double that of professional families. Children of skilled manual fathers (occupational class III M) run a 1.5 times greater risk. For the next eleven months of a child's life this ratio widens still further. For the death of every one male infant of professional parents, we can expect almost two among children of skilled manual workers and three among children of unskilled manual workers. Among females the ratios are even greater [. . .]

Now let us look at some other criteria for dividing the population which have a bearing on any attempt to describe the 'structure' of health among the population.

Sex differences in mortality

The gap in life expectancy between men and women is one of the most distinctive features of human health in the advanced societies. As Table 1 indicates, the risk of death for men in each occupational class is almost twice that of women, the cumulative product of health inequalities between the sexes during the whole lifetime. It suggests that gender and class exert highly significant but different influences on the quality and duration of life in modern society.

It is also a gap in life expectancy which carries important implications for all spheres of social policy, but especially health, since old age is a time

Table 1 *Death rates by sex and social (occupational) class (15–64 years) rates per 1000 population, England and Wales, 1971*

Social (occupational) class	Males	Females	Ratio M/F
I (Professional)	3.98	2.15	1.85
II (Intermediate)	5.54	2.85	1.94
III N (Skilled non-manual)	5.80	2.76	1.96
III M (Skilled manual)	6.08	3.41	1.78
IV (Partly skilled)	7.96	4.27	1.87
V (Unskilled)	9.88	5.31	1.86
Ratio V/I	2.5	2.5	

when demand for health care is at its greatest and the dominant pattern of premature male mortality adds the exacerbating problem of isolation for many women.

Although attempts have been made to explain the differences between the sexes, comparatively little systematic work exists on the aetiology of the mortality and morbidity differences between men and women and much remains to be disentangled. Women suffer uniquely from some diseases and it would be wrong, for example, to assume too readily that all wives share the same living conditions or even standards as their husbands. Some men have the advantage, for instance, not only of a preferential diet at home but subsidized meals at work. Where both husband and wife are in paid employment, the meals they get in the day, as well as working conditions and the nature of the work, may be radically different. There is a great deal more research to be undertaken to sort out these various influences.

Regional differences in mortality

Mortality rates also vary considerably between the regions which make up the United Kingdom. Using them as an indicator of health, the healthiest part of Britain appears to be the southern belt below a line drawn across the country from the Wash to the Bristol Channel [. . .]

Race, ethnicity and health

Another important dimension of inequality in contemporary Britain is race. Immigrants to this country from the so-called New Commonwealth, whose ethnic identity is clearly visible in the colour of their skin, are known to experience greater difficulty in finding work and adequate housing (Smith 1976). Given these disabilities it is to be expected that they might also record rather higher than average rates of mortality and morbidity.

This hypothesis is difficult to test from official statistics, since 'race' has rarely been assessed in official censuses and surveys. Moreover it is far from clear what indicator should be utilized in any such assessment – skin colour, place of birth, nationality – and the most significant may depend on the precise issue of interest . . . What little evidence that has been accumulated, however, does suggest that the children of immigrants do suffer from certain specific health disabilities related to cultural factors such as diet or to their lack of natural immunity to certain infectious diseases (Thomas 1968; Oppé 1967; Gans 1966). Studies based on small samples of immigrant children have pointed to the possibility of higher-than-average morbidity associated with material deprivation, but the evidence is scarce and somewhat inconclusive and needs to be augmented by further research (Hood *et al.* 1970) [. . .]

Summary

There are marked inequalities in health between the social classes in Britain . . . Mortality rates are taken as the best available indicator of the health of different social, or more strictly occupational classes and socio-economic groups. Mortality tends to rise inversely with falling occupational rank or status, for both sexes and at all ages. At birth and in the first month of life twice as many babies of unskilled manual parents as of professional parents die, and in the next eleven months of life four times as many girls and five times as many boys, respectively, die. In later years of childhood the ratio of deaths in the poorest class falls to between one and a half and two times that of the wealthiest class, but increases again in early adulthood before falling again in middle and old age.

A class 'gradient' can be observed for most causes of death and is particularly steep for both sexes in the case of diseases of the respiratory system and infective and parasitic diseases [. . .]

Inequality in the Availability and Use of the Health Service

One of the fundamental principles of the NHS is to 'divorce the care of health from questions of personal means or other factors irrelevant to it' (Cartwright and O'Brien 1976). Yet a number of studies have revealed significant social inequalities in the availability and use of health services. In 1968 Richard Titmuss argued, on the basis of evidence then available, that: 'Higher income groups know how to make better use of the Service: they tend to receive more specialist attention; occupy more of the beds in better equipped and staffed hospitals'. Subsequent studies, many of which we shall refer to, have cast further light on the issue and added to the evidence.

Unequal usage will never be more than a partial explanation of the overall inequalities in standards of health. Several commentators have shown, and we shall go on to show this later, that differences in health between sections of the population may be far more a function of 'variations in the socio-demographic circumstances of the population than the amount and type of medical care provided and/or available' (Martini *et al.* 1977). Nevertheless, any inequality in the availability and use of health services in relation to need is in itself socially unjust and requires alleviation. This remains true whatever the relative importance of health care in comparison with other areas of social policy.

Moreover, since equal access has always been a fundamental principle of the NHS, the extent to which it has been achieved is a matter of considerable interest. In sorting out the evidence we have found it useful to look separately at GP consultation rates, hospital care, preventive services and services for the disabled and infirm. This is partly because such a distinction reflects the availability of information and the foci of research, and also because, as we shall show, while some uncertainty remains as to the existence of inequalities in the first two cases, there are no grounds for doubt in the case of preventive services in particular.

Preventive and promotive services

Although neither administrative returns nor the NHS provide information on the utilization of community health and preventive services by social or occupational class, there is a substantial body of research on which to draw, and it is well established that those in the manual classes make considerably less use of them than do those higher up the occupational scale [. . .]

In the case of family planning and maternity services substantial evidence shows that those social groups in greatest need make least use of services and (in the case of antenatal care) are least likely to come early to the notice of the service. A study published in 1970 found clear class gradients in the proportion of mothers having an antenatal examination, attending a family planning clinic and discussing birth control with their GP (Cartwright 1970). Unintended pregnancies were also more common among working-class women. A second study, in 1973, appears to confirm these findings (Bone 1973). It found that women from the non-manual classes make more use of family planning services than those from the manual classes. This is true both for married and unmarried women. Scottish data also show that late antenatal booking is more common in poorer social groups, although the situation seems to be improving in all classes (Table 2). (They further suggest that late attendance for antenatal care is an effective predictor of subsequent infant morbidity and mortality within families (Brotherston 1976).)

Similar class differences have been found in attendance at postnatal examinations (Douglas and Rowntree 1949), and immunization, antenatal and postnatal supervision and uptake of vitamin foods (Gordon 1951). Among

Table 2 *Late antenatal booking. Percentage of married women in each occupational class making an antenatal booking after more than twenty weeks of gestation (Scotland 1971–3)*

Occupational class	1971	1972	1973
I	28.4	27.2	27.0
II	35.3	32.3	29.8
III	36.3	33.4	30.6
IV	39.3	137.8	35.3
V	47.1	44.2	40.5

Source: Brotherston 1976. Data from Scottish Information Services Division

Table 3 *Use of health services by children under 7 by occupational class of father (Great Britain 1965)*

	I	II	III N	III M	IV	V
Percent who had never visited a dentist	16	20	19	24	26	31
Percent not immunized against smallpox	6	14	16	25	29	33
polio	1	3	3	4	6	10
diphtheria	1	3	3	6	8	11

Source: Second Report of the NCDS

slightly older children the National Child Development Study (1958 birth cohort) found substantial differences in immunization rates in children aged 7, as well as in attendance at the dentist (Table 3).

These patterns are further confirmed in studies of screening for cervical cancer, even though working-class women are much more likely to die from it. A study in Greater Manchester, for instance, showed that while women from classes IV and V accounted for over one-third of all women living in the study area, they made up only about one-sixth of women who had a smear test done.

Further studies show that working-class people make less use of dental services (Gray *et al.* 1970; Bulman *et al.* 1968) and of chiropody (Clarke 1969) and receive inferior dental care (Sheiham and Hobdell 1969). Many of these studies are admittedly old, and their findings cannot necessarily be accepted as still valid. Nevertheless, taken together, and in the absence of later evidence to the contrary, a clear relationship between social class and use of preventive services seems to have been demonstrated.

Care of the infirm and disabled

There is little information on class inequalities in the care received by the infirm and disabled, though we now enter that awkward and neglected area where health care shades into the variety of other forms of social service provision. That is, to make comparisons of the care of services received by those who are disabled or infirm (including the aged infirm and the long-term chronic sick) would necessarily be to consider not only health care in the strict sense, but social work support, delivery of meals, home help, sheltered housing, mobility aids, sheltered work and rehabilitation etc., all or many of which may be crucial to the well-being of an infirm or disabled person [. . .]

In considering the needs of the disabled, aged, infirm and chronic sick, not only is it difficult clearly to distinguish needs for strictly medical services from needs for other supportive services, but it is similarly difficult to distinguish needs related to the condition 'itself' (i.e. medically defined) from those relating to its social and economic consequences. In this context it may be helpful to look at the circumstances of the long-term sick, that is those receiving sickness, invalidity and industrial injury benefits for periods of between a month and a year (Martin and Morgan 1975). This shows not only that the sample of benefit recipients as a whole contained a much higher proportion of semi-skilled and unskilled manual workers, which is to have been expected, but that the longer the spell of sickness, the higher the proportion of unskilled workers. Moreover, the longer the period of incapacity the less likely the sick person is to be able to return to the same type of work with the same employer as before, though skilled manual workers are more likely to have their jobs kept open for them than are semi-skilled or unskilled workers. Unsurprisingly also, receipt of sick pay from the employer is also related to duration of invalidity and to level of job (defined by occupational group) [. . .]

Conclusion

Class differentials in the use of the various services which we have considered derive from the interaction of social and ecological factors. Differences in sheer availability and, at least to some extent, in the quality of care available in different *localities* provide one channel by which social inequality permeates the NHS. Reduced provision implied greater journeys, longer waiting lists, longer waiting times, difficulties in obtaining an appointment, shortage of space and so on. A second channel is provided by the structuring of health care *institutions* in accordance with the values, assumptions and preferences of the sophisticated middle-class 'consumer'. Inadequate attention may be paid to the different problems and needs of those who are less able to express themselves in acceptable terms and who suffer from lack of command over resources both of time and of money. In all cases, for an individual to seek medical care, his (or her) perception of his (or her) need for care will have to outweigh the perceived costs (financial and other) both of seeking care and of the regime which may be prescribed. These costs are class-related.

It is the interaction of these two sets of factors which produces the inequalities documented.

From P. Townsend and N. Davidson (1982) *Inequalities in Health*, Harmondsworth: Penguin, pp. 51–64, 76–89.

Questions

1. What explanations can you suggest for *The Black Report*'s findings that:
   (a) 'for the death of every one male infant of professional parents, we can expect almost two children of skilled manual workers and three among children of unskilled manual workers'?
   (b) the manual classes make considerably less use of community health and preventive service than do non-manual classes?
2. Why might reduced provision from the NHS affect manual more than non-manual class groups?
3. Why do you think the government responded in a negative manner to *The Black Report*?

Reading 34

Domestic violence: A case against patriarchy

R. EMERSON DOBASH AND RUSSELL DOBASH

The Dobashes book Violence Against Wives *became one of the key feminist texts of the 1970s, presenting a feminist explanation of men's violence against women and, specifically, wives. In this extract the authors reflect on the historical and cultural roots of such violence and explicitly link domestic violence to past and continuing patriarchal social structures. They stress the importance of the patriarchal family as a cornerstone of male authority and control which they see as supported by other institutions and cultural beliefs or ideologies which legitimate violence against wives. Women's subordination, they argue, is institutionalised within marriage – which they see as a legal contract that cedes a woman's rights to her husband. The Dobashes also contend that the family is not a benign apolitical institution but rather a political one in which power is unequally distributed.*

Woman's Place in History: A Singular and Subordinate Status

Although there are very few historical references to women as important, powerful, meaningful contributors to the life and times of a people, history is littered with references to, and formulas for, beating, clubbing, and kicking them into submission. Women's place in history often has been at the receiving end of a blow. This history is a long and sad one – sad because of the countless women who have been browbeaten, bruised, bloodied, and broken and sad because the ideologies and institutional practices that made such treatment both possible and justifiable have survived, albeit somewhat altered, from century to century and been woven into the fabric of our culture and are thriving today.

It is not possible to understand wife beating today without understanding its past and the part the past plays in contemporary beliefs and behaviours. The essence of wife beating cannot, however, be distilled merely from a description of ancient wife beating practices or from a reiteration of the laws specifying chastisement. Understanding requires an account of how wife beating fits into the family and the entire society. It also requires an examination of the individual and institutional factors that reveal why wives, and not husbands, were beaten.

Legal, historical, literary, and religious writings all contribute to understanding the unique status of women, a status that composes the kernel of the explanation of why it is they who have become the 'appropriate' victims of 'marital' violence. Almost all of the writings about women discuss them in only one type of relationship, their personal relationship with men. The only roles truly allowed women in the real or the imaginary world have been those of wife, mother, daughter, lover, whore, and saint. Although the focus is almost always upon women in their so-called special and exclusive status as wives, mothers, daughters, and lovers, the artist, the historian, the legislator, and the clergyman have given differing forms and meanings to this status. Virginia Woolf noted the curious and contradictory position of women in the imaginary world of literature and the more realistic world as noted by the historian.

A very queer, composite being thus emerges. Imaginatively she is of the highest importance; practically she is completely insignificant. She pervades poetry from cover to cover; she is all but absent from history. She dominates the lives of kings and conquerors in fiction; in fact she was the slave of any boy whose parents forced a ring on her finger. Some of the most inspired words, some of the most profound thoughts in literature fall from her lips; in real life she could hardly read, could scarcely spell, and was the property of her husband [. . .]

In reality, women rarely had an identity apart from that given them as wives, mothers, and daughters, and departure from that identity was discouraged and punished. Rarely in historical or religious writings has a woman been named and discussed as an individual except in terms of an exceptional ability or inability to fulfil family obligations. For example, biblical references to Ruth, the Virgin Mary, as well as various named and unnamed whores, and historical references to women like Josephine and Cleopatra, all describe women in terms of their relationships with men and their membership in families. Women were rarely remembered as individuals, even when they did something memorable. They were nameless, undifferentiated, undistinguished, and indistinguishable. They were considered to be all alike; they were merely the members of some man's family. As such, there was little or nothing the historian thought he could write about any particular one of them.

Since the historian was not interested in a group of people who were seen as merely family members, they ignored women. On the other hand, writers and artists found the imaginary woman compelling. The contradictory and unrealistic picture of what it meant to be a woman may be found in literature and history, but something that was much closer to reality was reflected in laws and religion. Within legal and religious institutions, the only legitimate position for women in most Western societies has been in the family. Women have been relatively isolated and segregated in the home and socialized primarily for this position. Numerous mechanisms, moral and legal, have been developed to render women relatively unwilling or unable to leave or to change either the institution of the family or the particular family of which they were a member.

The status of women was not only separate and singular but also subordinate, and this subordination was institutionalized primarily in marriage and the family. In the family, the parameters of a woman's behaviour were set, her undifferentiated nature reiterated, her relationships with men defined, her subordination taught, and her deviations controlled. Saint Augustine wrote that in marriage 'woman ought to serve her husband as unto God, affirming that in no thing hath woman equal power with man . . . affirming that woman ought to be repressed.'

Although some women escaped this monolithic and secondary status, the pressures to enter marriage were great, alternatives few, and those who did not marry lost the only completely 'legitimate' and therefore socially unproblematic position open to them. It is significant that Augustine used the word woman in place of wife: it was almost inconceivable for an adult woman to be anything other than a wife, and he had no need to differentiate between a woman's gender and her marital status. Since women were usually deprived of alternatives to marriage and subordinated within it, they were completely trapped in inferiority. To be a wife meant becoming the property of her husband, taking a secondary position in a marital hierarchy of power and worth, being legally and morally bound to obey the will and wishes of one's husband, and thus, quite logically, subject to his control even to the point of physical chastisement or murder.

The seeds of wife beating lie in the subordination of females and in their subjection to male authority and control. This relationship between women and men has been institutionalized in the structure of the patriarchal family and is supported by the economic and political institutions and by a belief system, including a religious one, that makes such relationships seem natural, morally just, and sacred. This structure and ideology can be seen most starkly in the records of two societies that provided the roots of our cultural legacy, the Romans and the early Christians.

The Roman Legacy

The Romans have been credited with exceptionally good treatment of women. Women were educated, played an essential part in religious celebrations, could inherit property, and during some periods had limited rights of divorce. But this was the Rome after the Punic Wars of the second century BC. This Rome had undergone considerable economic, political, social and familial change and was quite different from the patriarchal society of the early Empire.

On the other hand, the early Roman family was the cornerstone of society and was one of the strongest patriarchies known. The family was a religious, educational, economic, and legal institution commonly spanning three generations and presided over by a male head, who was priest, magistrate, and owner of all properties, both material and human, and who had absolute power over everything and everyone. The patriarch decided when a newborn child was to be allowed to live and join the family or be put in the street to die. He could choose marriage partners for his children, divorce them without their consent, sell them into bondage, and punish or kill them for any wrongdoing.

There was a very clear and undisputed family hierarchy. The head of the household owned and controlled everything and obviously held the highest status in both his own family and the rest of the society. The training of children from a very early age reflected the fact that boys were to lead, to own, and to control and that girls were to be their subordinates, and there was a marked personal preference for male children, who would continue the family line, its property, and its religion. Name giving also reflected differential worth: males were given three names, designating the individual, the clan, and the family, females usually were given only two names. The one dropped was the first name, which denoted the individual; instead, she was called *maxima* or *minor*, *secunda* or *tertia.*

Children were usually educated informally by their parents. Special emphasis was placed upon morals, reverence of Gods and the law, obedience to authority, and self-reliance. Girls were educated almost entirely by their mothers, whereas at the age of seven boys accompanied their fathers into the field or to the forum and were tutored in agriculture, business, or government. When a boy reached manhood, about seventeen, this was marked by an important celebration that included a procession to the forum, a feast, a religious sacrifice, and the adoption of the toga of a man. There was no celebration when a girl reached womanhood, and she was given in marriage as young as twelve years of age.

The separation of the male and female roles are extreme. The singular role to be allocated to women, that of wives, was reflected in the girl's education. This contrasted with the more complex and worldly training of the boy. The subordination of the girl and her subsequent lack of importance were reflected in everything from her name to the conditions of her marriage. At marriage the guardianship of a woman was transferred from her father to her husband [. . .]

Enforcing the Patriarchal Order

Obedience, however, was something a wife could not withhold without serious consequences. It was the legal right of a husband to require that his wife obey him. She was his property and subject to whatever form of control was necessary for achieving obedience and what was deemed by himself and by the law to be appropriate behaviour. The laws specified the types of behaviour that were to be controlled, the legitimate means by which such control could be effected, and who had the right to control.

During the early patriarchal period, adultery and the drinking of wine were the gravest offenses a wife could commit and were punishable by divorce or death. Romulus considered adultery 'a source of reckless folly and drunkenness a source of adultery'. The severity of the punishment for the adulteress remained during later reforms, although its enforcement decreased. Drunkenness later became a less serious offense, punishable merely by divorce. Counterfeiting the household keys, making poison, abortion, attending public games without the husband's permission, and appearing unveiled in the streets also became punishable by divorce.

In all of these cases, it was the wife who was the offender and the husband the offended. In all cases it was the husband who had the right to control, the wife the obligation to obey [. . .]

Husbands and fathers could put a woman to death without recourse to public trial. Although such legally prescribed executions were rarely carried out, it seems reasonable to conjecture that these statutes reflected general acceptance of physical abuse of women and legitimized their subjugation through force. This subjugation is illustrated in a speech delivered by Cato to Caesar in which he indicated the correct response of husbands and wives to marital indiscretion: 'If you should take your wife in adultery, you may with impunity put her to death without a trial – but if you should commit adultery or indecency, she must not presume to lay a finger on you, nor does the law allow it.'

Roman husbands had the legal right to chastise, divorce, or kill their wives for engaging in behaviour that they themselves engaged in daily. But it did not take something as extreme as marital infidelity to rouse the man of the house to raise club and boot – or sandal – to the erring wife. If she were caught tippling in the family wine cellar, attending public games without his permission, or walking outdoors with her face uncovered, she could be beaten [. . .]

The Law of God

In some ways, the early Christians rejected the existing hierarchies and oppression of Rome and posited the very revolutionary principle of equality of all people (all souls were equal before God, husband and wife were helpmates). In other ways, they rejected the reforms of later Rome, which had given greater freedom to women and challenged the absolute patriarch, and they reaffirmed the earlier principles of marital hierarchy and inequality between husband and wife. This contradiction may be best summarized in the later writings of Paul, that great 'admirer' of women, who wrote that wives were subordinate to their husbands and 'let the wife see that she fear her husband'. This so-called Christian attitude toward women, which surely reinforced their subjugation through force, did not differ dramatically from the law of the early Romans.

Christian principles have had a most profound influence upon the cultural beliefs and social institutions of Western society. With respect to the relationship between husband and wife, it was not the revolutionary principles of equality but the retrogressive principles of patriarchy that were taken up most enthusiastically and vehemently by later Christians that have largely prevailed. The ancient right of the husband to control his wife was incorporated into the new 'nonbarbaric, humanistic' religion and the *Decretum* (c. 1140), one of the early and enduring systematizations of church law, gave this principle precedence over egalitarianism: 'Women should be subject to their men.' Once again women were relegated to the home, and their subordinate and inferior status was reaffirmed.

The Christian account of creation is particularly instructive concerning the separate, singular, and subordinate position of women. Woman was created after man; indeed, she was a by-product of him. And she was created in response to man's needs [. . .]

[The] scriptures provided a moral ideology that largely denigrated women and made their inferiority and subjugation to their husbands appear natural, just, and sacred. Although other scriptures were contradictory and espoused equality, they were not so enthusiastically embraced. This is perhaps not surprising considering the roots of early Christianity and the fact that the church itself was later to organize along hierarchical principles. The relationship between cleric and parishioner was almost identical to that of husband and wife (or children). The belief in the power, wisdom, and authority of one figure over others is, after all, fundamental to Christianity. God is the head and there are tiers of followers who more or less approximate Him and are given powers over their 'inferiors'. It is this religious ideology that was translated into the organization of the church, with its layers of authority: God, the clergy, the flock. Within the flock, and in accordance with the same hierarchical beliefs, the male head of household was the 'Godhead'; his wife and children were his 'flock'. He was believed to be responsible for them, to have authority over them, and ultimately to control them and keep them in subjection. The law of God provided a sacred and moral ideology to uphold the existing patriarchal structure of the family.

The Nature of Patriarchy and its Maintenance

The patriarchy is comprised of two elements: its structure and its ideology. The structural aspect of the patriarchy is manifest in the hierarchical organization of social institutions and social relations, an organizational pattern that by definition relegates selected individuals, groups, or classes to positions of power, privilege, and leadership and others to some form of subservience. Access to positions is rarely based upon individual ability but is institutionalized to such an extent that those who occupy positions of power and privilege do so either because of some form of ascribed status or because of institutionalized forms of advantage that give them the opportunity to achieve status [. . .]

One of the means by which this order is supported and reinforced has been to insure that women have no legitimate means of changing or managing the institutions that define and maintain their subordination. Confining women in the home, banning them from meaningful positions outside the family, and excluding them from the bench and the pulpit is to deny them the means of bringing about change in their status. The best they can hope for is a merciful master both inside and outside the home.

The maintenance of such a hierarchical order and the continuation of the authority and advantage of the few is to some extent dependent upon its 'acceptance' by the many. It is the patriarchal ideology that serves to reinforce this acceptance. The ideology is supportive of the principle of a hierarchical order, as opposed to an egalitarian one, and of the hierarchy currently in power. It is the rationalization for inequality and serves as a means of creating acceptance of subordination by those destined to such positions.

The ideology insures that internal controls regulate the complaints of most subordinates. Socialization into an acceptance of the 'rightful' nature of the order and its inequities can, if successful, allow such inequities to go unquestioned and unchallenged or to make challenges seem unnatural or immoral. Such a general acceptance of the hierarchical structure means that any challenges to it (from those who are not internally controlled by the idea of its rightfulness) will be met by external constraints in the guise of social pressures to conform (from those who do believe in its rightfulness) and by legitimate intervention to prevent and punish deviance. When the ideology legitimizes the order and makes it right, natural, and sacred, the potential conflict inherent in all hierarchies is more likely to produce conflict within the individual and less likely to emerge as overt resistance.

In this respect women in general and wives in particular largely have been denied the means to struggle effectively against their subordination. Although individual women do dissent – and their struggles could pose considerable personal difficulties for the husband faced with a wife who does not know her place – women usually have been sufficiently removed from power and influence as to pose no challenge to the laws or common practices. The development of a legitimate hierarchy based upon acceptance and genuine compliance has meant a far more secure and less problematic order for those in control. The successful socialization of men and women for their positions within marriage has provided a mechanism for both the legitimation and the reinforcement of the marital hierarchy.

Christianity, as well as most other religions, has provided the ideological and moral supports for patriarchal marriage, rationalized it, and actively taught men and women to fit into this form of marriage. On the other hand, the state has codified this relationship into law, and it regulates both the marital hierarchy and access to the opportunities to institute change in the hierarchy. The history of the patriarchal family shows the integration of the family in society and the way in which the family, the church, the economic order, and the state each have influenced and supported one another in maintaining their own hierarchies.

From R.E. Dobash and R. Dobash (1979) *Violence Against Wives: A Case Against Patriarchy*, New York: The Free Press, pp. 31–44.

Questions

1. In highlighting the contradictory position of women in literature and history, the Dobashes comment that 'she pervades poetry from cover to cover; she is all but absent from history'. What 'evidence' can you think of that might justify this comment?
2. What aspects of the 'cultural legacy' of the early Roman and Christian attitudes to women and the family have influenced contemporary family life?
3. How do the Dobashes suggest that the ideology of the family (as an institution based on mutual love and respect) serves the interests of the powerful members within it, i.e. husbands?

Reading 35

Young, female and Black

HEIDI MIRZA

Mirza's study Young, Female and Black *attempts to explain and understand how the process of inequality structures the lives of young Black women. This extract starts with Mirza arguing that explanations for Black female underachievement in terms of negative or low self-esteem provides, at best, only a partial picture. It then focuses on the role of the education system in maintaining social and economic disadvantage. Mirza outlines a number of different teacher responses to the race, gender and social backgrounds of pupils and examines how they can affect teachers' classroom relationships with Black female pupils.*

Of the many theoretical perspectives that have contributed to the debate on the nature of the educational experience, two ideological camps are distinguishable. On the one hand there are those that emphasise the institutional level, the structure, operation and functions of schooling; on the other, there are those that find analysis at the personal interactive level more important. These theorists, who emphasise the inner workings of the classroom, focus in particular on the relationships between teacher and pupil.

Attempts to describe the black educational experience have been characterised, in the main, by research designs ideologically disposed towards the latter perspective, with early studies investigating the causes and effects of negative black self-esteem (Milner 1975, 1983; Coard 1971). Employing the notion of the self-fulfilling prophecy and the mechanism of labelling, these studies focused on the effect a teacher might have on a pupil's own self-image.

A central proposition of such research is that pupils tend to perform as well or as badly as their teachers expect. The teacher's prediction of a pupil's behaviour, it is suggested, is communicated to them, frequently in unintended ways, influencing the actual behaviour that follows. Thus it is only logical to assume that if teachers hold stereotyped opinions and expectations of black children, this may lead to different teaching techniques and classroom treatment, which works to the detriment of these children's education.

Indeed, it was not uncommon to find teachers expressing openly their misgivings about the intellectual capabilities of the black girls in their care. During informal conversation and formal interviews that I had with them, 75 per cent of the teachers in the study made at least one negative comment about the black girls they taught. I was told by one fifth-year teacher and careers mistress that: 'Most of these girls will never succeed . . . they are just unable to remember, the girls just can't make it at this level ['O' level and CSE], never mind what is demanded in higher education. There is what I call "brain death" among them . . . unable to think for themselves.' With statements such as these, teachers provide easy targets, offering tangible and powerful evidence against themselves. It is not surprising, therefore, that they are assumed by many social commentators to be the central link in the transmission of social and racial inequality. This is a convenient and obvious causal assumption to make.

[. . .] [However] the findings of this study do not uphold the notion of the self-fulfilling prophecy as a central explanation for black underachievement.

The Pupil Perspective: A Challenge to the Self-fulfilling Prophecy

There appeared to be two major reasons why the self-fulfilling prophecy failed to provide an adequate understanding of the observed classroom process. Firstly, there was nothing in the evidence to suggest that teachers were successful in eroding black female self-esteem. Secondly, the findings do not show that teachers transmitted their apparent negative expectations to the black pupils they teach. According to the logic of the self-fulfilling prophecy, these two aspects of the labelling process are fundamental to its successful operation.

There was no indication that young black women had negative feelings about being black or female. The girls greatly valued their cultural and racial identity.

There was also little evidence of young black females suffering psychological damage from being 'put down' as a consequence of their teachers' negative evaluations of them. Clearly the girls did not accept the negative evaluations of themselves and their academic abilities, as the following example shows. Ms Wallace, when describing a predominantly black fifth-year class designated as of 'low ability', said: 'These girls have absolutely no motivation. They feel you are here to think for them.' Yet these same girls said of their teachers: 'They hold you back. Teachers always put you down, then they say, "You can't manage . . ."' (Dianne: aged 16); 'When you come you sit a test and then after that they never give you a chance to prove yourself' (Tony: aged 16).

[. . .] If the explanation for the way in which teachers affect pupil performance does not lie within an understanding of the notion of the self-fulfilling prophecy, the question remains as to how exactly does teacher–pupil interaction function to disadvantage the black child? The evidence seemed to suggest that the process of discrimination operated by means of the teachers' access to physical and material resources, restrictions to which would result in the curtailment of opportunities. Clearly teachers do have the power to effect changes and limit or enhance pupil opportunity. As an outcome of their power within the institutional infrastructure teachers are in a position to enforce their prejudices by restricting access to information and educational resources. The positive pupil perspective, which has been persistently overlooked in the trend to highlight black negative self-esteem, brings to the fore the importance of power and control in the classroom.

Racism and Reaction: A Teacher Typology

The findings of this study revealed many shades of teacher reaction to the race, gender and social class of their pupils.

In the following pages I attempt to analyse some of the attitudinal characteristics I found among staff in the schools, and assess the outcome of their specific beliefs and values on the black female pupils in their classrooms. Five general teacher responses were identified. These were grouped as follows: (1) the 'Overt Racists', (2) the 'Christians', (3) the 'Crusaders', (4) the 'Liberal Chauvinists' and (5) the 'Black Teacher'.

1 The 'overt racists'

As high a proportion as 33 per cent of teachers interviewed in the study held what can only be described as overtly racist opinions. It appeared that at the 'grass-roots' level of the staffroom, many teachers remained untouched by the vigorous anti-racist debates and campaigns that were taking place around them. In spite of attempts to inform them to the contrary, these teachers held fast to their convictions as to the intellectual and cultural inferiority of their black pupils, often expressing open resentment at their presence in their country and their school.

Examples of overt racist sentiment and practice were not always confined to isolated incidents or statements, but were often the consequence of long-standing, bitter feuds between certain members of staff and pupils, situations fuelled by racist action and pupil reaction.

Mr Davidson was a young History teacher who derived a definite pleasure from taunting the black pupils, particularly the boys. One black male pupil reported the following incident, apparently one of many, in confidence: 'Mr Davidson called me a wog. Me and my friend we turned round and saw Davidson looking at us and then he said get inside. He also said, "Don't drop peanuts or coconuts on the floor".' While Davidson's racist behaviour was more overt than that displayed by others, incidents of overt racism were by no means an exceptional occurrence. Many members of staff deeply resented the presence of black pupils in their school and often articulated this point of view.

The school secretary, Ms Simpson, had a reputation that preceded her. The girls in her school constantly complained of the way she reacted towards them: keeping their parents waiting, not answering politely, and generally being as unhelpful as possible. There is always the matter of character misrepresentation in such reports and I was careful not to believe everything I was told. However, I witnessed an incident in the corridor that confirmed the girls' reports to me of her negative attitudes towards them.

During a class change-over, at the end of a period, Ms Simpson pushed past me, making her way angrily towards a group of black girls walking slowly and chatting away loudly among themselves. Obviously enraged, she shouted loudly: 'WILL YOU STOP THAT AT ONCE! . . . Honestly, the way you people conduct yourself you wouldn't think you were part of civilisation!'

[. . .] Apart from the situations mentioned so far, the passing of references to assumed inherent characteristics of black students was often to be heard in the staffroom and openly stated to me. For example, one pleasant and helpful young male teacher (he was doing an MA in Education) warned, 'You have to watch them [that is, black girls], they can be sly.' [. . .]

2 *The 'Christians'*

The 'Christians' were a distinctive group who lived up to their name. These teachers were identifiable by their capacity for compassion towards and conviction about the equality of their black brothers and sisters. The particular concept of equality employed by the 'Christians' led to a consensus that in general, characterised this attitude: that is, the 'colour-blind' approach to the education of the black child. What guided this approach was the philosophy that 'We are all the same . . . there are no differences, *and there are no problems*': a celebration of 'sameness'. As one teacher pointed out, 'We see them as pupils first, not if they are black or white.'

[. . .] However, this attitude in itself, although limiting, was not necessarily harmful to the pupils. What gave this particular 'Christian' orientation its negative impact was the reaction it engendered from the teachers to any form of positive action that aimed to redress racial discrimination. At St Hilda's, for example, the setting-up of a Multi-Racial Working Party was objected to on the grounds of a general consensus that all pupils were treated equally in the school and that therefore there was no racial discrimination, in spite of evidence to the contrary [. . .]

The refusal to recognise the existence of racism and the effect that this oversight might have on black pupils can again be illustrated by the response of Mr Madden, the headmaster of St Hilda's, to my application to undertake to do research in his school. Mr Madden was very keen and interested about my wanting to do research in his school, and in particular my emphasis on black girls. He explained: 'I suppose you know and indeed we are very proud that we have several black girls here doing very well . . . we are pleased about that. It is good that you are here. I understand that there is a lot of interest in the performance of black girls. As you will see we are doing fine, very well. There is very little that I can tell you as everything is fine, as it should be, may I say. You know we don't make special cases and I am sure when it comes down to it that is why they do so well.'

However, the truth was far from Mr Madden's claims. While there were several black girls in the top achievement stream of the school, as he had said, these girls did not owe their placement in this Band 1 stream to the policy of non-recognition upheld by the headmaster and his staff. The educational achievements of the black girls in the school were in spite of and not because of the schooling they received [. . .]

The evidence was clear, the 'Christian' approach, despite its benevolent and passive characteristics, can have negative consequences for black pupils. By adopting a 'colour-blind' perspective, the staff and the schools concerned created an atmosphere where ignorance and fear remained unchallenged. Any reference to colour was, among the 'Christians', an accepted taboo, as its very mention implied that there existed racial differences.

3 *The 'Crusaders'*

In contrast to the 'Christians', the 'Crusaders' were prepared to acknowledge that racism was present within educational establishments. This group of teachers held strong beliefs that this racism among their colleagues and the pupils they taught should be challenged. These teachers were therefore dedicated to action; that is, action of a political sort and indeed action as sanctioned and prescribed by the ILEA.

Comparatively, the 'Crusaders' were few in number; just 2 per cent of the teachers in the study lived up to the reputation as active 'anti-racist campaigners'. The distinctive characteristics of the 'Crusaders' were their colour (white), their youth and their commitment to their cause [. . .]

There was little doubt that the 'Crusaders' were dedicated to the cause of anti-racism: however, their actions were not always in the best interests of the black pupils in their care. Often, because of the futility and frustrations of their actions, a great deal of the 'Crusaders' teaching energies were concentrated on their staffroom campaign. It was also clear that the well-meaning but self-conscious treatment of black pupils in their classroom did not satisfy the immediate needs of the black students [. . .]

In conclusion, the evidence suggests that the outcome of the 'Crusader' anti-racist campaign was less productive than they themselves believed. The efforts of these well-intentioned teachers were lost on both their colleagues and their pupils: the former alienated, and the latter they neglected, if not misunderstood.

4 *The 'Liberal Chauvinists'*

Unlike the 'Crusaders' the 'Liberal Chauvinists' were not campaigners for social justice. These teachers did, however, attempt to 'understand' (albeit only within the context of their own perspective), the cultural, class and gender characteristics of the various minorities they came into contact with. Armed with information, mostly gleaned from the secondary sources such as television, books, travels, friends, rather than personal experience, these liberally inclined teachers were often convinced, with a curious arrogance that characterised the 'Liberal Chauvinists', that when it came to their students, they knew best. There were many examples of such liberally orientated staff in the schools in the study. Approximately 25 per cent of the teachers held beliefs that would classify them in this category.

There were many different types of 'Liberal Chauvinism' to be found among the staff in both the schools, each form having its own unique characteristics and therefore specific outcome for the young black women who found themselves on the receiving end of this type of 'unintentional' racism. Turning to an examination of one of these forms of 'Liberal Chauvinism', I cite first the case of Mr Sutton.

Sutton, the fifth year head at St Hilda's, believed that he, better than any other member of staff, 'understood' *his* black female students. In his efforts to 'understand' the young black women in his classrooms, Mr Sutton had become preoccupied with the issue of the sexuality of the black female pupils in the fifth year, as indeed were many other members of staff. It seemed that for Mr Sutton the answer to everything, when it came to young black women – success, failure; good or bad behaviour, happiness or sadness – lay in an explanation that had as its central causal concern the dynamic of black female sexuality [. . .]

It was apparent that pictures of black pupils coming from, on the whole, socially deprived backgrounds, and thus in need of care and assistance, were being pieced together from information teachers read or saw and understood within their own cultural framework. These assessments of their pupils had important consequences for the black girls in their care. Their ideas impinged on the expectations and attitudes they had toward certain girls, who became labelled as problem children or not from the impressions that they derived, from often very limited contact with the parents of the girls [. . .]

In conclusion, there were numerous examples of teachers' negative assessments, most of which were based on what they believed to be 'informed judgement'. These negative assessments often led to the curtailment of opportunities that should have been available to the black girls in the study in view of their ability and attainment.

5 *The 'Black Teacher'*

There is an expectation that, with a positive policy of recruitment towards black teachers, not only will it present a more representative picture of the population of the inner city, but that they will also be placed in the forefront of the demand for a more progressive and egalitarian educational system. However, in the schools studied the black members of staff, who numbered only four, did not participate in the obvious arena that had been constructed to encourage such change. The anti-racist campaign, which on the whole was monopolised by the 'Crusaders', did not attract black support, as Mr Green, a young black male teacher at St Hilda's explained: 'I just let them get on with their business. I don't bother with them. They feel they know what it is all about so who am I to say. I find it just gets on my nerves, I keep well out of it.'

This negative feeling about the 'liberal white tokenism' that dominated the race issue in schools was articulated by the other black teachers: 'The ILEA has set about "investigating" the "problem of race". Everyone is rushing around "investigating race", talking about "running out of time", having to do it now. A curious way to go about things' (Ms Lewis: head of Biology Department, St Theresa's).

It was not that these black members of staff did not sympathise with the need to reassess the issue of race in the schools, but that they shared a definite and alternative perspective on the nature of the black educational dilemma and the solution to that problem. This orientation was clear from the statements these teachers made about the role and development of multi-racial education. For example, when Ms Lewis was asked what she felt about multi-racial education and equal opportunities policies, she said: 'So what about them? What needs to change, if you ask me, is ourselves and our attitudes as teachers, rather than the girls.' [. . .]

Conclusion: The Strategic Avoidance of Racism

The evidence of this study shows that while young black women (who clearly displayed their positive self-esteem), challenged their teachers' expectations of them (expectations that were often characterised by overt racism on the one hand or unintentional racism on the other), they were in no position in the 'power hierarchy' to counteract any negative outcome of these interpretations.

All too often the recognition of these negative assessments led the girls to look for alternative strategies with which to 'get by'. These strategies, such as not taking up a specific subject or not asking for help, were employed by the girls as the only means of challenging their teachers' expectations of them, and as such were ultimately detrimental to the education of the pupils concerned.

However, the attitudes and orientations of black teachers presented a positive example of how some of the processes of disadvantage could be avoided. These teachers neither patronised nor misinterpreted their black students' reactions and were insistent on the maintenance of high standards of teaching and learning.

From H.S. Mirza (1992) *Young, Female and Black*, London: Routledge, pp. 53–83.

Questions

1. Mirza outlines five types or models of teacher responses and applies them to Black female pupils. To what extent do you think that they could be applied to (a) Black male pupils and (b) White working-class pupils?
2. To what extent can you recognise these 'models' in teachers that you have come across?
3. Summarise Mirza's argument that the self-fulfilling prophecy does not provide a central explanation for the underachievement of Black females. Does she convince you? What counter-arguments can you make?

Reading 36

Women and the criminal justice system

ANN LLOYD

In this extract Ann Lloyd examines the 'chivalry' argument – that the criminal justice system deals with women offenders in a more lenient manner than male offenders. Although there is some evidence that some women offenders do receive 'lighter' sentences, many women offenders do not. Chivalrous treatment from criminal justice agencies such as the police and the courts seems to be limited to those women who are felt to conform to stereotypical views of how women should behave. In contrast Lloyd argues that those women offenders who do not fit this picture are dealt with with (even) less understanding than male offenders. As the title of her book suggests they are seen as 'doubly deviant' – offending against the law and against generally held notions of 'good women'.

The leniency or 'chivalry' argument is that women are treated more leniently by the courts simply because they are women. My argument is that, while chivalry may well be extended to some women – those who conform to approved stereotypes – leniency will not be shown to 'deviant' women.

'If a woman conforms to a judge's idea of what is appropriate for a woman he will have trouble convicting her,' Helena Kennedy told a conference at St George's Medical School in 1991. '"Chivalry" exists but it is very much limited to those women who are seen to conform.' She added that a woman who showed anger would be viewed as threatening by the court, which puts women who've been violent at particular risk of being treated more harshly than women who are perceived as conforming to notions of what constitutes proper womanhood.

Aggression and violence are seen as much more essentially masculine than mere law-breaking, so violent women must be 'unnatural' and are more likely than men fitting the same description to be psychiatrized, labelled psychopathic and to end up in a Special Hospital like Broadmoor. These women are treated more harshly than comparable men since an *indefinite* term in a Special is a much more frightening option than a fixed term of imprisonment. And women tend to stay longer in the Specials than men.

Dr Gillian Mezey, Consultant Psychiatrist at St George's Hospital and Medical School:

> For example, if somebody has committed a stabbing in the pub . . . and a man has done it, then you look at it and think, 'Oh God there's an argument involved, it's a drunken brawl' – most of the time these people don't get psychiatric disposals made. If a woman has done it . . . people immediately sit up and take notice . . . the solicitor thinks it's unusual . . . she gets referred to a psychiatrist . . . The impact of what she's done may well be translated from a sort of statistical abnormality, because so few women do it, into a psychological abnormality. She is unrepresentative of the majority of women and therefore something must be wrong with her.

However, it seems that my case is contradicted by, and the leniency argument supported by, current statistics:

In 1990 the average sentence length of prison sentences awarded for indictable offences at the Crown Court was 17.7 months for women aged 21 or over, and 20.5 months for men. *The average length was lower for females convicted of violence against the person* [my emphasis], burglary or robbery and theft and handling, but higher for criminal damage and drugs offences.

In 1990 the average sentence length for women aged 21 or over sentenced at magistrates' courts was 2.3 months compared with 2.6 months for men. *The average sentence length for women was lower for offences of violence against the person* [my emphasis] and burglary, but higher for criminal damage and fraud and forgery and drug offences. For theft and handling both sentence lengths were similar.

But what force have these statistics? How 'true' are they in the sense that they give us the whole picture? The Home Office itself seems a little hesitant about its findings:

On the face of it, these statistics suggest that the courts are inconsistent in their treatment of the sexes. However, consistency in sentencing does not mean that all offenders convicted of crimes within a particular offence category should automatically receive the same sentence.

Sentencing courts may legitimately take into account a large number of other factors in addition to the offence category, such as the seriousness of the particular offence when compared with other offences of the same general type (measured, for example, by the value of goods stolen), the circumstances of the offence and any other aggravating or mitigating factors. This is clearly an issue for which more detailed research is needed and further thought is currently being given to how this might be done.

Another point to bear in mind when analysing statistics of conviction and sentencing rates is the influence of conventional stereotypical ideas and assumptions about women.

The conviction and sentencing figures represent the end of a long process which begins with somebody deciding what is a crime and what isn't. And, throughout that process, there are opportunities for the operation of assumptions, value judgements, stereotypes and prejudices – not only to do with gender, but also to do with, for instance, class and race. How do you measure the influence of such, perhaps largely unconscious, assumptions and value judgements, etc.? They are inevitably going to be part of the process leading to conviction and sentencing but what can conviction and sentencing figures tell us about how much they were influenced by the process, resulting in a certain outcome in a particular case?

Farrington and Morris noted that some factors (notably previous convictions) had an independent influence on sentence severity and reconviction for both men and women . . . others only had an influence for one sex. In particular, marital status, family background and children were more important for women than for men.

Morris also found that divorced and separated women received relatively severe sentences, as did women coming from a deviant family background.

These may be the kind of women whom magistrates, especially female magistrates, disapprove of: they are women who do not conform to notions of 'respectable' women.

She then refers to the work of Kruttschnitt who analysed more than a thousand cases involving female offenders and found that 'the more "respectable" a woman was, the more lenient her sentence'. 'Respectability' referred to 'a good employment record, no alcohol or drug use and no psychiatric history' but, no matter what the offence, the less 'respectable' a woman was the more likely she was to get a severe sentence. She also found that 'the more economically dependent a woman was, the less severe her disposition'.

Working lawyers I've spoken to agree with these findings, and tell me that chivalry is very much limited to those women who are seen to conform. The criminal lawyer, the probation officer and the psychiatrist all know how the system works: judges and magistrates make decisions based on a division of 'good' and 'bad' women, so the defence team tailor what they do and say to try to ensure their clients approximate to that stereotype as closely as possible.

Lawyers may well be aware that these strategies are locking women into traditional stereotypes and may even question what they are doing to women in general. But their job is to do their best for the client. Helena Kennedy discusses these methods with women clients, trying to give them choices about what they want to do, telling them that if they turn up in a broderie anglaise blouse or a nice Marks and Spencer's dress they will be dealt with in a rather different way than if they turn up in bovver boots, sporting a spiky hair-do [. . .]

The idea that criminal justice is simply chivalrous to women on the grounds they are the gentler and morally superior sex and therefore to be treated in a privileged way is far less real than the figures make it appear. If you take into account that men's crimes tend to be more serious and more frequent, such leniency may well disappear. However, where women can be shown to be mentally and emotionally unstable, they are likely to be treated more sympathetically than men. This viewing of women as unstable, though it may be advantageous to individual women, is a high price for all women to pay insofar as it is premised on a belief in women's inherent instability *per se.* It also raises questions about the unfairness of treating men as if they had no inner lives and therefore of denying psychiatric help to men who could benefit from it.

Even when mothers commit infanticide – a category of crime tailor-made for leniency on the grounds of instability – they are very likely, if they do not conform to traditional ideas of good motherhood, to be more severely treated than other women. Along with other violent women offenders they are judged not only on the crimes they have committed but on the extent to which they are perceived by those involved in the criminal justice system as proper women.

From A. Lloyd (1995) *Doubly Deviant, Doubly Damned: Society's Treatment of Violent Women,* Harmondsworth: Penguin, pp. 56–70.

Questions

1. Why do you think that Lloyd suggests that although treating women offenders in terms of stereotypical views might benefit some women, 'it is a high price for all women to pay'?
2. Think of some high profile female offenders. Do they fit Lloyd's characterisation of 'bad' women?
3. Look at press reports of crimes which involve both male and female defendants. Can you find any evidence for the chivalry argument?

Reading 37

What makes women sick: Gender and health

LESLEY DOYAL

In this study Doyal presents an overview of women's experiences of health and health care in the context of various aspects of women's lives, such as reproduction and childbirth, paid work, caring responsibilities and sex. This extract is taken from the chapter 'Safe Sex?' and focuses on a contemporary sexual health issue of global concern: HIV infection. Doyal highlights differences among women in terms of race, socioeconomic class and nationality. She considers the health of women living in the Third World and argues that a key divide among women is linked to global inequalities – indeed global inequality interacts with gender in shaping women's experiences of HIV. Doyal argues that social, economic, biological and cultural factors put women at greater risk of HIV infection than men. The responses to the needs of women who are HIV positive reflect the lack of power women often have to demand adequate care and, therefore, their chances of survival.

Why are Women at Risk?

It is now clear that women are at greater risk than men of contracting the HIV virus from an individual act of intercourse and from each sexual partnership. This 'biological sexism' also applies to most other sexually transmitted diseases. A woman has a 50 per cent chance of acquiring gonorrhoea from an infected male partner while a man has a 25 per cent chance if he has sex with an infected woman. In the case of HIV there is still considerable debate about the precise size of this differential, but it is clear that women's risk is greater (Kurth 1993: 7) [. . .]

The male domination of most heterosexual encounters provides the cultural context within which women have to negotiate strategies to protect their health. Not surprisingly, many feel they have no right to assert their

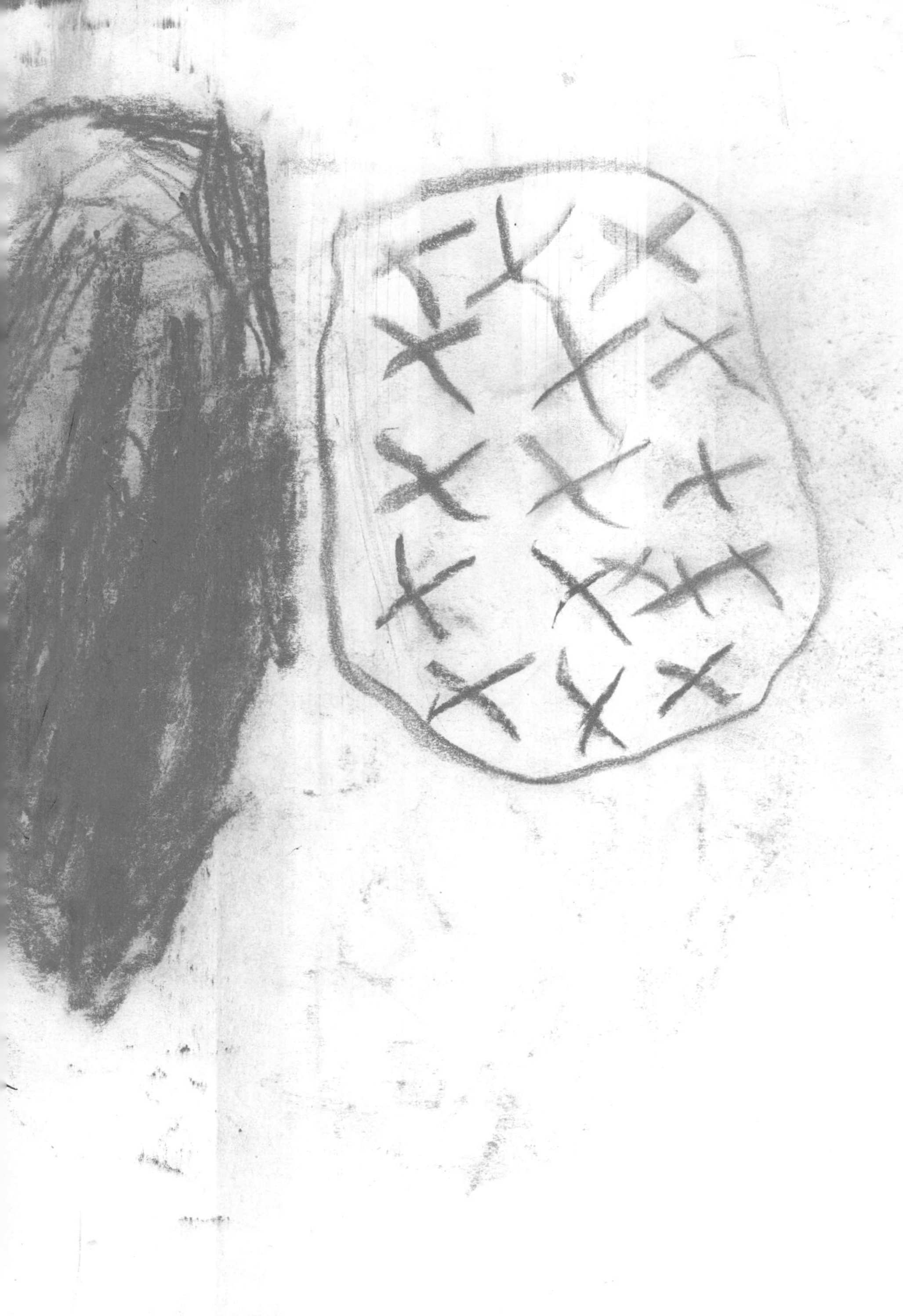

own needs and desires in a situation where society defines the male partner's wants as paramount. They feel unable to assert their wish for safe sex, for fidelity or for no sex at all. These beliefs may not simply kill a woman's desire, they may also lead to her contracting HIV.

Economics of HIV Transmission

This cultural domination of heterosex is reinforced by broader gender inequalities in income and wealth. For many women economic security, sometimes their very survival, is dependent on the support of their male partner. Sexual intercourse done in the way that he desires may well be the price they pay for that support. Hence many women's ability to control their exposure to HIV will be limited by their financial dependence. Requests for safer sex can be made, but if they are ignored most women will have few options, as Ugandan MP Miria Matembe reports:

> The women tell us they see their husbands with the wives of men who have died of AIDS. And they ask 'What can we do? If we say no, they'll say pack up and go. But if we do where do we go to?' They are dependent on the men and they have nowhere to go. What advice can you give these women? (Panos Institute 1990: vi)

These links between economic support and heterosex can take very different forms. Some sexual relationships have no financial implications at all while in commercial sex specific acts are performed solely for money. In most societies sex is implicitly assumed to be a husband's right in return for supporting his family, and there is usually a clear dichotomy between marriage and other forms of social and economic exchange. However in some communities there is a continuum of different types of sexual services (Seidel 1993: 188). In parts of Africa for instance, women may have long-term 'sugar daddies' on the explicit understanding that they will receive money in return, and some young girls use such arrangements as the only means of funding their education (Bassett and Mhloyi 1991: 150; de Bruyn 1992: 255). Whenever sex is part of an economic exchange women will be constrained in their attempts to protect themselves from sexually transmitted diseases – the greater the degree of financial dependence, the greater the constraint.

In many countries, social pressures are now pushing an increasing number of women towards selling sex for subsistence, under circumstances that may seriously damage their health. A recent study of women in mining towns in South Africa emphasised that the decision to provide sexual services is usually an economic one:

> Women talk of 'spanning donkeys' (hopana dipokola) or 'spanning oxen' (hopana dikhomo) when describing prostitution. In other words, women

> harness men's desires to work for and support them. Taking sexual partners is a way to supplement meagre salaries or replace them. (Jochelson *et at.* 1991: 167)

As one woman described it:

> I worked for six months and saw that it's better to span. I could send home money for my children to get something to eat, just think what it's like if you have no place, no money, no husband. (Jochelson *et at.* 1991: 167)

[. . .]

Poverty and Seropositivity

Thus women's sexual behaviour is the outcome of a complex set of internal calculations and interpersonal negotiations that cannot be understood outside the context of their cultural, social and economic environment. Not surprisingly it is the poorest women who have the least autonomy, run the most frequent risks and are most likely to be infected. As Bassett and Mhloyi have observed in Zimbabwe: 'For many women faced with divorce or dire poverty on the one hand and the risk of HIV infection on the other, the choice becomes one of "social death" or biological death' (Bassett and Mhloyi 1991: 146).

The growing numbers of women with HIV and AIDS are concentrated in the world's poorest countries. At present the majority are in Sub-Saharan Africa, where the migrant labour system, rapid urbanisation and frequent 'low intensity' wars have combined with growing landlessness and poverty to create an environment that is ripe for the spread of all sexually transmitted diseases, and of HIV in particular . . . Latest estimates suggest that nearly four million African women are now HIV positive – 83 per cent of HIV infections among women worldwide.

The interrelationship between these various factors is, of course, complex and has to be understood in relation to the detailed history of individual countries or regions. Broadly speaking however, the pattern is one where colonial policies of land expropriation, rural impoverishment and the forcible introduction of male migrant labour have led to changing patterns of family and sexual relations, often involving long separations and multiple partners. These developments have left many in situations of increasing poverty as world economic trends erode the limited gains made by independent African countries . . . The effects of this social upheaval and disorganisation are exacerbated by lack of access to adequate food and water supplies or to medical care, leaving both men and women without treatment for sexually transmitted (and other) diseases and an increased susceptibility to HIV/AIDS.

But HIV-positive women are not confined to the poorest parts of the world. In the United States, the richest country of all, some 130,000 women are now thought to be infected with the virus . . . Again it is the poor who are most at risk with women of colour accounting for about three quarters of all women with AIDS in the United States . . . As one US activist has put it:

> When you're talking about women and AIDS think women of color. Whenever you hear about women and AIDS think women of color. That should be your first image, because that gets lost. I have seen it get lost repeatedly on the part of people who are making policy for us. (Smith 1992: 85)

Many of these women are intravenous drug users or the partners of intravenous drug users. They may have little chance of achieving social equality, and sex may be the only commodity they can sell to support themselves and their families. For many this means unsafe sex with multiple partners, making the crackhouses of the 1990s as dangerous for women as the bathhouses of the early 1980s were for gay men. Drug use or sex with potentially infected men may be the only means of escape from the impoverishment and marginality of their daily lives. As a counsellor working in inner-city New York put it:

> If the only ways of escape people have are through drugs and sex which offer a rare chance to feel like a complete human being – and both of these are closely linked with AIDS – then what hope is there of addressing the issue of AIDS prevention without addressing the underlying issue of what people are trying to escape from? (Panos Institute 1990: 35)

Prevention and Power

We have seen that women are biologically more vulnerable than men to HIV infection. In most societies their own freedom of sexual choice is limited. Most have little power in sexual negotiations and can make only a limited impact on their partners' sexual activities. Under these circumstances HIV and AIDS prevention strategies have often failed to meet their needs. Such policies are based on the assumption that given accurate knowledge men and women will make rational decisions to practise safer sex and will act on those decisions. However a condom is only as useful as the capacity to negotiate its use and many women are unable to achieve this (Worth 1989).

Recent research among Latina women in New York has shown that many are becoming increasingly assertive in their interaction with sexual partners. One woman said of her boyfriend: 'Mine doesn't have a choice. Like it or not he has to use a condom with me. Or else nothing can happen. He will suffer for months.' An African American woman reported: 'I insist that he use protection. And if he doesn't want to, then he don't get the goodies.

That's all' (Kline *et al.* 1992: 453). But others feel unable to make such demands, and some men resist all attempts to change them [. . .]

In one piece of action research in Zaire, 60 married women in a church group attempted to persuade their husbands to use condoms. One third refused without discussion and many of these were angry and hostile; one refused his wife 'housekeeping' and suggested she go out and 'hustle for money'. One third of the men convinced their wives that there was no risk (perhaps correctly). Only one third agreed in principle to use the condom (Grundfest Schoepf *et al.* 1991: 199). In a national survey of Zimbabwean men, over 65 per cent said they had never used condoms and most saw them as appropriate only for use with prostitutes (Mbivso and Adamchak 1989).

Reports from many countries have documented women's fears of family conflict, violence and economic loss if they try to enforce condom use. Young girls in particular may also fear that they will be accused of mistrust, of 'not loving him enough', or of being too sexually assertive (Holland *et al.* 1990). For them, the problem may be not so much economic or social dependence as a fear of challenging dominant ideas about heterosex, of asserting their own needs and putting male pleasure in second place. After Holland and her coresearchers had studied the sexual behaviour of teenage girls in the United Kingdom, they suggested that the main thing standing between young women and safe sex was the men they were with.

Many prevention strategies also recommend faithfulness within a sexual relationship as a means of ensuring that sex is safe. In Uganda, for instance, government education campaigns have promoted monogamy or 'zero grazing' as the key to prevention of HIV (Kisekka 1990). However this will mean little to the millions of women who already confine their sexual activity to their husband or long-term partner. It has been estimated that between 50 per cent and 80 per cent of all HIV infected women in Africa have had no sexual partners other than their husbands (Reid 1992: 659).

In a recent study carried out in an HIV/AIDS clinic in Harare, in almost all cases it was the male partner who had been responsible for bringing HIV infection into the family unit. Among 75 couples there were only two in which the wife was seropositive and the husband negative. In both these instances the wife had an identifiable risk factor (blood transfusion and first marriage to a partner who died of an AIDS-like illness) (Latif 1989). Though women themselves are not always monogamous, economic, social and cultural factors often combine to make them more likely than men to limit their sexual contacts. Yet this does not prevent them from being at serious risk from infections picked up by their partners.

From L. Doyal (1995) *What Makes Women Sick: Gender and the Political Economy of Health*, London: Macmillan, pp. 77–83.

Questions

1. In what ways might 'social, economic and cultural forces work against women's health'? Consider women's situation in both the poorest nations and the richest.
2. How does Doyal suggest that economic inequality and power differentials in heterosexual relations lead to women facing an increased risk of HIV infection?

Reading 38

Images of Black women in everyday life

PAT HILL-COLLINS

Pat Hill-Collins argues that the experience of being Black provides a very revealing standpoint from which to undertake social analysis. This extract begins with a comment on the ways in which conventional, Western evaluations of beauty privilege White women rather than Black women. However, she warns of the dangers of lumping all Black women together, and looks at the different treatment accorded to light- and dark-skinned Black women. In particular, she argues that Western cultural institutions seem to 'prefer' lighter-skinned 'lesser Black' women to darker-skinned Black women and react to them in a different manner.

Controlling Images in Everyday Life: Color, Hair, Texture and Standards of Beauty

Like everyone else, African-American women learn the meaning of race, gender, and social class without obvious teaching or conscious learning. The controlling images of Black women are not simply grafted onto existing social institutions but are so pervasive that even though the images themselves change in the popular imagination, Black women's portrayal as the Other persists. Particular meanings, stereotypes, and myths can change, but the overall ideology of domination itself seems to be an enduring feature of interlocking systems of race, gender, and class oppression (Omi and Winant 1986: 63).

African-American women encounter this ideology through a range of unquestioned daily experiences. But when the contradictions between Black women's self-definitions and everyday treatment are heightened, controlling images become increasingly visible. Karen Russell, the daughter of basketball great Bill Russell, describes how racial stereotypes affect her:

> How am I supposed to react to well-meaning, good, liberal white people who say things like: 'You know, Karen, I don't understand what all the fuss is about.

> You're one of my good friends, and I never think of you as black.' Implicit in such a remark is, 'I think of you as white,' or perhaps just, 'I don't think of your race at all'. (Russell 1987: 22)

Ms Russell was perceptive enough to see that remarks intended to compliment her actually insulted African-Americans. As the Others, African-Americans are assigned all of the negative characteristics opposite and inferior to those reserved for whites. By claiming that Ms Russell is not really 'black', her friends unintentionally validate this system of racial meanings and encourage her to internalize those images.

Although Black women typically resist being objectified as the Other, these controlling images remain powerful influences on our relationships with whites, Black men, and one another. Dealing with issues of beauty – particularly skin colour, facial features, and hair texture – is one concrete example of how controlling images denigrate African-American women. A children's rhyme often sung in Black communities proclaims:

> Now, if you're white you're all right.
> If you're brown, stick around,
> But if you're black, Git back! Git back! Git back!

Externally defined standards of beauty long applied to African-American women claim that no matter how intelligent, educated, or 'beautiful' a Black woman may be, those Black women whose features and skin colour are most African must 'git back'. Blue-eyed, blond, thin white women could not be considered beautiful without the Other – Black women with classical African features of dark skin, broad noses, full lips, and kinky hair.

Race, gender, and sexuality converge on the issue of evaluating beauty. Judging white women by their physical appearance and attractiveness to men objectifies them. But their white skin and straight hair privilege them in a system in which part of the basic definition of whiteness is its superiority to blackness. Black men's blackness penalizes them. But because they are men, their self-definitions are not as heavily dependent on their physical attractiveness as those of all women. But African-American women experience the pain of never being able to live up to externally defined standards of beauty – standards applied to us by white men, white women, Black men, and, most painfully, one another.

Exploring how externally defined standards of beauty affect Black women's self-images, our relationships with one another, and our relationships with Black men has been one recurring theme in Black feminist thought. The long-standing attention of musicians, writers, and artists to this theme reveals African-American women's deep feelings concerning skin colour, hair texture, and standards of beauty. In her autobiography, Maya Angelou records her painful realization that the only way she could become truly beautiful was to become white:

> Wouldn't they be surprised when one day I woke out of my black ugly dream, and my real hair, which was long and blond, would take the place of the kinky mass that Momma wouldn't let me straighten? . . . Then they would understand why I had never picked up a Southern accent, or spoke the common slang, and why I had to be forced to eat pigs' tails and snouts. Because I was really white and because a cruel fairy stepmother . . . had turned me into a too-big Negro girl, with nappy black hair. (Angelou 1969: 2)

Gwendolyn Brooks also explores the meaning of skin colour and hair texture for Black women. During Brooks's childhood, having African features was so universally denigrated that she writes, 'when I was a child, it did not occur to me even once, that the black in which I was encased . . . would be considered, one day, beautiful' (Brooks 1972: 37). Early on Brooks learned that a clear pecking order existed among African-Americans, one based on one's closeness to whiteness. As a member of the 'Lesser Blacks', those farthest from white, Brooks saw first-hand the difference in treatment of her group and the 'Brights':

> One of the first 'world' truths revealed to me when I at last became a member of SCHOOL was that, to be socially successful, a little girl must be Bright (of skin). It was better if your hair was curly, too – or at least Good Grade (Good Grade implied, usually, no involvement with the Hot Comb) – but Bright you marvellously *needed* to be. (1972: 37)

This division of African-Americans into two categories – the 'Brights' and the 'Lesser Blacks' – affects dark-skinned and light-skinned women differently. Darker women face being judged inferior and receiving the treatment afforded 'too-big Negro girls with nappy hair'. Institutions controlled by whites clearly show a preference for lighter-skinned Blacks, discriminating against darker ones or against any African-Americans who appear to reject white images of beauty. Sonia Sanchez reports, 'sisters tell me today that when they go out for jobs they straighten their hair because if they go in with their hair natural or braided, they probably won't get the job' (Tate 1983: 141).

Sometimes the pain most deeply felt is the pain that Black women inflict on one another. Marita Golden's mother told her not to play in the sun because 'you gonna have to get a light husband anyway, for the sake of your children' (1983: 24). In *Color,* a short film exploring the impact of skin colour on Black women's lives, the dark-skinned character's mother tries to get her to sit still for the hot comb, asking 'Don't you want your hair flowing like your friend Rebecca's?' We see the sadness of a young Black girl sitting in a kitchen, holding her ears so that they won't get burned by the hot comb that will straighten her hair. Her mother cannot make her beautiful, only 'presentable' for church. Marita Golden's description of a Black beauty salon depicts the internalized oppression that some African-American women feel about African features:

> Between customers, twirling in her chair, white-stockinged legs crossed, my beautician lamented to the hairdresser in the next stall, 'I sure hope that

> Gloria Johnson don't come in here asking for me today. I swear 'fore God her hair is this long.' She snapped her finger to indicate the length. Contempt riding her words, she lit a cigarette and finished, 'Barely enough to wash, let alone press and curl.' (Golden 1983: 25)

African-American women who are members of the 'Brights' fare little better, for they too receive special treatment because of their skin colour and hair texture. Harriet Jacobs, an enslaved light-skinned woman, was sexually harassed because she was 'beautiful', for a Black woman. Her straight hair and fair skin, her appearance as a dusky white woman, made her physically attractive to white men. But the fact that she was Black, and thus part of a group of sexually denigrated women, made her available to white men as no group of white women had been. In describing her situation, Jacobs notes, 'if God has bestowed beauty upon her, it will prove her greatest curse. That which commands admiration in the white woman only hastens the degradation of the female slave' (Washington 1987: 17).

This difference in treatment of dark-skinned and light-skinned Black women creates issues in relationships among African-American women. Toni Morrison's (1970) novel *The Bluest Eye* explores this theme of the tension that can exist among Black women grappling with the meaning of externally defined standards of beauty. Freida, a dark-skinned, 'ordinary' Black girl, struggles with the meaning of these standards. She wonders why adults always got so upset when she rejected the white dolls they gave her and why light-skinned Maureen Peal, a child of her own age whose two braids hung like 'lynch-ropes down her back', got the love and attention of teachers, adults, and Black boys alike. Morrison explores Freida's attempt not to blame Maureen for the benefits her light skin and long hair afforded her as part of Freida's growing realization that the 'Thing' to fear was not Maureen herself but the 'Thing' that made Maureen beautiful.

Gwendolyn Brooks (1953) captures the anger and frustration experienced by dark-skinned women in dealing with the differential treatment they and their lighter-skinned sisters receive. In her novel *Maud Martha*, the dark-skinned heroine ponders actions she could take against a red-headed Black woman whom her husband found so attractive. 'I could,' considered Maud Martha, 'go over there and scratch her upsweep down. I could spit on her back. I could scream. "Listen," I could scream, "I'm making a baby for this man and I mean to do it in peace".' (Washington 1987: 422). But Maud Martha rejects these actions, reasoning 'if the root was sour what business did she have up there hacking at a leaf?'

This 'sour root' also creates issues in relationships between African-American women and men. Maud Martha explains:

> It's my colour that makes him mad. I try to shut my eyes to that, but it's no good. What I am inside, what is really me, he likes okay. But he keeps looking at my colour, which is like a wall. He has to jump over it in order to meet and

> touch what I've got for him. He has to jump up high in order to see it. He gets awful tired of all that jumping. (Washington 1987: 421)

Her husband's attraction to light-skinned women hurt Maud Martha because his inability to 'jump away up high' over the wall of colour limited his ability to see her for who she truly was.

From P. Hill-Collins (1990) *Black Feminist Thought: Knowledge, Consciousness and the Politics of Empowerment*, London: Unwin Hyman, pp. 78–82.

Questions

1. Why might the comment 'I never think of you as Black' be offensive to Black people?
2. What examples can you think of from recent films or TV programmes that back up Hill-Collins' view that light- and dark-skinned Black women are presented and treated differently?
3. How might Black women resist conventional definitions of beauty?

Reading 39

The history of Black people in Britain

PETER FRYER

In his historical study, Staying Power: The History of Black People in Britain, *Peter Fryer demonstrates that the presence of Black people in Britain is not a recent, post-Second World War phenomenon. In this extract he looks at the first settlement of Africans in England in the sixteenth century and examines the contemporary myths about Africa and Africans. He then details the subsequent attempt by Queen Elizabeth I to expel Black people from Britain – an attempt which can perhaps be seen as anticipating the politics of repatriation and racism faced by later generations of, among others, Jewish, Irish, Asian and Afro-Caribbean immigrants. In our extract, Fryer also refers to Septimus Severus, the Roman Emperor who was reputedly frightened by a Black soldier near Hadrians Wall in 210 AD. Fryer's historical study uses the language of the period to illustrate the attitude and reaction to Black people. We have included his 'translations' in most instances but not for the lengthy extracts from Queen Elizabeth I's letter to the Lord Mayor of London toward the end of the Reading.*

Africans in England

It was the summer of 1555 – before we had potatoes, or tobacco, or tea, and nine years before Shakespeare was born. Queen Mary was on the throne, had recently married Philip of Spain, and was much occupied with having heretics burnt. Some of her subjects were more interested in getting rich than in arguing about religion, and it was the pursuit of riches that caused them to bring her a group of five Africans. The visitors came from the small town of Shama, which can be found in any large atlas, on the coast of what nowadays we call Ghana. Three of them were known as Binne, Anthonie, and George; the names, real or adopted, of the other two have not come down to us. A contemporary account speaks of 'taule and stronge men' who 'could well agree with owr meates and drynkes' although 'the coulde and moyst ayer dooth sumwhat offende them' (tall and strong men [who] could well agree with our kind of food and drink [although] the cold and damp air gives them some trouble).

The same account refers to these five Africans as slaves. Whatever their status, they had been borrowed, not bought. Englishmen were not to start trafficking in slaves for another eight years. For the time being, English merchants were simply after a share in the profits to be gained from African gold, ivory, and pepper. The Portuguese had been hogging this lucrative West African trade for more than 100 years and had long managed to keep their rich pickings secret from their European neighbours. Now the secret was out. Portugal had ardent competitors to face. But the English needed African help if they were to succeed in breaking the Portuguese monopoly. That was why John Lok, son of a prominent London merchant and alderman, brought the group of West Africans over here in 1555. The idea was that they should learn English and then go back to Africa as interpreters and, as it were, public relations men.

In fact, three of them were taken home after a few months by another London merchant, William Towerson, whom they were soon helping by persuading fellow-Africans that it was safe to venture on board the *Hart* and the *Tiger* for trading purposes: the going rate for three ounces of gold was 39 brass or copper basins and two small white saucers. An eyewitness account tells how the three returning travellers were welcomed by their countrymen. At Hanta, not far from Shama, 'our Negroes were well knowen, and the men of the towne wept for joy, when they saw them'. And at Shama itself one of them was greeted by an aunt, another by a sister-in-law, and these ladies 'receiued them with much ioy, and so did all the rest of the people, as if they had bene their naturall brethren' (received them with much joy, and so did all the rest of the people, as if they had been their blood relatives).

If we can detect a note of surprise here at Africans' behaving with such human warmth, that is because sixteenth-century English people were poorly informed about Africa and those who lived there. Of course, as more and more Englishmen went to Africa, were surprised and impressed by the riches and living standards of the rulers and merchants they met, and started publishing their findings in travel books, sober facts began to get mixed with the accepted myths. When Vice-Admiral Thomas Wyndham reached Benin in 1553 he found the king (*oba*) able to speak good Portuguese, which he had learnt as a child, and perfectly willing to let the Englishmen have 80 tons of pepper on credit until their next voyage. Yet the same books that contained matter-of-fact reports providing accurate details of the Africans' houses, manners, dress, crops, and crafts – of their civilization, in short – gave equal weight to the fabulous Presterjohn, King of Ethiopia, who had attained the age of 562 back in the twelfth century. And these books reprinted, virtually unchanged, the ancient folklore of the elder Pliny (AD 23–79), a popular English version of whose description of Africa and Africans was published in 1566, entitled *A Summarie of the Antiquities, and wonders of the Worlde.*

What kind of light did this throw on the 'dark' continent? Readers were told that some Ethiopians had no noses, others no upper lips or tongues, others again no mouths. The Syrbotae were eight feet tall. The Ptoemphani were ruled by a dog. The Arimaspi had a single eye, in the forehead. The Agriophagi lived on the flesh of panthers and lions, the Anthropophagi on human flesh. There were people in Libya who had no names, nor did they ever dream. The Garamantes made no marriages; the men held the women in common. The Gamphasantes went all naked. The Cynamolgi ('dog-milkers') had heads like dogs' heads. The Blemmyes had no heads at all, but eyes and mouths in their breasts. 'The laste of all the Affriens Southewarde', according to another book of the time, were the Ichthyophagi, or fish-eaters. 'Like vnto beastes', after a meal of fish washed up on the shore and baked by the sun, they would 'falle vpon their women, euen as they come to hande withoute any choyse; vtterly voide of care, by reason they are alwaye sure of meate in good plentye' (like animals ... [they would] fall upon their women, just as they come to hand, without any choice; utterly free from care because they are always sure of plenty of food).

Such fantasies tended to cement in the minds of English people the notion that Africans were inherently carefree, lazy, and lustful. By the middle of the sixteenth century this notion was taken for granted, just as some English people took it for granted that every male African had an enormous penis; the tiny naked figures of Africans on more than one fifteenth-century map attest to the antiquity of that belief.

We can be sure that the five Africans who visited England in 1555 were stared at very hard indeed by the local inhabitants, as was the elephant's head brought over on the same voyage – along with about 250 tusks, 36 casks of malaguetta pepper, and over 400lb of 22 carat gold – and put on display in the house of Sir Andrew Judd, a prosperous London merchant and alderman. The English were prepared to swallow all kinds of yarns about elephants, too – for instance, that they were continually at war with dragons, 'which desyre theyr bludde bycause it is very coulde' (which desire their blood because it is very cold). Having live Africans in their midst, and finding them human enough to tolerate English food and drink while complaining of the weather, must have taught their hosts more about Africa than staring at a dead elephant's head. From that time on, those mythical carefree, lazy, lustful cannibals were always, so to say, beyond the next river or the next mountain range.

So, although knowledge about African peoples and cultures was increasing, the pale-skinned islanders disposed to make ethnocentric generalizations about dark-skinned people from over the sea found the persistent folk myths a convenient quarry. Such myths eased English consciences about enslaving Africans and thereby encouraged the slave trade. To justify this trade, and the use of slaves to make sugar, the myths were woven into a more or less coherent racist ideology. Africans were said to be inherently inferior, mentally, morally, culturally, and spiritually, to Europeans. They were sub-human savages, not civilized human beings like us. So there could be no disgrace in buying or kidnapping them, branding them, shipping them to the New World, selling them, forcing them to work under the whip. English racism was born of greed.

The first Englishman to line his pockets by trafficking in black slaves was an unscrupulous adventurer called John Hawkyns. On that first English triangular voyage, in 1562–3, he acquired at least 300 inhabitants of the Guinea coast. Some he bought from African merchants whose wares included domestic slaves; some he hijacked from Portuguese slavers; some he simply seized. He took these people to the Caribbean island of Hispaniola (now Haiti and the Dominican Republic), where he sold them to the Spaniards for £10,000 worth of pearls, hides, sugar, and ginger. His profit on the venture was about 12 per cent. Queen Elizabeth I is said, on rather slender authority, to have warned him that carrying off Africans without their consent would be 'detestable, and would call down the Vengeance of Heaven upon the Undertakers'. However that may be, she was quite happy to lend Hawkyns, for his second slave-hunting voyage (1564–5), the *Jesus of Lubeck*, a 600-ton vessel with a complement of 300 men that had been bought for the English navy and was valued at £4000. And Clarenceux King-of-Arms lost no time in augmenting Hawkyns's coat of arms with a crest showing 'a demi-Moor proper [i.e. a halflength figure in natural colouring] bound captive, with annulets on his arms and in his ears'. Three black men shackled with slavecollars were displayed on the coat of arms itself – a singular honour for the city of Plymouth, whose freeman Hawkyns was, and for the English navy, whose treasurer and comptroller he was soon to become.

Though it would be another 100 years before English merchants were trafficking in slaves in a really organized way, and longer still before they succeeded in dominating the slave trade, they had started dabbling. And, as a by-product of this dabbling, African slaves were brought to England from the 1570s onwards. In the late sixteenth century they were used here in three capacities: as household servants (the majority); as prostitutes or sexual conveniences for well-to-do Englishmen and Dutchmen; and as court entertainers. There is no evidence of black people being bought and sold in this country until 1621, which is not to say that it did not happen before that year. But there is clear evidence that black people were living here – and not only in London – in the last 30 years of the sixteenth century [. . .]

Towards the end of the sixteenth century it was beginning to be the smart thing for titled and propertied families in England to have a black slave or two among the household servants. One of the first to acquire such an exotic status symbol was Lady Ralegh, wife of the Sir Walter Ralegh who figures in the history books for other innovations. Her example was soon followed by the Earl of Dorset and others, but the practice was not to become general until the second half of the seventeenth century. In 1599 one Denis Edwards wrote to the Earl of Hertford's secretary: 'Pray enquire after and secure my negress: she is certainly at the "Swan", a Dane's beershop, Turnbull Street, Clerkenwell.' This cryptic reference has been read as suggesting the presence of black prostitutes in Elizabethan London, and there is, perhaps, supporting evidence in the fact that the part of the 'Abbess de Clerkenwel' – 'abbess', in this context, means brothel-keeper – in the Gray's Inn revels at Christmas 1594 was played by a woman called Lucy Negro (whom one authority identifies as Shakespeare's Dark Lady). There were certainly black entertainers at court well before the turn of the century, like the 'lytle Blackamore' for whom, not long after 1577, a 'Gascon coate' was made, of 'white Taffata, cut and lyned under with tincel, striped down with gold and silver, and lined with buckram and bayes, poynted with poynts and ribands'. In the 1570s Queen Elizabeth was shown with a group of black musicians and dancers entertaining her courtiers and herself. The seven musicians and three boy dancers dressed in scarlet can be seen on a painted panel supposed to depict *Queen Elizabeth and her court at Kenilworth Castle,* attributed to Marcus Gheeraerts the elder and dating from about 1575; it clearly isn't Kenilworth, but such a group was by now a standard feature of every self-respecting European court, as will appear. To disguise themselves as black women in masquerades became a favourite pastime among the queen's ladies-in-waiting.

Queen Elizabeth's Response

However entertaining she may have found them at court, the queen was soon expressing strong disapproval of the presence of black people elsewhere in her realm and, indeed, ordering that 'those kinde of people' should be deported forthwith. This episode rarely figures in the history books, and it is easy to see why. Elizabeth's professed reasons were that there were enough people in England without 'blackmoores' (the population was around 3,000,000); that they were taking food out of her subjects' mouths (there had been a series of bad harvests); and that in any case most of them were 'infidels'. A further reason has been suggested: the widespread belief, more firmly held than ever in the reign of a virgin queen of exceptional pallor, that whiteness stood for purity, virtue, beauty, and beneficence, whereas anything black was bound to be filthy, base, ugly, and evil. Like Septimius Severus, many English people did tend to think that way. But was Elizabeth's action merely crude xenophobia? To answer this question we have to examine the documents, which have rarely been printed (and the most accessible version of one of which is marred by errors of transcription).

On II July 1596, Elizabeth caused an open letter to be sent to the lord mayor of London and his aldermen, and to the mayors and sheriffs of other towns, in the following terms:

> Her Majesty understanding that several blackamoors have lately been brought into this realm, of which kind of people there are already too many here . . . her Majesty's pleasure therefore is that those kind of people should be expelled from the land, and for that purpose instruction is given to the bearer, Edward Banes, to take ten of those blackamoors that were brought into this realm by Sir Thomas Baskerville on his last voyage, and transport them out of the realm. In this we require you to give him any help he needs, without fail.

But that was only the beginning. A week later an open warrant was sent to the lord mayor of London and all vice-admirals, mayors, and other public officers, informing them that a Lubeck merchant called Casper van Senden, who had arranged for the release of 89 English prisoners in Spain and Portugal, was asking in return 'licence to arrest the same number of blackamoors here in this realm and to transport them to Spain and Portugal'. Her Majesty,

> considering the reasonableness of his requests to transport so many blackamoors from here, thinks it a very good exchange and that those kind of people may be well spared in this realm . . . [Public officers] are therefore . . . required to aid and assist him to arrest such blackamoors as he shall find within this realm, with the consent of their masters, who we have no doubt – considering her Majesty's good pleasure to have those kind of people sent out of the land . . . and that, with christian love of their fellow-men, they will prefer to be served by their own countrymen rather than by those kind of people – will yield those in their possession to him.

This was an astute piece of business, which must have saved the queen a lot of money. The black people concerned were being used as payment for the return of 89 English prisoners. The government simply confiscated them from their owners – there is no mention of compensation – and handed them over to a German slave-trader.

In so far as this was a serious attempt to deport all black people from England, it failed completely. For within five years the English queen and her advisers were engaged in a second deal of the same kind. In 1601 Elizabeth issued a proclamation in which she declared herself

> highly discontented to understand the great numbers of negars and Blackamoores which (as she is informed) are crept into this realm . . . who are fostered and relieved [i.e. fed] here to the great annoyance of her own liege people, that want the relief [i.e. food], which those people consume, as also for that the most of them are infidels, having no understanding of Christ or his Gospel.

The queen had therefore given 'especial commandment that the said kind of people should be with all speed avoided [i.e. banished] and discharged out of this Her Majesty's dominions'. And, once again, Elizabeth commissioned handy Casper van Senden to arrest and transport them. But this second attempt to get rid of black people was no more successful than the first. From that day to this, there has been a continuous black presence in Britain.

From P. Fryer (1984) *Staying Power: The History of Black People in Britain*, London: Pluto Press, pp. 4–12.

Questions

1. Why do you think Fryer has written a book providing such detail about the history of Black people in Britain?
2. To what extent does this historical account alter any preconceptions that you held about Black people in Britain?
3. What do you think Fryer means when he says that the 'folk myths' surrounding Africa could be used as a 'coherent racist ideology' to justify slavery?

Reading 40

Ethnic diversity and disadvantage in Britain

TARIQ MODOOD AND RICHARD BERTHOUD

The Policy Studies Institute have charted the experiences of ethnic minorities in Britain since the 1960s. The 4th Report, from which this reading is taken, continues to provide detailed and accurate information and, as Bhiku Parekh puts it in his Forward to the Report, 'provides the most reliable and comprehensive picture of the ways in which ethnic minorities are carving out a place for themselves in British society'. This extract is taken from the concluding chapter and shows that the established patterns of ethnic minority disadvantage in conjunction with diversity between different ethnic minority groups have continued. It starts with a summary of the circumstances of the major ethnic minority groups in Britain in terms of the established issues of employment, housing, education and racial harassment and then goes on to identify the main areas of progress and the obstacles and limitations (including racial prejudice and discrimination) faced by the ethnic minority population. The extract concludes by considering changes in what is understood by the concept of racial equality.

Pakistanis and Bangladeshis: Serious Poverty

The Pakistanis and, especially, the Bangladeshis continue to be severely disadvantaged. While the men in these groups have experienced some improvement in their job levels since 1982, it is from a very low base. They continue to be disproportionately in manual work, with twice as many in manual work as in non-manual work, while white men are now evenly split between these kinds of jobs. Indeed, Pakistanis are twice as likely, and Bangladeshis more than five times as likely, as white men to be in semi-skilled manual work. Self-employment reduces these ratios a little, but, even so, Pakistani and Bangladeshi men are less than two-thirds as likely to be professionals, managers and employers as white men. They are less than half as likely to supervise staff, and as employees have only two-thirds the pay packet of white men, and as self-employed only three-quarters of the incomes of whites.

While the Bangladeshis are strongly represented in self-employment with employees, this is owing largely to their concentration in one business, namely, restaurants. Self-employment among Bangladeshi men is half as common as among white men; Pakistani men on the other hand have the same rate of self-employment as white men. For both these groups, though, self-employment is relatively more important than it is for whites because so few of them have jobs as employees.

Bangladeshi and Pakistani men had unemployment rates of about 40 per cent in 1994. This was the highest of all groups; more than two and a half times higher than white men.

Only a third as many Pakistani women and only a tenth as many Bangladeshi women are in paid work compared with other women. This is probably the single most important economic division between women from different ethnic groups. It is a result of very low levels of economic activity as well as very high levels of unemployment among these two groups of women.

The full scale of the economic plight of the Bangladeshis and Pakistanis becomes apparent when one analyses household incomes and standard of living. The new data reveal that there is severe and widespread poverty among these two groups. Thus more than four out of five Pakistani and Bangladeshi households have an equivalent income below half the national average – four times as many as white nonpensioners.

Pakistanis nevertheless continue to have high levels of home-ownership. The proportion of Bangladeshis who own their own house is still low, though it has increased since 1982; many of them rent from councils or housing associations. Regardless of tenure, however, and despite the general improvements in amenities and accommodation space, Pakistanis and Bangladeshis continue to be the worst housed, and, when owners, continue to be concentrated in terraced housing. They are also still disproportionately located in inner-city areas, and are the most residentially segregated of all groups. Six out of ten Bangladeshi women, nearly half of Pakistani women and more than a fifth of the men in these groups do not speak or have only limited English. In each case this is much higher than for other Asians.

Indians and Caribbeans: Good News and Bad News

The circumstances of these two groups are far from identical. The point of grouping them together is that they occupy a middle position: their circumstances are better than those of the Bangladeshis and the Pakistanis, but they continue to experience some disadvantage. By some measures one or the other of these groups can be as poorly placed as any group studied here, but by other criteria they may have parity with the white population.

Job levels are a case in point. Caribbean men have a similar manual work profile to the Pakistanis and, despite some progress, are less likely to be professionals, managers and employers than Pakistanis. Indian men on the other hand are distinctly better represented in that category, as well as in more junior non-manual work. While of all men they have probably made the most progress up the jobs hierarchy in this period, Indians remain disadvantaged compared with white men. Yet Caribbean male employees are slightly better placed than Indians in relation to supervisory duties and earnings, with Caribbeans averaging just over 90 per cent, and Indians 85 per cent, of white male employees' earnings.

The position of Caribbean women relative to white and other women is much better than that of Caribbean men compared with other men. For though Caribbean women are much less likely to be in senior non-manual jobs than white women, they are also much less likely to be in manual work (or part-time work). In fact, of all groups, Caribbean women are most likely to be in intermediate and junior manual posts. Indian women, by contrast, are more likely to be in manual work – in fact they have a similar jobs profile to the Pakistanis. Despite these differences Indian and Caribbean women have slightly higher average earnings from full-time work than white women, and Caribbean women are also more likely to be supervisors. These are not new developments, for the same was true in 1982; then as now, Caribbean women averaged the highest female earnings (the Chinese female earnings may be higher: the sample size is too small for confidence). The Indian average earnings, however, hide a polarisation: Indian women were twice as likely as white women to be earning less than £115 per week in 1994, but were also three times as likely to earn more than £500 per week.

The gender asymmetry in the comparisons between these two minority groups and whites does not manifest itself so much in unemployment. Indian men and women were nearly a third more likely to be unemployed than whites in 1994 Caribbean men and women had double the white unemployment rate. The unemployment rate of younger Caribbeans, especially men, is a particular cause of concern.

Self-employment is a further point of divergence between these two groups. While Caribbeans have the lowest rate of self-employment, the Indians have among the highest. Caribbean men are half as likely and women a quarter as likely to be self-employed as whites, while the proportion of Indian men and women who are self-employed is 50 per cent higher than whites [. . .]

The average Indian household has a slightly higher total income than a white household, but this is largely only because the white population includes many more pensioners. If pensioners are excluded, Indian households are

8 per cent worse off than whites. By the same measure, Caribbean households are as much as a quarter worse off than whites. This is certainly because of the high proportion of lone-parent Caribbean households. Yet even among non-pensioner, non-lone-parent households, once household size is taken into account, Caribbeans have one and a half times and Indians twice the poverty rate of whites.

Despite these inequalities, Indians have significantly improved their position in the housing market. They have added to an already high rate of home-ownership, and are now as likely as whites to occupy detached or semi-detached properties. The Caribbeans, from a low base, have increased their level of home ownership. Many younger Caribbeans, however, rent in the social sector. Though improvements are discernible, both these minority groups experience housing disadvantage relative to white people in terms of quality of areas and of accommodation.

African Asians and Chinese: Upward Social Mobility

African Asian men are as likely as white men to be professionals, managers and employers, and Chinese men half as likely again. Chinese women are nearly twice as likely as white women to be so placed, though African Asian women are only three-quarters as likely. This is reflected in the employee earnings of these minority groups, which are now equivalent to those of white men and women.

Similarly, African Asians and whites have similar rates of unemployment, and the Chinese have the lowest of any ethnic group. The position of these two minority groups in the economy certainly owes something to self-employment, for both have among the highest rates and report better financial returns than whites.

A comparison of non-pensioner household average incomes confirms this picture, showing the African Asians to be only slightly worse off than whites and the Chinese to be the best off of all. Income distribution among the minority groups, however, is more polarised. For example, African Asian employees are much more likely than whites to be earning more than £500 per week in 1994, and African Asian and Chinese self-employed more likely to be making profits of £500 per week. Conversely, once family size has been taken into account, more African Asian and Chinese than white households are in poverty.

The African Asians still have an above-average proportion of households in poorer accommodation and in less desirable areas. There have, however, been considerable improvements, and, like the Indians, they have increased an already high rate of home ownership, and are now as likely as whites to own and live in detached or semi-detached houses. The Chinese, despite their high income levels, have a low rate of home-ownership, and are concentrated to a surprising extent in poor quality rented accommodation.

Progress and its Limits

The trends identified by the earlier surveys seem, then, to continue. On the one hand, there is some improvement for most groups by most measures, and roughly along previous lines. The disadvantaged location, exacerbated by the loss of manufacturing jobs from the mid-1970s, has not entirely disappeared for any of these minorities, but it continues to characterise strongly only some of them. These two features, improvement and persisting disadvantage, were also simultaneously present in the previous decades and applied to different groups in different degrees, but the cumulative effect has been to deepen socio-economic divergence.

This divergence is reflected in whether people thought that life in Britain had got better or worse for their ethnic group in the previous five years. This is about a general sense of well-being (or lack of it), and may reflect as much the mood prevalent in the country as any thing specifically to do with race relations. It is worth bearing in mind, therefore, that the economy performed well in the late 1980s, but unemployment rose again between 1990 and the end of 1993. So 1994 was not a time of deep gloom, but the 'feel-good factor' was still proving elusive. What is interesting is that, while in 1974 there was optimism in each of the minority groups, and in 1982 there was across-the-board gloom, there was no such uniformity in 1994. About a third in all groups thought that the previous five years had not resulted in any change for their group. Of the remainder, Indians and African Asians were evenly divided on whether life for Asians in Britain was better than it was five years ago, while twice as many Pakistanis and Bangladeshis thought it had got worse than thought it had got better. The Caribbeans were mid-way between the Asian groups, thus revealing a three-way split roughly corresponding to the actual fortunes of the various groups in the previous decade.

Having emphasised divergence, it is important to add something missing from the previous section. The survey found one important point in common between all the ethnic minorities. Men from all minorities are seriously under-represented as managers and employers in large establishments. These represent the top 10 per cent of all jobs in terms of status, power and earnings. Even the best-off minorities are only half as likely to hold these top jobs as white men. Even so, the minorities are better represented in these top 10 per cent of jobs today than they were in the top 25 per cent of jobs in 1974. While some minority groups are better represented in professional occupations than white people, there may nevertheless be a 'glass ceiling' effect, holding back all groups that are not white. Insofar as there is a continuing 'black-white' boundary in employment today, this is where it may be said to be. It is partially compensated by the success in self-employment that some groups have achieved: the Chinese, African Asians and Indians combined are almost twice as likely as whites to make profits of over £500 per week.

Education offers another example of similarity between the minorities. While attainment levels and progress are uneven, all minority groups have responded to their circumstances and to discrimination in the jobs market by staying on in or returning to post-compulsory education. Moreover, relative to group starting-points, the greatest progress in getting qualifications has been made by women and by Caribbean men. Qualification levels continue, however, to vary between groups. For example, the Chinese, African Asians and Indians are much more likely to have degrees than white people, while Bangladeshis and Pakistanis, especially women, are much less likely than whites to have any qualifications at all. Educational achievement, therefore, encapsulates the twin phenomena of progress and disadvantage. Perhaps the most important point here is that the progress at least partly reflects the varied educational profile of the migrant generation.

The second report's expectations (quoted above) about the consequence of education for the employment prospects of different groups seem to have proven true. The qualifications, job levels and earnings spread in 1994 are roughly what one would have predicted from the spread of qualifications in 1974, if racial exclusion was relaxed. Those ethnic groups that had an above-average middle-class professional and business profile before migration seem to have been able to re-create that profile despite the occupational downgrading that all minority groups initially experienced.

Our chapter on employment showed that ethnic minorities are still to some extent in jobs below their qualifications levels, but that some minority groups are more likely to be in professional occupations than their white peers, and the possession of qualifications, especially higher qualifications, strongly shaped earnings in 1994. The growing influence of qualifications on employment is therefore one of the factors in the reduction of racial disadvantage. An increase in educational achievement does not guarantee socio-economic equality, but it seems to be a prerequisite. It has the potential to feed directly into job levels and thence to earnings, to household income, and thus to housing, health and standard of living. These effects take different periods of time (entering a professional career will bring those other improvements in its train rather than on day one), but all can be seen in this survey to be taking place for some groups. Or, sometimes, for parts of groups: internal polarisation means that Indians, and perhaps other South Asians, are well represented simultaneously among both the prosperous and the poor. Indians are nearly twice as likely as whites to be financially in the top seventh of self-employed, and yet also twice as likely as whites to be in the poorest fifth of non-pensioner households.

It is worth pointing out that qualification attainment levels have depended not just upon the minorities themselves. They have, for example, depended also upon how white people – especially teachers, but also white peers, employers, sporting fraternities, the music and fashion industries, the police and so on – have identified the characteristics of various minorities and encouraged or excluded them in respect of various spheres of activity. There is considerable evidence that, for example, teachers, fellow pupils and others have encouraged black males to excel in sports and discouraged them from commitment to academic goals. Young black men have been stereotyped as violent and disruptive, challenging the authority of teachers and the police; or they have been praised and emulated as macho, 'cool' and exemplars of youth culture. It has recently been argued that young black men's success as leaders of youth cultures and fashion has been socially self-defeating for it has taken them away from a 'classroom culture' to a 'street culture' (Wambu 1996).

South Asians' perceived commitment to classroom discipline and academic goals has made them particularly vulnerable to racial harassment at the hands of fellow pupils, but it has also made them more attractive to teachers (Gillborn and Gipps 1996: 49–50, 56–7). Hence minority groups have been stereotyped, often in contrast to each other, in ways which have a positive as well as a negative dimension (Bonnett 1993: 25–6). Insofar as ethnicity is a factor in explaining the various minorities' qualifications profile, it is an interactive ethnicity, shaped partly by and in reaction to white people, institutions and society. Nor has it just depended upon race relations. Ethnic minorities' access to higher education has been assisted by the major expansion in the number of places available in the system.

If qualifications, and in particular the proportion of a group with degrees, are as important to the socio-economic advancement of ethnic minorities as our analysis suggests, then the qualifications profile of the young and admissions into higher education give a strong hint of the kind of socio-economic profile we should expect in ten or 20 years' time. This survey found that ethnic minority men aged 16–24 who already had some qualifications are nearly three times as likely as white men, and ethnic minority women more than one and a half as likely as white women, to be in full-time education. This applies to the disadvantaged groups, especially the Pakistanis and the Bangladeshis, as much as to those whose adult members have been relatively successful. Recent admissions data for higher education show movement in the same direction: for example, in 1994 nearly twice the proportion of young Pakistani men entered university as white men. Yet among men aged 16–24 this survey also found that twice as many Pakistani men were without an O-level equivalent GCSE pass as white men. Other research continues to show that young Caribbean men experience disproportionate problems in school (Gillborn and Gipps 1996). We found that younger Caribbeans have very high rates of unemployment, especially if they have no qualifications. So there is a continuing pattern of disadvantage and advantage not just between the ethnic minorities but within them too [. . .]

Health: New Topic, Similar Findings

This is the first time that detailed information on the health of the ethnic minorities has been available from a large, fully representative national survey. It shows that the relative health of groups follows the general socio-economic pattern. The Chinese, African Asians and Indians have a similar state of health to that of whites, and the Bangladeshis, Pakistanis and Caribbeans have poorer health than whites. The analysis shows that the categories used in previous surveys ('Black' or 'Asian') are extremely misleading because they combine minorities with very different health profiles. They thereby suggest that some 'healthy' groups have poor health and, most importantly, obscure the extent of the unhealthy circumstances of the worst-off groups.

We also found some medical conditions which are more prevalent in some groups than in others. Pakistanis and Bangladeshis are more likely to have heart disease symptoms than anyone else. The relative risk of diagnosed hypertension among Caribbean women is much higher than for other men and women. Diabetes is one condition that all minority groups seem to suffer more than whites; while white people and Caribbeans are more prone to respiratory problems than other minority groups. Nevertheless, the main finding was that the health differences between ethnic groups follow socio-economic contours. The differences seem to be less connected to the distinctive cultural practices of each group than to divisions in employment, income and standards of living [. . .]

Racial Prejudice and Exclusion

There are several indicators suggesting that British society, both white people and minorities, believes to an increasing extent that there is racial prejudice and discrimination. Most people think that employers discriminate, and many members of minority groups think that they personally have been discriminated against. Increases in these beliefs since 1982 have been greatest among South Asians – the group which was least concerned about the issue in the previous survey. It is not clear, however, that increased reports of discrimination represent a change in the actual extent of discrimination rather than a rising level of consciousness. Objective tests show that it is still common, but no more so than in earlier periods (Brown and Gay 1985; Simpson and Stevenson 1994). Nor does there seem to be a simple correlation between the reports of discrimination and the extent of disadvantage in employment. Bangladeshis report little discrimination – less than that of Indians and African Asians far above them in the occupational ladder. It was Caribbeans, whose economic position is in the middle range, who were most likely to report discrimination. The perception of discrimination may be affected by the extent to which the different minorities feel themselves to be defined by 'race' or 'colour' [. . .]

Racism can go beyond mere prejudice and discrimination. This survey found that individuals in all ethnic minority groups suffer from racial harassment and violence from those in their immediate neighbourhoods, as their workplace, from strangers in public places and sometimes even from police officers. In contrast to reports of discrimination in employment, there is much less variation in the extent of harassment reported by different minority groups, with the South Asians nearly as likely to mention incidents as the Caribbeans; as with discrimination in employment, however, the Bangladeshis are the least likely to mention it. For the first time in any survey, we were able to gauge the extent of racial insults and abuse, as well as of more directly criminal attacks on people or on property. As many as 12 per cent of the ethnic minorities interviewed said they had been racially abused or threatened in these ways at least once in the previous year. This suggests a minimum of a quarter of a million racist incidents year. Nearly a quarter of those who had been racially harassed had been victimised five or more times in the past year.

Not surprisingly, therefore, a quarter of all ethnic minority adults worry about being racially harassed. A measure of the effect of racial harassment upon them – and upon ethnic relations in this country – is that many take steps to reduce their vulnerability: making their home more secure and avoiding going out at night or travelling in areas where mostly white people live [. . .]

A specially worrying example of this wider culture of racism is what the interviewees said about the police. Among the 98 attacks on the person in which the perpetrator was seen, it was claimed that three were by police officers. Only a quarter of people who had been racially attacked in the last year had reported the incident to the police. Half of those who had reported an incident to the police were dissatisfied with the police response, the predominant feeling among them being that the police had shown a lack of interest in the victim's complaint, or even an implicit sympathy with the perpetrators. The majority of young members of the minority groups do not believe they can rely on the police to protect them from racial harassment. In fact, regardless of age, a majority of Caribbeans and (especially) of South Asians believe that they should organise self-defence groups [. . .]

Equality and Ethnicity

People who are not white in Britain are often conceived as sharing similar circumstances. Yet this study of the six main groups of immigration-based minorities shows that the differences are even more important. This diversity is not a hotch-potch, with different groups being better or worse off than each other in different areas of social life. There is an element of this kind of random or extreme diversity, but in the main there is a systematic pattern with particular groups being severely disadvantaged across a number of measures. While the fundamental division cannot be characterised as black–white, or as black–Asian–white, there continues to be evidence of racial inequality. Some of the processes involved, such as the under-employment of the talents and resourcefulness of minority persons, contribute directly to diversity – to the high level of business ownership among some groups, for example [. . .]

The concept of equality has been under intense theoretical and political discussion, especially in the English-speaking world; what is often claimed today in the name of racial equality is more than would have been recognised as such in the 1960s. Iris Young expresses well the new political climate when she describes the emergence of an ideal of equality based not just on allowing excluded groups to assimilate and live by the norms of dominant groups, but based on the view that 'a positive self-definition of group difference is in fact more liberatory' (Young 1990: 157) [. . .]

The shift is from an understanding of equality in terms of individualism and cultural assimilation to a politics of recognition, to equality as encompassing public ethnicity. Equality is not having to hide or apologise for one's origins, family or community but expecting others to respect them and adapt public attitudes and arrangements so that the heritage they represent is encouraged rather than contemptuously expected to wither away [. . .]

Britain has undoubtedly made some progress towards developing multiracial equality in the last three decades. This has included a movement away from the policy of colour-blindness – the idea that equality could be achieved by simply outlawing colour-discrimination – to a recognition of racial disadvantage as a multidimensional condition that sometimes requires positive, targeted policies if a level playing-field is to be created. Concurrently, there has been increasing recognition that minorities cannot simply be understood in terms of racism. The latest period of settlement has seen the maturation of groups with distinctive values, orientations, economic niches and policy agendas. Two decades ago, in a PSI survey report, David Smith asked whether the uniformity of Britain would turn out to be more important to Asians and Caribbeans than the diversity of their origins and heritages (Smith 1977: 331). The conclusion of this survey has to be that, while the circumstances of the minorities show some common sources of inequality, the diversity is proving to be extremely resilient and is far from confined to aspects of private culture.

From T. Modood, R. Berthoud *et al.* (1997) *Ethnic Minorities in Britain: Diversity and Disadvantage*, London: Policy Studies Institute, pp. 342–59.

Questions

1. List the main areas of racial disadvantage that have 'survived' the past 30 years.
2. What patterns of diversity between ethnic minority groups have emerged?
3. Summarise the role that education has played in the changing patterns of achievement of different ethnic minority groups.

Reading 41

Nationalism and ethnicity

MICHAEL IGNATIEFF

Michael Ignatieff's book Blood and Belonging *is based on the BBC television series of the same name in which he visited the former Yugoslavia, the Ukraine, Germany, Quebec, Kurdistan and Northern Ireland in order to explore the state of modern nationalism. This extract starts with two examples from his journey. In the first a Chetnik Serb reveals the pride and satisfaction a father can derive from the loss of his sons and in the second a wealthy German talks of his fear for the multicultural future of his country. In both cases, national pride and national identity are asserted at the expense of ethnic others. The extract ends with Ignatieff's 'conclusion' that in nations where the differences between ethnic groups are not clearly visible (for instance, by colour of skin) there is a greater need to exaggerate cultural differences in order to remind people of who they are. As he puts it, 'A Croat, thus, is someone who is not a Serb. A Serb is someone who is not a Croat. Without hatred of the other, there would be no clearly defined national self to worship and adore.'*

An Old Man's Wallet

I am standing directly in front of the Moscow Hotel in downtown Belgrade in the middle of a listless, slowly disintegrating demonstration against the Milosevic regime. A crowd of several hundred people has been there all morning and is slowly discovering that it is too small to make anything happen. In the middle of the crowd is an old man wearing a Chetnik hat. I go up and talk to him. He is in his 70s and he fought with Mihailovic against Tito during the Second World War. Does he have sons, I ask him, and if so, have they seen fighting this time?

Calmly, he takes out his wallet and shows me three passport-size colour pictures: each of his sons, all young men in their 20s. Two are dead, killed on the front during the Croatian war. The third is in prison. Why? Because, the old man says with grim satisfaction, he took his vengeance. He found the killer of one of his brothers, and killed him. Then he takes out a small folded news clipping from a Croatian newspaper, and there is a passport-size photo of another young man's face. 'The bastard who killed my son. But we got him. We got him,' he says, neatly folding the picture of his son's assassin back into the wallet with pictures of his sons.

From father to son, from son to son, there is no end to it, this form of love, this keeping faith between generations which is vengeance. In this village war, where everyone knows each other, where an old man keeps the picture of his son's killer beside the picture of the son who avenged them both. There is no end, for when he dies, this old man knows, and it gives him grim satisfaction, there will be someone to do vengeance for him too [. . .]

Herr K's White Horse

'Why are we the only people in Europe that cannot be allowed to be proud of ourselves?' Herr K asks me bitterly. The question – I have heard it a dozen times around Frankfurt already – hangs in the air between us. We are in his bungalow in a village outside Frankfurt, and he glares at me, as if I am to blame for the fact that he is not allowed to be proud to be German. The trouble is, I haven't said a word.

Then he gets up and says brightly, 'Would you like to see my horse?' Herr K loves his horse, a white Arab stallion he keeps in a paddock behind his house in a dormitory village north of Frankfurt. His love for his horse – romantic, extreme and innocent – is rather like his love of Germany [. . .]

Like most Germans of his age (*he is 53 years old*), he tells me proudly that he belongs to the first German generation lucky enough to have been born too late. Too late for what? I ask. Too late to be guilty of anything he replies, with a mirthless chuckle.

He just remembers the red glow of burning Berlin in the winter of 1945. As the Russians moved into the city, he and his mother fled to this village in the verdant hills north of Frankfurt. Now, after twenty-five years in the prison service, he is standing as a candidate for the right-wing Republikaners in the round of municipal elections to be held in Hesse. German politics is being driven right-wards and the people driving it in that direction are men like Herr K. He knows he will be elected: he is a good politician, he can feel the wind turning his way [. . .]

Ten kilometres away from Herr K's immaculate villa is a tent city for asylum seekers. He drives there, and we stand outside the fence and look at the rows of tents, the board walks in the mud, and a pair of sad Africans giving each other a haircut in the rain. Herr K particularly wants me to know that

German women, in need of pin money, come here to do the cleaning. Can you imagine? he says. A black man knocking his cigarette ash on the floor and a German woman on her knees sweeping it up. No, this cannot go on.

Then his bonhomie returns and his shoulders shake with his strange mirthless laughter, and he says that the asylum law is a 'typical piece of German megalomania'. What other country would dream of making itself the world's welfare officer?

He is remarkably cheerful for someone who believes the German way of life is under attack. He should be, for he knows his party cannot lose. The constitutional right of asylum has been abridged, and the Republikaner have taken the credit for saying out loud what other parties only said under their breath.

Yet tightening up the asylum process, Herr K says, will not get to the root of the problem. The real issue is that Germans no longer feel at home in their own country. Thirty per cent of the population of Frankfurt is foreign. Why do you think I live in the countryside? he says.

Multiculturalism is the problem. We will have no culture at all if we go on 'in this way'.

But Turks in your country speak German, live in a German way. Why can't you admit them as citizens?

'We are Germans. They are Turks.'

Racism is too simple a word for Herr K's view of the world. A racist usually has some fantasy about the way 'they' smell, or the way 'they' cook. Herr K doesn't seem prey to any phobias. Ethnic essentialism is a fancier term for his position, and perhaps more accurate. He believes that being German defines the limits of what he can possibly know, understand or sympathize with. Kerr K is hardly alone. All week long I met liberal Germans who would not be seen dead with the likes of Herr K, for mixed reasons of social snobbery and political conviction, who nevertheless spoke Herr K's language. They all feel that the liberal German conscience has reached its hour of truth with the asylum crisis. 'This cannot go on,' they all said to me. 'We will end up not knowing who we are.' [. . .]

It strikes me that it would be nice for Germans to like themselves and like their nation, so long as they accept the Germany that actually exists, the Germany of the post-1945 borders, the Germany that is home to millions of foreigners. The problem with Herr K is not that he is a nationalist, but that he is a German nationalist who actually despises the Germany he lives in.

He wants a Germany for the Germans, when there are already 6 million foreigners here. He wants a Germany that is law-abiding, clean, orderly, where women stay at home, where the television does not preach sex and violence to its adolescents. It is a Germany, in other words, in which not just the 1930s, but the 1960s never happened. It is a Germany, he keeps saying, that is at home with itself, at peace with itself. ('How do you say it in English?' He searches for the word, 'Ah, yes,"serene".') [. . .]

The Hungry and the Sated

I end my journey where I started, thinking about the relation between arguments and consequences, between nationalist good intentions and nationalist violence. A rationalist tends to believe that what people do results from what they say they intend. Thus when nationalists say violence is warranted in self-defence and in seeking self-determination, a rationalist concludes that this is why violence occurs.

I am no longer so sure. So often it seemed to me, the violence happened first, and the nationalist excuses came afterwards [. . .]

Everywhere I've been, nationalism is most violent where the group you are defining yourself against most closely resembles you. A rational explanation of conflict would predict the reverse to be the case. To outsiders at least, Ulstermen look and sound like Irishmen, just as Serbs look and sound like Croats – yet the very similarity is what pushes them to define themselves as polar opposites. Since Cain and Abel, we have known that hatred between brothers is more ferocious than hatred between strangers. We say tritely that this is so because hatred is a form of love turned against itself. Or that we hate most deeply what we recognize as kin. Or that violence is the ultimate denial of an affiliation we cannot bear. None of this will do. There are puzzles which no theory of nationalism, no theory of the narcissism of minor differences can resolve. After you have been to the wastelands of the new world order, particularly to those fields of graves, marked with numberless wooden crosses, you feel stunned into silence by a deficit of moral explanation [. . .]

There was a bewildering insincerity and inauthenticity to nationalist rhetoric everywhere I went, as if the people who mouthed nationalist slogans were aware, somewhere inside, of the implausibility of their own words. Serbs who, in one breath, would tell you that all Croats were Ustashe beasts would, in the next, recall the happy days when they lived with them in peace. In this divided consciousness, there was a plane of abstract fantasy and a plane of direct experience which were never allowed to confront each other. Nationalism's chief function as a system of moral rhetoric is to ensure this compartmentalization and in so doing to deaden the conscience. Yet it never entirely works. The very people who absorb such generalizations with such apparently unthinking zeal often still hear the inner voice which tells them that, actually, in their own experience, these generalizations are false. Yet if most people hear this inner voice, few seem able to act upon it. The authority of nationalist rhetoric is such that most people actively censor the testimony of their own experience.

Nationalism is a form of speech which shouts, not merely so that it will be heard, but so that it will believe itself. It was almost as if the quotient of crude historical fiction, violent moral exaggeration, ludicrous caricature of the enemy was in direct proportion to the degree to which the speaker was himself aware that it was all really a pack of lies. But such insincerity may be a functional requirement of a language which is burdened with the task of insisting upon such a high volume of untruths. The nationalist vision of an ethnically pure state, for example, has the task of convincing ordinary people to disregard stubbornly adverse sociological realities, like the fact that most societies are not and have never been ethnically pure. The nationalist leaders' call to ardent communitarian fellow-feeling has to triumph over the evidence, plain to every one of his listeners, that no modern society can beat to the rhythm of a single national will. That such fantasies do take hold of large numbers of people is a testament to the deep longing such people have to escape the stubborn realities of life.

Nationalism on this reading, therefore, is a language of fantasy and escape. In many cases – Serbia is a flagrant example – nationalist politics is a full-scale, collective escape from the realities of social backwardness. Instead of facing up to the reality of being a poor, primitive, third-rate economy on the periphery of Europe, it is infinitely more attractive to listen to speeches about the heroic and tragic Serbian destiny and to fantasize about the final defeat of her historic enemies.

The political systems of all societies – advanced and backward, developed and undeveloped – are prey to the lure to fantasy, and the only reliable antidote is the cold bath of economic, political or military disaster. Even then, societies cannot awaken from nationalist fantasy unless they have a political system which enables them to remove the fantasists. Societies with adequate democratic tradition have proven themselves vulnerable to the politics of fantasy. But a democratic system does provide at least for the punishment of fantasists whose lies catch up with them. At the same time, however, one cannot think of democracy as a reliable antidote to nationalism [. . .]

My journeys have also made me re-think the nature of belonging. Any expatriate is bound to have moments of longing for a more complete national belonging. But I have been to places where belonging is so strong, so intense that I now recoil from it in fear. The rational core of such fear is that there is a deep connection between violence and belonging. The more strongly you feel the bonds of belonging to your own group, the more hostile, the more violent will your feelings be towards outsiders. You can't have the intensity of belonging without violence, because belonging of this intensity moulds the individual conscience: if a nation gives people a reason to sacrifice themselves, it also gives them a reason to kill.

Throughout my travels, I kept remembering the scene in *Romeo and Juliet* when Juliet is whispering to herself on the balcony in her night-gown, unaware that Romeo is in the shadows listening. She is struggling to understand what it means for her, a Capulet, to fail in love with a Montague. Suddenly she exclaims,

> 'This but thy name that is my enemy;
> Thou art thyself though, not a Montague.
> What's Montague? it is nor hand, nor foot,
> Nor arm, nor face, nor any other part
> Belonging to a man. O! be some other name!
> What's in a name?

In the front lines of Bosnia, in the estates of Loyalist and Republican Belfast, in all the places where the tribal gangsters – the Montagues and Capulets of our day – are enforcing the laws of ethnic loyalty, there are Juliets and Romeos who still cry out 'Oh, let me not be a Croatian, Serbian, Bosnian, Catholic or Protestant. Let me only be myself.'

Being only yourself is what ethnic nationalism will not allow. When people come, by terror or exaltation, to think of themselves as patriots first, individuals second, they have embarked on a path of ethical abdication.

Yet everywhere, in Belfast, in Belgrade and Zagreb, in Lvov, in Quebec and Kurdistan, I encountered men and women, often proud patriots, who have stubbornly resisted embarking on that path. Their first loyalty has remained to themselves. Their first cause is not the nation, but the defence of their right to choose from their own frontiers for their belonging.

But such people are an embattled minority. The world is not run by sceptics and ironists, but by gunmen and true believers and the new world they are bequeathing to the next century already seems a more violent and desperate place than I could ever have imagined . . . I began the journey as a liberal, and I end as one, but I cannot help thinking that liberal civilization – the rule of laws not men, of argument in place of force, of compromise in place of violence – runs deeply against the human grain and is only achieved and sustained by the most unremitting struggle against human nature. The liberal virtues – tolerance, compromise, reason – remain as valuable as ever, but they cannot be preached to those who are mad with fear or mad with vengeance. In any case, preaching always rings hollow. We must be prepared to defend them by force, and the failure of the sated, cosmopolitan nations to do so has left the hungry nations sick with contempt for us.

Between the hungry and the sated nations, there is an impassable barrier of incomprehension. I've lived all my life in sated nation states, in places which have no outstanding border disputes, are no longer ruled by foreigners or oppressors, are masters in their own house. Sated people can afford to be cosmopolitan; sated people can afford the luxury of condescending to the passions of the hungry. But among the Crimean Tartars, the Kurds and the Crees, I met the hungry ones, peoples whose very survival will remain at risk until they achieve self-determination, whether in their own nation state or in someone else's.

What's wrong with the world is not nationalism itself. Every people must have a home, every such hunger must be assuaged. What's wrong is the kind of nation, the kind of home that nationalists want to create and the means they use to seek their ends. A struggle is going on wherever I went between those who still believe that a nation should be a home to all, and that race, colour, religion and creed should be no bar to belonging, and those who want their nation to be home only to their own. It's the battle between the civic and the ethnic nation. I know which side I'm on. I also know which side, right now, happens to be winning.

From M. Ignatieff (1994) *Blood and Belonging: Journeys into the New Nationalism,* London: Vintage, pp. 40–1, 71–3, 185–9.

Questions

1. In the section of the reading entitled 'The Old Man's Wallet', why do you think the old man takes 'grim satisfaction' in vengeance?
2. In the section entitled 'Herr K's White Horse', what do you think Germans mean when they say 'we will end up not knowing who we are'?
3. In the final part, 'The Hungry and the Sated', what do you think Ignatieff means when he says that 'Nationalism . . . is a language of fantasy and escape'?
4. List some of the ways in which 'minor' nationalist differences may be used to exaggerate ethnic divisions between groups.

Reading 42

How the other half dies

SUSAN GEORGE

This text was first published in 1976 but has since been revised and reprinted. In it Susan George asks the question 'Why are so many people of the world hungry?' Her answer, essentially, is because food is controlled by the rich. The extract here demonstrates George's emphasis on the need to acknowledge the divide between the Third World and the rich nations, the exploitation of the Third World by powerful Western institutions and governments and the contingent dependency of Third World nations. In it she challenges the notion that large scale agribusiness is an efficient system for food production in global terms. Indeed, she suggests it is one of several crucial strands in creating hunger in poor nations.

Hunger is not an unavoidable phenomenon like death and taxes. We are no longer living in the seventeenth century when Europe suffered shortages on an average of every three years and famine every ten. Today's world has all the physical resources and technical skills necessary to feed the present population of the planet or a much larger one. Unfortunately for the millions of people who go hungry, the problem is not a technical one – nor was it wholly so in the seventeenth century, for that matter. Whenever and wherever they live, rich people eat first, they eat a disproportionate amount of the food there is and poor ones rarely rise in revolt against this most basic of oppressions unless specifically told to 'eat cake'. Hunger is not a scourge but a scandal.

The present world political and economic order might be compared to that which reigned over social-class relations in individual countries in nineteenth-century Europe – with the Third World now playing the role of the working class. All the varied horrors we look back upon with mingled disgust and incredulity have their equivalents, and worse, in the Asian, African and Latin American countries where well over 500 million people are living in what the World Bank has called 'absolute poverty'. And just as the 'propertied classes' of yesteryear opposed every reform and predicted imminent economic disaster if eight-year-olds could no longer work in the mills, so today those groups that profit from the poverty that keeps people hungry are attempting to maintain the *status quo* between the rich and poor worlds [. . .]

It is absolutely true that the developed, industrialized countries (mostly Western, whether market economy or socialist, plus Japan and a handful of others), which we'll call DCs, consume a lot more food than the three continents of so-called Third World nations, which we'll call UDCs, or *underdeveloped countries.* In general, they are neither 'less developed' or 'developing' – their situation is frequently growing worse – and there is no reason to adopt polite, euphemistic initials to describe them.

In recent years, the world has produced about 1300 million tons of food and feed grains annually, and the DCs eat half although they account for only about a quarter of the world's population. Their animals eat fully a quarter of all the grain, or, as some journalist has undoubtedly already told you, because we all get our figures from the same UN documents, 'the equivalent of the total human consumption of China and India put together' – some 1.3 billion people. If the Chinese, who raise about four times as many pigs as the Americans, collectively went mad tomorrow and began to feed their pigs on grain as Americans do, there would be very little grain left in the world for humans anywhere. UDC people eat their grain directly as bread or other pastry. On the average (although averages aren't much use in UDCs as well shall see) they consume about 506 lb annually (1969–71). During the same period, in the USA, people averaged 1760 lb of grain intake, nine-tenths of it in the form of meat, poultry or dairy products. Figures are just slightly lower for Europe and Japan. In the past ten years alone the average American has *added* 350 lb of grain to his annual diet – about the equivalent of the yearly consumption of a poor Indian. Obviously, this American was not seriously malnourished in 1966 and this addition has not been imperative. If *you* are eating too much meat and animal fat, this is a matter between you and your doctor. If *millions* of consumers are eating such a proportion of the world's cereal grains in this form, it is a matter between them, their governments and those economic agents their governments primarily serve. It is also a matter in which the consumer generally has very little to say. Taking the individual meat-eater to task for starving his brethren is on about the same intellectual plane as, 'Think of the hungry children in India, darling, and finish your lovely peas and carrots.' So please put your guilt, if you are harbouring any, aside while we try to understand the *structural* nature of DC agriculture and how it relates to hunger.

The United States is generally credited with having one of the world's most efficient food-production machines – and there is plenty of evidence that it is attempting to generalize its own system in other DCs and in the Third World as well. It may be efficient, but it is also extremely costly. If you still think of farming in terms of 'We plough the fields and scatter the good seed on the land/But it is fed and watered by God's almighty hand', you are barking up an entirely wrong tree. Agriculture as practised in the US today is hardly 'agricultural' at all – it is rather a highly sophisticated, highly energy-intensive *system for transforming one series of industrial products into another series of industrial products which happen to be edible.* Farming itself, inside this system, has become almost incidental: it occupies under 4 per cent of the American population on 2,800,00 farms. Not quite 4 per cent of those farms produce *half* of all the food that feeds the other 96 per cent, the farming population itself, and provides millions of tons for export besides. Forty years ago there were 6.8 million farms in America. The 4 million that have disappeared were, of course, small family farms. Such 'inefficient' producers have been increasingly replaced by superfarmers: 1 per cent of US feedlots now raise 60 per cent of the beef cattle, and three streamlined producers reportedly grow 90 per cent of all the lettuce in American salads, to give only two examples. Fewer and fewer 'farmers' are out in the fields in overalls and straw hats – they are, rather, in corporate boardrooms in grey pinstripes and conservative ties. Many of them are in farming only because of the tax advantages it offers. In 1972, only 39 per cent of US farms with more than $40,000 turnover reported *any profits at all* – profits are eaten up in 'costs' which are made up in other phases of the business. One of the huge 'corporate farmers' is the Tenneco conglomerate whose total operating revenues went over the $55.5 billion mark in 1975. Although it is a major grower of citrus fruits, grapes, almonds, etc., this is just a tiny fraction of its business; for as a modern 'integrated' company, its other divisions can supply tractors, fertilizers and pesticides on the input end – and packaging, marketing and even ships to carry food exports on the output end. Big processing companies like Del Monte and Minute Maid supply most of their own factories' needs from their own farms. Such farms need very little labour but they are intensely dependent on manufactured inputs like machinery, irrigation systems, fertilizers and the like.

As to the modern way to raise animals, another giant, now under development in North Carolina, will cover a total of 150,000 hectares but will employ only 1000 people, one for every 15 hectares (37 acres). 'Grains will be sown, nurtured and harvested by machines, including airplanes. They will be fed to the (50,000) cattle and hogs . . . those animals will never touch the ground. They will be bred, suckled and fed to maturity in specially designed pens.' The agricultural economist in charge of the farm (which belongs to a New York investor) says, 'Meeting a need and making a profit from it is the American way . . . The era of the family farm is gone and people might as well forget it. It takes risk-capital to farm nowadays and capital investment requires a profit. The house wife will be paying more for food, but Americans spend less on food now than any other nation. The American consumer is spoiled rotten, but it's going to change.'

It is not the 'spoiled-rotten' American consumers' choice that the only chicken, pork or beef they can now buy is raised on industrially processed feed on industrial feedlots. Twenty years ago, one-third to one-half of the *entire continental United States* was classed by the Department of Agriculture as pastureland – and thus only marginally fertile for raising anything but animals. But because it takes 'too long' to fatten an animal on grassland, much of this marginal land now goes to waste and nearly all US animals which may be regarded as animated machines for consuming inputs are concentrated on feedlots where up to 100,000 ill-fated beasts can be conveniently stuffed with high-protein feeds and chemical additives. The animal feedstuff industry is the 'ninth largest in the United States'. This system wastes pastureland and it wastes grain that would be suitable for humans, but is this the individual consumer's fault? The profligate nature of this kind of livestock raising is further demonstrated by the fact that feedlot animal wastes do not even go back into the soil as fertilizer but into the waters as pollution.

This energy- and capital-intensive food system model, expressly geared to consuming enormous amounts of grain and industrial products, is the one the US is trying to inflict upon the rest of the world. In Europe, the family farm still holds an honourable place and most European cattle are still pasture fed, but this is no longer the case for Europe's pigs and chickens that have become dependent on industrially processed feeds like US-produced soya meal. Feedlots for beef have already been successfully implanted in Iran and in the Italian Piedmont; the Soviet Union has also adopted this model: its massive grain purchases in 1972 and 1975 were aimed at feeding livestock, not people. Chickens in Argentina are now being fed just like those in Alabama. Other countries – unless their governments recognize the dangers of dependency on feedgrains they do not themselves produce, and unless their consumers can learn to organize *now* – may well follow suit. Why? Because the commercial survival, and thus status as a world power, of the United States depends enormously and increasingly on its ability to sell its farm and agro-industrial products abroad. Feedgrains are among its major crops.

Some experts claim that US farming uses more than a calorie of energy for every calorie of food it produces. The Club of Rome says the ratio can go as high as twelve to one. If you count everything that goes into producing tractors, fertilizers, agri-chemicals and even the scientific research that contributes so much to increased yields, you can make a very convincing case for this statement. Yet these inputs, 'upstream' from actual food growing, are only half the picture: the whole industrial processing, packaging, marketing and distribution system for food 'downstream' from the farm is the other. The biggest integrated corporate farmers can handle their produce from seeds to supermarket.

Most of the 2,800,000 farms left in the US are still, however, family operated and according to *Fortune* many large-scale growers have concluded 'there is more money to be made as a packer and marketer than as a farmer'. These marketers (again including Tenneco) provide brand-name, pre-packed fresh fruits and vegetables grown by themselves or by smaller farmers under contract. This produce will cost more at the supermarket 'as consumers are persuaded to upgrade their purchases. And the costs of carrying out such marketing programs could also accelerate the trend to concentration in produce wholesaling that has already taken place at the retail level.' For the smaller-scale farmer, this concentration can only mean 'the prospect of an even greater imbalance in the relative bargaining power of many sellers and few buyers' (*Fortune*). Food- and feedgrain-producing family farms are already largely in thrall to this system characterized by a limited number of possible customers [. . .] Upstream, grain and energy are squandered; downstream, farmers and consumers are squeezed. Here is how the Secretary of the US National Farmers Union described at Congressional hearings what he calls the 'social inefficiency' of the food industry:

> I went shopping at the Giant Supermarket on the weekend. I found General Mills asking $75.04 per bushel for corn! ('Cocoa Puffs' – cornmeal, sugar, corn syrup, cocoa, salt, etc.). Farmers averaged $2.95 a bushel for corn last month. The farm price had been multiplied by more than 25 times by the time the corn was offered to the consumer.
>
> I don't care whether General Mills makes 90% profit or 50% or 1% or goes broke on its Cocoa Puffs. I think that charging consumers $75.04 a bushel for corn represents a monumentally inefficient performance. General Mills isn't the only nutritional and economic incompetent in the breakfast food business. Quaker Oats was charging . . . a whopping $110.40 per bushel for what? Plain puffed wheat! Nabisco, Kelloggs, Posts were all in the same league. The performance of the breakfast food industry only illustrates the kind of social inefficiency that characterizes much of our present-day food product design and merchandising practices.

The American food-system model has nearly reached the outer limits of what it can induce people to consume in *physical* terms, but since its only alternatives are expansion or stagnation and eventual collapse, it must increase the *value* of what is eaten. Although very few Americans are still involved in *farming* (the figures are also steadily decreasing in the other DCs), fully three out of ten are employed in *food* input production-processing-distribution – which makes 'agriculture' in this sense easily the largest industry in America. It is this whole system, wherever it may be used, that is implied by the term 'agribusiness'.

Another characteristic of such highly sophisticated agricultural systems is their *flexibility*. They can adapt to market demand or, the lack of it, in an amazingly short period, considering that food still must, after all, be *grown*. Canadian officials have said they could increase food production by 50 per cent in five years if necessary. During the 1960s, the huge US food-production machine ran out of control and began to amass surpluses that could not be got rid of in the world market. The government responded by taking 20 million hectares out of production and as late as the spring of 1973 was still paying farmers not to produce: subsidies stood at $3 billion that year and the country was operating at only a fraction of its real agricultural capacity. But when world grain prices shot up and world food stocks dwindled to alarming levels, those hectares were put back into production. Between 1972 and 1973 (according to USDA estimates) the wheat crop increased by 12 per cent and soybeans by fully 25 per cent. Both 1975 and 1976 were bumper years; the US planted 'fence to fence'. Industrialized agriculture can, in other words, respond with exceptional sensitivity to increased demand for farm products when this demand is expressed in money.

From S. George (1991) (1976) *How the Other Half Dies: The Real Reasons For World Hunger*, London: Pelican, pp. 23–9.

Questions

1. Summarise the reasons that George offers for the growth of corporate farmers and farming and the decline of the small family farm.
2. The comment from the Secretary of the US National Farmers Union (p. 271, lines 14–27) provides some examples of the packaging and marketing of basic foodstuffs. What other popular food items can you think of that involved such packaging and marketing?

Reading 43

Sociology and disability

LEN BARTON

In this reading, Barton advocates an 'emancipatory' approach to the study of disability; an approach that considers how a sociological imagination can contribute to the benefit of disabled people. Disability tends to have been viewed in medical and psychological, rather than sociological, terms and to that extent has had very limited impact within sociology. This reading looks at how our own, 'able bodied', experiences of encounters with disabled people have influenced how we define and relate to disability; and how such definitions can encourage discriminatory practices. It also looks at the social restrictions faced by the disabled and how disabled people have fought against discrimination and prejudice and challenged existing power relations.

Mainstream sociology has historically shown little interest in the issue of disability. A range of possible reasons can be identified for this situation. Sociologists have tended to accept the dominant hegemony with regard to viewing disability in medical and psychological terms. Thus the issue is perceived as pre- or non-sociological. A great deal of sociological work has been based on the assumption of individuals as 'rational' actors (Barbalet 1993). Individuals categorised in terms of being 'subnormal' or 'mentally handicapped' were excluded from this work or viewed as examples of exotic behaviour (Quicke 1986). Finally, sociological work concerned with the generation of theories of social reproduction and the pursuit of change has ignored the ways in which disabled people operate as a powerful social movement (Barton and Oliver 1992).

Even where the question of disability has been addressed it has not been without some concern. For example, Jenkins (1991) makes hardly any reference to the existing work produced by disabled sociologists. If he was aware of it, he chose not to use it.

A great deal of the sociological work accomplished so far has been undertaken by the contributors to this book. Few of these work within mainstream sociology departments or publish in recognised sociology outlets. It is a sobering thought to consider the limited extent to which this work has had any important impact on the discipline itself [. . .]

Definition, History and Difference

How we relate to disabled people is influenced, for example, by our past experience of such encounters and the way in which we define 'disability'. Our definitions are crucial in that they may be part of and further legitimate disabilist assumptions and discriminatory practices. Disabled people have been the recipients of a range of offensive responses by other people. These include horror, fear, anxiety, hostility, distrust, pity, over-protection and patronising behaviour.

One of the dominant influences shaping both professional and commonsense definitions has been the medical model. This approach as Hahn notes: 'imposes a presumption of biological or physiological inferiority upon disabled persons' (1986: 89). It emphasises individual loss or inabilities thereby contributing to a dependency model of disability. Labels such as 'invalid', 'cripple', 'spastic', 'handicapped' and 'retarded' all imply both a functional loss and a lack of worth. Such labels have tended to legitimate individual medical and negative views of disability, to the neglect of other perspectives, in particular, those of disabled people.

Disability is a social and political category in that it entails practices of regulations and struggles for choice, empowerment and rights. This approach provides a very different understanding of disability and entails an alternative set of assumptions, priorities and explanations, as Hahn clearly shows. He maintains that:

> disability stems from the failure of a structured social environment to adjust to the needs and aspirations of citizens with disabilities *rather* than from the inability of a disabled individual to adapt to the demands of society. (1986: 128)

Being disabled involves experiencing discrimination, vulnerability and abusive assaults upon your self-identity and esteem.

Disability is thus a form of oppression which entails social restrictions, as Oliver has so powerfully argued:

> All disabled people experience disability as social restriction whether these restrictions occur as a consequence of inaccessible built environments, questionable notions of intelligence and social competence, the inability of the general public to use sign language, the lack of reading material in Braille or hostile public attitudes to people with non-visible disabilities. (1990: xiv, Introduction)

This perspective challenges both professional and public perceptions of disability. It involves more than changes to access and resource issues.

In a discussion of changing definitions of difference in relation to the history of people classified as 'mentally handicapped', Ryan and Thomas contend that these definitions: 'have always been conceived by others, never are they the expression of a group of people finding their own identity, their own history' (1980: 13).

Rather than seeking an explanation in terms of an individual's inabilities they place the emphasis on the *power* of significant groups in defining the identity of others. In this instance, the outcome of such interventions by professionals has been one of disempowerment, marginalisation and dependency.

Medical values and interpretations have, historically, contributed to a view which gives priority to impairments, physical and/or intellectual, as being the cause of disability (Rieser and Mason 1990). In this brief attempt to highlight some of the unacceptable features of this approach, it must not be assumed that disabled people do not need, or see, at specific points in their lives, the necessity of medical support. What is being challenged are the social conditions and relations in which such encounters take place, the enveloping of their identity in medical terms, the importance of their voice being heard and a much more effective participation in decisions which affect them [. . .]

Another gap requiring more sociological work concerns the politics of difference. The disability movement has begun to be analysed in terms of a new social movement in modern societies (Oliver 1990; Shakespeare 1993). This includes the question of collective solidarity. Particular criticisms have been made concerning the degree to which people with learning difficulties, gay and lesbian disabled people and disabled women are adequately represented and feel part of the movement (Morris 1991). Thus, for example, the degree of marginalisation is intensified in the lives of disabled women, as Begum, a disabled black woman, so powerfully reminds us:

> Disabled women have become perennial outsiders, our powerless position has not been seriously addressed by either the disability rights or the women's movement. The simultaneous neglect is unforgivable. (1992: 73)

Disabled women mediate their experiences within gendered relations. These compound the oppressions involved. This results in differences in perception and understanding. Oppression involves relations of domination and the absence of choices in the lives of the oppressed. Disability, like race, is part of an overarching structure of domination. This involves a rejection of an additive approach to oppression in favour of an interlocking perspective. How we see oppressed groups *relationally* is of central importance. Challenging disabilist oppression is a necessary step in the struggle to eradicate all forms of oppression [. . .]

The struggle of disabled people is against discrimination and prejudice as it is expressed in individual and institutional forms. This essential but difficult task is as Shakespeare notes, for example:

> about the 'victim' refusing that label, and instead focusing attention on the structural causes of victimisation. It is about the subversion of stigma: taking a negative appellation and converting it into a badge of pride. (1993: 253)

Disabled people are thus involved, in varying degrees of intensity and effectiveness, in a struggle to capture the power of naming difference itself. An emancipatory meaning of difference is one of the goals of social justice. This entails challenging definitions which isolate and marginalise and replacing them with those which engender solidarity and dignity.

This is part of the endeavour for effective participation in society on the part of disabled people which involves challenging the existing power relations and conditions as well as developing a positive self-identity. Johnny Crescendo, the disabled singer, has captured these concerns in the following vivid way:

> It's about being comfortable in who you are as a disabled person. It's about having the self respect and the self confidence to challenge the system that screws me and you . . . There's a war going on for our right to be included in the human race. Stay Strong. Stay Proud. Stay Angry. GET INVOLVED. (Cassette, entitled PRIDE)

Thus there is a refusal to accept the deficit and dependency role which has powerfully shaped policies and practices. The language used to describe these endeavours is that of a war, struggle, a battle. The use of such discourse reminds us of the stubbornness and pervasiveness of that which is being opposed. It highlights the degree of commitment required by those engaged in such efforts. It reinforces the social and political nature of the task and the importance of collective solidarity. Finally, it assumes that there are no easy, quick answers to what are fundamentally complex and often contradictory issues.

These sentiments are reflected by Barnes, a disabled analyst, in a powerful statement in which he maintains that:

> The abolition of institutional discrimination against disabled people is *not* a marginal activity; it strikes at the heart of social organisations within both the public and private sectors. It would not be possible to confront this problem without being involved in political debate and taking up positions on a wide range of issues [my emphasis]. (1991: 233)

In an analysis of social policy in the past decade Glendinning argues that the case of disabled people has actually got *worse* in that:

> The economic and social policies of the last decade have done little to enhance, and much to damage, the quality of life of disabled people. Despite the rhetoric of 'protecting' the most 'deserving', 'vulnerable', or 'needy', much of this 'protection' has been illusory. (1991: 16)

These events have culminated in a serious reduction in the degree of autonomy and choice of disabled people and an increase and intensification of 'scrutiny and control by professionals and others' (p. 16).

Projects undertaken since this serious criticism was made continue to reinforce such concerns. For example, in a project examining the extent to which community care can promote independent living for disabled people, Morris (1993) interviewed disabled people, all of whom required assistance in daily living tasks. Several consistent findings confirmed the sense of hopelessness and helplessness that many disabled people experience when trying to get access to statutory services. These services were often not able to respond to the particular or changing requirements of disabled people. The ideology of 'caring' for someone which underpins practice in the social and health services predominantly means 'taking responsibility for them, taking charge of them' (Morris 1993: 38). This necessarily involves relations of dependence and an emphasis on 'fitting the client to the service' (p. 20). These factors contributed to a custodial notion of caring. Too often statutory services were based on the assumption that 'physical impairment is the barrier to asserting choice and control' (p. 42) rather than how it is responded to. In another research project Bewley and Glendinning (1994) explored how far disabled people are consulted about the preparation of Community Care Plans. The research included a survey of Community Care Plans in LEAs in England and Wales and detailed studies of a number of authorities. Some of the main findings revealed that very little energy and resources have gone into the production of appropriate materials for people with learning difficulties. Many disabled people gave examples of how they had been effectively excluded by the format of the meetings, the predominance of paperwork, technical terminology, professional jargon and the shared understandings of social services staff. Thus, there was little opportunity for disabled people to define those issues relating to Community Care which they thought were important. Finally, there was a clear failure to recognise the unequal power relations between those who control the provision of services and the disabled people for whom these services are essential to maintain their personal independence.

Disabled people, both individually and through their organisations, have been campaigning for a range of changes with such professional bodies. These include demands for greater choice in the nature and amount of services provided, more control over allocations of resources, especially in relation to independent living, and new forms of accountability of service providers to disabled people involving clear mechanisms for handling disagreements.

Conclusion

To be disabled means to be discriminated against. It involves social isolation and restriction. Disability is a significant means of social differentiation in modern societies. The level of esteem and the social standing of disabled people is derived from their position in relation to the wider social conditions and relations of a given society.

Particular institutions can have a significant influence on social status. Status is influenced by the cultural images which, for example, the media portray of particular groups, as well as the legal rights and protection offered them. How a society excludes particular groups or individuals involves processes of categorisations in which the inabilities, and the unacceptable and inferior aspects of a person are generated and legitimated.

Disabled people are increasingly involved in challenging such stereotypes and developing an alternative dignified perspective, one which recognises disability as a human rights issue. This involves the struggle for choice, social justice and participation. The voices of disabled people are unmistakably clear on these issues. Listen to these:

> In a sense it is startlingly simple. We live in a world which depends for its smooth functioning on marginalising all those for whom its living, working and leisure space was not designed. But we are not just marginalised, we are oppressed and the oppression and abuse have one central identical effect – to make the victims blame themselves and feel that they are bad. (Cross 1994: 164)

or again:

> Our vision is of a society which recognises our rights and our value as equal citizens rather than merely treating us as the recipient of other people's goodwill. (Morris 1992: 10)
>
> This commitment to human rights is based on the belief that the world is changeable and that we need to find effective ways of struggling to get things changed. (Richardson 1991)

Part of this struggle must be concerned with establishing a public confirmation that discrimination against disabled people is not acceptable. This will require anti-discrimination legislation and political action. In a book entitled *Meeting Disability: A European Response,* Daunt 'explores the intersection between the political integration of Europe and the social integration of disabled people'. He also maintains that:

> everything we do in relation to disability should be founded on two complementary principles . . .
>
> 1. The principle that all measures should be founded on the explicit recognition of the *rights* of disabled people.
> 2. The principle that all people are to be regarded as of *equal* value in the society and to the society. (1991: 184)

The extent to which we recognise the value of such principles and seek to implement them in our everyday lives will be contingent upon the degree to which we recognise the profound seriousness of the oppression of disabled people.

In this chapter there has been an encouragement to develop a self-critical approach to the sociological engagement with the issue of disability. An adequate sociology of disability will entail an exploration of issues of power, social justice, citizenship and human rights. Ultimately, fundamental questions need to be asked about the current structural and social conditions and relations of society and how these in complex, and often contradictory ways, establish and legitimate the creation of barriers. The economic, material and ideological forces involved need to be challenged and changed if institutional discrimination is to be overcome.

The issue of disability raises difficult questions that are not only to be examined and engaged with at a societal or policy level, but also at an individual one. What vision do you have with regard to your society and to what extent is your concern over the question of disability inspired by a human rights approach? An important way to begin to seriously engage with such questions is to listen to the voices of disabled people as they are expressed, for example, through their writings, songs and plays.

From L. Barton (1996) 'Sociology and disability: some emerging issues's in L. Barton (ed.) *Disability and Society: Emerging Issues and Insights*, Harlow: Addison Wesley Longman, pp. 6–14.

Question

1. Explain the criteria you think should be used in defining disability.
2. Barton makes the point that establishing relationships with people raises certain questions for the 'non-disabled' researcher, such as 'What rights have I to undertake this work?' and 'What responsibilities arise from the privileges I have as a result of my social position?' How would you respond to these questions?
3. In concluding Barton suggests that 'to be disabled means to be discriminated against'. List some of the ways in which disabled people are discriminated against.

Part III Differences and Inequalities

Further Reading

As this section has encompassed such a wide range of material – indeed, as we pointed out in the introduction, differences and inequalities have been arguably the most pervasive themes of sociological inquiry – it is particularly difficult to select a handful of supporting readings. The following titles, then, are merely examples of sociological work in this vast field.

On social class, the collection of papers edited by David Lee and Bryan Turner, from which two of our readings (29 and 30) are taken, makes available many of the key contributions to sociological debate about the concept of class and its relevance to late twentieth century industrial societies.

Lee, D.J. and Turner, B.S. (eds) (1996) *Conflicts About Class: Debating Inequality in Late Industrialism*, Harlow: Addison Wesley Longman.

The readings we included on gender illustrated some of the areas of social life where women experience oppression and differential treatment. The following text provides a feminist introduction to sociology and introduces and summarises the extent of inequalities faced by women:

Richardson, D. and Robinson, V. (1993) *Introducing Women's Studies: Feminist Theory and Practice*, London: Macmillan.

A good starting point for consideration of equal opportunities and social policy in the areas of gender, race and disability is:

Bagilhole, B. (1997) *Equal Opportunities and Social Policy*, Harlow: Addison Wesley Longman.

A clear empirical overview of the position of ethnic minority groups in contemporary Britain and the theoretical debates concerning race is provided by the following texts:

Back, L. and Solomos, J. (1989) *Race and Racism in Contemporary Britain*, London: Macmillan.

Mason, D. (1995) *Race and Ethnicity in Modern Britain*, Oxford: Oxford University Press.

For a wider collection of material on race the following reader is recommended:

Skellington, R. (ed.) (1992) *'Race' in Britain Today*, London: Sage.

Activity

The first reading in Part Three is taken from Ralph Dahrendorf's important study *Class and Class Conflict in an Industrial Society*. In this extract Dahrendorf argues that, contrary to Marx's expectations and hopes, there has been a 'remarkable spread of social equality in the past century' and a clear tendency toward a leveling of social differences, which has meant that 'the concepts of social stratification and class structure tend to lose their meaning'.

Look at the data and arguments provided in some of the other readings and make a case **for** and **against** Dahrendorf's view that (a) there has been a remarkable spread of social equality; and (b) social stratification has lost its importance in modern society.

This activity might work best as a structured class debate on 'class in Britain'. As a starting point, each class member would be given time to read and then summarise (perhaps on one sheet of A4 and/or in 5 minutes) one of the readings in this section. In the summary, points that contribute to the debate on the importance of and role of class in contemporary society should be highlighted. This could be an individual task for each student, or one undertaken in pairs.

A refinement could be to ask half of the group to look for material that supports Dahrendorf's comments and the other half to look for material to make a case against them.

Part IV

Sociological Research

44 Introduction

Sociological analysis is dependent on sociological research and the key role of research has generated a great deal of debate around questions and issues such as: How should sociologists collect the material and data on which to base their findings and theorising? How should this material and data be interpreted and analysed? To what extent do methods of research reflect and in turn inform sociological theorising? As these questions imply, there is no general agreement as to what are the most effective methods for sociologists to adopt. The Readings in Part Four explore some of the main issues that accompany sociological research.

Durkheim, more than any other of the 'classic' sociological writers, was concerned with establishing and promoting sociology as an academic discipline in its own right. A particular aspect of this concern was to establish sociological research as of equal status to research in other disciplines and thereby to advance sociology's claim as a 'scientific' discipline. As Durkheim comments in the Introduction to *The Rules of Sociological Method*, 'until the present [the study was first published in 1895], sociologists have given little thought to describing and defining the method they employ in the study of social facts'. The great sociologists who influenced Durkheim, such as Comte and Spencer, offered no detail on, for instance, the precautions they took in their observations, the manner in which they formulated problems or the specific methods of work that enabled them to reach their conclusions. Reading 45 is taken from Durkheim's attempt to define and then elaborate on the nature of social facts and his consideration of how they should be observed.

One of the key areas of debate for sociological research, and indeed for sociology in general, has been the extent to which it should adopt the same or similar methods to those used in the natural sciences. Should sociology use scientific techniques of hypothesising and deduction to discover 'scientific laws' which could explain the causes, functions and consequences of social phenomena? Karl Popper, philosopher of science and Professor of

Logic and Scientific Method at the London School of Economics until his retirement in 1969, has been perhaps the foremost advocate of the positivist position that favours the adoption of the scientific method of research in sociology and the social sciences. He believed that sociology should follow the 'hypothetico-deductive' model and that sociologists should proceed by gathering facts so as to refute hypotheses. Reading 46 includes extracts from his famous study *The Poverty of Historicism* in which he sets out the doctrine of 'historicism' (in Parts I and II) – essentially the idea that there are fixed laws of historical development and that it is possible to make and then act upon predictions about social and historical development – and then criticises it as a 'poor method unable to yield the results it promises' (in Parts III and IV). The reading includes extracts from both 'sections' of this study – the explanation of historicism and his contention that this doctrine is based on a misunderstanding of the methods of the natural sciences and specifically physics.

There are a range of different methods or techniques for obtaining information which can be used in pursuing social research. Some, such as in-depth interviews and participant observation, allow sociologists to examine social interaction and small numbers of people in great detail (qualitative research). Other methods, such as surveys, involve the study of large representative samples of a wider population but tend to provide less detailed and descriptive information (quantitative research). Readings 47 and 48 are taken from surveys into the same broad area – poverty and labour in London – that were undertaken in very different historical periods. The first is from Charles Booth's pioneering study in the late-nineteenth century and the second from a study roughly one hundred years later led by Peter Townsend.

Charles Booth's position as first a member and then President of the Royal Statistical Society indicates his importance in the history of social research. His monumental study of the people in London at the end of the nineteenth century, which utilised a number of techniques of social research, has become perhaps the seminal example of the social survey. This classic study extended to seventeen volumes and has been acknowledged as a landmark of empirical research. In spite of this, Booth is rarely acknowledged as a key figure in the development of sociology. In part this was because he was seen as a social reformer with little interest in theorising about social change; but perhaps also because he was a wealthy businessman not a university academic. However, Robert Park, the leader of the Chicago School of the 1920s and 1930s, described Booth's studies as 'a memorable and permanent contribution to our knowledge of human nature and society'.

In 1889 the first volume of what became known as the 'Poverty Series' was published, and it is from this that Reading 47 is taken. This along with a second volume and a detailed appendix shared the title: *Labour and Life of the People.* The major sources of data for the statistics on poverty were the 1881 Census and the School Board Visitors. Although Booth's focus was on the practical problems and issues faced by the people of London – and in particular the problem of poverty – his methods and findings have relevance at the theoretical and methodological level for contemporary sociology.

In similar vein to Booth's survey is the research led by Peter Townsend in the 1980s (Reading 48). Starting in late 1985 and extending into early 1987 information was gathered from interviews with a random sample of 2700 people representing the population of Greater London, interviews with random samples of 400 adults living in each of two London boroughs – one 'rich', Bromley, and the other 'poor', Hackney – and interviews with employers in Bromley and Hackney to obtain their views, experiences and predictions. This more contemporary research suggested that London's economy was in deeper crisis in 1987 than it had been for a hundred years and that there were widening inequalities in the standards of living of Londoners.

Research into the pattern of inequality does not just involve surveying the extent and nature of poverty but also that of wealth. However, it is probably fair to say that it is generally less easy to research wealth. Wealthy people might wish to avoid publicising the fact; and it is likely that they will have some degree of influence and power that will enable them to keep their affairs relatively secret – from prying social scientists anyway! Reading 49 is taken from John Scott's investigation of the relationship between poverty and wealth. Although wealth is generally seen in purely statistical terms (e.g. the richest 1 per cent of the population may be designated wealthy), Scott argues that, like poverty, wealth is a relative concept; as he puts it, 'Just as "poverty" must be distinguished from starvation and absolute want, so "wealth" must be distinguished from any absolute level of luxury that it might be possible to identify.' In our extract, Scott highlights some of the definitional difficulties that need to be considered when researching both wealth and poverty.

Before looking at examples of qualitative sociological research, Reading 50 highlights some of the important concerns that have to be considered when using surveys to research social issues. Sara Arber uses a piece of research that she was involved with – a survey of tenants in public housing that was funded by a local authority in south-east England – to describe and illustrate some of the practical methodological issues that are attendant on survey-based research. Issues such as gaining access, selecting samples, designing questionnaires and undertaking interviews (including the managing of other interviewers whom it may be necessary to employ in order to cover a large sample). The focus of Arber's examination of all of these issues is on the practicalities of how to gain reliable data.

An example of small-scale, qualitative research is provided by Simon Holdaway's participant observation study *Inside the British Police*, from which Reading 51 is taken. Holdaway was a police sergeant before becoming a sociology lecturer at the University of Sheffield and he undertook much of his research while he was a uniformed officer in a socially deprived inner-city area (which he called Hilton). He was, therefore, in an ideal position to carry out an investigation into day-to-day policing and, in particular, the 'occupational culture' of the police. In our extract, Holdaway describes some of the dilemmas he encountered as a participant observer.

Participant observation has been widely and successfully used in research into unusual and deviant, including criminal, behaviour. One reason for this has been because those who engage in such behaviour are likely to want as few people as possible to know what they do – to avoid legal or social recrimination. This raises particular problems for the study of criminal and deviant behaviour – problems that include the locating of and gaining access to people who participate in crime and deviance; and dealing with the potential ethical dilemmas that might arise from uncovering behaviour or information that might be illegal and, perhaps, place other people at risk. It is for these sort of reasons that the more formal and structured methods of obtaining information are often less appropriate in this area of sociological research. Reading 52 is taken from Ned Polsky's ground-breaking study, *Hustlers, Beats and Others* in which he describes his research into the lives and 'occupations' of people involved in different types of deviance in USA in the 1960s, including poolroom hustlers, prostitutes and drug-users. We will refer to Polsky's research into poolroom hustlers as an illustration of his approach. Polsky's fieldwork (his preferred term) involved observing hustlers as they engaged in hustling (essentially a betting and cheating racket), talking with hustlers and participant observation. Polsky was in an ideal position to study poolroom hustling by participant observation as he was a regular and very adept billiard and pool player and he knew a number of hustlers as a result of playing in the main pool rooms in New York. In our extract Polsky considers some of the difficulties faced when doing fieldwork and suggests some procedures that he has found useful in overcoming them.

Of course there is a range of behaviour that the participants have particular reason to keep hidden and there are a number of reasons why people want to keep their behaviour hidden – perhaps because it is against the law or because it would undermine their position, either in terms of their private relationships or their social/occupational positions. Prostitution might fit all of those areas of concern and Reading 53 is taken from the first chapter of McKeganey and Barnard's study of prostitutes and their clients, in which they describe their method of establishing contact with and gaining useful information from prostitute women and male clients. As with Polsky, their research illustrates both the ethical and practical dilemmas that can face social researchers.

The next three Readings indicate some of the key issues that have been addressed by feminist research. Reading 54 taken from Liz Stanley and Sue Wise's study *Breaking Out Again: Feminist Ontology and Epistemology*, which was published as a second edition in 1993, ten years after the first edition *Breaking Out*. This has become one of the key feminist methodology texts and represents a critique of orthodox sociological research methodology, and in particular positivism. It argues for a valuing of experience, involvement and emotion in the research process and illustrates the continuing concerns and practice of feminist researchers to adopt a reflexive approach, making visible 'themselves', emotions and all, in this process. This is an approach adopted by Liz Kelly in her research into sexual violence *Surviving Sexual Violence*. Kelly identifies her involvement in and emotional response to the research and also stresses the value of the emotional responses of the women in her research. Reading 55 provides an example of feminist research in practice set in the context of some more general reflections on such research. As with Kelly's research, Reading 56, taken from Anna Pollert's study of women workers at a tobacco factory in Bristol, *Girls, Wives, Factory Lives*, illustrates the commitment of feminist research to doing something to improve women's position and to raising women's consciousness. In this Reading, Pollert sets out the aims of her research and then describes how she attempted to carry them out. She makes it quite clear that she does not adopt a 'neutral' position in her study. This is demonstrated in her willingness to challenge the (predominantly male) managers and the (female) workers over their assumptions and practices.

A number of these readings have touched on the problems and dilemmas faced by social scientists' pursuing of social research. The last Reading in Part Four is taken from Roger Homan's examination of the ethics of social research and considers the 'effects' of such research on those involved, including the risks that both researchers and subjects of research can be faced with. It also includes Homan's consideration of the tension between personal moral standards and professional ethical norms.

Reading 45

The observation of social facts

EMILE DURKHEIM

In his classic study on the sociological method, The Rules of Sociological Method, *Durkheim argues that there is a genuine distinction between the natural and the social sciences and that the methods of science applicable to the natural sciences are also valid in the social field. In the introduction, from which this Reading is taken, he points out that social phenomena, which he terms 'social facts', are not the product of an individual's own ideas or opinions; indeed they can and do have a constraining influence on both individuals and collective groups. In this extract Durkheim sets out what he means by the term 'social fact'. Essentially it is something that exists outside of an individual's consciousness. Even if it may be felt very deeply by an individual – such as a religious belief – it is not unique to or dependent on her or him, in that it has existed and will continue to do so irrespective of the particular individual. For Durkheim the study of social facts helps to distinguish sociology from those disciplines – such as biology and psychology – which focus on phenomena that depend more exclusively on the individual consciousness.*

Before inquiring into the method suited to the study of social facts, it is important to know which facts are commonly called 'social'. This information is all the more necessary since the designation 'social' is used with little precision. It is currently employed for practically all phenomena generally diffused within society, however small their social interest. But on that basis, there are, as it were, no human events that may not be called social. Each individual drinks, sleeps, eats, reasons; and it is to society's interest that these functions be exercised in an orderly manner. If, then, all these facts are counted as 'social' facts, sociology would have no subject matter exclusively its own, and its domain would be confused with that of biology and psychology.

But in reality there is in every society a certain group of phenomena which may be differentiated from those studied by the other natural sciences. When I fulfil my obligations as brother, husband, or citizen, when I execute my contracts, I perform duties which are defined, externally to myself and my acts, in law and in custom. Even if they conform to my own sentiments and I feel their reality subjectively, such reality is still objective, for I did not create them; I merely inherited them through my education. How many times it happens, moreover, that we are ignorant of the details of the obligations incumbent upon us, and that in order to acquaint ourselves with them we must consult the law and its authorized interpreters! Similarly, the church-member finds the beliefs and practices of his religious life ready-made at birth; their existence prior to his own implies their existence outside of himself. The system of signs I use to express my thought, the system of currency I employ to pay my debts, the instruments of credit I utilize in my commercial relations, the practices followed in my profession, etc., function independently of my own use of them. And these statements can be repeated for each member of society. Here, then, are ways of acting, thinking, and feeling that present the noteworthy property of existing outside the individual consciousness.

These types of conduct or thought are not only external to the individual but are, moreover, endowed with coercive power, by virtue of which they impose themselves upon him, independent of his individual will. Of course, when I fully consent and conform to them, this constraint is felt only slightly, if at all, and is therefore unnecessary. But it is, nonetheless, an intrinsic characteristic of these facts, the proof thereof being that it asserts itself as soon as I attempt to resist it. If I attempt to violate the law, it reacts against me so as to prevent my act before its accomplishment, or to nullify my violation by restoring the damage, if it is accomplished and reparable, or to make me expiate it if it cannot be compensated for otherwise.

In the case of purely moral maxims., the public conscience exercises a check on every act which offends it by means of the surveillance it exercises over the conduct of citizens, and the appropriate penalties at its disposal. In many cases the constraint is less violent, but nevertheless it always exists. If I do not submit to the conventions of society, if in my dress I do not conform to the customs observed in my country and in my class, the ridicule I provoke, the social isolation in which I am kept, produce, although in an attenuated form, the same effects as a punishment in the strict sense of the word. The constraint is nonetheless efficacious for being indirect. I am not obliged to speak French with my fellow-countrymen nor to use the legal currency, but I cannot possibly do otherwise. If I tried to escape this necessity, my attempt would fail miserably. As an industrialist, I am free to apply the technical methods of former centuries; but by doing so, I should invite certain ruin. Even when I free myself from these rules and violate them successfully, I am always compelled to struggle with them. When finally overcome, they make their constraining power sufficiently felt by the resistance they offer. The enterprises of all innovators, including successful ones, come up against resistance of this kind.

Here, then, is a category of facts with very distinctive characteristics: it consists of ways of acting, thinking, and feeling, external to the individual, and endowed with a power of coercion, by reason of which they control him. These ways of thinking could not be confused with biological phenomena, since they consist of representations and of actions; nor with psychological phenomena, which exist only in the individual consciousness and through it. They constitute, thus, a new variety of phenomena; and it is to them exclusively that the term 'social' ought to be applied. And this term fits them quite well, for it is clear that, since their source is not in the individual, their substratum can be no other than society, either the political society as a whole or some one of the partial groups it includes, such as religious denominations, political, literary, and occupational associations, etc. On the other hand, this term 'social' applies to them exclusively, for it has a distinct meaning only if it designates exclusively the phenomena which are not included in any of the categories of facts that have already been established and classified. These ways of thinking and acting therefore constitute the proper domain of sociology [. . .]

Since the examples that we have just cited (legal and moral regulations, religious faiths, financial system, etc.) all consist of established beliefs and practices, one might be led to believe that social facts exist only where there is some social organization. But there are other facts without such crystallized form which have the same objectivity and the same ascendancy over the individual. These are called 'social currents'. Thus the great movements of enthusiasm, indignation, and pity in a crowd do not originate in any one of the particular individual consciousnesses. They come to each one of us from without and can carry us away in spite of ourselves. Of course, it may happen that, in abandoning myself to them unreservedly, I do not feel the pressure they exert upon me. But it is revealed as soon as I try to resist them. Let an individual attempt to oppose one of these collective manifestations, and the emotions that he denies will turn against him. Now, if this power of external coercion asserts itself so clearly in cases of resistance, it must exist also in the first-mentioned cases, although we are unconscious of it. We are then victims of the illusion of having ourselves created that which actually forced itself from without. If the complacency with which we permit ourselves to be carried along conceals the pressure undergone, nevertheless it does not abolish it. Thus, air is no less heavy because we do not detect its weight. So, even if we ourselves have spontaneously contributed to the production of the common emotion, the impression we have received differs markedly from that which we would have experienced if we had been alone. Also, once the crowd has dispersed, that is, once these social influences have ceased to act upon us and we are alone again, the emotions which have passed through the mind appear strange to us, and we no longer recognize them as ours. We realize that these feelings have been impressed upon us to a much greater extent than they were created by us. It may even happen that they horrify us, so much were they contrary to our nature. Thus, a group of individuals, most of whom are perfectly inoffensive, may, when gathered in a crowd, be drawn into acts of atrocity. And what we say of these transitory outbursts applies similarly to those more permanent currents of opinion on religious, political, literary, or artistic matters which are constantly being formed around us, whether in society as a whole or in more limited circles.

To confirm this definition of the social fact by a characteristic illustration from common experience, one need only observe the manner in which children are brought up. Considering the facts as they are and as they have always been, it becomes immediately evident that all education is a continuous effort to impose on the child ways of seeing, feeling, and acting which he could not have arrived at spontaneously. From the very first hours of his life, we compel him to eat, drink, and sleep at regular hours; we constrain him to cleanliness, calmness, and obedience; later we exert pressure upon him in order that he may learn proper consideration for others, respect for customs and conventions, the need for work, etc. If, in time, this constraint ceases to be felt, it is because it gradually gives rise to habits and to internal tendencies that render constraint unnecessary; but nevertheless it is not abolished, for it is still the source from which these habits were derived. It is true that, according to Spencer, a rational education ought to reject such methods, allowing the child to act in complete liberty; but as this pedagogic theory has never been applied by any known people, it must be accepted only as an expression of personal opinion, not as a fact which can contradict the aforementioned observations. What makes these facts particularly instructive is that the aim of education is, precisely, the socialization of the human being; the process of education, therefore, gives us in a nutshell the historical fashion in which the social being is constituted. This unremitting pressure to which the child is subjected is the very pressure of the social milieu which tends to fashion him in its own image, and of which parents and teachers are merely the representatives and intermediaries [. . .]

Currents of opinion, with an intensity varying according to the time and place, impel certain groups either to more marriages, for example, or to more suicides, or to a higher or lower birthrate, etc. These currents are plainly social facts. At first sight they seem inseparable from the forms they take in individual cases. But statistics furnish us with the means of isolating them. They are, in fact, represented with considerable exactness by the rates of births, marriages, and suicides, that is, by the number obtained by dividing the average annual total of marriages, births, suicides, by the number of persons whose ages lie within the range in which marriages, births, and suicides occur. Since each of these figures contains all the individual cases indiscriminately, the individual circumstances which may have had a share in the production of the phenomenon are neutralized and, consequently, do not contribute to its determination. The average, then, expresses a certain state of the group mind (*l'ame collective*).

From E. Durkheim (1964) (1895) *The Rules of Sociological Method,* New York: Free Press, pp. 1–8.

Questions

1. Durkheim comments that he is 'not obliged to speak French . . . nor to use the legal currency, but I cannot possibly do otherwise. If I tried to escape this necessity, my attempt would fail miserably.'
   (a) List some of the 'social facts' that determine your own everyday behaviour.
   (b) How do they differ from biological or psychological facts?
   (c) How do they constrain you?
   (d) What would the effects be of not following them?
2. 'Social currents' are seen by Durkheim as a particular form of social fact. Describe some of the social currents that are influential in contemporary society.

Reading 46

Sociology and the scientific method

KARL POPPER

This reading is made up of extracts from Karl Popper's study The Poverty of Historicism *which is, essentially, an examination and criticism of the doctrine of historicism. First, Popper sets out what he means by historicism – the belief that it is possible to make long-term predictions about social development and, consequently, that the methods of the natural sciences, and especially physics, cannot be applied to the social sciences. For example, he argues that although the principal of 'generalization' is central to physical science, reflecting a notion of the general uniformity of nature, historicism sees such a principal as useless in sociology, in that social conditions depend on specific historical situations. The social sciences Popper argues, should be less ambitious and not look for laws of social and historical development but rather aim to make modest contributions to social reform. He 'blames' this doctrine (of historicism) for what he calls the 'unsatisfactory state of the theoretical social sciences'. While he admits that there are clearly some differences between sociological and physical methods, in the second part of the Reading, from the sub-heading 'The Variability of Experimental Conditions', Popper criticises historicism by highlighting where principles such as generalisation do not even apply to the physical sciences. He points out that we cannot 'prove' irrefutably that any laws are truly universal even in the natural sciences: even such an 'obvious regularity' as day following night breaks down when the polar circle is crossed.*

Introduction

Scientific interest in social and political questions is hardly less old than scientific interest in cosmology and physics; and there were periods in antiquity (I have Plato's political theory in mind, and Aristotle's collection of constitutions) when the science of society might have seemed to have advanced further than the science of nature. But with Galileo and Newton, physics became successful beyond expectation, far surpassing all the other sciences; and since the time of Pasteur, the Galileo of biology, the biological sciences have been almost equally successful. But the social sciences do not as yet seem to have found their Galileo.

In these circumstances, students who work in one or another of the social sciences are greatly concerned with problems of method; and much of their discussion of these problems is conducted with an eye upon the methods of the more flourishing sciences, especially physics [. . .]

I think that the crucial mistakes in most methodological discussions arise from some very common misunderstandings of the methods of physics. In particular, I think they arise from a misinterpretation of the logical form of its theories, of the methods of testing them, and of the logical function of observation and experiment. My contention is that these misunderstandings have serious consequences [. . .]

What I mean by 'historicism' will be explained at length in this study. It will be enough if I say here that I mean by 'historicism' an approach to the social sciences which assumes *that historical prediction* is their principal aim, and which assumes that this aim is attainable by discovering the 'rhythms' or the 'patterns', the 'laws' or the 'trends' that underlie the evolution of history. Since I am convinced that such historicist doctrines of method are at bottom responsible for the unsatisfactory state of the theoretical social sciences (other than economic theory), my presentation of these doctrines is certainly not unbiased. But I have tried hard to make a case in favour of historicism in order to give point to my subsequent criticism [. . .]

The Anti-naturalistic Doctrines of Historicism

In strong opposition to methodological naturalism in the field of sociology, historicism claims that some of the characteristic methods of physics cannot be applied to the social sciences, owing to the profound differences between sociology and physics. Physical laws, or the 'laws of nature', it tells us, are valid anywhere and always; for the physical world is ruled by a system of physical uniformities invariable throughout space and time. Sociological laws, however, or the laws of social life, differ in different places and periods. Although historicism admits that there are plenty of typical social conditions whose regular recurrence can be observed, it denies that the regularities detectable in social life have the character of the immutable regularities of the physical world. For they depend upon history, and upon differences in culture. They depend on a particular *historical situation.* Thus one should not, for example, speak without further qualification of the laws of economics, but only of the economic laws of the feudal period, or of the early industrial period, and so on; always mentioning the historical period in which the laws in question are assumed to have prevailed.

Historicism asserts that the historical relativity of social laws makes most of the methods of physics inapplicable to sociology. Typical historicist arguments on which this view is based concern generalization, experiment, the complexity of social phenomena, the difficulties of exact prediction, and the significance of methodological essentialism. I will treat these arguments in turn.

Generalization

The possibility of generalization and its success in the physical sciences rests, according to historicism, on the general uniformity of nature: upon the observation – perhaps better described as an assumption – that in similar circumstances similar things will happen. This principle, which is taken to be valid throughout space and time, is said to underlie the method of physics.

Historicism insists that this principle is necessarily useless in sociology. Similar circumstances only arise within a single historical period. They never persist from one period to another. Hence there is no long-run uniformity in society on which long-term generalizations could be based – that is, if we disregard *trivial regularities*, such as those described by the truism that human beings always live in groups, or that the supply of certain things is limited and the supply of others, like air, unlimited, and that only the former can have any market or exchange value.

A method which ignores this limitation and attempts a generalization of social uniformities will, according to historicism, implicitly assume that the regularities in question are everlasting; so that a methodologically naïve view – the view that the method of generalization can be taken over from physics by the social sciences – will produce a false and dangerously misleading sociological theory. It will be a theory denying that society develops; or that it ever changes significantly; or that social developments, if there are any, can affect the basic regularities of social life [. . .]

The historicist opposes them by maintaining that social uniformities differ widely from those of the natural sciences. They change from one historical period to another, and *human* activity is the force that changes them. For social uniformities are not laws of nature, but man-made; and although they may be said to depend on human nature, they do so because human nature has the power to alter and, perhaps, to control them. Therefore things can be bettered or worsened: active reform need not be futile [. . .]

Experiment

Physics uses the method of experiment; that is, it introduces artificial controls, artificial isolation, and thereby ensures the reproduction of similar conditions, and the consequent production of certain effects. This method is obviously based on the idea that where circumstances are similar, similar things will happen. The historicist claims that this method is not applicable in sociology. Nor would it be useful, he argues, even if it were applicable. For, as similar conditions occur only within the limits of a single period, the outcome of any experiment would be of very limited significance. Moreover, artificial isolation would eliminate precisely those factors in sociology which are most important. Robinson Crusoe and his isolated individual economy can never be a valuable model of an economy whose problems arise precisely from the economic interaction of individuals and groups.

It is further argued that no really valuable experiments are possible. Large-scale experiments in sociology are never experiments in the physical sense. They are not made to advance knowledge as such, but to achieve political success. They are not performed in a laboratory detached from the outside world; rather, their very performance changes the conditions of society. They can never be repeated under precisely similar conditions since the conditions were changed by their first performance [. . .]

Novelty

In the world described by physics nothing can happen that is truly and intrinsically new. A new engine may be invented, but we can always analyse it as a rearrangement of elements which are anything but new. Newness in physics is merely the newness of arrangements or combinations. In direct opposition to this, social newness, like biological newness, is an intrinsic sort of newness, historicism insists. It is real newness, irreducible to the novelty of arrangements. For in social life, the same old factors in a new arrangement are never really the same old factors. Where nothing can repeat itself precisely, real novelty must always be emerging. This is held to be significant for the consideration of the development of new stages or periods of history, each of which differs intrinsically from any other.

Historicism claims that nothing is of greater moment than the emergence of a really new period. This all-important aspect of social life cannot be investigated along the lines we are accustomed to follow when we explain novelties in the realm of physics by regarding them as re-arrangements of familiar elements. Even if the ordinary methods of physics were applicable to society, they would never be applicable to its most important features: *its division into periods, and the emergence of novelty*. Once we grasp the significance of social newness, we are forced to abandon the idea that the application of ordinary, physical methods to the problems of sociology can aid us in understanding the problems of social development [. . .]

Complexity

The methodological situation just sketched has a number of further aspects. One which has been discussed very frequently (and which will not be discussed here) is the sociological role of certain unique personalities. Another of these aspects is the complexity of social phenomena. In physics we are dealing with a subject matter which is much less complicated; in spite of that, we further simplify matters artificially by the method of experimental isolation. Since this method is not applicable in sociology we are faced with a twofold complexity – a complexity arising out of the impossibility of artificial isolation, and a complexity due to the fact that social life is a natural phenomenon that presupposes the mental life of individuals, i.e. psychology, which in its turn presupposes biology, which again presupposes chemistry and physics. The fact that sociology comes last in this hierarchy of sciences plainly shows us the tremendous complexity of the factors involved in social life. Even if there were immutable sociological uniformities, like the uniformities in the field of physics, we might very well be unable to find them, owing to this twofold complexity. But if we cannot find them, then there is little point in maintaining that they nevertheless exist [. . .]

The Variability of Experimental Conditions

The historicist contends that the experimental method cannot be applied to the social sciences because we cannot, in the social field, reproduce at will precisely similar experimental conditions. This brings us a little closer to the heart of the historicist position. I admit that there may be something in this contention: no doubt there are some differences here between physical and sociological methods. Nevertheless, I assert that the historicist contention rests upon a gross misunderstanding of the experimental methods of physics.

Let us first consider these methods. Every experimental physicist knows that very dissimilar things may happen under what appear to be precisely similar conditions. Two wires may at first sight look exactly alike, but if the one is exchanged for the other in a piece of electrical apparatus, the resulting difference may be very great. Upon closer inspection (say, through a microscope), we may perhaps find that they were not as similar as they first appeared [. . .]

Are Generalizations Confined to Periods?

I begin my criticism of the historicist contention with the admission that most people living in a certain historical period will incline to the erroneous belief that the regularities which they observe around them are universal laws of social life, holding good for all societies. Indeed, we sometimes only notice that we are cherishing such beliefs when, in a foreign country, we find that our habits regarding food, our greeting-taboos, etc., are by no means as acceptable as we naïvely assumed. It is a rather obvious inference that many of our other generalizations, whether consciously held or not, may be of the same kind, though they may remain unchallenged because we cannot travel into another historical period . . . In other words, it must be admitted that there may be many regularities in our social life which are characteristic of our particular period only, and that we are inclined to overlook this limitation. So that (especially in a time of rapid social change) we may learn to our sorrow that we have relied on laws that have lost their validity [. . .]

If the historicist's contentions went no further than this, we could only accuse him of labouring a rather trivial point. But unfortunately, he asserts more. He insists that the situation creates difficulties which do not occur in the natural sciences; and more particularly that, in contrast to the natural sciences, in the social sciences we must never assume that we have discovered a truly universal law, since we can never know whether it always held good in the past (for our records may be insufficient), or whether it will always hold good in the future.

In opposition to such claims, I do not admit that the situation described is in any way peculiar to the social sciences, or that it creates any particular difficulties. On the contrary, it is obvious that a change in our physical environment may give rise to experiences which are quite analogous to those which arise from a change in our social or historical environment. Can there be a more obvious and proverbial regularity than the succession of day and night? Yet, it breaks down if we cross the polar circle. It is perhaps a little difficult to compare physical with social experiences, but I think that such a breakdown may be quite as startling as any that might occur in the social realm. To take another example, the historical or social environments of Crete in 1900 and of Crete three thousand years ago can hardly be said to differ more than the geographical or physical environments of Crete and of Greenland. A sudden unprepared removal from one physical environment into the other would, I think, be more likely to produce fatal results than a corresponding change in the social environment.

It seems clear to me that the historicist overrates the significance of the somewhat spectacular differences between various historical periods [. . .]

To this, the historicist may reply that the differences in social environment are more fundamental than the differences in physical environment; for if society changes, man changes too; and this implies a change in all regularities, since all social regularities depend on the nature of man, the atom of society. Our answer is that physical atoms also change with their environment (for example, under the influence of electromagnetic fields, etc.), not in defiance of the laws of physics, but in accordance with these laws. Besides, the significance of this alleged changes of human nature is dubious, and very hard to assess.

We now turn to the historicist contention that in the social sciences we must never assume that we have discovered a truly universal law since we cannot be sure whether its validity extends beyond the periods in which we have observed it to hold. This may be admitted, but only in so far as it applies to the natural sciences as well. In the natural sciences, it is clear, we can never be quite certain whether our laws are really universally valid, or whether they hold only in a certain period (perhaps only in the period during which the universe expands) or only in a certain region (perhaps in a region of comparatively weak gravitational fields). In spite of the impossibility of making universal validity, we do not add in our formulation of natural laws a condition saying that they are asserted only for the period for which they have been observed to hold, or perhaps only within 'the present cosmological period'.

From K. Popper (1961) *The Poverty of Historicism*, London: Routledge, pp. 1–3, 5–12, 93, 99–103.

Questions

1. Unlike physical laws, or the 'laws of nature', social rules differ in different places and periods. The historicist position is that this historical relativity makes the methods of physics inapplicable to sociology.

   Make a case for and against the following historicist arguments:
   (a) generalisation 'is necessarily useless in sociology'.
   (b) the method of experiment 'is not applicable in sociology'.
   (c) 'social newness' is more than the 're-arrangements of familiar elements'.
   (d) social phenomena have a far greater complexity than the subject matter of the natural sciences.

2. Popper's *The Poverty of Historicism* was first published in 1957.
   (a) To what extent do you think his contention that the social sciences lack the status of the natural sciences is still valid?
   (b) Do you think that sociology has not yet 'found its Galileo'?

Reading 47

Social surveys (1): Poverty and labour in London in the 1880s

CHARLES BOOTH

Social surveys involve the systematic collection of information about a given population; and they generally gain this information through some form of sampling. Such surveys have a long history in social research with perhaps the most famous examples being the large-scale descriptive surveys such as Charles Booth's. This study is a classic of both early British social research and of empirical research in general. Booth used observation, interviews and statistical analysis in producing his massive survey of poverty in late Victorian London. This reading starts with a brief discussion of School Board visitors – one of Booth's major sources of data. School Board visitors visited all the houses in their designated areas and provided details on families with school-age children. Booth then explains how the mass of information gathered was utilised to produce a social map of East London and to classify the population into different class groupings.

The Inquiry of which I am now able to publish the results, was set on foot in 1886, the subject being the condition and occupations of the inhabitants of London, and my grateful thanks are due to those friends who helped me at the outset in laying down the principles on which the inquiry has been conducted. It was decided to employ a double method, dividing the people by districts and again by trades, so as to show at once the manner of their life and of their work. Most of 1886 was occupied with preliminary work, 1887 sufficed to complete the district inquiry in East London, and 1888 was spent on the trades and special subjects.

For the district inquiry, resulting in the division of the people into 8 classes, I have relied upon information obtained from the School Board visitors, of whom there are 66 in the East London district, and my tables are based on three assumptions:

The School Board visitors perform amongst them house-to-house visitation; every house in every street is in their books, and details are given of every family with children of school age. They begin their scheduling two or three years before the children attain school age, and a record remains in their books of children who have left school. The occupation of the head of the family is noted down. Most of the visitors have been working in the same district for several years, and thus have an extensive knowledge of the people. It is their business to re-schedule for the Board once a year, but intermediate revisions are made in addition, and it is their duty to make themselves acquainted, so far as possible, with new corners into their districts. They are in daily contact with the people, and have a very considerable knowledge of the parents of the school children, especially of the poorest amongst them, and of the conditions under which they live. No one can go, as I have done, over the description of the inhabitants of street after street in this huge district (East London), taken house by house and family by family – full as it is of picturesque details noted down from the lips of the visitor to whose mind they have been recalled by the open pages of his own schedules – and doubt the genuine character of the information and its truth. Of the wealth of my material I have no doubt. I am indeed embarrassed by its mass, and by my resolution to make use of no fact to which I cannot give a quantitative value. The materials for sensational stories lie plentifully in every book of our notes; but, even if I had the skill to use my material in this way – that gift of the imagination which is called 'realistic' – I should not wish to use it here. There is struggling poverty, there is destitution, there is hunger, drunkenness, brutality, and crime; no one doubts that it is so. My object has been to attempt to show the numerical relation which poverty, misery, and depravity bear to regular earnings and comparative comfort, and to describe the general conditions under which each class lives.

In order that the true, and not more than the true, significance and value may be given to the facts and figures produced, it may be useful to explain exactly the method that has been adopted in collecting them.

The 46 books of our notes contain no less than 3400 streets or places in East London, and every house and every family with school children is noted, with such information as the visitors could give about them.

From notes such as these the information given in our schedules was tabulated, and from them also was coloured the map which now forms a part of that published in connection with these volumes. The people – that is those of them who had school children – were classified by their employment and by their apparent status as to means; the streets were classified according to their inhabitants. Such is the nature of our information, and such the use made of it. It was possible to subject the map to the test of criticism, and it was mainly for this purpose that it was prepared. It was exhibited at Toynbee Hall and Oxford House, and was seen and very carefully studied by many who are intimately acquainted, not with the whole, but each with some part, of the district portrayed. Especially, we obtained most valuable aid in this way from the Relieving Officers and from the agents of the Charity Organization

Society. The map stood the test very well. There were errors, but on reference these were, in almost every case, found to be due to mistake in the transfer of verbal into graphic description, or consequent on our having made a whole street the unit of colour, whereas different parts of the same street were of very different character. The map was revised, and now equally represents the facts as disclosed by this inquiry, and as agreed to by the best local authorities.

Our books of notes are mines of information. They have been referred to again and again at each stage of our work. So valuable have they proved in unforeseen ways, that I only regret they were not more slowly and deliberately prepared; more stuffed with facts than even they are. As it was, we continually improved as we went on, and may be said to have learnt our trade by the time the work was done. At first, nothing seemed so essential as speed. The task was so tremendous; the prospect of its completion so remote; and every detail cost time. In the Tower Hamlets division, which was completed first, we gave on the average 19¾ hours' work to each School Board visitor; in the Hackney division this was increased to 23½ hours. St George's-in-the-East when first done in 1886 cost 60 hours' work with the visitors; when revised it occupied 83 hours. At the outset we shut our eyes, fearing lest any prejudice of our own should colour the information we received. It was not till the books were finished that I or my secretaries ourselves visited the streets amongst which we had been living in imagination. But later we gained confidence, and made it a rule to see each street ourselves at the time we received the visitors account of it. With the insides of the houses and their inmates there was no attempt to meddle. To have done so would have been an unwarrantable impertinence; and, besides, a contravention of our understanding with the School Board, who object, very rightly, to any abuse of the delicate machinery with which they work. Nor, for the same reason, did we ask the visitors to obtain information specially for us. We dealt solely with that which comes to them in a natural way in the discharge of their duties.

The amount of information obtained varied with the different visitors; some had not been long at the work, and amongst those who had been, there was much difference in the extent of their knowledge, some might be less trustworthy than others: but taking them as a body I cannot speak too highly of their ability and good sense. I wish also to express my warm thanks for the ready manner in which all the Divisional Committees themselves, the District Superintendents, and the Visitors, lent themselves to my purpose. For without this nothing could have been done. The merit of the information so obtained, looked at statistically, lies mainly in the breadth of view obtained. It is in effect the whole population that comes under review. Other agencies usually seek out some particular class or deal with some particular condition of people. The knowledge so obtained may be more exact but it is circumscribed and very apt to produce a distortion of judgement. For this reason, the information to be had from the School Board visitors, with all its inequalities and imperfections, is excellent as a framework for a picture of the Life and Labour of the People [. . .]

The special difficulty of making an accurate picture of so shifting a scene as the low-class streets in East London present is very evident and may easily be exaggerated. As in a crowd, the details of the picture change continually, but the general effect is much the same, whatever moment is chosen. I have attempted to produce an instantaneous picture, fixing the facts on my negative as they appear at a given moment, and the imagination of my readers must add the movement, the constant changes, the whirl and turmoil of life. In many districts the people are always on the move; they shift from one part of it to another like 'fish in a river'. The School Board visitors follow them as best they may, and the transfers from one visitor's book to another's are very numerous. On the whole, however, the people usually do not go far, and often cling from generation to generation to one vicinity, almost as if the set of streets which lie there were an isolated country village.

Statistics of Poverty

[. . .] The inhabitants of every street, and court, and block of buildings in the whole of London, have been estimated in proportion to the numbers of the children, and arranged in classes according to the known position and condition of the parents of these children. The streets have been grouped together according to the School Board subdivisions or 'blocks' . . . The numbers included in each Block vary from less than 2000 to more than 30,000, and to make a more satisfactory unit of comparison I have arranged them in continuous groups, 2, 3, or 4 together, so as to make areas having each about 30,000 inhabitants, these areas adding up into the large divisions of the School Board administration. The population is then classified by Registration districts, which are likewise grouped into School Board divisions, each method finally leading up to the total for all London.

The classes into which the population of each of these blocks and districts is divided are the same as were used in describing East London, only somewhat simplified. They may be stated thus:

A The lowest class – occasional labourers, loafers and semi-criminals.
B The very poor – casual labour, hand-to-mouth existence, chronic want.
C & D The poor – including alike those whose earnings are small, because of irregularity of employment, and those whose work, though regular, is ill-paid.
E & F The regularly employed and fairly paid working class of all grades.
G & H Lower and upper middle class and all above this level.

The classes C and D, whose poverty is similar in degree but different in kind, can only be properly separated by information as to employment which was obtained for East London, but which, as already explained, the present inquiry does not yield. It is the same with E and F, which cover the various grades of working-class comfort. G and H are given together for convenience.

Outside of, and to be counted in addition to, these classes are the inmates of institutions whose numbers are specially reported in every census, and finally there are a few who, having no shelter, or no recognized shelter, for the night, elude official enumeration and are not counted at all.

From C. Booth (1967) (1889) *On the City: Physical Pattern and Social Structure*, Chicago: University of Chicago Press, pp. 173–83.

Questions

1. List the benefits and disadvantages of using the records of School Board visitors as a source of data.
2. How useful is Booth's categorisation of social classes into eight groupings, A to H?
3. What do you consider to be the strengths and weaknesses of Booth's study of the condition of the inhabitants of London?

Reading 48

Social surveys (2): Poverty and labour in London in the 1980s

PETER TOWNSEND, PAUL CORRIGAN AND UTE KOWARZIK

The survey undertaken by Peter Townsend and his colleagues, although not as volumous as Booth's (Reading 47), also utilised the classic social survey methods of sampling and collecting data. And although the context of this study – Thatcher's Britain – might seem very different from the late-Victorian period, the findings on the extent of poverty make equally depressing reading. After setting the scene, the Reading includes details on how the sampling was undertaken and how, as with Booth's survey, the data was gathered with the help of a number of different bodies and support groups. It concludes with a brief comment on how the findings relate to the official, governmental 'picture'.

Introduction

The third survey of poverty and the London labour market began in late 1985 and is due to be completed during 1987. Every day interviewers have been bringing back evidence of severe deprivation among the population of 6½ million. There are people who are homeless and even some, early in 1986, who were sleeping in the open at the end of one of the hardest winters of this century. There are disabled and elderly people too poor to keep the heating on during the day and too frightened to walk the surrounding streets on their own. There are unemployed people whose desperation to keep their families fed and clothed is acute. There are increasing numbers of people earning low pay in bad or thoroughly unsatisfactory working conditions.

Yet these were precisely the concerns of the books being written about the London of 1886. It was on April 17 of that year that Charles Booth established his Board of Statistical Research and began his huge survey of Life and Labour in London, which was to be published eventually in a total of 17 volumes.

Our work is carried out within that tradition. We believe it is necessary to gather together empirical evidence about working and social conditions in our capital city. Like Booth, we believe it is necessary because there are sections of the population who are not aware that anything is wrong with those conditions or do not believe there are problems of consequence, and are implicitly or explicitly condoning developments which are liable to do even greater harm to society in the future than they are doing at the present. We consider such people are out of touch with events for reasons which may not always be their own fault. Whenever there is a major conflict in any society about how to deal with its internal problems there is always the possibility of insisting on making observations and measures of those problems so that the rift in perceptions of the problems at least might be bridged. Also like Booth we advocate a painstaking approach to the documentation of information about the lives of people, in this case by interviewing a representative sample of the population, so that the work carries conviction and authority with specialists as well as with the public at large. When our work is complete we will be able to describe and analyse the lives of London's people with some considerable confidence.

The London Survey – Summary of Methods

By any reckoning the problems of poverty, unemployment and multiple deprivation have become huge and deserve careful scientific examination. The surveys in London are aimed at illuminating contemporary discussion of all three. We interviewed a general sample of the adult population of the city; a total of 2700 people have been interviewed at considerable length. Addresses were chosen at random from 30 wards selected at regular intervals from the total of 755, ranked by the index of multiple deprivation that we discuss below. All the adults at each of these addresses were invited to answer questions about employment, income and experiences of, as well as attitudes towards deprivation. We are also undertaking research in depth in the borough of Hackney and Bromley, representing, as demonstrated in the pages above, the impoverished and prosperous ends of the London spectrum. In that stage of the research we invited cross-sections of the borough populations to furnish an extensive job history, as well as comment on the local labour market and other immediately local conditions. And at this stage information will also be sought from employers in those boroughs so that a better theory of institutional developments can be built up.

This study was not simply carried out within the confines of a University or Polytechnic department, with some input from the GLC thrown in. It was important from the beginning that the whole methodology was discussed fully with all of those who had some important input to make. Thus the Women's Committee Support Unit, the Disability Resources Unit, the Ethnic Minorities Unit and the Industry and Employment Branch of the Greater London Council were all actively involved. This made the research a lot more representative of different interests in London, and also more accountable for the direction it took. Certain approaches and sets of questions depended heavily on this advice; and the combined knowledge and experience of these groups went into the specifics of the questionnaire. At no stage did we feel any intellectual freedoms were curtailed in any way. All the decisions about the form and content of the surveys rested finally with the research team. More positively it must be acknowledged that such inputs enrich the form and nature of social studies such as our own.

It was equally important that our study had to begin within a clear scientific and theoretical framework. As we explain in the next section, we chose to look at living standards in relationship to the labour market. We also chose to study living standards across the board. While much of what we have to say will inevitably concentrate upon the poorer sections of London's society, we have data about and are interested in the rich and people with middle incomes as well and the institutions which govern and afford opportunities in their lives. Although such people may be separated by wealth and location from the poorer people in London, they are inextricably linked through the networks of economic and social organisations and relationships of the capital city. Fundamentally the poor can be understood and their numbers explained not only according to the ways by which they but also the rich actually earn their wealth and live their lives. Of course we recognise this is a proposition which itself requires substantiation and explanation throughout our analysis.

Our study also calls into question many of the 'taken for granted' categories of social life. For example, within this interim report we put considerable emphasis on the problem of 'unemployment'. The question of who is and who is not unemployed has become an issue of considerable political importance. The Government has changed the precise definition (now 19 times) since 1980 – which has had a marked effect upon the numbers officially recognised as unemployed. This study allows the numbers produced by different definitions to be compared. It also allows estimates to be made of the numbers in the population who are not doing any work because they have given up expecting the possibility of labour – for example, many women and older people. While our study can properly reflect what are the official definitions of social relations it can also demonstrate how far the 'official' fails to come to grips with the 'real'.

From P. Townsend with P. Corrigan and U. Kowarzik (1987) *Poverty and Labour in London*, London: Low Pay Unit, pp. 3–6.

Questions

1. What are the advantages of involving interest and support groups in social research? What are the possible problems with this?
2. Assess the strengths of Townsend's research methods compared to Booth's of a century earlier.

Reading 49

Measuring wealth and poverty

JOHN SCOTT

Scott suggests that the sociological examination of wealth has to adopt a similar approach to that which has been established in research into poverty. Privilege, he argues, is a parallel condition to deprivation and has, therefore, to be understood in relative terms. As he puts it, 'privilege . . . is a condition in which people are able to enjoy advantaged powers and opportunities, life chances that are superior to those that are normal in their society'. In this reading, Scott discusses some of the definitional issues raised by the notion of 'wealth' and tries to relate them to the more established sociological work on the nature of poverty.

I am concerned with the distribution of economic resources and specifically, with the conditions of poverty and wealth that arise from this distribution. My usage of the term 'wealth' . . . accords with the everyday idea that a person is 'wealthy' when he or she is particularly advantaged in the distribution of economic resources. Wealth, like poverty, is a feature of a particular pattern of inequality. This usage is something of a departure from the definition of wealth that is generally employed in studies of distribution. In these studies a distinction is generally made between 'income' and 'wealth', where income is the *flow* of economic resources that a person receives in a particular period, and wealth is the total *stock* of such resources that a person has accumulated. 'Income', then, is the total daily, weekly, or annual value of such things as earnings from employment, interest on savings and investments, grants, state benefits, and so on. Income can be measured both 'before' and 'after' the taxes are applied to its various components. After-tax income, or net income, is the 'disposable income' that a person has available for spending. Personal 'wealth', on the other hand, refers to the monetary value of the physical and financial assets that belong to a person and that he or she has been able to accumulate from income and from other sources. I have used such terms 'personal assets' or 'personal property' for this idea, in order to retain the word 'wealth' to refer to its original meaning of the advantaged possession of personal assets.

In defining income and personal assets I have referred to the 'person' who receives or owns them. In many cases, however, the family or household is the more meaningful unit of analysis, and many studies do, in fact, refer to family income or household assets. Where such differences are relevant, they will be made apparent in my discussion. Matters are further complicated by the fact that official statistics often refer to 'tax units' or other categories that may include individuals, couples, families, or households, and which may be difficult to translate into more meaningful terms. Fortunately, *trends* in such figures generally move in the same direction, whichever unit is used, and so a clear view of overall trends can be obtained. Wherever this is not the case, I have tried to indicate the differences that exist. More problematic is the varying level of inequality that is apparent from statistics based upon different units of analysis. All that can be done in many cases is to put the differing estimates alongside one another with an indication of the respects in which they differ.

Other definitional matters relating to income and personal assets need not detain us here; they will be introduced in the main text whenever they are relevant. It is, however, necessary to say something about the definitions of poverty and wealth that I have adopted. 'Poverty' – as I have already shown – is a highly contested term. In its most general sense, poverty refers to a lack of the economic resources that are necessary for the enjoyment of a basic standard of living, however this is seen in the particular society in question. The poor are those who are 'deprived' of the conditions necessary for an adequate life in the society in which they live. One implication of the work of Marshall and Townsend is that it is possible to conceptualise 'wealth' in parallel terms. To be wealthy is to enjoy a standard of living that is greater than that normal for members of a particular society. If deprivation is the condition of life of the poor, 'privilege' is the condition of life of the wealthy.

Deprivation and privilege should be seen as complementary terms and as indicating contrasting departures from the normal lifestyle of the citizen. If it is possible to recognise a 'poverty line', it may also be possible to recognise a 'wealth line': the poverty line defines the level at which deprivation begins, and the wealth line defines the level at which privilege begins. From this point of view, deprivation and privilege are polarised conditions of life that reflect the polarisation of wealth and poverty. A recognition of this fact forces us to recognise that the causes of poverty cannot be separated from the causes of wealth: indeed, the one may be a necessary condition of the other. Townsend's work has developed the powerful idea of poverty as 'relative deprivation', the concept being designed to overcome the inadequacies of attempts to define poverty in simple subsistence terms as an ahistorical absolute. My contention is that an analogous concept of wealth as 'relative privilege' can go a considerable way towards overcoming the difficulties faced in the assessment of wealth.

From J. Scott (1994) *Poverty and Wealth: Citizenship, Deprivation and Privilege*, Harlow: Longman, pp. 16–18.

Questions

1. Scott distinguishes between income and wealth. Give examples of people who might be wealthy but not have a high income.
2. What difficulties do you think there are in measuring wealth? How might they be surmounted?
3. Scott suggests that, in a similar vein to the idea of a 'poverty line', it should be possible to establish a 'wealth line' – a line at which privilege begins. What sort of 'indicators' could be used to define the wealthy?

Reading 50

The research process: Planning social surveys

SARA ARBER

In this Reading, Sara Arber describes the stages involved in planning a large-scale social survey. Her discussion uses her own research into local authority housing policy to illustrate the planning process. The Reading starts by considering how research issues and hypotheses are derived and conceptualised and then looks at the practical considerations of gaining access, designing samples and questionnaires and gathering reliable data from interviews. The focus of the extract is on the practicalities of doing research, rather than the theoretical issues related to what is being researched.

[This reading] presents a personal account of one piece of research as an example of planning the research process. This study had very specific policy-related aims, but also examined theoretical issues relating to inter-generational housing mobility [. . .]

The Survey of Tenants in Public Housing

The genesis of this study was a number of policy questions which were of interest to a Local Authority in South-East England. The funder specified a survey of public housing tenants. The research had to be completed quickly so that the results could be fed into their policy and planning cycle [. . .]

The aim of the survey as specified by the Local Authority was to examine the satisfaction of public housing tenants with a range of services, including the repairs service, a newly introduced scheme to encourage residents' associations and tenant participation, and a new tenants' magazine. The Authority was interested in tenants' preferences about improvements such as central heating and replacement windows, and whether tenants would opt for a private landlord rather than remaining with the Local Authority, a possibility opened up by the 1988 Housing Bill. A representative sample survey was the most appropriate research strategy for these objectives, since it would provide accurate estimates of the views of all tenants in this Local Authority area. In addition, our own sociological goals were adequately met using a survey approach, for example, to test the hypothesis that mobility out of public sector housing was associated with labour market position [. . .]

From our analysis of documentary sources, official statistics and the existing sociological literature, we derived a number of sociological hypotheses which could be explored with data from this policy oriented survey. The main theoretical issue we chose to pursue was the housing mobility of tenants in public housing, that is, the pattern of moves between different sectors of the housing market (owner occupation, public housing and private renting). We wanted to examine whether the adult children of tenants tended to be restricted to public housing because they were unable to break into owner occupation in a high cost housing area. Social mobility is a mainstay of sociology, with numerous studies of the relationship between the occupation of fathers and the occupational achievement of their adult children (e.g. Goldthorpe 1980; Heath 1981; Payne 1987), yet there is no comparable work on intergenerational housing mobility [. . .]

To examine housing mobility required the introduction of two new sets of questions. First, a set on the housing history of the tenant: when they first entered Local Authority tenure, their previous tenure, and their housing tenure at age 14. These questions were asked about each adult in the household. Second, a set of questions about the housing history of each adult child who had left home.

Gaining Access

Gaining access requires detailed planning and may take several months of preparatory work to achieve, especially if access is required to organisations such as hospitals or to an institutional setting. Gaining access includes a number of discreet issues. First, access to a group of research subjects or a setting may require extensive negotiation and the permission of 'gatekeepers'. Second, cooperation from individual members of the study sample or the participants in a setting is required in order to maximize response, while ensuring informed consent. Third, access to documentary materials – for example, memoranda and committee minutes – which are not publicly available requires negotiation and permission. In the Public Housing survey, an additional access issue was the need to obtain permission to use the research data for our own sociological publications.

Access to the names and addresses of public housing tenants was provided by our sponsor, the Local Authority. However, it was still essential to prepare the ground to ensure the respondents' informed consent. The Local Authority sent out letters in advance to each tenancy selected for the study, providing information about the research, stressing that it was an independent piece of work being undertaken by the University on behalf of the Local Authority, and reassuring respondents that all information would be treated entirely confidentially. Tenants were assured that they had the right to decline to take part in the research [. . .]

Before beginning the interview, the interviewers read an Introduction which reiterated many of the points made previously in the letter and reminded respondents that they did not need to answer any questions if they did not want to.

An issue relating to access was the researchers' rights to data collected in a survey which was financed entirely by the Local Authority for its own purposes. As academic researchers we would not have embarked on this research unless we were sure we could publish our academic findings. This was raised as an essential prerequisite at the initial meeting with the Local Authority and was written into the research contract, signed by the Local Authority and the University, using a form of words which was acceptable to both parties. This stipulation generated extensive discussions and held up the final signing of the contract. The contract required publications to have prior written consent from the Local Authority, but consent could only be withheld for specific reasons. In the event, no changes to publications have been required.

It is essential that researchers consider carefully all issues relating to access prior to embarking on a research study, and if necessary, include the researchers' publication rights in a written contract.

Designing Samples

The purpose of sampling is usually to study a representative subsection of a precisely defined population in order to make inferences about the whole population . . . In this research, the 'population' consisted of current tenancies in the Local Authority area. We had to decide how to select a sample from the population of approximately 9000 tenancies in the Local Authority area and who to interview in the case of joint tenancies.

Where there was a sole tenant, it was clear who should be interviewed, but the decision was more difficult for joint tenancy or where the tenant was married or living as married. One alternative was to interview both tenants (either separately or at the same time). This would have provided a fuller and more accurate picture of the views and characteristics of tenants, but was ruled out because of the higher interviewing costs and the likelihood that the response rate would have decreased if interviews with both parties were required.

Having decided on one interview per household, we could have interviewed whoever opened the door, but this would probably have biased the sample towards women. Or we could have specified interviews with the Head of Household, or the prime wage earner, but this would have biased the sample towards men. Because women and men are likely to be concerned about different types of issues, the most appropriate sample was one which included equal proportions of 'husbands' and 'wives'. To achieve this, we required interviewers to obtain equal numbers of interviews with 'husbands' and 'wives' in their area [. . .]

The 'sampling frame' was an up-to-date list of current tenancies in the Local Authority area, listed by house number within street. The sponsors wanted separate results for tenancies in different parts of the area, for example, in rural areas and in some smaller estates which had recently undergone a house modernisation programme. There were also some very big estates which were quite homogeneous in the characteristics of their tenants. Since reliable results were required about the views of tenants living on different estates, and the estates were of varying size, we proposed a 'disproportionate stratified sample' (Moser and Kalton 1971). The whole area was divided into three sections or strata, which were assigned varying probabilities of selection: tenancies in the rural areas and some estates of particular interest had a one in three chance of selection, those in town estates had a one in six chance of selection, and those in the very big estates had a one in nine chance of selection. This yielded a selected sample of 1225 tenancies. We assumed that we would achieve interviews with 80 per cent of the selected tenancies, which would thus produce the desired sample size of 1000.

Designing Questionnaires

Before starting work developing a questionnaire, the researcher should decide on its approximate length and the nature of the questions. Large scale surveys generally require identical question wording for each respondent so that results are reliable and so that comparable information is obtained from each respondent, facilitating data entry and statistical analysis.

Survey questionnaires can include any of three broad types of questions: 'closed' questions, where the respondent selects a response from a set of alternative answers; 'open' questions, which allow the respondents to give whatever answer they like with the response either written down verbatim or tape-recorded; and 'pre-coded' or 'field coded' questions, where the respondents give whatever answer they like and the interviewer codes their answer into one of a number of response categories provided on the interview schedule.

Open questions in a survey require subsequent coding 'in the office' after the interview is complete, a process known as post-coding. The costs of this coding and the time it takes need to be considered when designing the questionnaire. It was decided that the interview schedule would be mainly pre-coded, with a minimum of questions requiring post-coding [. . .]

The process of designing questions to measure the concepts under study was one of gradual development, partly by 'trial and error'. Questions were drafted to cover the issues identified by the Local Authority, for example, a section on the repairs service. Our first version of this section asked about the three most recent repairs undertaken by the Local Authority and, for each repair, about how the repair was reported, the response of the repairs staff, how quickly the work was done, the quality of the workmanship, and so on. Because during development work we realised that asking about three repairs was very time consuming and most respondents had had a similar experience for each repair, we decided only to ask detailed questions about the last repair. The questions also needed to be re-formulated to take into account respondents who had not had any repairs, and the concern expressed by many tenants that they were given very short notice of the date on which a repair would be done.

The interview schedule was then piloted on tenants who were not in the sample. These pilot interviews provided invaluable insights for altering question wording, adding questions about issues which were of particular concern to respondents but which we had not thought of, omitting or changing questions, and altering the order of questions to a more logical flow [. . .]

Measuring Attitudes

Attitudes were measured using a number of different measurement strategies. One was the Likert scale, where the respondents say whether they 'strongly agree, agree, disagree or strongly disagree' with a series of statements, for example about the quality of services and facilities provided on the Local Authority estates [. . .]

A second strategy used in measuring attitudes was to assess the 'salience' of particular issues for respondents, that is, what they considered most important. For example, respondents were asked what they most liked about their present home. Up to three items could be specified. During the pilot work we found that some tenants were entirely dissatisfied with all aspects of their home and gave responses such as 'It should be knocked down' and 'nothing'. Likert scales cannot give such a graphic illustration of the priorities and concerns of respondents as can this kind of field coded question.

Interviewing and Managing Interviewers

The public housing survey aimed to achieve 1000 interviews each lasting about an hour and a quarter. Interviews had to be completed within a six week time period, so it was necessary to recruit and train a large number of interviewers. Forty interviewers were recruited on the assumption that the average interviewer would complete 25 interviews, although some might do substantially less and others more.

Interviewers were recruited from various sources, including Masters students, older undergraduate students, interviewers who had worked for other departments in the University, and people responding to advertisements in the local paper. Interviewer briefing notes were prepared which provided detailed information about the survey, specific information about individual questions, and practical information including the amount and method of payment of interviewers and their travelling expenses.

A two-day training programme was held for interviewers. Then objectives of the research were described and it was explained that the intention of the Local Authority was to make policy on the basis of the survey results. The interview schedule was discussed in detail, and the trainees then watched a mock interview with a public housing tenant. The method of sampling was explained, including the requirement to interview equal numbers of 'husbands' and 'wives' in each interviewer area. Administrative arrangements and the methods to be used in filling in interview record sheets were outlined. Finally, each interviewer had an opportunity to run through an interview and raise queries [. . .]

Most of the interviews were completed within the planned six week period. Areas where potential interviewers remained were reallocated to more experienced interviewers and completed within the following two weeks. Interviews were achieved in 83 per cent of the selected sample of tenancies; this was a higher response rate than originally anticipated.

From S. Arber (1993) 'The research process', in N. Gilbert (ed.) *Researching Social Life*, London: Sage, pp. 33–43.

Questions

1. Arber's research was financed by the Local Authority. What were the Local Authority's aims for the research and what other aims did Arber herself have?
2. List the advantages and disadvantages of gaining outside funding for academic research?
3. What would you suggest are the potential weaknesses of the research process described by Arber?

Reading 51

Participant observation (1): Inside the British police

SIMON HOLDAWAY

One of the central issues that faces participant observers is whether they should conduct their research covertly or not. Objections to covert research range from moral indignation – it betrays the trust of participants in the research, who are 'used' in that data is gained from them without their consent – to concerns of a more practical nature – it imposes a great deal of strain on the researcher. This issue faced Simon Holdaway when he pursued research into his own occupation– policing – and at his own place of work. This Reading is taken from the first chapter of Holdaway's study Inside the British Police Force *in which he discusses his methodology and the constraints he experienced. In particular he highlights the dilemma caused by the divided loyalties he felt: between the opportunities to pursue his research and his commitment to the police force, who had, among other things, supported his secondment to university. Holdaway adopted a covert strategy, a decision that he justifies in the first part of the reading by pointing out that, first, the police are a powerful group who would perhaps be better able to 'protect' themselves from research than other groups and, second, traditionally policing has been a secretive activity. He then goes on to indicate some of the 'ethical issues' he had to deal with – for example, whether to record instances of police malpractice that came to his notice. He also considers how being a sociologist and researcher affected his relationships and interactions with his police colleagues and the pressures he felt in keeping his researcher role hidden.*

Researching Hilton

'Getting the seat of your pants dirty in real research' is a hazardous business. My research began after graduation, when I returned from university secondment to my force and to work as a sergeant. During my undergraduate studies I learned to conceptualize what seemed highly questionable police practices as the 'occupational culture' of policing – a term well suited to the seminar but less appropriate in the station office and charge room [. . .]

When I returned from university to my new police posting my 'First' was, I suspect, bristling somewhat. The senior officers who welcomed me had rather different preoccupations. They did not seem to know much about where I had been during my absence from operational policing; neither did they know or think much about my subject. If I was glowing with academic pride, the senior officer of my new station was critical about the bristles I now sported. One greeted me with the words: 'The last thing I want is men with beards. I spend half my time telling men to get their hair cut'; and he continued, 'You will have no time for research. We have to get on with policing the ground and haven't time for experiments. What I want is people who can lead men.' I left my initial interviews with senior staff feeling intensely frustrated, hurt and not a little angry. Despite having read numerous articles on the methods of participant observation, not least on ways of gaining access to research, I found myself torn between opportunities for research and commitment to the police service, which had sponsored me at university [. . .]

After weighing all the options – requesting permission for research access from Headquarters and/or from my lower-ranked colleagues, resignation and so on – I decided to begin my fieldwork by adopting a covert strategy . . . The argument that all individuals have a right to privacy (that is to say, freedom from observation, investigation and subsequent publication based on the investigation) is strong but should be qualified when applied to the police. Research and my previous experience of police work demonstrated the power of the lower ranks, not least their resistance to external control of their work. Any effective research strategy would have to pierce their protective shield if it was to be successful.

This problem is encountered during research of many organizations; however, the case for covert research is strengthened by the central and powerful situation of the police within our social structure. The police are said to be accountable to the rule of law, a constitutional constraint which restricts their right to privacy but which they can neutralize by maintaining a protective occupational culture. When such an institution is over-protective, its members restrict the right to privacy that they possess. It is important that they be researched [. . .]

The covert researcher of the police has to be reminded that he is working within an extremely powerful organization which begs revelation of its public and private face by first-hand observation – risky as that observation might be. In part, therefore, my covert research is justified by my assessment of the power of the police within British society and the secretive character of the force. This does not mean that covert research into powerful groups is ethical while that into less powerful ones is not (Young 1970); neither is it to advocate a sensational type of sociology in which rigorous analysis of evidence gives way to moral crusading. Although I came to this uncomfortable conclusion when my research began ten or more years ago, I would still argue in similar terms, despite widespread changes in police policy.

Defining the Limits of Research

Having made the decision in principle to conduct covert research, I had to face its practical implications and responsibilities. This was none the easier for my being a police sergeant, holding all the legal powers of that office as well as being responsible for the supervision of a large number of officers who would be working according to their 'street-wise' rules. I was not a sociology lecturer masquerading as a schizophrenic, an alcoholic, a millenarian, a Pentecostalist or a factory worker; I was actually a police sergeant who had no idea when or if he would leave the field for other work (Festinger *et al.* 1956; Homan 1980; Loftland 1961; Rosenhan 1973; Roy 1960).

Unlike experimental, questionnaire and other controlled methods, covert research is equivocal; those who are being researched control the situation as much as, if not more than, the researcher. When the subject of research is the police, whose job is highly unpredictable and varied (no less so when the researcher is a serving police officer), the definition of the limits of ethical tolerance is a significant matter [. . .]

During my first week's duty I worked as a station officer . . . [In one incident] I dealt with a man who had threatened his wife with a pistol. He pleaded his innocence, and a police officer kicked him on the backside, not with excessive force but just to remind him that his explanation was not acceptable. The incident was recorded, but I omitted from my notes the fact that the prisoner had been kicked; for good or ill, it was too sensitive an issue for me to accept. Similar situations arose, and I recorded in my diary:

> It is still a problem working with another police officer who has very different ideas about civil liberties – patrolling with Sergeant – in this case. Every time we stopped someone I had to manage a situation in which the possibilities of corners being cut were real. This causes a strain for the sociological observer.

I was that impersonal observer; the realization that I was actually involved in grappling with such ethical issues was slow to dawn.

But incidents like these were not the only experiences that informed my covert research. I also gained access to, and recorded, very private and – I do not use the word lightly – precious moments of people's lives. One day a mother called the police after the sudden death of her young baby. In her grief-stricken state she made some remarks about her marriage – I did not record them. I recall wrapping the baby in a blanket and holding it in my arms as two silent colleagues drove with us to the mortuary. The mortuary attendant took the child and, in a routine fashion, placed it in a refrigerator. One of my colleagues said that he felt like 'putting one on' the attendant for the way he treated the child. I later classified the conversations about the incident as jokes and stories; they proved to be the genesis of an idea about the use of humour in managing the personal stress of police work. I should also add that incidents like this reminded me of the demanding work required of the police, and of their humanity – I needed to be reminded of that.

The first couple of months of research were exceedingly tough. Despite support from my academic supervisors, I could not make much sense of that data that I was collecting. I applied for an academic post which, thankfully, I did not get. The PCs had noticed that my ideas about policing were rather different from their own. (When tea mugs belonging to the shift were changed we were presented with colours to suit our personality: my mug was yellow. 'Why yellow?' I asked naïvely. 'Because you're scared.'). Senior officers found me truculent, and my chief doubted my suitability for the police service. I later complained of his insensitivity to another senior officer, who responded: 'You might disagree with Mr—, but do you disagree with 99 per cent of the officers at the station?' He explained, 'There are two important things about police work. First, policemen must be willing to cut corners or else they would never get their job done. Secondly, it's because policemen have been happy to gild the lily that the law has been administered in this country.' He was right. On these points I did indeed disagree with him, and he knew it. A new officer soon came to command my division, and he transferred me from my station and pilot study in participant observation into a new subdivision and, unknowingly, to the beginning of a substantive research project.

My new station was much larger, and I now worked with an inspector, three other sergeants and about twenty-five constables. From the outset it seemed to me important to tell my colleagues about my attitude to the use of force and to the manner in which evidence is gathered, suspects are handled in the station and so on. This was often done by engaging them in conversation about a particular issue or job in which they were involved. For example, one of my fellow sergeants was known to use 'unorthodox techniques' when questioning suspects. When we chatted about this issue he gave me a full description of what he was and was not willing to do, citing examples to illustrate each point. His explanations proved to be very useful because I was able to compare his accounts with his subsequent behaviour and that of others. Fortunately, he enjoyed discussing such issues and drew on my opinions about sociology; he became an important informant, who was always happy to provide details of the actions of particular officers and of particular incidents [. . .]

Stress – the Life Blood of Participant Observation

Covert research and the ethical questions it raises create conditions of stress within which the sociologist has to live with himself. For example, tension resulted from working with officers who did not share my values and assumptions about policing. Such, it might be said, is the nature of a nasty world; but I had some direct responsibility for the manner in which these officers behaved. I occasionally retreated from conversations and incidents over which I had no control and which I found distasteful. At times I had to deal with an officer whose behaviour exceeded the bounds of what I considered reasonable conduct. These situations could easily get in the way of research and increased the pressure of my work.

Then the constant reflection involved in participant observation added to the pressure of working in a busy station. Gold (1958) and others who have written on participant observation encourage us to consider a continuum with overt and covert observation and participation at either end. In my covert research a constant triadic dialogue took place between the balancing of personal ethical limits, the aims of research and my duty as a police officer. There were times when research suffered because I was engrossed in police work and times when police work took second place to the recording of detailed evidence. The resulting tension was demanding and wearing.

This risk of 'going native' was always present, and at the beginning of each tour of duty I reminded myself of my research and its themes. There were days when I was less attentive than usual; but when I became too involved in policing I was often pulled back by a particularly distasteful event. On one occasion, after hearing a conversation about race relations, I wrote in my diary:

> I reacted badly to the conversation yesterday and want nothing to do with such sentiments. I remember saying to myself, 'Underneath, these policemen are ruthless and racist.' I seem to have slipped into the mould easily during the last couple of weeks and wonder if I should have been so easy with my feelings. The balance of participant observation is one which can so easily be submerged and forgotten. Now it has been brought before me in glaring lights, and all the old issues of ethics – when to speak out, how involved one should get, whose perspective one takes on – loom large.

Finally, as a covert researcher of the police I was documenting the work of people who regarded me as a colleague. The risk of being found out was always present and I had to be sensitive to any indication that others – sometimes friends – might know what I was doing. I kept shorthand notes on a scrap of paper in the back pocket of my trousers; if I had to leave the station or charge office to make notes, I listened for approaching footsteps [. . .]

Into Civvie Street: Analysis and Publication

Leaving the police service proved to be a comparatively comfortable move, but it has left a nagging doubt in my mind: as I publish, I may hurt those who have unknowingly co-operated in my research [. . .]

Covert researchers therefore take risks when they publish their work: they risk the charges that they are simply engaging in a polemical exposé of an easily accessible 'whipping boy' and that their data are unreliable; they risk the possibility of action for attempting to convey the truth about a powerful institution in British society; they risk the consequences of a calculated deception of trust. I have attempted to argue that my research is based on reasoned and acceptable ethical decisions. These decisions do not sanction research into any group of people. The question we should ask when deciding on any research strategy is this: 'If I were to place myself in the situation of those whom I wish to research, would I object to the covert method?' If we begin from this question and pit our evidence against it, preferably in debate with others concerned with the research, a good decision may well be made. In the end the individual researcher may have to make the decision to adopt a covert stance, accepting the risks that it involves.

From S. Holdaway (1983) *Inside the British Police: A Force at Work*, London: Blackwell, pp. 3–14.

Questions

1. Why do you think that Holdaway suggests that covert research of the police is particularly justifiable because of the 'central and powerful situation of the police within our social structure'?
2. How did Holdaway's position as a sergeant help him to gain data? How might it have hindered him?
3. What were the major practical problems Holdaway faced and how did he resolve them?
4. How did Holdaway's 'personal ethical limits' get in the way of the aims of his research?

Reading 52

Participant observation (2): Deviant lives and careers

NED POLSKY

In this Reading, Ned Polsky reflects on the difficulties faced when undertaking field research on deviants and criminals and sets out some of the 'rules' and procedures that sociologists engaged in such research should follow in order to overcome such difficulties. He illustrates these with examples from his own field research into deviant subcultures, including hustlers, drug addicts and prostitutes. In reading this extract bear in mind that Polsky was researching and writing about deviance in the USA in the early 1960s and the language that both he and his subjects use reflects that period: terms such as 'squares', 'hustlers', 'junkies' and 'beat scene' have a rather dated and almost quaint feel to them.

Most difficulties that one meets and solves in doing field research on criminals are simply the difficulties one meets and solves in doing field research. The basic problem many sociologists would face in field work on criminals, therefore, is an inability to do field work. I cannot try to solve that problem here, but shall briefly indicate what I think is its nature before discussing problems peculiar to research on criminals.

Successful field research depends on the investigator's trained abilities to look at people, listen to them, think and feel with them, talk with them rather than at them. It does *not* depend fundamentally on some impersonal apparatus, such as a camera or tape recorder or questionnaire, that is interposed between the investigator and the investigated. Robert E. Park's concern that the sociologist become first of all a good reporter meant not that the sociologist rely on gadgets to see, hear, talk and remember for him; quite the contrary, it asked the sociologist to train such human capacities in himself to their utmost and use them to their utmost in direct observation of people he wants to learn something about. But the problem for many a sociologist today – the result of curricula containing as much scientism as science – is that these capacities, far from being trained in him, have been trained out of him. He 'knows' that Park-style sociology produced merely 'reportage' (this is less than a half-truth at best) and insists that the real way for him to learn about people is to place one or more screens between him and them. He can't see people any more, except through punched cards and one-way mirrors. He can't talk with people any more, only 'survey' them. Often he can't even talk *about* people any more, only about 'data'. Direct field study of social life, when he is forced to think about it at all, is something he fondly labels 'soft' sociology, as distinguished from his own confrontation of social reality at several removes, which in his mysterious semantics is 'hard' sociology.

Colleagues in older disciplines have begun to give up such scientism – for example, psychologists studying child development have lately come out of the laboratory in droves to look at the child in his natural habitat – and when sociology has finished anxiously proving it is scientific it too will abandon scientism.

In what follows I shall take this problem of trained incapacity for field work as already solved. This means I shall assume, at the outset, that the sociologist is not a man who needs an NIMH grant to find a criminal, that he can humanly relate to nonsociologist humans and by asking around can quickly get introduced to a career criminal or at least find out where one or more can be met.

But suppose he finds, say, a tavern where a jewel thief or loan shark or fence hangs out, and has him pointed out or is even introduced. What then? The problems have just begun.

Perhaps the largest set of problems arises from the fact that a criminal judges the judges, puts down the people who put him down. Any representative of the square world initially encounters some covert if not overt suspicion or hostility; it is best to assume such feelings are there (in the criminal) even if they don't show, and that you are not going to get far unless and until you overcome those feelings. This problem, although it exists in studying a criminal enmeshed with the law, is usually magnified in dealing with an uncaught criminal in his natural surroundings, for the following reasons: (1) You are more of an intruder. As far as he is often concerned, it's bad enough that he has to put up with questioning when in the hands of the law, and worse when squares won't even leave him in peace in his own tavern. (2) He is freer to put you down and you are more on your own; you have no authority (police, warden, judge, parole board) to back you up. (3) There is more of a possibility that he might be hurt by you, that is, he has more to lose than someone already in jail.

At least potentially going for you, on the other hand, is the fact that because you are not working in a law-enforcement setting you might *possibly* be all right; and the sooner you firmly establish in his mind that you are not any kind of cop or social worker, the sooner that fact begins going for you.

The following paragraphs will not solve for every researcher these and related problems, but will give some procedures – in no special order – that I have found useful to overcome such problems and often to prevent them from arising in the first place. They should be understood as a first attempt to state formally what I have arrived at on a more or less intuitive and trial-and-error basis in dealing with uncaught criminals. They might not work for every researcher, but I think they would work for most.

1. Although you can't help but contaminate the criminal's environment in some degree by your presence, such contamination can be minimized if, for one thing, you use no gadgets (no tape recorder, questionnaire form) and, for another, do not take any notes in the criminal's presence. It is quite feasible to train yourself to remember details of action and speech long enough to write them up fully and accurately after you get home at the end of the day (or night, more typically). Historians accept an account by a disinterested eye-witness written immediately after the event as decent evidence, even when by an untrained observer, and there is no good reason to deny validity to similar accounts by trained observers.

2. Most important when hanging around criminals – what I regard as the absolute 'first rule' of field research on them – is this: initially, keep your eyes and ears open *but keep your mouth shut.* At first try to ask no questions whatsoever. Before you can ask questions, or even speak much at all other than when spoken to, you should get the 'feel' of their world by extensive and attentive listening – get some sense of what pleases them and what bugs them, some sense of their frame of reference, and some sense of *their* sense of language (not only their special argot, as is often mistakenly assumed, but also how they use ordinary language). Even after all this has been learned, if the researcher is a compulsive talker or otherwise longwinded, if he can't shut up for considerable periods, he will be seriously handicapped; his sheer verbosity, even if in 'correct' language, will bother most informants (as it will lower-class people generally).

   Until the criminal's frame of reference and language have been learned, the investigator is in danger of coming on too square, or else of coming on too hip (anxiously over-using or misusing the argot). The result of failure to avert such dangers is that he will be put on or, more likely, put down, and end by provoking the hostility of his informant. True, sometimes a skilful interviewer can deliberately provoke hostility to good effect. But that technique is difficult except after long experience with the particular type of deviant one is studying; and in any case, outside anticrime settings it should be tried, if at all, only with milder kinds of deviants.

3. Once you know the special language, there is a sense in which you should try to forget it. You cannot accurately assess any aspect of a

deviant's lifestyle or sub-culture through his argot alone, although many investigators mistakenly try . . . Such attempts result in many errors, because there is often a good deal of cultural lag between the argot and the reality.

One cannot, for instance, assume that every important role in a deviant sub-culture is represented by a special term. An example:

A distinctive role in the male homosexual sub-culture is played by that type of woman, not overtly lesbian, who likes to pal around with male homosexuals and often serves as a front for them in the heterosexual world; but although this role has, according to older homosexuals I know, existed for decades, it is only within the past several years that homosexual argot has developed special terms for such a woman (today eastern homosexuals often refer to her as a 'faghag' and western homosexuals refer to her as a 'fruit fly') [. . .]

Thus the presence or absence of special language referring to deviance is conclusive evidence for nothing except the presence or absence of such special language. It may sensitize you as to what to look for in actual behaviour, but the degree of congruence between the language and the reality of deviance is an empirical matter to be investigated in each case.

Also, the researcher should forget about imputing beliefs, feelings, or motives (conscious or otherwise) to deviants on the basis of the origins of words in their argot. Whether the etymologies are genuine or fancied (what linguists call 'folk' or 'false' etymologies), they tell us nothing about the psychic state of the users of the words. One form of analysis, a kind of parlour version of psychoanalysis, implicitly denies this. I have seen it seriously argued, for example, that heroin addicts must unconsciously feel guilty about their habit because they refer to heroin by such terms as 'shit', 'junk', and 'garbage'. Actually, the use of any such term by a heroin addict indicates, in itself, nothing whatever about his guilt feelings or the lack thereof, but merely that he is using a term for heroin traditional in his group.

At best, deviant argot is supporting evidence for behavioural phenomena that the investigator has to pin down with other kinds of data.

4. In my experience the most feasible technique for building one's sample is 'snowballing': get an introduction to one criminal who will vouch for you with others, who in turn will vouch for you with still others. (It is of course best to start at the top if possible, that is, with an introduction to the most prestigious person in the group you want to study.)

Getting an initial introduction or two is not nearly so difficult as it might seem. Among students whom I have had perform the experiment of asking their relatives and friends to see if any could provide an introduction to a career criminal, fully a third reported that they could get such introductions. (This experiment also produced rather startling information about parental backgrounds of some of today's college students!) Moreover, once your research interests are publicly known you get volunteer offers of this sort. From students, faculty, and others, I have had more offers of introductions to career criminals – in and out of organized crime – than I could begin to follow up. And that is hardly anything compared to introductions obtainable via criminal lawyers and crime reporters (to say nothing of law enforcement personnel).

Be that as it may, there are times when you don't have an introduction to a particular scene you want to study, and you must start 'cold'. In such a situation it is easier, usually, to get acquainted first with criminals at their play rather than at their work. Exactly where this is depends on your individual play interests. Of course, initiating such contact means recognizing that criminals are not a species utterly different from you; it means recognizing not only that there but for the grace of God (or whoever else you think runs the show) goes you, but that you do have some leisure interests in common with criminals. It means recognizing the reality of a criminal's life (as distinguished from the mass-media image of that life), which is that he isn't a criminal twenty-four hours a day and behaves most of the time just like anyone else from his class and ethnic background.

In fact, one excellent way of establishing contact involves a small bit of fakery at the beginning, in that you can get to know a criminal on the basis of common leisure pursuits and *then* let him know of your research interest in him. (But this latter should be done quite soon, after the first meeting or two.) Where and how you start depends, other things being equal, on what you do best that criminals are also likely to be interested in. For example, in trying to make contact with criminals in a neighbourhood new to me, I of course find it best to start out in the local poolroom. But if you can drink most people under the table, are a convivial bar-room companion, etc., then you should start out in a tavern. If you know horses, start out at a horse parlour. If you know cards, ask around about a good poker game. If you know fighters, start out at the local fight gym.

5. If you establish acquaintance with a criminal on some basis of common interest, then, just as soon as possible, let him know of the differences between you if he hasn't guessed them already; that is, let him know what you do for a living and let him know why, apart from your interest in, say, poker, you are on his scene. This isn't as

ticklish as it seems to people who haven't tried it – partly because of that common interest and partly because the criminal often sees, or can easily be made to see, that there may be something in it for him. For example, he may have some complaint about the outside world's mistaken view of him that you, as someone who has something in common with him, might sympathetically understand and correctly report. (Sometimes these complaints are in fact accurate – as, say, when a pimp complains that, contrary to public impression, his girls drum up their own business.) Or he may want to justify what he does. (For example, a numbers operator justified his activity to me on the basis of a localistic sort of patriotism; he feels that he, like local bookies, benefits local businessmen because, when a player wins he spends some money with a neighbourhood merchant before blowing the rest in further gambling, whereas race-tracks merely drain money out of the neighbourhood and in fact out of the city.) Or he may be motivated by pride and status considerations, e.g., want to let you know that his kind of criminality is superior to other kinds. (Examples: A burglar tells me his line of work is best because 'If you do it right, there are no witnesses.' Another, indicating his superiority to pimps, told me that among his colleagues a common saying about a girl supporting a pimp is that 'Maybe she'll get lucky and marry a thief'. And a robber, indicating his scorn of con men, proudly informed me of one of his scores that 'I didn't *talk* him out of it – I *took* it off him.').

These and similar motives are present not far below the surface in most criminals, and are discoverable and usable by any investigator alert for them.

6. In studying a criminal it is important to realize that he will be studying you, and to let him study you. Don't evade or shut off any questions he might have about your personal life, even if these questions are designed to 'take you down', for example, designed to force you to admit that you too have knowingly violated the law. He has got to define you satisfactorily to himself and his colleagues if you are to get anywhere, and answering his questions frankly helps this process along.

   Sometimes his definitions are not what you might expect. (One that pleased but also disconcerted me: 'You mean they pay you to run with guys like me? That's a pretty good racket.') The 'satisfactory' definition, however, is usually fairly standardized one reason being that you are not the first non-criminal he's met who didn't put him down and consequently he has one or more stereotyped exceptions to his usual definitions of squares. And with a bit of experience you can angle for this and get yourself defined as, for example, 'a square who won't blow the whistle' or 'a square who likes to play with characters' or 'a right square'.

One type of definition you should always be prepared for (though it is by no means always overtly forthcoming) is the informant's assumption that you want to be like him but don't have the nerve and/or are getting your kicks vicariously. Thus one of the better-known researchers on drug addiction has been described to me by junkies as 'a vicarious junkie', criminals often define interested outsiders as 'too lazy to work but too scared to steal', and so on. This type of definition can shake you if there is any truth in it, but it shouldn't; and indeed you can even capitalize on it by admitting it in a backhanded sort of way, that is, by not seriously disputing it.

7. You must draw the line, to yourself and to the criminal. Precisely where to draw it is a moral decision that each researcher must make for himself in each research situation. (It is also to some extent a decision about personal safety, but this element is highly exaggerated in the thinking of those who haven't done field work with criminals.) You need to decide beforehand, as much as possible, where you wish to draw the line, because it is wise to make your position on this known to informants rather early in the game. For example, although I am willing to be told about anything and everything, and to witness many kinds of illegal acts, when necessary I make it clear that there are some such acts I prefer not to witness. (With two exceptions I have had this preference respected.) To the extent that I am unwilling to witness such acts, my personal moral code of course compromises my scientific role – but not, I think, irreparably.

8. There is another kind of compromise that must be made, this by way of keeping faith with informants. As the careful reader of some other parts of this book will gather, in reporting one's research it is sometimes necessary to write of certain things more vaguely and skimpily than one would prefer. But that is more of a literary than a scientific compromise; there need be no distortion of the *sociological* points involved.

9. Letting criminals know where you draw the line of course depends on knowing this yourself. If you aren't sure, the criminal may capitalize on the fact to manoeuvre you into an accomplice role. The possibility of such an attempt increases directly as his trust of you increases. For example, I knew I was really getting somewhere with one criminal when he hopefully explained to me why I would make a fine 'steerhorse' (which in his argot means someone who fingers a big score for a share of it). To receive such indication of 'acceptance' is of course flattering – and is meant to be – but the investigator must be prepared to resist it or the results can be far more serious than anything he anticipates at the beginning of his research. I have heard of one social worker with violent gangs who was so insecure, so unable to 'draw the line' for fear of being put

down, that he got flattered into holding and hiding guns that had been used in murders.

10. Although I have insisted that in studying criminals you mustn't be a 'spy', mustn't pretend to be 'one of them', it is equally important that you don't stick out like a sore thumb in the criminal's natural environment. You must blend in with the human scenery so that you don't chill the scene. One consequence is that often you must modify your usual dress as well as your usual speech. In other words, you must walk a tightrope between 'openness' on the one hand and 'disguise' on the other, whose balancing point is determined anew in each investigation. Let me illustrate this with an example.

    During the summer of 1960, in the course of the research reported on in the next chapter, I spent much time with people involved in heroin use and distribution, in their natural settings: on rooftops, in apartments, in tenement hallways, on stoops, in the streets, in automobiles, in parks and taverns . . . On the one hand, I did not dress as I usually do (suit, shirt and tie), because that way of dressing in the world which I was investigating would have made it impossible for many informants to talk with me, e.g., would have made them worry about being seen with me because others might assume I represented the law. But on the other hand, I took care always to wear a short-sleeved shirt or T-shirt and an expensive wristwatch, both of which let any newcomer who walked up know immediately that I was not a junkie.

11. A final rule is to have few unbreakable rules. For example: although the field investigator can, to a large extent, plan his dress, speech and other behaviour beforehand so as to minimize contamination of the environment he is investigating, such plans should be seen as provisional and subject to instant revision according to the requirements of any particular situation. Sometimes one also must confront unanticipated and ambiguous situations for which one has no clear behavioural plan at all, and abide the maxim *On s'engage et puis on voit.*

From N. Polsky (1971) *Hustlers, Beats and Others*, Harmondsworth: Penguin, pp. 124–33.

Questions

1. In what ways might 'scientism' criticise procedures 1, 7 and 8 detailed by Polsky?
2. What practical difficulties could be faced by sociologists trying to follow procedures 2, 4 and 6?
3. What ethical issues and dilemmas are highlighted by Polsky's account?

Reading 53

Researching prostitutes and their clients

NEIL McKEGANEY AND MARINA BARNARD

Prostitution has an ambiguous legal position in that the behaviour itself is not illegal but many of the activities associated with it, such as soliciting or running a brothel, are. And although prostitution is an activity that the parties involved – usually the prostitute and her client – want to occur, generally speaking they do not want other people, including the police, to know about it. It is for these sorts of reasons that it is particularly difficult for the researcher to gain access to people involved in prostitution. In this reading, McKeganey and Barnard discuss how they had to create 'an acceptable social role in order to be in the red-light area'. They did this by adopting a 'quasi-service-provider' role which involved providing prostitutes with information and supplies of condoms and sterile needles. McKeganey and Barnard did manage to establish good working relationships with many women prostitutes but found it much more difficult to do so with male clients, who were, in most cases, extremely reluctant to provide any information. They found that anonymous contact via advertised phone lines was the most effective – and often the only – way of researching male clients. The Reading concludes with a brief reflection on the research project and, in particular, how specific issues and problems that faced McKeganey and Barnard determined their responses and the research methods they adopted.

Researching Female Prostitutes

In the early days of our research we took a decision which shaped all of our subsequent work, namely to try and contact women directly on the streets. Often other researchers studying prostitution have contacted women in a variety of formal settings and have, for example, interviewed women attending genito-urinary clinics, or attending court proceedings for solicitation. As an alternative we decided to go to those parts of the city where women were working and to approach them directly to see if they would be prepared to be interviewed.

To do this necessitated the creation of an acceptable social role in order to be in the red-light area in the first place. With the agreement of the local health board and having informed the local police of what we intended to do, we adopted a quasi-service-provider role which entailed providing women working on the streets with supplies of condoms, sterile injecting equipment, information on HIV risk reduction and telephone numbers of a variety of local services. Each night's fieldwork within the red-light area consisted of walking round all of the streets where sex was being sold, approaching as many women as possible, introducing ourselves and offering them the various items we were carrying. In this way we gradually became familiar to the women and this in turn facilitated the build-up of sufficiently good relationships with the women to allow the research to proceed [. . .]

In total we carried out more than 800 hours of fieldwork in the main red-light areas in Glasgow spread over a three-year period. We carried out our work from the sunniest days in Glasgow to near blizzard conditions (when sex would still be being traded), from midday to 2 a.m. or 3 a.m [. . .]

In the early days of our fieldwork, the unpredictability of the area created a sense of tension on our part [. . .]

Violence involving the women, their clients, and sundry others was an ever present feature of the area. Indeed . . . there was hardly a night in our fieldwork when at least one of the women was not bearing the sign of some kind of recent assault. In a way our own situation mirrored that of the women; both we and they had to avoid becoming so anxious about the possibility of violence as to make it impossible to carry on working, while at the same time not becoming so blasé about the dangers as to take unnecessary risks. This balance had to be struck without ever really knowing the actual level of threat involved [. . .]

Contacting the Women

How to approach the women? What to say? How would they react? Would there be pimps in the area and if so what would they make of what we were trying to do? These were just some of the questions which characterized the first days of our work. As is often the case, most of these uncertainties receded once the work began in earnest. As it turned out, it was surprisingly easy to contact the women and although there were some individuals who remained wary of us, we did manage with time, and through our continued presence in the area, to build up good working relationships with many of our women [. . .]

Working in the red-light area over an extended period of time enabled us to build up fairly close research relationships with many of the women. While such relationships proved valuable in our research, they also constrained our work in ways of which we were not always fully aware. We began to wonder if the kind of relationships we were establishing with the women, and the fact that those relationship occurred within the red-light area itself, might be influencing the kind of information we were getting from the women. For example, we routinely asked women about their use of condoms with clients, only to be provided with the unanimous response that condoms were always used. It seemed likely to us that despite such claims there must have been occasions when condoms were not used and certainly many of the women we spoke to alleged that there were women working in the area who were not using condoms [. . .]

The nature of our fieldwork also raised certain ethical dilemmas (Barnard 1992, McKeganey *et al.* 1994). We have already outlined the fact that we were providing women with, among other things, sterile injecting equipment. Combining the role of researcher and outreach service provider in this way was problematic on more than one occasion [. . .]

By providing (a) young girl with sterile injecting equipment we might have been guilty of encouraging her to inject; however, in refusing to do so we might equally have been increasing her chances of needing to share needles and syringes with other people and placing her at increased risk of HIV as a result. There are no guidelines covering what we should have done on such occasions and as a result we acted in the way which seemed most appropriate to ourselves at the time.

Researching Male Clients

The difficulties we anticipated in the early days of our research contacting female prostitutes were nothing compared to the difficulties we faced in contacting the clients. As with our work with the women, we intended to contact men directly in the red-light area, this we felt was at least one way of getting round the problem of men concealing the fact of their having paid for sex. While it was relatively easy to identify men repeatedly returning to the red-light area to contact women selling sex, most of the men we approached declined to be interviewed or provided a plainly spurious reason for being in the area. At times our approach would be very low key ('This is an area used by working women and I was wondering if you had been approached?') at other times more direct ('I'm carrying out a study of men who have paid for sex – would you mind being interviewed?'). Whichever version we used, the response was almost always the same, a more or less polite 'get lost'. There were, though, some notable successes which were frequent enough to persuade us that it was worth continuing with the fieldwork without being so numerous as to be sufficient for our study.

The major boost in our efforts at contacting men who had paid for sex came as a result of an advertisement we placed in a tabloid newspaper. This asked men who had recently paid for sex to ring us on a specific number. From early morning on the day our advert appeared, the phone hardly stopped ringing, enabling us to interview a further 66 clients. With the cloak of anonymity which the telephone provided, the men's reticence at talking about having paid for sex disappeared and it was possible to ask them not only straight-forward factual information about the number of women they had bought sex from and the kind of sex purchased, but also the more sensitive areas of what attracted them to paid sex, what they looked for in a prostitute, and their concerns in relation to HIV.

Conclusion

Looking back at this period of field research it is apparent that a good deal of what was achieved was arrived at through a process of trial and error. There was no blueprint for us to follow and no one to smooth our entrance into this different world. The mix of research methods we used was largely a response to the particularities of gathering information in the context of street prostitution. As in all things there were disadvantages as well as advantages for each method used. Similarly each research problem would raise different issues for us to grapple with. So, for example, the incorporation of a service provider role provided us with a means of sustained contact with the women. In turn this had ramifications for the way in which the women perceived us and consequently had some influence on the kinds of information provided. So, too, the provision of needles and syringes was not unproblematic in that it raised ethical issues concerning the provision of means to inject illegal drugs, an issue which was particularly present in the case of the 14 year-old girl asking us for needles. Our responses to such issues were based on a pragmatic reasoning of how best to serve the interests of the research while not undermining those of the women researched. Sometimes we got it right, other times we had to think again. Over time we achieved a more sure-footed familiarity with the world we were researching; we knew many of the women and understood something of the culture of the area. There were never any illusions though. We were privileged in being able to glimpse their world, but knew we were never more than bystanders at its very margins.

From N. McKeganey and M. Barnard (1996) *Sex Work on the Streets: Prostitutes and their Clients*, Buckingham: Open University Press, pp. 5–16.

Questions

1. What issues of validity and reliability are raised by McKeganey and Barnard's methods of research into (a) female prostitutes and (b) male clients?
2. List the practical problems and ethical dilemmas faced by McKeganey and Barnard.

   How did they attempt to resolve them?

   How successful do you think they would be?

Reading 54

Feminist principles (1): A reflexive approach

LIZ STANLEY AND SUE WISE

Stanley and Wise argue that the place of the personal within research has to be acknowledged; as they put it 'the presence of the researcher, with the usual complement of human attributes, can't be avoided'. They believe that research should aim to utilise this presence, rather than ignore it. This Reading starts with a critique of conventional social scientific (with the emphasis on scientific) research and the pressures on researchers to fit in with this convention. Stanley and Wise then highlight some basic principles that feminist research should adopt – in particular, a reflexivity that includes an acknowledgement that 'we see the presence of the researcher's self as central in all research'.

Presenting the research process as orderly, coherent and logically organized has consequences. One of these is that most social science researchers start off by believing that what is presented in these descriptions is a reasonable representation of the reality of research. Most of us get a nasty shock when we come to do research ourselves. However, the point at which we begin to realize that this 'hygienic research' in which no problems occur, no emotions are involved, is 'research as it is described' and not 'research as it is experienced', is frequently a crucial one. It tends to be the point at which we are required to present our research products to academic colleagues, supervisors, publishers and so forth. And so it is precisely the point at which we are most vulnerable, most likely to find pressures to conform to 'normal science' most difficult to resist, should we want to.

One problem all researchers have to cope with is their actual experiences of the research process. If these fail to correspond to textbook descriptions, then we have to face the possibility that this is because we are inadequate researchers. That these descriptions are over-simplistic and misleading isn't usually the first possibility that occurs to us. This problem is generally 'solved' because most of us fail to confront the contradiction between consciousness and research ideology. Our research simply gets written up in exactly the same way that previous researchers have written up theirs. By doing so, of course, we help to perpetuate the research ideology of 'hygienic research'. We become a part of the research community by enacting the same rituals that others have done before us.

We aren't suggesting that this is deliberate, usually. Nor are we suggesting that it is some kind of con trick. Instead we feel that social science researchers are taught to mistrust experience, to regard it as inferior to theory, and to believe that the use of 'research techniques' can provide data unclouded by values, beliefs and involvements [. . .]

People who work within a particular paradigm use its descriptions of research as a means of structuring their own. And regardless of which of the basic research models we adopt, we present our research as 'scientific' in whatever way 'normal science' is regarded in the paradigm we work within. By 'scientific' we mean that we fit our research into current concerns and relevancies, and also we adopt the ways of writing and discussing which are current too. We address ourselves to 'the issues' as these are seen by our colleagues. We present our data and our arguments so as to address these, we omit what are seen as irrelevancies. Another way of describing this is to say that we present *our* science as courageous, radical even, but not outrageous. We attempt to say something new and exciting, but not threatening. To do this would mean that our credibility would be impugned, we would not be taken seriously, our membership of that particular scientific community perhaps even withdrawn – excommunication!

As part of this we also attempt to be 'objective'. Within both positivism and naturalism this usually means that we present our work as scholarly and detached from what we have conducted research on. It may now be all right to be involved, committed even, but we must necessarily preserve 'scholarly detachment'. We must present our research in such a way that we strip 'ourselves' from descriptions, or describe our involvements in particular kinds of ways – as somehow 'removed' rather than full-blown members of the events and processes we describe [. . .]

Basic to feminism is that 'the personal is the political'. We suggest that this insistence on the crucial importance of the personal must also include an insistence on the importance, and also the presence, of the personal *within research experiences* as much as within any other experiences. But, more than this, the personal is not only the political, it is also the crucial variable which is absolutely present in each and every attempt to 'do research', although it is frequently invisible in terms of the presentation of this research. It mustn't be absent from presentations of feminist research, because this is to deny the importance of the personal elsewhere. In other words, academic feminism must take feminist beliefs seriously, by integrating these within our research [. . .]

And so we believe that all research is 'grounded' in consciousness, because it isn't possible to do research (or life) in such a way that we can separate ourselves from experiencing what we experience as people (and researchers) involved in a situation. There is no way we can avoid deriving theoretical constructs from experience, because we necessarily attempt to understand what is going on *as* we experience it. The research experience itself, like all other experiences, is necessarily subject to on-going 'theorizing', on-going attempts to understand, explain, re-explain, what is going on. This is what consciousness is all about; this is what people do in new situations and researchers do no differently from anyone else [. . .]

We see the presence of the researcher's self as central in all research. One's self can't be left behind, it can only be omitted from discussions and written accounts of the research process. But it *is* an omission, a failure to discuss something which has been present within the research itself. The researcher may be unwilling to admit this, or unable to see its importance, but it nevertheless remains so: if nothing else, we would insist on the absolute reality of this: that being alive involves us in having emotions and involvements; and in doing research we cannot leave behind what it is to be a person alive in the world.

So how – and why – should we use consciousness within the research process as a resource and topic in our exploration of feminism and social reality? This question has been tackled by Dorothy Smith, who argues that 'women's perspective' on and in social reality makes available to us, women, a radical critique of sociology (1974). We feel that this critique can to a large extent be extended to other social sciences too [. . .]

In other words, the social sciences claim to provide us with objective knowledge independent of the personal situation of the social scientist. But, of course, women's perspective, women's knowledge, and women's experience, provide an irrefutable critique of such claims. Within such products of social science research women's lives are omitted, distorted, misunderstood, and in doing this men's lives too are similarly distorted.

If the social sciences cannot avoid being situated, being located within a particular time, space and place, and formed by the experiences specific to these, then Smith argues that they must make full use of this. Indeed, she argues that the situated nature of the researcher should form the very beginning and basis of social science work. This would require a thorough examination of where the social scientist is actually situated; and then making her direct experience of the world, and the research process, the basis of her knowledge as a social scientist.

From L. Stanley and S. Wise (1993) *Breaking Out Again: Feminist Ontology and Epistemology*, London: Routledge, pp. 152–63.

Questions

1. In what ways can the researcher's personal and emotional involvement in their research enhance the quality and scope of that research?
2. What potential difficulties might there be with this personal involvement?
3. (From your reading of social scientific research) What do you think Stanley and Wise mean by the 'rituals of the research community'?

Reading 55

Feminist principles (2): Researching sexual violence

LIZ KELLY

In similar vein to Stanley and Wise, Liz Kelly also provides a critique of conventional social scientific research in explaining her research into sexual violence. This Reading documents how and why Kelly has pursued this research project. It starts with a brief comment on her involvement in a Women's Liberation Group and then considers some of the specific details and practicalities of the research – such as what sort of questions to ask, what style of interviewing to adopt, and how to check and correct the transcripts. The Reading finishes with a comment on the impact of the research on Kelly herself. When reading this last section it would be useful to consider other ways in which the research process can effect the individual researcher.

Getting and Staying Involved

In 1973, after five months in a Women's Liberation Group, I joined a group which aimed to set up a refuge for battered women. I did not consciously choose to work on the issue of violence. I simply wanted to 'do something'. I became one of the founder members of the refuge group in my home town and, to the amazement of some (though not me), I am still an active member. Whilst in the subsequent fourteen years the group and I have changed enormously, it was there that I gained self-confidence, skills and an understanding of sexual violence and it is still the base for my feminist work and politics [. . .]

Throughout the research and the writing of this book I have remained involved in both my local refuge group and several national campaigning groups. I was not involved in these groups because I was doing research and I did not 'use' them as sources of data. Involvement did, however, contribute in very direct ways as there was a continual exchange of information, ideas and support. Within the literature on research methods there is no term which covers this form of contribution, perhaps best described as 'active participation'. There is equally no term to cover the fact that I have talked to at least as many women again informally about their experiences of sexual violence as the 60 I interviewed. Whilst I kept no records of these conversations, I made mental notes if new insights emerged. As most women were interested in the research, I was able to discuss my current ideas and receive valuable comment and feedback [. . .]

How the Research was Conducted – Feminist Research Practice

To record truthfully and fully the history of a research project would require a book in itself! Most accounts appear in appendices and are reconstructed and sanitized descriptions of the research methodology; the problems, doubts, changes of direction that beset all research are censored out. This has been referred to as 'hygienic' research or 'the chronological lie'. Nevertheless, some honest accounts have appeared in volumes which deal with the 'reality' of sociological research practice. The discussion of the methodology of this project will be presented in the context of a description of my feminist research practice.

The first stage of this project involved the construction of an interview guide and four pilot interviews. Two decisions I made at this point had major impacts on the project methodology. First, I decided to do the pilot interviews with friends and meet a second time to discuss the interview style and content. Second, I decided to discuss the redrafted interview guide, revised following the pilot interviews, with both academic colleagues and friends. The women who did the pilot interviews felt that hearing their own tape gave them time to reflect on and add to what they had said and this resulted in the decision to return a transcript of the interview to each woman and to do follow-up interviews with them. The discussions on the revised interview guide resulted in the inclusion of a final section which focused on the future rather than the past. This meant that potentially distressing interviews could end on a positive, forward-looking note. It was the co-operative framework in which the pilot interviews and discussions took place which resulted in these crucial methodological developments.

The final draft of the interview guide began with reflections on childhood and moved through adolescence to adulthood. Questions about a range of possible experiences of sexual violence were thus placed in the context of women's lives. The wording and placement of questions about sexual violence was carefully chosen in order not to presume shared definitions. For example, a question on whether women had ever felt pressured to have sex came much earlier in the interview than the question about ever having been raped.

My interviewing style reflects that used by other feminist researchers; a rejection of the 'objective' aloofness and the refusal to enter into dialogue. It is difficult for me to envisage being detached when I remember how shaken many women were during or after the interviews. Many commented that they had never talked through their experiences in such depth before and on a number of occasions interviews had to be stopped because women were visibly distressed (all chose to complete the interview). I often spent as much time talking with women informally as in recording the interviews. These conversations ranged from specific requests for information, to reflections on aspects of the interview, to discussions of preliminary research findings.

Interviewing and transcribing the tapes was much more time-consuming and emotionally draining than I had anticipated. I had little idea of how complicated and frustrating these activities could be. For example, several interviews were done with young children in the room, all of whom insisted on playing with or shouting into the microphone, and several women had speech patterns which meant parts of sentences were inaudible.

Interviewing is a skill. My skill developed over time as I sensed where to ask a further question, when to just listen, and where to leave space for women to think. It is not just talking, although a good interview may feel like a stimulating conversation. It involves the interviewer being aware of a number of things at the same time and juggling priorities. After transcribing several tapes I became aware of how problematic it is to directly transpose the spoken to the written word. Mishearing one word can change the meaning of a whole passage of speech, and meaning in the spoken word is often conveyed by tone of voice and gesture. Several women also commented on this when discussing reading their transcript. In order to retain as much of this meaning as possible I developed a method for coding expression and tone of voice. Whilst transcribing I also noted any questions or points that required clarification on a follow-up sheet and wrote any more general insights or questions on file cards.

When copies of the transcript were sent to women, a note was included asking them to note any corrections, qualifications or additions they wanted to make. Follow-up interviews were done with 47 women. Each of these interviews began with a series of questions about participation in the project, reactions to reading the transcript, whether or not there were any changes women wanted to make and whether or not they had remembered anything in the intervening time. Questions specific to each woman's first interview followed.

Almost 75 per cent of the women had remembered additional incidents of sexual violence, or aspects of incidents they had discussed, between the original interview and the follow-up. Several women made detailed comments and revisions on the original transcript; one woman sent me her transcript 18 months later and added important information which she had not trusted me with at either of our two formal meetings. No one felt the interview had been a negative experience; 85 per cent described it in very positive terms and felt that they had learnt things through their participation. A number of women stated explicitly that they valued having the transcript, both as a record of the past and a marker for the future.

> Actually I'm quite surprised. I've found it really helpful. I can't think about it so talking is the only way of admitting it ever happened . . . I have never talked in that concentrated way before . . . I think I like myself a lot more, I feel quite brave really.

> I felt a lot better after I'd talked about it because it's been a lot of years and I've never really talked openly about it to anyone.

It is in the style of interviewing, the return of the transcripts, and the content of the follow-up interviews that my feminist research practice is reflected. The return of the transcripts meant that the women who participated controlled the content of their interview. Follow-up interviews allowed what Shulamith Reinharz calls 'joint interpretation of meaning' to take place, and I was able to assess the impact of the research on women [. . .]

Reflexive Experiential Analysis

I have already noted the importance for feminist researchers of locating themselves within their research questions. Shulamith Reinharz has documented her journey through a variety of sociological methods to what she calls 'experiential analysis'. She argues that rather than ignoring our own feelings, responses and experience, we should focus on these human responses as they are precisely what enables us to understand social reality [. . .]

[This reading ends with an example of the impact that doing this research had on Liz Kelly herself.]

I had anticipated that listening to women's experiences of sexual violence would affect me emotionally. I did not expect to be affected by the discussions of childhood and family relationships that began each interview. My reactions were certainly linked to my personal history – I grew up in a Catholic, working-class, extended family; my mother died when I was 12.

Coming to discussions of mother/daughter relationships without a mother, yet being one, undoubtedly gave me a particular perspective. I either reacted with envy when women talked of developing close relationships with their mothers or felt upset if women were negative and judgmental about their mothers. In trying to understand these responses I realized how I had cut off from my feelings about my mother's death. This occurred at the same time as I was trying to make sense of the immense amount of mother-blame in the literature on incest. I slowly came to see the trap that most mothers are in and why some (but by no means all) abused young women blame their mothers. To children, mothers are powerful and children develop unrealistic expectations of them. Mothers are expected to know, in an almost telepathic way, when something is wrong and to be able to solve the problem. When, for whatever reason, children feel their mother fails to understand or protect them, they may experience this as betrayal. Incest survivors are certainly not the only women who feel betrayed by or angry with their mothers.

At this point, I was beginning to look at forms and experiences of violence in terms of a continuum. I noticed how many women's fathers were controlling, seductive and/or physically violent: father–daughter incest being an extension of this much more common and acceptable pattern. Feminists have been surprisingly silent about fathers, almost without noticing reinforcing the traditional psychological view that mothers are the all-important influence in children's lives. I suspect that fathers play a crucial role, particularly in relation to daughters; they lay the basis, subtly, coercively or violently, of our fear of male anger and, therefore, our awareness of the risks of challenging men.

It is impossible to describe in words the emotions and reactions that doing this piece of research evoked, and I have only selected a few examples here. It is just as important, though, to make clear that there was another side to this experience: positive feelings and interactions that were sustaining. The completion of the project was, in part, the result of trust that many of the women who were interviewed placed in me and their interest in, and support for, the research in general and me in particular. It was extremely important that the interviews contained both a record of victimization and of women's strength in survival.

Moving between the interviews and my own experiences and reactions was an integral part of the research methodology. Had I 'tuned out' these responses I would probably not have noticed or fully understood the importance of aspects of women's experience of sexual violence.

From L. Kelly (1988) *Surviving Sexual Violence*, Cambridge: Polity, pp. 2–19.

Questions

1. Liz Kelly researched women who had survived sexual violence. Suggest the sort of differences there might be between the findings of researchers who were emotionally involved with women victims and those who aimed to remain 'detached' and 'objective'.
2. Liz Kelly discusses how pursuing this research led to her reflecting on her own personal relationships. How else might doing such research impact on the researcher?
3. How has the sociological research that you have read about (both here and elsewhere) helped you to understand your own personal history?

Reading 56

Feminist principles (3): Research for women

ANNA POLLERT

Anna Pollert's study Girls, Wives, Factory Lives *examines the situation of women in the labour force – specifically women in unskilled manual factory work – and their exploitation therein. She discusses the extent to which the experiences of women workers are different to, and worse than, those faced by male factory workers. Throughout the study Pollert considers what it is to be defined as 'girls' and 'wives' in a man's world; and she makes it clear that her personal commitment lies in supporting these women workers. The Reading starts with Pollert setting out the aims of her research and the questions that she hoped to address; she then describes how she gained access to and carried out research in the factory. Our extract focuses, in particular, on how the factory management and the workforce responded to the presence of a (female) researcher and how, in turn, Pollert reacted to and dealt with those responses.*

The facts about women's participation in the labour force are now well documented. What remains to be done is to turn this lived experience into an understanding of the interplay between working women's oppression and exploitation. This book sets out to do that.

It is about factory life, about women doing unskilled, manual work in contemporary Britain. Throughout two themes are explored: the common areas of wage labour for men and women, and the way being a woman alters this. First, there are forces which affect all workers selling their 'generalised' (unskilled) labour power in modern capitalism. How are their lives affected by big business and a corporate economy? How does the employers' strategy in a time of economic crisis affect them? Second, all these questions must be asked again, but with additions, now talking to women. Does it make any difference being a *woman* worker? Is work seen or felt differently from a man? How does marriage and the family come into work? What is the atmosphere of a 'women's factory'? Do women deal with supervision, discipline and control at work in the same way as men? How does women's participation in trade unions differ from men's? What are the economic prospects of women in a time of rising unemployment? What, in short, is distinctive about wage labour for a woman, because of her socialisation as a woman and her oppression as a woman?

The study is based on informal interviews and observations on the shop-floor of a Bristol tobacco factory during 1972 and subsequent contact. It is a glimpse into the everyday working lives of the young girls and older women who worked there: about how they got on with their jobs, their bosses and each other – and in a background sense, their boyfriends, their husbands and their families – and how all these strands wove together into their experience and consciousness.

I myself was not employed there, and made no secret of the fact that I was a researcher. In this sense my method was not strictly one of 'participant observation'.

Why did I not get a job in the factory? The reason is simple: I had already approached both the union and management, and the latter would not entertain the idea. I was permitted onto factory premises, with the strict proviso that this should not interfere with production. This suited me quite well. First, I did not have much chance of learning how to do the work (weighing, for example) in short period of time, and become adroit enough to talk, observe or think about anything except keeping up. The women's work in the factory – while termed 'semi-skilled' – thoroughly intimidated me. Second, had I got a job, the advantage of experiencing for myself what it felt like, and possibly becoming very close to a small work-group around me, would have been heavily outweighed by the disadvantages of restricted movement, abiding by the rule preventing entry into another department (without permission), and losing the privileges of the outsider, of speaking to other employees in the factory, including chargehands, supervisors and managers. Third, the proviso of not interrupting production meant I was not offered an interviewing room. I *had* to talk to workers as they worked: whether I liked it or not, I had my nose in the shop-floor, got to know informal groups as well as individuals, and witnessed the subtleties of factory relations within the inexorable pace of work.

There were difficulties. The initial interviews with the trade-union official at Transport House and with the factory management were gruelling, largely because I was a woman trying to convince men (and the woman personnel officer) that I was interested in women factory workers. Fortunately, sociologists are regarded as cranks anyway, so they indulged my femaleness and oddness without grilling me too deeply about my motives, my politics or feminism. But this introduction was nothing to the terror of walking on to the shop-floor. Although partly mitigated by the fact that I was a woman among women, nothing could alter the artificiality of the situation: that I was middle class, had a middle class accent and was not there to earn money. My position was the more awkward because management had simply told their frontline spokesmen – the supervisors – to instruct the women that 'someone was coming to talk to them' and to co-operate. I had no trade-union introduction. A letter I had duplicated, explaining that I wanted to write a book on what it was like to be a woman factory worker, and which I specifically asked both the union officer and management to pass on to the girls via the stewards, never reached them. This was the best I could do, not having managed to meet the stewards beforehand. And even this failed: a significant beginning to my research which told a lot about the level of union organisation and the way the women and younger girls were regarded.

To begin with I was naturally scrutinised with a mixture of hostility, suspicion and cruelty. My manner was necessarily apologetic and explanatory, and I answered more questions than I asked. As my motives became clearer – that I really felt most people who had not worked in a factory had no idea of what it was like, and that this was what I wanted to communicate – suspicions softened to incredulity, some amusement and some sympathy. Many still could not see what I was on about, but saw little harm it; but several older women were positively encouraging – 'Go on, my love, write your book.' and 'I think it's a good thing: people ought to know how people live. Don't just think about yourself.' More than anything, however, the women were shy and self-effacing; they simply could not see what they had to offer.

Being a woman researcher was vitally important to my study. Not only did it affect my relationships with women but it also coloured my contact with men. Class and gender were both significant here; what men – managers, supervisor, foremen and shop stewards – reported to me about the factory, and the women workers, was an interaction between my questions and their definitions of me as middle class, educated, apparently endowed with the rather threatening X-ray eyes of the 'professional', social scientist, but at the same time an academic ignoramus about the 'real world'. Such cocktails of images undoubtedly went through the women's heads as well; this is the 'interactionist' assumption that any outside observer must expect. But with the men it was important that they could not assume automatic sympathy or unspoken understanding from a female interrogator in a way they might expect from a man. The fact that I was a woman and my approach feminist, in that I closely questioned and challenged taken-for-granted and throw-away remarks, often forced men to pull out justifications and defences which they were unused to examining. Their responses would be a subject in itself; but my main preoccupation was not with men or masculine identity for themselves but only in the ways they were woven into the women's experience.

With the women my being female was one factor in slowly breaking down barriers. More than this, however, was the realisation that while I was different and was not working in the factory, I did not set myself up just as a reporter but tried to be open with my own opinions. In this sense my study could be put in the category of 'interventionist research'. It was (I hope) less patronising than the attitude which comprises the fascination of seeing 'how the masses think'; I genuinely wanted to argue with and challenge attitude as well as to learn. We discussed not only the concrete work situation, attitudes to employment, home life, but also the company, the economy and the unions – in short, 'politics' both in the here and now and in the outside world.

Several times I was hauled over the coals by management for apparently asking the 'wrong' questions, not obviously relevant to research on 'women workers'. (How they found out about this I never knew.) These were about unemployment, whether the women felt they had a right to their jobs, and, more specifically, what was being organised about threatened redundancies at the factory. Did management consider it out of keeping for women to trouble themselves about class, about industrial action and solidarity among workers, about the government and who runs the country, about what was 'right' and what was 'wrong', and what people could do about it? Often the stream of conversations flowed with the women's interests, not my own questions. My aim was not just to learn what they thought and felt, but also to discover how they argued with an outsider – and how complex their ideas were. My concern was not to freeze for posterity some photographic representation of 'consciousness', nor could I hope to get a complete picture of people's lives or to proffer total explanations. Rather, it was the conflicts and loose-ends in consciousness, and how these changed, that I wanted to understand and portray.

As well as this, I wanted to gain insight into the social relations of the factory, both between the women, and between the women and the men, including male workers, foremen and management. In this I wanted to discover whether a system of male domination operated – and if it did, how it collided with women's consciousness and collective spirit. In other words, how was sexual oppression reproduced and tied to exploitation in the workplace, and, also, how was it challenged?

From A. Pollert (1981) *Girls, Wives, Factory Lives*, London: Macmillan, pp. 5–9.

Questions

1. Why do you think Pollert says she 'was naturally scrutinised . . . with hostility, suspicion and curiosity'?
2. What were the barriers which Pollert had to break down in order to pursue her research; and how did she go about this?
3. How might Pollert's feminist approach have: (a) helped her to gain the trust of the workforce and (b) hindered her?

Reading 57

The effects of social research

ROGER HOMAN

In this Reading Roger Homan discusses the ways in which the conduct of social research can effect all those involved, including the subjects and professionals, and considers some of the implications of such research. For participants, there are 'risks of strain or harm both during the research process and in the aftermath of publication' and Homan highlights some of them. For instance, students or employees such as research assistants might be implicated in projects that are hazardous or likely to involve great strains on them – as Homan's account of the famous research projects led by Milgram and Rosenhan illustrates. Or publication of the research findings can expose both subjects and researchers to unwelcome and potentially dangerous attention – as Roy Wallis found as a consequence of his research into the Church of Scientology.

Effects on Subjects

Professional guidelines

The professional associations all counsel their members to have due care for the interests of subjects, whom they should apprise of the nature and purpose of their research and the procedures by which they sampled their respondents. Voluntariness in participation, the entitlement to be informed and to have privacy respected are principles stressed in all guidelines.

Beyond that, some go further than others and the British Sociological Association (1982) does not go very far at all. The BSA reminds practitioners of the dangers of raising false hopes and causing undue anxieties.

It is in psychology, where the work of Stanley Milgram (1974) has exercised professionals to consider ethical problems, that the code gives a better sense of some of the possibilities. The principles of the British Psychological

Society (1978) stress the responsibility that psychologists have when working with human subjects to anticipate harmful effects including strain, consult with experienced and disinterested professionals at the design stage, and break off an experiment for such consultation if evident effects exceed those anticipated. Experimenters are obliged to stress the voluntariness of participation in proportion to the magnitude of physiological or psychological stress likely to be suffered. They must also observe the highest standard of safety in procedure, equipment and premises. Milgram justified his procedures by distinguishing between intended and unintended effects: what is therefore significant about the BPS principles is that they hold psychologists responsible for both [. . .]

The legend of Stanley Milgram

In 1954 a correspondent to the *American Psychologist* raised a number of questions concerning the protection of experimental subjects in an attempt to alert fellow psychologists to neglected ethical issues. He referred to what he called 'the miniature social situation' in which an experimenter may use dissimulation or deceit in the control of behaviour variables. He wanted to establish what were the proper bounds of deceit. He noted reports of 'standard' reassurances given to subjects after experiments implying that they went away happy but he pointed to practices which compelled the attention of conscientious professionals although, as he observed at the time, 'So far as I can tell no one is particularly concerned about this' (Vinacke 1954: 155).

The professional concern which was dormant as Vinacke wrote came to life as reports appeared of the experiments on obedience conducted by Stanley Milgram. These were always explicit as acts of research although they involved the deception of subjects at a number of stages. Subjects were recruited by means of a newspaper advertisement which described the project as 'a Study of Memory' (Milgram 1974: 15) and their briefing for the laboratory sessions was in terms of theories of learning (Milgram 1974: 18). At the superficial level this was honest in that the role which the subject then acted was that of teacher operating under supervision.

However, the real purpose of Milgram's experiments was to study the degree to which subjects were prepared to administer to a 'learner' punishments in the form of electric shocks. Subjects were put in charge of a control panel from which they understood that they could administer to a learner shocks ranging from 15 volts to 450 volts. Subjects were themselves given a token shock of 45 volts before the outset. In fact, the person in the role of learner had been trained to show various reactions and was not suffering the shocks that subjects believed they were administering. That subjects chose the role of teacher was manipulated by allowing them to draw a scrap of paper from two, both of which carried the word 'teacher'. As the learner continued to give wrong answers, so the subject, following instructions, increased the degree of shock. If subjects had scruples about inflicting pain and possibly damage, they were told 'Although the shocks may be painful, there is no permanent tissue damage, so please go on' (Milgram 1974: 21). The learner or 'victim', as he is called in the study, showed no discomfort but only mild grunts as the level of shock rose to 105 volts. Then,

> at 120 volts the victim shouted to the experimenter that the shocks were becoming painful. Painful groans were heard on administration of the 135-volt shock and at 150 volts the victim called out, 'Experimenter, get me out of here! I won't be in the experiment any more! I refuse to go on!' Cries of this type continued with generally rising intensity, so that at 180 volts the victim cried out, 'I can't stand the pain,' and by 270 volts his response to the shock was definitely an agonized scream . . . At 300 volts, the victim shouted in desperation that he would no longer provide answers to the memory test. (Milgram 1974: 23)

In this circumstance the experimenter instructed what the study calls 'the naïve subject' to treat non-response as incorrect response and continue the punishment. Those who have faith in human nature will be reassured to know that only a small number of subjects were prepared to go as far as to administer the maximum shock.

Milgram made a point of giving his subjects a debriefing or 'dehoax' at the end of the experiment when thy were reconciled with the 'victim' and it was explained that their behaviour was perfectly normal (Milgram 1974: 194). Some time later he surveyed those who had taken part and it was found that 83.7 per cent were glad or very glad they had done so, while only 1.3 per cent were sorry or very sorry (Milgram 1974: 195).

On the issue of whether or not there was a likelihood of enduring harm to the subjects of the Milgram experiments, the discussion wants the view of an experienced psychologist. It was not long after the appearance of Milgram's first report (Milgram 1963) that Diana Baumrind delivered her judgement that Milgram's standards of concern and care for the well-being of his subjects fell short of professional requirements. She declared herself to be alarmed by the detached and unfeeling manner in which Milgram reported the extraordinarily disturbing experiences of his subjects and she was unconvinced by his casual assurance that he was able to calm subjects before they left his laboratory . . . In Baumrind's professional opinion there was a distinct possibility that the emotional disturbance suffered by subjects could be permanently harmful, perhaps effecting alterations of the self-image of subjects and their ability to trust other adult authorities (Baumrind 1964: 433) [. . .]

Persistent effects

The long and continuing debate over the ethical aspects of Milgram's work has drawn attention to the effects of participation in research, especially in contrived or non-naturalistic settings. The hazards have been widely heeded by psychology professionals who have endeavoured to put their house in order but the problem is by no means confined to the use of experimental methods.

We have already observed a study in which children aged 11 years and above were asked how often they experienced sexual intercourse (Udry and Billy 1987: 852) and commented that the question itself may be interpreted as a message about what is expected or accepted as normal. The introduction of human subjects to attitudes and habits which they may not already have formed is a serious by-product of some research procedures and the problem is especially acute when the subjects are particularly vulnerable. West, Gunn and Chernicky (1975) offered their subjects $2000 to take part in burglary though they took no part themselves. Sherif (1980: 409–11) expresses a similar concern in the comparable case of Malamuth *et al.* who exposed student respondents to false depictions of rape: though available in popular pornography it was not to be known whether respondents had previously encountered such images and she wonders about the effect upon a young man who is aroused by a cruelly violent depiction and then told in debriefing that it is totally false. These are instances of the formation of undesirable habits or attitudes and of psychological damage to subjects but we must observe also that physical danger may be persistent, particularly where researchers use as informants members of a potentially hostile community who would not corporately cooperate in an enquiry: this may be the case in research on deviant groups and Warwick (1983: 327) suggests that in places like Argentina and Chile a social researcher may be endangering the lives of those who participate in politically sensitive research.

In many cases, however, the most injurious and persistent effects of social research arise not from participation but from publication. The issue of a research report can have serious implications for the lives of subjects, be they factory workers such as Ditton's subjects at 'Wellbreads' or the residents of a small town like West's 'Plainville'. Those communities of subject both felt that life could never be the same again. 'Plainville' was soon identified and became a curiosity and visiting place for sightseers. Ditton (1977) anticipated the effect of this report of fiddling and pilferage in the Preface to his book:

> I don't expect that many of the men at Wellbread's will look too kindly on the cut in real wages that this work will mean to them, and my bakery self would agree with them.

[. . .]

Effects on Researchers

Participation in social research often incurs strain as well for those who conduct it as for those who are their subjects [. . .]

The strains of doing research

Research in social fields can be lonely, arduous, inescapable and dangerous. Those who become involved may regret having done so but have no means of turning back. They may not have been realistically apprised of what to expect, which perhaps not even their directors could have envisaged.

The case which instances a number of these possibilities is the work of Rosenhan who engaged eight colleagues to experience mental health care by professing symptoms of insanity and becoming admitted to institutions. It seemed a good idea at the time but the eight had more difficulty getting out than getting in. The arrangement was that they would have to secure discharge by their own means by persuading the authorities they were sane. The psychological stress was severe and all but one of the pseudo-patients desired to be discharged almost immediately after admission. However, the average period of hospitalisation was 19 days and one of the colleagues whom Rosenhan engaged took 25 days to get released (Rosenhan 1973: 19).

Not the least considerable source of strain, however, are the subjects themselves who may be very resentful of researchers in their midst. They may be intent either upon driving the researcher away or upon controlling or discrediting any reports that might issue from the investigation.

Pressures of this kind are vividly detailed by Roy Wallis in his autobiographical paper 'The moral career of a research project' (Wallis 1977). Wallis had been conducting his doctoral research initially on aspects of the new religious movements and later more specifically on Scientology. He responded to an invitation by post to take a short course at the Church of Scientology's British headquarters at Saint Hill Manor, East Grinstead. To the extent that he did not declare himself a sociologist who was researching the situation, he used the method of covert participant observation, although after two days he abandoned the course and slipped away during a dinner break. He also made contact with and interviewed a number of former members. Wallis was mindful that Scientology was particularly active in the field of public relations and would have defined his interest within this field had a formal approach been made. He also wanted to know how the visitor off the street was treated, not how a sociologist from a university was received (Wallis 1977: 153–5).

Evidently prompted by the publication of an article on the basis of his early research, the Church of Scientology then took an active interest in Wallis. According to his account, a man turned up at the University of Stirling where he was lecturing, said that he was researching religion in Scotland, asked to join Wallis's classes and even to stay at his home. Wallis recognised him from Saint Hill Manor. The man asked students whether Wallis was involved in the drug scene. Wallis confronted him and he claimed to be a defector and afterwards disappeared (Wallis 1977: 157).

After this some forged letters supposedly by Wallis were put into the hands of his university employers suggesting in one case that he was involved in a homosexual love affair and in another that he was a spy for the drugs squad (Wallis 1977: 158).

When Wallis published an article in *New Society* in 1973 scientologists wrote to the Social Science Research Council which had partly funded his research complaining on a number of grounds including the fact that Wallis had not secured informed consent before embarking on his research.

From R. Homan (1991) *The Ethics of Social Research*, Harlow: Longman, pp. 160–8.

Questions

1. In what circumstances do you think it is justifiable for researchers to use deceit in conducting social research?
2. Consider the following comment:

   > As the researchers in the projects and experiments discussed by Homan knew what they were doing – for instance, Rosenhan's pseudo-patients and Milgram's subjects were volunteers and Wallis chose to research Scientology – the difficulties and dilemmas they faced were no more than the sort of 'professional hazards' faced in many occupations. All workers have to face issues of loyalty and honesty.

   To what extent do you think that this is a fair comment?

Part IV Sociological Research

Further Reading

Of the classic, founding sociologists, Durkheim provides the most explicit discussion of the sociological method and it is well worth looking at his key work (from which Reading 45 is taken) in full:

Durkheim, E. (1964) (1895) *The Rules of Sociological Method*, New York: Free Press.

One of the main areas of debate within sociological research, and the discipline of sociology in general, has concerned the extent to which sociologists should adopt the scientific method in pursuing their research. Karl Popper (Reading 46) has been one of the foremost advocates of the view that scientific knowledge is the only valid form of knowledge. His arguments have been disputed by many, but perhaps most notably by Thomas Kuhn. Kuhn has argued that scientists hold theoretical positions that are informed by the beliefs and interests of themselves and of the scientific community they are a part of. Again, it is well worth reading the original sources and Kuhn's position and argument is clearly set out in his most renowned work:

Kuhn, T.S. (1962) *The Structure of Scientific Revolutions*, Chicago: Chicago University Press.

There are a number of different methods of research that sociologists can utilise when investigating social issues and phenomena and some of these are illustrated in the readings in this section. The following titles provide fuller discussion of the different research methods:

Gilbert, N. (ed.) (1993) *Researching Social Life*, London: Sage.

Hammersley, M. (ed.) (1993) *Social Research: Philosophy, Politics and Practice*, London: Open University Press.

Hammersley, M. (1990) *Reading Ethnographic Research: A Critical Guide*, London: Longman.

The papers in Gilbert's reader are written by experienced social researchers who reflect on their research experiences and provide a comprehensive guide to the different methods of social research (Reading 50 is taken from Sara Arber's chapter in this book). Hammersley's edited collection includes both classic and contemporary contributions that highlight some of the key debates within the social research community, including: What are and are not the most appropriate methods? and How should research relate to policy making? Hammersley himself has been one of the foremost figures in the promotion of ethnographic and qualitative methodology and in *Reading Ethnographic Research* he provides a clear introduction to the nature of ethnography and a guide to how we should read ethnographic studies. The study considers some of the controversial issues that have surrounded ethnographic work, such as: Is it scientific? How can the validity of such work be assessed given the difficulty of replicating ethnographic research?

For a more specific discussion of data analysis we would recommend these introductory texts:

Dey, I. (1993) *Qualitative Data Analysis*, London: Routledge.

Marsh, C. (1988) *Exploring Data: An Introduction to Data Analysis for Social Scientists*, Cambridge: Polity Press.

Rose, D. and Sullivan, O. (1993) *Introducing Data Analysis for Social Scientists*, Milton Keynes: Open University Press.

In her introduction, Catherine Marsh uses a range of examples of quantitative social research, taken from well-known studies that have examined issues of social inequality, to illustrate the techniques of data analysis. She considers how analysis of quantitative data can illuminate sociological concerns and debates and discusses some of the problems of exploring such data. Another useful introduction to data analysis is Rose and Sullivan's text. It is designed for social science students and requires no previous knowledge of statistics or computer use. In contrast to those two texts, Dey focuses on the analysis of qualitative data and considers, in particular, the computer-based analysis of such data.

While many research textbooks discuss and evaluate different methods of social research, few focus on student projects in the world outside the classroom. The following text details the important practical steps involved in negotiating research projects and gaining access to research settings. It considers all the main styles of social research and provides guidance on the analysis and presentation of data:

Hall, D. and Hall, I. (1996) *Practical Social Research*, London: Macmillan.

On feminist research the following readers are recommended:

Maynard, M. and Purvis, J. (eds) (1994) *Researching Women's Lives*, London: Taylor & Francis.

Ribbens, J. and Edwards, R. (eds) (1997) *Femininst Dilemmas in Qualitative Research: Public Knowledge and Private Lives*, London: Sage.

Both these books include papers that detail the current debates within feminist research. Ribbens and Edwards' collection addresses, in particular, the dilemma of how feminist researchers can produce work of academic rigour and credibility while remaining faithful to the private experiences and accounts provided by their research participants.

Lee, R.M. (1993) *Doing Research on Sensitive Topics*, London: Sage.

This title provides a comprehensive introduction to the methodological, ethical and practical issues involved in undertaking research on sensitive topics. Lee covers both quantitative and qualitative research methods and considers the relationship between research and issues of social and political power, the ways in which research can encroach on people's lives, including the potential implications such research may have for the researcher.

Activity

(A) Find two sociological studies that involve first-hand research into a specific area of sociological interest (e.g. education and ethnicity, gender roles, football hooliganism, etc.).

Read the introduction and any other references to the research methodology used. There may be a separate chapter or part of a chapter on this or there may be discussion of methodology in an appendix.

Consider these questions:

How much detail do the authors give on their method of research?

To what extent do they justify their particular approach?

To what extent do they consider alternative methods?

Do they relate their research method and approach to any theoretical position?

(B) The next part of this activity involves you in designing and then undertaking a small piece of research into the same or similar areas to one of the two studies considered in A, using both the survey method and observation.

Steps: (a) think of a question or hypothesis that you could investigate.
(b) design a short questionnaire and an observation schedule.
(c) do the research – administer the questionnaires and do the observation. There is no need to analyse your findings – just collect the data.

Consider the following questions:

What (if any) difficulties/dilemmas did you face?

How did you (or could you in future) resolve them?

(C) Now write a short methodological report (up to 300 words) that could serve as an introduction to your research.

Notes to Students

- You may have already done a small-scale piece of research as part of a project/assignment on a sociology course. If so, you could go back to that work and use it for this activity.
- You may want to use this activity to plan/try out a future piece of work/assignment that is required on a course you are currently studying.
- In your report (part C) there is no need to analyse or write up your findings. This activity is intended to highlight issues in the gathering of data.

References

Part II Sociological Theories

Introduction

Layder, D. (1994) *Understanding Social Theory*, London: Sage.

Parsons, T. (1951) *The Social System*, New York: Free Press.

Reading 24 City Cultures and Postmodern Lifestyles

Boyer, M.C. (1988) 'The return of aesthetics to city planning', *Society*, 25(4).

Douglas, M. and Isherwood, B. (1980) *The World of Goods*, Harmondsworth: Penguin.

Elias, N. (1978) *The Civilizing Process. Volume I: The History of Manners*, Oxford: Blackwell.

Elias, N. (1982) *The Civilizing Process. Volume II: State Formation and Civilization*, Oxford: Blackwell.

Goudsblom, J. (1987) 'On high and low in society and sociology', *Sociologisch Tijdschrift*, 13(1).

Marwick, A. (1988) *Beauty*, London.

Schwartz, B. (1983) *Vertical Classification*, Chicago: Chicago University Press.

Williams, R. (1983) *Towards 2000*, London: Chatto and Windus.

Part III Differences and Inequalities

Introduction

Bailey, J. (ed.) (1998) *Social Europe*, 2nd edn, Harlow: Addison Wesley Longman.

Brown, C. (1984) *Black and White Britain: The Third Policy Studies Institute Survey*, London: Heinemann.

Daniel, W.W. (1968) *Racial Discrimination in England*, Harmondsworth: Penguin.

Dobash, R.E. and Dobash, R. (1992) *Women, Violence and Social Change*, London: Routledge.

Edwards, P. (1992) 'The early African presence in the British Isles', in J.S. Gundara and I. Duffield (eds) *Essays on the History of Blacks in Britain*, Aldershot: Avebury.

Glass, D.V. (ed.) (1954) *Social Mobility in Britain*, London: Routledge & Kegan Paul.

Goldthorpe, J. (1987) *Social Mobility and Class Structure in Modern Britain*, 2nd edn, with C. Llewellyn and C. Payne, Oxford: Clarendon Press.

Heath, A. (1981) *Social Mobility*, London: Fontana.

Marshall, G., Newby, H., Rose, D. and Vogler, C. (1988) *Social Class in Modern Britain*, London: Hutchinson.

Smith, D.J. (1977) *Racial Disadvantage in Britain*, Harmondsworth: Penguin.

Whitehead, M. (1987) *The Health Divide*, in P. Townsend and N. Davidson (eds) *Inequalities in Health*, Harmondsworth: Penguin.

Reading 27 Changes in the Structure of Industrial Societies since Marx

Davis, K. (1949) *Human Societies*, New York: Macmillan.

Drucker, P.F. (1950) *The New Society: The Anatomy of the Industrial Order*, New York.

Fayol, H. (1916) *Administration industrielle et generale*, Paris.

Horkheimer, M. and Adorno, T. (1947) *Dialektik der Aufklarung*, Amsterdam.

Kluth, H.B. (1955) 'Arbeiterjugend – Begriff und Wirklichkeit', in H. Schelsky (ed.) *Arbteiterjugend – gestern und heute*, Heidelberg.

Philip, A. (1955) *La democratie industrielle*, Paris.

Schelsky, H. (1955) 'Industrie and Betriebssoziologie', in A. Gehlen and H. Schelsky (eds) *Sozologie*, Dusseldorf and Cologne.

Taylor, F.W. (1947) 'The principles of scientific management', in *Scientific Management*, New York and London: Harper and Row.

Whyte, W.H. (1957) *The Organization Man*, New York: Simon and Schuster.

Reading 29 Are Social Classes Dying?

Birch, D. (1979) *The Job Generation Process*, Cambridge, MA: MIT Program on Neighbourhood and Regional Change.

Cherlin, A.J. (1981) *Marriage, Divorce and Remarriage*, Cambridge: Harvard University Press.

Clark, T. and Inglehart, R. (1991) 'The new political culture: an introduction'. Prepared for T. Clark and V. Hoffmann-Martinot (eds), *The New Political Culture* (draft volume).

Dahrendorf, R. (1959) *Class and Class Conflict in Industrial Society*, London: Routledge & Kegan Paul.

Featherman, D. and Hauser, R. (1978) *Opportunity and Change*, New York: Academic Press.

Forse, M. (1986) 'La diversification de la societe française vue a travers le mariage et l'ideologie', *Tocqueville Review*, 7: 223–33.

Hout, M. (1988) 'More universalism, less strutural mobility', *American Journal of Sociology*, 93: 1358–1400.

Lipset, S. (1960) *Political Man: The Social Bases of Politics*, New York: Doubleday.

Lipset, S. and Bendix, R. (1991) (1959) *Social Mobility in Industrial Society*, New Brunswick, NJ: Transition Books.

Nisbet, R. (1959) 'The decline and fall of social class', *Pacific Sociological Review*, 2(1): 11–17.

Parkin, F. (1979) *Marxism and Class Theory: A Bourgeois Critique*, London: Tavistock.

Peters, T. and Waterman, R. (1982) *In Search of Excellence*, New York: Warner Books.

Richta, R. *et al.* (1969) *Civilization at the Crossroads*, White Plains NY: International Arts and Sciences Press.

Wilson, W. (1978) *The Declining Significance of Race*, Chicago: University of Chicago Press.

Reading 30 The Persistence of Classes in Post-Industrial Societies

Bianchi, S. (1981) *Household Composition and Racial Inequality*, New Brunswick: Rutgers University Press.

Block, F. (1990) *Postindustrial Possibilities*, Berkeley: University of California Press.

Connell, R. (1987) *Gender and Power*, Stanford: Stanford University Press.

Crystal, G. (1991) *In Search of Excess; Executive Compensation in the 1980s*, New York: Norton.

Davis, M. (1991) *City of Quartz*, London: Verso.

Engbersen, G. (1989) 'Cultures of long-term unemployment in the West', *Netherlands Journal of Social Sciences*, 25: 75–96.

Esping-Anderson, G. (1990) *The Three Worlds of Welfare Capitalism*, Princeton: Princeton University Press.

Featherman, D. and Hauser, R. (1978) *Opportunity and Change*, New York: Academic Press.

Hochschild, A. (1989) *The Second Shift: Working Parents and the Revolution at Home*, New York: Viking.

Hout, M. (1982) 'The association between husbands' and wives' occupations in two-earner families', *American Journal of Sociology*, 88: 397–409.

Hout, M. (1988) 'More universalism, less structural mobility', *American Journal of Sociology*, 93: 1358–400.

Jencks, C. and Petersen, P. (eds) (1991) *The Urban Underclass*, Washington DC: Brookings Institute.

Lipset, S. (1981) *Political Man: The Social Bases of Politics*, 2nd edn, Baltimore: John Hopkins University Press.

Lipset, S. (1990) 'The death of the third way: everywhere but here that is', *National Interest*, 20: 25–7.

Mare, R.D. (1980) 'Social background and educational continuation decisions', *Journal of the American Statistical Association*, 75: 295–305.

Mare R.D. (1981) 'Change and stability in educational stratification', *American Sociological Review*, 46: 72–87.

Markland, S. (1990) 'Structures of modern poverty', *Acta Sociologica*, 33: 125–40.

Massey, D.S. (1990) 'American apartheid: segregation and the making of the underclass', *American Journal of Sociology*, 96: 329–57.

Mills, C. Wright (1946) 'The middle class of middle-sized cities', *American Sociological Review*, 11: 520–9.

Mingione, E. (1991) 'The new urban poor and the crisis of citizenship/welfare systems in Italy'. Paper presented at Conference on 'Pauvrété, immigrations et marginalities urbaines dans les societies advancées', Paris, Maison Suger.

Nisbet, R. (1959) 'The decline and fall of social clas', *Pacific Sociological Review*, 2(1): 11–17.

Parkin, F. (1979) *Marxism and Class Theory: A Bourgeois Critique*, London: Tavistock.

Przeworski, A. and Sprague, J. (1986) *Paper Stones: A History of Electoral Socialism*, Chicago: University of Chicago Press.

Raftery, A. and Hout, M. (1993) 'Maximally maintained inequality: expansion, reform and opportunity in Irish education 1921–1975', *Sociology of Education*, 66: 41–62.

Reich, R. (1991) *The Work of Nations*, New York: Knopf.

Sabel, C. (1982) *Work and Politics*, New York: Cambridge University Press.

Shaiken, H. (1984) *Work Transformed: Automation and Labor in the Computer Age*, New York: Holt, Rinehart & Winston.

Shavit, Y. and Blossfeld, H. (eds) (1992) *Persistent Inequality: Changing Educational Attainment in Thirteen Countries*, Boulder, Colorado: Westview Press.

Smeeding, T. (1991) 'Cross-national comparisons of inequality and poverty position', in L. Osberg (ed.) *Economic Inequality and Poverty: International Perspectives*, Armonk, New York: Sharpe.

Thistle, S. (1992) 'Between two worlds', unpublished PhD dissertation, Department of Sociology, University of California, Berkeley.

Townsend, P., Corrigan, P. and Kowarzik, U. (1987) *Poverty and Labour in London*, London: Low Pay Unit.

Wacquant, L. (1993) 'Red belt, black belt: articulating color, class and place in Chicago's ghetto and the Parisian periphery', *International Journal of Urban and Regional Research*.

Weakliem, D. (1991) 'The two lefts? Occupation and party choice in France, Italy and Netherlands', *American Journal of Sociology*, 96: 1327–61.

Weizman, L. (1985) *The Divorce Revolution*, Stanford: Stanford University Press.

Wilson, W. (1987) *The Truly Disadvantaged: The Inner City, the Underclass and Public Policy*, Chicago: University of Chicago Press.

Wright, E. (1985) *Classes*, London: Verso.

Zuboff, S. (1988) *In the Age of the Smart Machine: The Future of Work and Power*, New York: Basic.

Reading 31 The Meritocratic Ideal – Unequal but Fair?

Davis, K. and Moore, W.E. (1967) 'Some principles of stratification', in R. Bendix and S. Lipset (eds) *Class, Status and Power*, London: Routledge & Kegan Paul.

Durkheim, E. (1960) (1893) *The Division of Labour in Society*, New York: Free Press.

Halsey, A.H. (1986) *Change in British Society*, 3rd edn, Milton Keynes: Open University Press.

Hayek, F. (1976) *The Constitution of Liberty*, London: Routledge & Kegan Paul.

Herrnstein, R. and Murray, C. (1994) *The Bell Curve: Intelligence and the Class Structure*, New York: Free Press.

Marshall, G. and Swift, A. (1993) 'Social classes and social justice', *British Journal of Sociology*, 44: 206.

Nozick, R. (1974) *Anarchy, State and Utopia*, Oxford: Blackwell.

Parsons, T. (1937) *The Structure of Social Action*, New York: McGraw Hill.

Young, M. (1958) *The Rise of the Meritocracy, 1870–2033*, London: Thames & Hudson.

Reading 32 Social Stratification in Europe

Ardagh, J. (1988) *Germany and the Germans*, Harmondsworth: Penguin.

Atkinson, A.B. (1983) *The Economics of Inequality*, 2nd edn, Oxford: Oxford University Press.

Boltanski, L. (1987) *The Making of a Class: Cadres in French Society*, Cambridge: Cambridge University Press.

Bottomore, T. and Brym, R.J. (eds) (1989) *The Capitalist Class: An International Study*, Brighton: Harvester Wheatsheaf.

Dahrendorf, R. (1963) 'Recent changes in the class structure of European societies', in S. Graubard (ed.) *A New Europe?*, Boston: Beacon Press.

Dahrendorf, R. (1987) 'The erosion of citizenship', *New Statesman*, 12 June: 12–15.

Erikson, R., Goldthorpe, J.H. and Portocarero, L. (1979) 'Intergenerational class mobility in three western European societies', *British Journal of Sociology*, 30(4): 415–41.

Giddens, A. (1982) *Profiles and Critiques in Social Theory*, London: Macmillan.

Goldthorpe, J.H. (1982) 'On the service, its formation and future', in A. Giddens and G. Mackenzie (eds) *Social Class and the Division of Labour*, Cambridge: Cambridge University Press.

Goldthorpe, J.H., Lockwood, D., Bechhofer, F. and Platt, J. (1969) *The Affluent Worker in the Class Structure*, Cambridge: Cambridge University Press.

Lawson, R. and George, V. (1980) 'An assessment', in V. George and R. Lawson (eds) *Poverty and Inequality in Common Market Countries*, London: Routledge and Kegan Paul.

Marceau, J. (1989) *A Family Business? The Making of an International Business Elite*, Cambridge: Cambridge University Press.

Reading 33 Inequalities in Health

Bone, M. (1973) *Family Planning Services in England and Wales*, London: HMSO.

Brotherston, J. (1976) 'Inequality is inevitable?', in Carter and Peel (eds) *Equalities and Inequalities in Health*, London: Academic Press.

Bulman, J.S., Richards, N.D., Slack, G.L. and Willcocks, A.J. (1968) *Demand and Need for Dental Care*, Oxford: Oxford University Press.

Cartwright, A. (1970) *Parents and Family Planning Services*, London: Routledge.

Cartwright, A. and O'Brien, M. (1976) 'Social class variations in health care', in M. Stacey (ed.) *The Sociology of the NHS*, Sociological Review Monograph 22.

Clarke, M. (1969) *Trouble with Feet*, Occasional papers on social administration, Bell.

Douglas, J.W.B. and Rowntree, G. (1949) 'Supplementary maternal and child health services', *Population Studies*, 2.

Gans, B. (1966) 'Health problems and the immigrant child', in CIBA Foundation, *Immigration: Medical and Social Aspects*.

Gordon, I. (1951) 'Social status and active prevention of disease', *Monthly Bulletin of the Ministry of Health*, 10.

Gray, P.G. *et al.* (1970) *Adult Dental Health in England and Wales in 1968*, London: HMSO.

Hood, C., Oppé, T.E., Pless, I.B. and Apte, E. (1970) 'West Indian immigrants: A study of one-year olds in Paddington', *Institute of Race Relations.*

Martin, J. and Morgan, M. (1975) *Prolonged Sickness and the Return to Work*, London: HMSO.

Martini, C.J.M. *et al.* (1977) 'Health indexes sensitive to medical care variation', *International Journal of Health Services*, 7: 293.

Oppé, T.E. (1967) 'The health of West Indian children', *Proceedings of the Royal Society of Medicine*, 57.

Sheiham, A. and Hobdell, M.H. (1969) 'Decayed, missing and filled teeth in British adult populations', *British Dental Journal*, 126: 401.

Smith, D. (1976) *The Facts of Racial Disadvantage*, London: PEP.

Thomas, H.E. (1968) 'Tuberculosis in immigrants', *Proceedings of the Royal Society of Medicine*, 61.

Titmuss, R.M. (1968) *Commitment to Welfare*, London: Allen and Unwin.

Reading 35 Young, Female and Black

Coard, B. (1971) *How the West Indian Child is made ESN in the British School System*, London: New Beacon Books.

Milner, D. (1975) *Children and Race*, Harmondsworth: Penguin.

Milner, D. (1983) *Children and Race: Ten Years On*, London: Ward Lock Educational.

Reading 36 Women and the Criminal Justice System

Farrington, D. and Morris, A. (1983) 'Sex, sentencing and reconviction', *British Journal of Criminology*, 23(3): 229–48.

Kennedy, H. (1992) *Eve was Framed*, London: Chatto & Windus.

Kruttschnitt, C. (1981) 'Prison codes, inmate solidarity and women: a re-examination', in M. Warren (ed.) *Comparing Female and Male Offenders*, Newbury Park, Ca.: Sage.

Morris, A. (1987) *Women, Crime and Criminal Justice*, Oxford: Blackwell.

Reading 37 What Makes Women Sick: Gender and Health

Bassett, M. and Mhloyi, M. (1991) 'Women and AIDS in Zimbabwe: the making of an epidemic', *International Journal of Health Services*, 21(1): 143–56.

de Bruyn, M. (1992) Women and AIDS in developing countries, *Social Science and Medicine*, 34(3): 249–62.

Grundfest Schoepf, B., Engundu, W., wa Nkera, R., Ntsomo, P. and Schoepf, C. (1991) 'Gender, power and risk of AIDS in Zaire', in M. Turshen (ed.) *Women and Health in Africa*, Trenton NJ: Africa World Press.

Holland, J., Ramazanoglou, C., Scott, S., Sharpe, S. and Thomson, R. (1990) 'Sex, gender and power; young women's sexuality in the shadow of AIDS', *Sociology of Health and Illness*, 12(3): 336–50.

Jochelson, K., Mothibeli, M. and Leger, J.-P. (1991) 'Human immunodeficiency virus and migrant labour in South Africa', *International Journal of Health Services*, 21(1): 157–73.

Kisekka, M. (1990) 'AIDS in Uganda as a gender issue', in E. Rothblum and E. Cole (eds) *Women's Mental Health in Africa*, New York: Hogarth Park Press.

Kline, A., Kline, E. and Oken, E. (1992) 'Minority women and sexual choice in an age of AIDS', *Social Science and Medicine*, 34(4): 447–57.

Kurth, A. (1993) 'Introduction: an overview of women and HIV disease', in A. Kurth (ed.) *Until the Cure: Caring for Women with HIV*, London and New Haven: Yale University Press.

Latif, A. (1989) 'Genital ulcers and transmission of HIV among couples in Zimbabwe', *AIDS*, 3: 519–23.

Mbivso, H. and Adamchak, D. (1989) 'Condom use and acceptance: a survey of male Zimbabweans', *Central African Journal of Medicine*, 35: 519–58.

Panos Institute (1990) *Triple Jeopardy: Woman and AIDS*, London: Panos Publications.

Reid, E. (1992) 'Gender, knowledge and responsibility', in J. Mann, D. Tarantola and T. Netter (eds) *AIDS in the World: A Global Report*, Cambridge, Mass: Harvard University Press.

Seidel, G. (1993) 'The competing discourses of HIV/AIDS in Sub-Saharan Africa: discourses of right and empowerment vs discourses of control and exclusion', *Social Science and Medicine*, 36(3): 175–94.

Smith, B. (1992) 'Choosing ourselves: black women and abortion', in M. Gerber Fried (ed.) *Abortion to Reproductive Freedom: Transforming a Movement*, Boston: South End Press.

Worth, D. (1989) 'Sexual decision making and AIDS: why condom promotion among vulnerable women is likely to fail', *Studies in Family Planning*, 20(6): 297–307.

Reading 38 Images of Black Women in Everyday Life

Angelou, M. (1969) *I Know Why the Caged Bird Sings*, New York: Bantam.

Brooks, G. (1953) *Maud Martha*, Boston: Atlantic Press.

Brooks, G. (1972) *Report from Part One: The Autobiography of Gwendolyn Brooks*, Detroit: Broadside Press.

Golden, M. (1983) *Migrations of the Heart*, New York: Ballantine.

Morrison, T. (1970) *The Bluest Eye*, New York: Pocket Books.

Omi, M. and Winant, H. (1986) *Racial Formation in the United States: From the 1960s to the 1980s*, New York: Routledge & Kegan Paul.

Russell K.K. (1987) 'Growing up with privilege and prejudice', *New York Times Magazine*, 14 June: 22–8.

Tate, C. (ed.) (1983) *Black Women Writers at Work*, New York: Continuum Publishing.

Washington, M.H. (ed.) (1987) *Invented Lives: Narratives of Black Women 1860–1960*, Garden City NY: Anchor.

Reading 40 Ethnic Diversity and Disadvantage in Britain

Bonnett, A. (1993) *Radicalism, Anti-Racism and Representation*, London: Routledge.

Brown, C. and Gay, P. (1985) *Racial Discrimination: 17 Years After the Act*, London: PSI.

Gillborn, D. and Gipps, C. (1996) *Recent Research on the Achievements of Ethnic Minority Pupils*, London: Office for Standards in Education.

Simpson, A. and Stevenson, J. (1994) 'Half a chance still? Jobs, discrimination and young people in Nottingham', Nottingham: Nottingham and District Racial Equality Council.

Smith, D.J. (1977) *Racial Disadvantage in Britain*, Harmondsworth: Penguin.

Wambu, O. (1996) 'Students of the street academy', *Voice*, 4 June: 12.

Young, I.M. (1990) *Justice and the Politics of Difference*, New York: Princeton University Press.

Reading 43 Sociology and Disability

Barbalet, J. (1993) 'Citizenship, class inequality and resentment', in B. Turner (ed.) *Citizenship and Social Theory*, London: Sage.

Barnes, C. (1991) *Disabled People in Britain and Discrimination: A Case for Anti-Discrimination Legislation*, London: Hurst.

Barton, L. and Oliver, M. (1992) 'Special needs; personal trouble or public issue?' in M. Arnot and L. Barton (eds) *Voicing Concerns: Sociological Perspectives on Contemporary Education Reform*, Wallingford: Triangle Books.

Begum, N. (1992) 'Disabled women and the feminist agenda', *Feminist Review*, 40: 70–84.

Bewley, C. and Glendinning, C. (1994) 'Representing the views of disabled people in community care planning', *Disability and Society*, 9(3): 301–14.

Cross, M. (1994) 'Abuse', in L. Keith (ed.) *Mustn't Grumble*, London: The Women's Press.

Daunt, P. (1991) *Meeting Disability: A European Response*, London: Cassell.

Glendinning, C. (1991) 'Losing ground: social policy and disabled people in Great Britain 1980–1990', *Disability, Handicap & Society*, 6(1): 3–20.

Hahn, H. (1986) 'Public support for rehabilitation programs: the analysis of US disability policy', *Disability, Handicap & Society*, 1(2): 121–38.

Jenkins, R. (1991) 'Disability and social stratification', *British Journal of Sociology*, 42(4): 557–80.

Morris, J. (1991) *Pride Against Prejudice: Transferring Attitudes to Disability*, London: Women's Press.

Morris, J. (1992) *Disabled Lives, Many Voices, One Message*, London: BBC.

Morris, J. (1993) *Community Care or Independent Living*, York: Joseph Rowntree Foundation.

Oliver, M. (1990) *The Politics of Disablement*, London: Macmillan.

Quicke, J. (1986) 'A case of paradigmatic mentality? A reply to Mike Oliver', *British Journal of Sociology of Education*, 7(1): 81–6.

Richardson, R. (1991) 'Introduction: a visitor yet a part of everybody – the tasks and goals of human rights education' in H. Starkey (ed.) *The Challenge of Human Rights Education*, London: Cassell.

Rieser, R. and Mason, M. (eds) (1990) *Disability, Equality in the Classroom: A Human Rights Issue*, London: ILEA.

Ryan, J. and Thomas, F. (1980) *The Politics of Mental Handicap*, Harmondsworth: Penguin.

Shakespeare, T. (1993) 'Disabled people's self organisation: a new social movement?', *Disability, Handicap and Society*, 8(3): 249–64.

Part IV Sociological Research

Reading 49 Measuring Wealth and Poverty

Marshall, D. (1965) *The English Poor in the Eighteenth Century*, London: Routledge & Kegan Paul.

Townsend, P. (1979) *Poverty in the United Kingdom*, Harmondsworth: Penguin.

Reading 50 The Research Process: Planning Social Surveys

Goldthorpe, J. (1980) *Social Mobility and the Class Structure in Modern Britain*, Oxford: Oxford University Press.

Heath, A. (1981) *Social Mobility*, Glasgow: Fontana.

Moser, C.A. and Kalton, G. (1971) *Survey Methods in Social Investigation*, 2nd edn, London: Heinemann.

Payne, G. (1987) *Mobility and Change in Modern Society*, London: Macmillan.

Reading 51 Participant Observation (1): Inside the British Police

Festinger, L., Riechen, H.W. and Schachter, S. (1956) *When Prophecy Fails*, London: Harper & Row.

Gold, R.L. (1958) 'Roles in sociological field observations', *Social Forces*, 36: 217–33.

Homan, R. (1980) 'The ethics of covert research: Homan defends his methods', *Network*, January.

Lofland, J. (1961) 'Comment on initial interaction with newcomers in AA', *Social Problems*, 8: 236–49.

Rosenhan, D.L. (1973) 'On being sane in insane places', *Science*, 179: 250–8.

Roy, D. (1960) 'Banana time: job satisfaction and informal interaction', *Human Organization*, 18: 156–68.

Young, J. (1970) The Zookeepers of Deviancy, *Catalyst*, 5: 38–46.

Reading 53 Researching Prostitutes and their Clients

Barnard, M. (1992) 'Working in the dark: research in female street prostitution', in H. Roberts (ed.) *Women's Health Matters*, London: Routledge.

McKeganey, N., Barnard, M. and Bloor, M. (1994) 'How many prostitutes? Epidemiology out of ethnography', in M. Boulton (ed.) *Challenge and Innovation: Methodological Advances in Social Research in HIV/AIDS*, London: Taylor & Francis.

Reading 54 Feminist Principles (1): A Reflexive Approach

Smith, D. (1974) 'Women's perspective as a radical critique of sociology', *Sociological Quarterly*, 44: 7–13.

Reading 55 Feminist Principles (2): Researching Sexual Violence

Reinharz, S. (1993) 'The principles of feminist research: a matter of debate', in C. Kramarae and D. Spender (eds) *The Knowledge Explosion: Generations of Feminist Scholarship*, Hemel Hempstead: Harvester Wheatsheaf.

Reading 57 The Effects of Social Research

Baumrind, D. (1964) 'Some thoughts on ethics of research: after reading Milgram's behavioural study of obedience', *American Psychologist*, 19: 421–3.

British Psychological Society (1978) 'Ethical principles for research with human subjects'

British Sociological Association (1982) 'Statement of ethical principals and their application to sociological practice'

Ditton, J. (1977) *Part Time Crime: An Ethnography of Fiddling and Pilferage*, London: Macmillan.

Milgram, S. (1963) 'Behavioural study of obedience', *Journal of Abnormal and Social Psychology*, 67: 371–8.

Milgram, S. (1974) *Obedience to Authority*, London: Tavistock.

Rosenhan, D.L. (1973) 'On being sane in insane places', *Science*, 179: 250–8.

Sherif, C.W. (1980) 'Comment on ethical issues in Malamuth, Heim and Feshbach's "Sexual Responsiveness of College Students to Rape Depictions: Inhibitory and Disinhibitory Effects"', *Journal of Personality and Social Psychology*, 38(3): 409–12.

Udry, J.R. and Billy, J.O.G. (1987) 'Inhibition of coitus in early adolescence', *American Sociological Review*, 52: 841–55.

Vinacke, W.E. (1954) 'Deceiving experimental subjects', *American Psychologist*, 9: 155.

Wallis, R. (1973) 'Religious sects and the fear of publicity', *New Society*, 24: 545–7.

Wallis, R. (1977) 'The moral career of a research project', in C. Bell and H. Newby (eds) *Doing Sociological Research*, London: Allen & Unwin.

Warwick, D.P. (1983) 'The politics and ethics of field research', in M. Bulmer and D.P. Warwick (eds) *Social Research in Developing Countries: Surveys and Censuses in the Third World*, Chichester: Wiley.

West, S.G., Gunn, S.P. and Chernicky, P. (1975) 'Ubiquitous watergate: An Attributional Analysis', *Journal of Personality and Social Psychology*, 32(1): 55–65.

Index